The Logic of Capital

The Logic of Capital presents the main economic argument developed by Marx in the three volumes of *Capital* in a coherent and comprehensive manner. It also delves into three long-standing debates in Marxist political economy: the transformation problem, the Okishio theorem and theories of exploitation and oppression.

Starting with discussions of methodology, including dialectics and historical materialism, this book explains key concepts of Marxist political economy: commodity, value, money, capital, reserve army of labour, accumulation of capital, circuit of capital, reproduction schemas, prices of production, profit, interest and rent. Scholars of economics, sociology, geography, political science, anthropology and other kindred disciplines will find here an accessible yet rigorous treatment of Marxist political economy.

Deepankar Basu is associate professor in the Department of Economics at the University of Massachusetts Amherst. His research interests span classical political economy, development economics and applied econometrics. He has published widely in peer-reviewed journals. He is associate editor of the *Review of Social Economy* and has co-edited, with Debarshi Das, *Conflict Demand and Economic Development: Essays in Honour of Amit Bhaduri*, a collection of essays on heterodox macroeconomics and political economy.

The Logic of Capital

An Introduction to Marxist Economic Theory

DEEPANKAR BASU

CAMBRIDGE
UNIVERSITY PRESS

Shaftesbury Road, Cambridge CB2 8EA, United Kingdom

One Liberty Plaza, 20th Floor, New York, NY 10006, USA

477 Williamstown Road, Port Melbourne, VIC 3207, Australia

314–321, 3rd Floor, Plot 3, Splendor Forum, Jasola District Centre, New Delhi – 110025, India

103 Penang Road, 07/06–05#, Visioncrest Commercial, Singapore 238467

Cambridge University Press is part of Cambridge University Press & Assessment, a department of the University of Cambridge.

We share the University's mission to contribute to society through the pursuit of education, learning and research at the highest international levels of excellence.

www.cambridge.org
Information on this title: www.cambridge.org/9781108832007

© Deepankar Basu 2021

First published 2021
Paperback edition 2023

A catalogue record for this publication is available from the British Library

ISBN 978-1-108-83200-7 Hardback
ISBN 978-1-009-41811-9 Paperback

Contents

List of Figures and Tables   ix
Acknowledgements   xi

1 Introduction   1

    1.1 Motivation   1

    1.2 Organization of the Book   4

    1.3 What Is Different in This Book   11

    1.4 How to Use This Book   14

Part I Foundations

2 Some Methodological Issues   19

    2.1 Marx's Route to Political Economy   19

    2.2 The Structure of *Capital*   40

3 The Generation and Accumulation of Surplus Value   47

    3.1 The Commodity   48

    3.2 Money-Form of Value   77

    3.3 Capital, or Self-Valorizing Value   100

    3.4 Production under Capitalism   125

    3.5 Accumulation of Capital   135

    3.6 The Primary Accumulation of Capital   156

3.7	Conclusion	158
3.A	Appendix A: Reduction of Complex to Simple Labour	160
3.B	Appendix B: Comparison of MEV over Time and Space	166
3.C	Appendix C: Labour as the Substance of Value	170

4 Realization of Surplus Value — **179**

4.1	Circulation of Capital	180
4.2	The Problem of Aggregate Demand	192
4.3	Use-Value Basis of the Reproduction of Capital	194
4.4	Conclusion	207

5 Distribution of Surplus Value — **209**

5.1	Emergence of Prices of Production	211
5.2	Detour: Technical Change	220
5.3	Commercial Profit	228
5.4	Productive and Unproductive Labour	232
5.5	Interest and Fictitious Capital	241
5.6	Ground-Rent	248
5.7	Estimates of Surplus Value and Its Components	263
5.8	Conclusion	267

Part II Further Explorations in Political Economy

6 Capitalism and Technical Change — **273**

6.1	Technical Change	275
6.2	Progressive Technical Change and Capitalism	281
6.3	Technical Change and the Rate of Profit	283
6.4	A Marx-Okishio Threshold	285
6.5	Constant Rate of Exploitation	291
6.6	Conclusion	294

7 The Transformation Problem   **296**

7.1   Ricardo, Marx and Bortkiewicz   298

7.2   The Standard Interpretation   302

7.3   Sraffa-Based Critique   324

7.4   Marxist Responses to the Sraffa-Based Critique   325

7.5   The New Interpretation   326

7.6   Three Less Appealing Approaches   335

7.7   Conclusion   341

7.A   Appendix A: General Treatment   344

7.B   Appendix B: R Code for Examples Discussed in Text   363

8   Exploitation and Oppression   **372**

8.1   Theories of Exploitation   373

8.2   A Critique of the Commodity Exploitation Theorem   389

8.3   Manifold Exploitations?   399

8.4   Exploitation and Distributive Justice   401

8.5   Conclusion   407

Bibliography   409

Index   423

Figures and Tables

Figures

3.1 Concrete and abstract labour   56

3.2 Visual representation of Marx's metaphor of the working day that is divided between necessary and surplus labour   117

3.3 Visual representation of Marx's metaphor of the working day expanded to take explicit account of the non-market component of labour-power   119

3.4 Time series plots of the rate of exploitation, the OCC and the rate of profit for India's organized manufacturing sector, 1981–82 to 2016–17   122

3.5 The labour market in a typical capitalist economy   140

3.6 Four measures of the reserve army of labour in the post-war US economy, 1948–2016   150

3.7 Four measures of the reserve army of labour, as a proportion of the labour force, in the post-war US economy, 1948–2016   153

3.8 Time series plots of the monetary expression of value (MEV) for the US economy, 1964–2018   168

4.1 The circuit of capital   186

5.1 Categories of social activities   234

5.2 Depiction of the marginal product of capital outlay on the i-th and j-th plots of land   253

5.3 Ground-rent in agriculture on the i-th plot of land measured in units of corn   256

ix

5.4 Ground-rent in agriculture on the n-th plot (that is, worst-quality plot) of land measured in units of corn 258

5.5 Decomposition of ground-rent in agriculture on the i-th plot of land, measured in units of corn, when rent is specified as a lump-sum monetary payment 261

5.6 Components of surplus value in the US CB sector, 1948–2018 265

5.7 Components of surplus value in the US NFCB sector, 1948–2018 267

5.8 Components of surplus value in India's organized manufacturing sector, 1981–82 to 2016–17 268

6.1 The relationship between progressive technical change and capitalistically viable technical change 282

6.2 Scatter plot for the US CB sector between 1979 and 2019 of (a) the difference between ratio of real wage rate in consecutive years and the Marx-Okishio threshold for that year and (b) change in the rate of profit 290

Tables

3.1 Reserve army of labour in the post-war US economy 152

4.1 Three stages of the circuit 185

4.2 Marx's example of simple reproduction 196

4.3 Marx's first example of expanded reproduction 199

5.1 Unequal rates of profit 217

5.2 Equalized rates of profit and prices of production 218

5.3 Value added in the US CB sector (billion USD) 264

Acknowledgements

This book draws on two sources.

I have been teaching courses in Marxist economics at the undergraduate and graduate levels in the Department of Economics at the University of Massachusetts Amherst since 2009. The lecture notes for these courses, which have evolved year after year with critical input from colleagues and feedback from students, formed the first source material for the book.

In June 2017, Bernard D'Mello asked me to contribute an article for a special issue of the fantastic journal *Economic and Political Weekly* to mark the 150th year of the publication of Volume I of Karl Marx's *Capital*. I took this opportunity to develop an article-length presentation of Marx's argument in the three volumes of *Capital*. This article, which was published in the *Economic and Political Weekly* on 16 September 2017, formed the second source material for this book.

The first part of this book is a substantial and substantive expansion of the presentation in my 2017 *Economic and Political Weekly* article. In working out the expansion, I have drawn on and developed much of the material from the lecture notes for Marxist economics classes that I have taught at the University of Massachusetts Amherst since 2009.

First and foremost, therefore, I would like to thank all the students at the University of Massachusetts Amherst, both graduate and undergraduate, who have engaged with my lectures, provoked me to think more deeply by raising critical questions and helped me to always connect abstract debates in political economy with real life struggles of ordinary working people. In the same vein, I would like to thank Bernard D'Mello and the *Economic and Political Weekly* for inviting me to contribute to the special issue of the journal on the 150th year of the publication of Volume I of Karl Marx's *Capital*. This invitation provided the impetus to my attempt to develop a coherent presentation of Marx's argument in the three volumes of *Capital*.

I would like to take this opportunity to thank two extraordinary scholars who have been a source of support in my long journey towards Marxist economics: Duncan Foley and Debarshi Das.

Duncan Foley not only has inspired me by his work in Marxist economics, an influence which can be seen in this book, but has also been extraordinarily generous with his time. Over the years, I have discussed almost all aspects of Marxist economics with him and I have been amazed by his willingness to engage, explain, learn and teach. He has been kind enough to read many chapters of this book and has provided useful insights about various aspects of the argument presented in the chapters. While writing this book, and more generally in developing various arguments in Marxist economics that I have presented previously in published and unpublished papers, I have benefitted from the constant support and engagement of Debarshi Das. He has been kind enough to read several chapters of this book and has provided detailed comments that have made the arguments stronger.

The development of my ideas on Marxism, economics and the social sciences, more broadly, has been influenced by numerous persons over the past three decades. It is only fitting that I should acknowledge that influence at this point in my academic life and career. I was introduced to Marxism, and radical social thought and practice in the early 1990s, for the first time, by my remarkable teachers in, of all places, the Indian Institute of Technology: A. P. Shukla, Deshdeep Sahadev, Sandeep Pandey and Mohini Mullick. I continued this journey in the Centre for Economic Studies and Planning, Jawaharlal Nehru University, with insights and input from another set of remarkable teachers: Amit Bhaduri, Prabhat Patnaik and Utsa Patnaik.

My overall development as a social scientist has also been helped and supported by numerous friends and comrades: Michael Ash, Amit Basole, Anindya Bhattacharya, Palash Bhattacharya, Rajesh Bhattacharya, Manali Chakrabarty, Pratyush Chandra, Nandini Chandra, the late Dan Clawson, Mary Ann Clawson, David Kotz, Jesse Knutson, Jinee Lokneeta, P. T. Manolakos, Sangay Mishra, Alita Nandi, Karen Pfeiffer, Ashok Prasad, Rakesh Ranjan, Abhay Shukla, Poonam Srivastava, Rahul Varman, Ramaa Vasudevan, Mwangi wa Githinji and many others.

Finally, I would like to thank Priyanka Srivastava, my companion, love and fellow traveller, for the constant support and encouragement through the years. This book, like much else I have managed to accomplish over the last two decades, would not have been possible without her companionship and support.

1

Introduction

1.1 Motivation

The global economic crisis that was triggered by the financial crisis in the United States in 2007 has revived political movements critical of many harmful aspects of the capitalist system, like income and wealth inequality, unjust burdens of student debt, disparity in access to housing and health care, racial oppression and discrimination of immigrants, unequal trade and investment treaties, and policies of economic austerity. Parallel with the growth of such political movements has been a growing interest – among activists, scholars and the general public – in currents of critical social and political thought that can make sense of such issues and offer alternatives to the unjust and exploitative capitalist-imperialist system. It is in this context that there has been a revival of interest in Marxism, one of the most consistently radical strands of critical social thought, one moreover, that offers a coherent and comprehensive framework for understanding the social world we live in.

Marxism is a creative synthesis of three strands of nineteenth-century European thought – classical German philosophy, British political economy and French socialism. It offers a theory of history, referred to as the materialist conception of history or historical materialism, which puts an understanding of the material conditions of life at the centre of historical analysis. To understand both the structure of society at a point in time and the logic of large-scale historical change, Marxism asks us to start from an understanding of how the production and reproduction of material life is organized. In studying the production and reproduction of material life, Marxism pays attention to both technology, what it calls the forces of production, and the relationships people enter into during the process of production, which it calls the relations of production. Starting from the relations of production, it explains the structure of political and legal institutions of modern, bourgeois society; and, starting from the contradiction between the forces and relations of production, which is expressed through and in the conflicts of fundamental social classes, it explains large-scale historical change in the political and social domains of life.

Guided by this powerful theory of history, which he had developed in the first phase of his studies in the mid-nineteenth century, Marx spent the rest of his life developing a detailed analysis of the production and reproduction of material life in capitalist economies. The most complete and comprehensive picture of the results of this lifelong study of the structure and dynamics of capitalism is available in Marx's mature economic writings, especially in the three volumes of *Capital*. In this work, conceived of and worked out over the span of more than a decade, we find a startlingly relevant analysis of capitalism. Its pages offer us a coherent framework to understand a range of contemporary issues – from exploitation of workers to globalization of production, from the centrality of relentless technological change in capitalism to the degradation of work and dehumanization of workers, from the brutalities of primary accumulation of capital to the speculative frenzies of the financial system, from the power of rentier interests to the despoliation of nature.

In this book, I present an exposition and extension of the argument developed by Marx in the three volumes of *Capital*. In presenting the exposition of Marx's argument, I wish to attain two objectives simultaneously. First of all, I want to pay close attention to the text – the three volumes of *Capital* – so as to present the contours of *Marx's* argument. But in my engagement with the text of *Capital*, the main goal is to draw out the *analytical* core of Marx's arguments. Hence, while I follow the text closely and provide relevant quotations from the three volumes, this book is tilted far more in the direction of analysis than exegesis. Ultimately I am motivated, in my engagement with Marx's text, by the need to reconstruct the logic of Marx's argument, so that it becomes a tool for the analysis of contemporary capitalism. Hence, this book is not a contribution to the history of economic thought, but should be read instead as a contribution to contemporary political economic analysis from a Marxist perspective.

My second objective is to draw on the work of later Marxist scholars to extend, deepen and enrich Marx's political economy. As I develop the argument of the three volumes of *Capital*, at various points I will engage with work by later Marxist scholars to illuminate some important issues that Marx either did not discuss or discussed only partially. Three areas of work that have generated an enormous literature in Marxist economic theory over the past several decades will, in particular, be discussed in great detail: the relationship of value and price, which goes by the name of the so-called transformation problem; the relationship of technical change and profitability, which goes by the name of the Okishio theorem; and the theory of exploitation. I will also pause at different points and indicate to the reader some fruitful ways to engage with contemporary debates and discussions from within the framework of Marxist political economy. Here is a quick overview of some of these points.

- In Marx's argument in Volume I about surplus value and capital, an important place is held by an understanding of the value of the unique commodity labour-power. A very fruitful way to engage with feminism and to understand the oppression of women is to explore the Marxist–feminist literature on labour-power and social reproduction. I present a discussion of labour-power in section 3.3.3.

- Marx's argument in Volume I about the effect of capitalist social relations on the organization and technology of production offers a nice entry point for discussions of a range of contemporary issues: alienation of work, degradation of work and deskilling of workers; the roots of the contemporary ecological crisis; and commodification of knowledge and information. A discussion of the characteristics of production under capitalism is presented in section 3.4.

- Marx's discussion of primary accumulation of capital at the very end of Volume I finds resonance in contemporary debates over primitive accumulation and accumulation by dispossession under neoliberal capitalism. This discussion is especially relevant to popular struggles against dispossession in the periphery of the global capitalist system. For an introduction to the discussion of primitive accumulation of capital, see section 3.6.

- Marx's discussion of the circulation of capital in Volume II has the potential to become a framework for the analysis of problems of macro dynamics of capitalist economies – a framework that is different from both the neoclassical and the Keynesian frameworks. I discuss some of these issues in Chapter 4.

- Marx's argument about the development of finance and fictitious capital in Volume III provides a useful framework to think about the growth of the financial sector and the attendant problems of financial instability and crisis in contemporary capitalism. An introduction to Marx's ideas on interest income and fictitious capital can be found in section 5.5.

- Marx's discussion about ground-rent in Volume III can be a very good entry point into the study of rent in contemporary capitalism and can be applied to the study of oil and natural gas sectors, real estate prices and the dynamics of the housing market. It can also throw some light into discussions of 'rent' in the knowledge sector. For an introduction to a novel presentation of Marx's theory of ground-rent, see section 5.6.

1.2   Organization of the Book

This book is divided into two parts. The first part, called *Foundations*, presents the main argument developed by Marx in Volumes I, II and III of *Capital*; it consists of four chapters, Chapters 2 through 6. The second part, called *Further Explorations in Political Economy*, delves deeper into three important and long-standing debates in Marxist political economy: capitalism and technical change, value and prices, and exploitation and oppression. The second part comprises three chapters, Chapters 7 through 9.

1.2.1   Part I of the Book

Chapter 2 is the introductory chapter in the first part of the book. It acquaints readers with some methodological issues through a discussion of Marx's route to political economy and the structure of his mature work, *Capital*. After completing his PhD in Philosophy in 1841, and unable to get an academic position due to his political activism, Marx turned to journalism. As a contributor to, and later editor of, the radical-democratic newspaper *Rheinische Zeitung*, Marx was confronted with issues of 'material interest'. His previous training in literature, jurisprudence and philosophy had not prepared him well enough to deal with such issues. It was an acute awareness of this lack that propelled him to a lifelong engagement with political economy.

We can divide Marx's scholarly life into two phases: the first spanning the early 1840s and the second running from the early 1850s to the end of his life in 1883. In the first phase of his initial engagement with political economy, Marx developed two important methodological ideas: the dialectical method and the materialist conception of history. In the second phase of his scholarly life, which was focused primarily on economic studies, these methodological ideas continued to guide his research and thinking. The importance of these methodological ideas come from their role in identifying both the object and method of study for the mature Marx. The materialist conception of history suggested the object of study: the structure and dynamics of capitalism. Dialectics suggested the method of study: unpacking the contradiction between capital and labour. But the object and method did not automatically suggest the best way to present the results of his research to the broader public.

Marx was clear that the presentation of his analysis would not necessarily follow the emergence of forms and relations of economic life in history. Rather, the correct presentation required him to uncover the relationships of economic life as they presented themselves in contemporary capitalist societies. His methodological researches suggested that the best way to present his research would be to pay attention to different levels of abstraction. This method of presentation is regularly used by scientists, where features of a complex entity are abstracted from, that is ignored as a first approximation, to uncover what the researcher thinks as the fundamental processes at work. In this abstracted form, the fundamental logic of the complex entity is explained. As a second step, the features that had been abstracted from are brought back into the analysis, and we then try to understand how the fundamental logic works in, or is modified by, the presence of these features.

Marx's presentation follows this method. That is why his mature economic work, *Capital*, came to be organized at two levels of abstraction: (*a*) a high level of abstraction called 'capital in general', where competition between capitals and relations of credit are abstracted from – this is the level at which Volume I and II are located and (*b*) a more concrete level designated as 'many capitals', which explicitly considers competition and credit – this is the level at which the analysis in Volume III resides. Within this layered structure and using surplus value as the central concept, we can see that Volumes I, II and III deal with, in turn, the generation, realization and distribution of surplus value. Taken together, the three volumes of *Capital* present an integrated, comprehensive argument about the structure and dynamics of capitalism.

Chapter 3 of this book develops the main argument of Volume I of *Capital*. Posed at the level of abstraction of 'capital in general', Marx investigates three big questions in Volume I: (*a*) What is the origin of surplus value? (*b*) What is the use of surplus value? (*c*) What is the logic of emergence of a system of social production that rests on the generation and accumulation of surplus value? To understand the generation of surplus value, we need to first understand value; and to understand value, we need to understand the commodity. That is why Marx begins Volume I of *Capital* with an investigation of the commodity – the basic form of wealth in a capitalist economy. The commodity presents two aspects: use-value and exchange value. Analysis of these two aspects leads to the concept of value and the development of the labour theory of value, which, in turn, gives rise to the concept of money. With an understanding of money, Marx is then able to pose the question of capital – which is just another way of posing the question of the generation of surplus value. One of the key arguments developed by Marx in Volume I is that surplus value is the monetary expression of the unpaid labour of workers – hence, capitalism rests on the exploitation of the working class. Once we understand how surplus value is generated, we are led to the question: What does the capitalist class do with the surplus value? The answer: recommit the surplus value into the generation of more surplus value, a process referred to by Marx as the accumulation of capital. Analysis of the accumulation of capital leads Marx to develop the important concept of the reserve army of labour, or what he calls the relative surplus population, and highlight the degrading effects of capitalist conditions of production on the workers. Once we have understood the generation and accumulation of surplus value, we can then pose the question that Marx investigates at the very end of Volume I: How does a system governed by the ceaseless interplay between the generation and accumulation of capital emerge in the first place? Marx offers the concept of 'primary accumulation of capital' to answer this question. At the heart of this process, argues Marx, lies the forcible separation of primary producers (peasants) from their means of production (land) – a process we see being replicated in the periphery of the contemporary global capitalist system.

Chapter 3 has three appendices that deal with some important issues in the labour theory of value. In Appendix 3.A, I discuss the issue of the reduction of complex to simple labour. This is conceptually important because without a consistent procedure for comparing the labour of skilled and unskilled labour, a researcher will not be able to compute aggregate value magnitudes. In Appendix 3.B, I present a detailed discussion of an important concept that was developed in the main chapter: monetary expression of value. This is an important concept that Marx implicitly assumed in his economic analysis, and it is only later scholars like Duncan Foley who have highlighted its importance in Marxist economics. In Appendix 3.C, I return to a detailed discussion of the question: Why did Marx single out labour and use it as the foundation for the theory of value? I provide both negative and positive arguments in support of the claim that labour should be used as the (social) substance of value. I also present common critiques of the labour theory of value and offer Marxist responses to those critiques.

Chapter 4 of this book presents the main argument of Volume II of *Capital*. In analysing the generation and accumulation of surplus value in Volume I of *Capital*, Marx had abstracted from the question of aggregate demand, that is, under what conditions can the commodity that has been produced by the capitalist system sell for a price that realizes its full value (and surplus value)? Marx returns to this question about realization of value in Volume II of *Capital*. Since commodities realize their value through sale, Marx begins his analysis in Volume II of *Capital* with a general treatment of the circulation of capital, that is, sale and purchase of commodities as a means to realizing surplus value. The general treatment of circulation allows Marx to investigate two important questions – the temporal pattern of flow of value and the aggregate proportionalities between different branches of production that are needed to facilitate smooth reproduction of the whole capitalist system. In investigating the first issue, Marx develops the *circuit of capital* analysis; in addressing the second issue, Marx develops the *reproduction schemas*. In this chapter, I discuss the reproduction schemas in some detail. These schemas represent an elaboration of ideas about sectoral linkages that were first developed by the Physiocrats in eighteenth-century France. They highlight the proportional relationships that need to hold between branches producing means of production and means of consumption to ensure smooth reproduction of the aggregate system. The analyses of both the circuit of capital and the reproduction schemas have proved fruitful entry points for analyses of crisis tendencies in capitalist economies. In Chapter 4, I provide an algebraic treatment of Marx's reproduction schemas and show how the numerical problems in the examples Marx used to study expanded reproduction, that is, an expanding capitalist economy, can be easily corrected.

Chapter 5 of this book presents the main argument of Volume III of *Capital*, which deals with the distribution of surplus value. Marx's argument about the distribution and redistribution of surplus value is developed in two steps. In the first step, Marx explains how the total surplus value generated in production and realized through sale is distributed across sectors of the economy involved in capitalist commodity production by the emergence of a *uniform rate of profit* and *prices of production*. The mechanism underlying this first step in the distribution of surplus value is the competition between capitals, manifested as the mobility of capital across sectors in search of higher rates of profit. The argument about the emergence of prices of production, in turn, moves through two levels of abstraction. In the higher level of abstraction, we will abstract from commercial capital, that is, capital only involved in trade but not in production (broadly understood). After developing the argument in this simplified set-up, we return to the argument and incorporate commercial capital into the analysis to see that the competitive process leads to the total surplus value being divided between industrial and commercial capital in the form of *industrial profit* and *commercial profit*, respectively. In the second step of the argument about the distribution of surplus value, Marx shows that the surplus value realized as industrial or commercial profit is further redistributed into two income streams. One part of the industrial (or commercial) profit is appropriated by money capitalists as *interest*, with the part of surplus value remaining with industrial capital known as *profit of enterprise*. Another part is appropriated by owners of nonreproducible resources, like land, in the form of *ground-rent*. In both cases, the key mechanism that facilitates these latter appropriations of surplus value by money capitalists (as interest) or resource owners (as ground-rent) is the process of bargaining between different factions of the ruling class.

By the end of Part I of this book, the reader would have become familiar with the details of Marx's argument in the three volumes of *Capital*. The reader would be able to see that capitalism is an exploitative system, just like previous class-divided socieites were, in the precise sense that Marx wanted us to understand. Exploitation in capitalism arises from the surplus, in the form of surplus value, being appropriated by a tiny section of society, the capitalist class, who then decide upon its disposition. The reader would be able to understand how the reserve army of labour is not an anomaly of capitalism, but that it is a necessary feature of capitalism. The reader would be able to see not only how capitalism might solve problems of aggregate demand by maintaining correct proportionality between branches of production but also that such solutions are temporary, so that crisis tendencies always loom large over the horizon. And finally, the reader would be able to distinguish surplus value from the different forms it takes, which will then help hammer home the point that no matter what form the income of the factions of the ruling class takes, profit, interest or rent, its ultimate source is surplus value, that is, the unpaid labour of the workers.

1.2.2 Part II of the Book

The second part of this book presents a detailed analysis of three important and long-standing debates in Marxist economic theory. Here the discussion moves beyond Marx's own work in the three volumes of *Capital* and engages with the work of later Marxist scholars. This discussion is a little more technical than the presentation in the first part of the book. At many places, I use mathematical arguments to clarify ideas and substantiate claims.

In Chapter 6, the first chapter in the second part of the book, I discuss an issue that has generated long-lasting controversy and discussion: the law of the tendential fall in the rate of profit. In Volume III of *Capital*, Marx had argued that the progress of capitalist production will impart a downward tendency to the average rate of profit. It is widely believed in heterodox economic circles that the contribution of the Japanese scholar, Nobuo Okishio, in the early 1960s refuted Marx's argument about the tendency for the rate of profit to fall over time – this result is known as the *Okishio theorem*. Drawing on work by Marxist scholars like Duncan Foley and David Laibman, I show that such a conclusion is misleading. In fact, depending on factors relating to the nature of technological change and changes in the labour market, the rate of profit might rise or fall. Hence, both Marx and Okishio can be accommodated in a more comprehensive theoretical framework.

In Chapter 7, I provide an account of the so-called *transformation problem* – understood by Marx as the process of redistribution of surplus value but which the later literature has identified with the vexed question of the relationship between value (Volume I) and long run, equilibrium prices (Volume III). It is widely believed that Marx's value theory is internally inconsistent because of a contradiction between his accounts in Volume I and III. I argue in this chapter that this belief is mistaken. While Marx's account does have some algebraic mistakes, they can be easily corrected, and with a redefinition of the value of labour-power, as proposed by the New Interpretation (developed independently in the late 1970s by Gérard Duménil and Duncan Foley), a consistent labour theory of value can be constructed.

Marx's numerical examples in Volume III of *Capital* about the transformation of value to prices of production had two errors: first, he had converted output from value to prices but had neglected doing the same for the inputs; and second, he had computed the rate of profit in value terms, whereas it should have been computed in terms of prices. These two problems can be easily addressed, as was shown by the work of Ladislaus von Bortkiewicz in 1907. Marxist scholars like Nobuo Okishio, Micho Morishima and Francis Seton extended the approach of von Bortkiewicz much further in the 1970s, which developed into the Standard Interpretation of Marx's value theory. While the Standard Interpretation demonstrated all of the key claims of Marx, it was nonetheless open to the criticism by Sraffian scholars that value magnitudes were redundant for the analysis of capitalism.

In Chapter 7 of this book, I provide a detailed account of the Standard Interpretation and highlight both its conceptual strengths and limitations. I explain the Sraffian critique and discuss various Marxist responses. I argue that the New Interpretation is the most consistent response to the Sraffian critique. After presenting the New Interpretation, I also present three other interpretations – Macro-monetary Interpretation, Temporal Single System Interpretation and Simultaneous Single System Interpretation – and argue why these are less appealing than the New Interpretation. By the end of this chapter, the reader would have become familiar with the details of the more than century long debate on the so-called transformation problem. The reader will be able to see that contrary to the widespread belief in mainstream and even some heterodox economics circles, the transformation problem is not fatal to Marxist economics.

In Chapter 8, the final chapter of the book, I discuss the questions of exploitation and oppression. The issue of exploitation is central to Marxism. In Chapter 3, we had encountered the claim that surplus value rests on the exploitation of the working class. In Chapter 8, we return to this issue and explore it in greater detail. What is exploitation? Can we define it rigorously? Can we quantify exploitation? I discuss both qualitative and quantitative aspects of the question of exploitation in this chapter. In this chapter, I also discuss two other issues related to the theory of exploitation.

First, I discuss the so-called commodity exploitation theorem. In the early 1980s, a strand of Analytical Marxist thinking developed an ingenious critique of Marx's labour theory of value. The Analytical Marxist argument had two claims. The first claim was that any basic commodity, that is, a commodity that is directly or indirectly used to produce every commodity, can be used to construct a theory of value. Hence, there was nothing special about labour so far as it was, according to Marx, the substance of value. The second claim was that the basic commodity that was used to construct a theory of value would be exploited, just like labour is understood as being exploited when we use the Marxist labour theory of value. In this chapter, I show that both these claims rest on simple conceptual errors.

Second, I discuss the relationship between the concepts of exploitation and oppression. I argue that Marx was a lifelong fighter against all forms of oppression and would support the struggle against all types of oppression even today. But his political project was deeper than a fight against distributive injustice. He conceived of the transcendence of capitalism as the abolition of class-divided society, a fundamental change in the property relations of society, not merely a more equitable distribution of income, wealth and power, though the latter might be an effect of the transcendence of classes.

1.3   What Is Different in This Book

There are well-known texts on Marxist political economy. A reader is therefore justified in asking: What is different in this book? By way of answering this question, I wish to highlight the key novelties of this book.

There are several texts on Marxists political economy in the English language. In particular, I would like to mention the following: Paul M. Sweezy's 1942 book, *The Theory of Capitalist Development*, Ernest Mandel's 1962 book, *Marxist Economic Theory*, and Duncan K. Foley's 1986 book, *Understanding Capital: Marx's Economic Theory*. These three books are, in my opinion, classic texts of Marxist political economy in the English language. They have been used by generations of Marxist scholars and activists to learn the basic principles of Marxist political economy. But all three books are partly outdated by the passage of time. While the contours of the main argument in each book might remain relevant today, the details require updating. My book takes up that task. The presentation in this book is informed by debates and discussion in Marxist political economy over the past several decades since the publication of these books. Thus, my book updates and suitably amends, where necessary, the arguments in the classic texts of Marxist political economy.

There is another respect in which this book is different from the classic texts of Sweezy, Mandel and Foley. Unlike each of these three books, I present Marx's argument of the three volumes of *Capital* in an integrated fashion. I explain the logic of the structure of the three volumes as a whole and then develop the argument in a step-by-step manner, carefully following the logic and structure of the three volumes of *Capital*. While the books by Sweezy, Mandel and Foley touch on all the three volumes of *Capital*, they do not do so in an integrated manner, they do not present Marx's argument in its totality.

An integrated presentation of Marx's argument can also be found in Michael Heinrich's 2012 book, *An Introduction to the Three Volumes of Karl Marx's Capital*. This is a clearly written recent book on Marx's argument and covers much of the same ground that is discussed in the first part of my book. The presentation in this book differs from Heinrich's book in two important respects. First, while Heinrich's presentation avoids engaging with quantitative aspects of Marxist political economy, I integrate qualitative and quantitative aspects of Marxist political economy into a holistic presentation. This is important not only because Marx emphasized both qualitative and quantitative aspects in the three volumes of *Capital* but also because many important debates in Marxist political economy, for example, the transformation problem, or the Okishio theorem or the theory of ground-rent, have been related to quantitative aspects of political economy. Second, Heinrich's book spends lot more time in philosophical discussions than I think is necessary. The philosophical jargon makes the text unnecessarily complicated, and, in my opinion, does not help in developing the political economy argument. This can be seen clearly by contrasting my discussion of 'abstract labour' in Chapter 3 of this book from Heinrich's. While I give due importance to Marx's philosophical ideas, especially those related to dialectics and historical materialism, I do not let philosophical jargon overly encumber the political economy argument.

One important respect in which classical Marxist political economy differs from both mainstream economics and from several strands of heterodox economics is the centrality it accords to the labour theory of value. Over the years, the labour theory of value has been attacked from various quarters for its apparent lack of conceptual coherence. Much of this criticism has been organized around debates on two issues: (*a*) the so-called transformation problem (which relates to the relationship between value and price) and (*b*) the Okishio theorem (which relates to Marx's claim about the tendency of the average rate of profit to fall over time). Given the theoretical importance of these two debates in the history of Marxist political economy, I offer chapter-length treatments of each. In Chapter 6, I discuss issues surrounding the Okishio theorem and in Chapter 7, I present a detailed discussion of the transformation problem. In both these chapters, the discussion is relatively comprehensive in that I have covered all of the main points of the debates. I have also tried to strike a balance between rigour and accessibility with a judicious use of mathematics.

At various points in the book, I have borrowed from my ongoing research to present novel arguments about various issues in Marxist political economy. In Chapter 3, I have used a simple model of production to clarify Marx's discussion of the relationship between the complexity, productivity and intensity of labour to the value creation process. I believe this is a novel presentation of this issue and helps in clarifying some problems in Marx's, and later Marxist, discussion about the effect of intensification of labour on the value of commodities. I show that an increase in the intensity of labour has an ambiguous impact on the value of each unit of the commodity. Depending on the relative magnitudes of what I call the value-creating and use-value handling capacity of intensified labour, the value of each unit of the commodity can either increase, decrease or remain unchanged. This also allows us, in section 3.4, to understand the impact of an intensification of labour on the rate and form of surplus value.

In Chapter 5, I present a novel theory of ground-rent. My presentation clarifies long-standing debates on the concept of 'absolute rent' that figures so prominently in Marx's theory of ground-rent. Previous presentations of Marx's theory of ground-rent have been mired in controversy partly because of the difficulty in defining the components of ground-rent, that is, what Marx identified as differential rent of the first and second varieties and absolute rent. I present an integrated framework for quantifying ground-rent and decomposing it into three components. I also show that once the theory allows capitalist farmers to choose investment in a profit-maximizing way, there will be no absolute rent. The novel presentation of Marx's theory of ground-rent will, I believe, be of interest to scholars not only in political economy but also in sociology, geography and urban studies.

A strand of Marxist thinking, which I will call Analytical Marxist for lack of a better term, developed a whole set of arguments in the 1970s and 1980s that was interpreted as raising serious doubts on the labour theory of value. One argument in this broader class of Analytical Marxist thinking is what I have called a commodity theory of value (CTV), which claims, first, that any 'basic' commodity can be used to construct a consistent theory of value, and second, that such a value theory will show that, in a capitalist economy, profits will be positive if and only if the basic commodity (which is the substance of value) is exploited (commodity exploitation theorem). In Chapter 8, I provide a critique of this argument by highlighting two conceptual flaws on which it rests: (*a*) the failure to distinguish between labour and labour-power and (*b*) the inability to distinguish between the commodity labour-power and all other commodities.

1.4   How to Use This Book

This book can be used either for self-study or for teaching a one-semester course in Marxist political economy, both at the undergraduate and at the graduate level. The presentation in this book builds up Marx's argument almost from scratch. No prior knowledge of economics or Marxism is assumed. Hence, the book can be used by anyone interested in understanding the details of Marx's argument, no matter what their disciplinary background or prior training. When teaching a course in Marxist political economy, this book can be used in disciplines as varied as economics, sociology, geography, urban studies, race studies, critical social theory and, in fact, any other discipline that engages with classical political economy and Marxism. At some places in the book, mathematical arguments are used to clarify concepts and ideas. All the mathematical arguments, other than in Chapter 7 and Appendix 7.A, will be accessible to anyone familiar with high school algebra. The arguments in Chapter 7 and Appendix 7.A use some basic matrix algebra and the discussion of the theory of ground-rent in Chapter 5 uses a little calculus.

A one-semester undergraduate course in Marxist political economy could use the first part of the book and supplement it with readings from contemporary debates on social reproduction, class analysis, financialization, the ecological crisis, the knowledge economy, imperialism and other relevant topics that could vary with the course and the instructor. A one-semester graduate course in Marxist political economy could use the whole book and supplement it with readings from the three volumes of *Capital* and other Marxist scholars. At the end of every major section of the book, I have provided suggestions for further readings to assist instructors who plan on using the book in a course or for those who are using it for self-study.[1]

---

[1]All data sets used to construct charts and tables are available for download from https://people.umass.edu/dbasu/logic-of-capital.html.

Part I

Foundations

2

Some Methodological Issues

In this introductory chapter, we will discuss some methodological issues that will prepare us for the study of Marx's economics. We will begin by acquainting ourselves with Marx's life in general and, in particular, understanding Marx's route to the study of political economy. This will allow us to grasp the motivations that propelled Marx to the study of political economy. On the way we will engage with two important ideas: dialectical method and historical materialism. In the second part of this chapter, we will study the logic behind the structure of his mature work, *Capital*. The structure of Marx's presentation in *Capital* reflects his understanding of some important aspects of the methodology of social sciences. A proper understanding of the structure of *Capital* can potentially prevent us from misunderstanding some of Marx's economic arguments.

2.1 Marx's Route to Political Economy

How and why did Karl Marx come to the study of political economy? In this section, we look, very briefly, at the life and times of Karl Marx and try to understand the motivations that underlay his lifelong study of political economy.

2.1.1 First Phase of Studies

Marx came to the study of economics via jurisprudence, philosophy, history and journalism. After completing his PhD in philosophy from the University of Jena in 1841, he quickly gave up hopes of an academic position. He realized that there was no real prospect of an academic job materializing in Germany due to his radical political views. So he turned to journalism, writing for and then becoming the editor of a radical democratic newspaper *Rheinische Zeitung* (Rhineland Gazette). As editor of the newspaper, he found himself ill prepared to deal with issues of what he called 'material interest'.

> Although I studied jurisprudence, I pursued it as a subject subordinated to philosophy and history. In the year 1842–43, as editor of *Rheinische Zeitung*, I first found myself in the embarrassing position of having to discuss what is known as material interests. The deliberations of the Rhenish Landtag on forest thefts and diversion of landed property; the official polemic started by Herr von Schaper, then Oberprasident of the Rhine Province, against *Rheinische Zeitung* about the condition of the Moselle peasantry, and finally the debates on free trade and protective tariffs caused me in the first instance to turn my attention to economic questions. (Marx, 1976, pp. 19–20)

Working as a young radical activist and journalist in the early 1840s, Marx seems to have realized that the lack of his knowledge of economics was a serious handicap. It is to address this lacuna in his understanding that Marx initiated his lifelong study of political economy in 1842–43. But when we look at the details of Marx's studies during the 1840s, we see that political economy was only one of three sets of issues that engaged his attention. His studies of this period focused on two more large topics: (*a*) French theories of socialism and communism and (*b*) classical German, especially Hegelian, philosophy. How do we make sense of this?

In mid-nineteenth-century German radical and democratic circles, French theories of socialism were popular. Marx had been exposed to some of these theories in his adolescence by his father and his to-be father-in-law. He encountered them again as a young university student in Bonn and Berlin. While being positively disposed to such theories because of their egalitarian thrust, Marx's impression was that they lacked in theoretical rigour and empirical content. When these theories made their way into the pages of the *Rheinische Zeitung* or came up in debates with other conservative newspapers (like the *Allgemeine Augsburger Zeitung*), he found that his previous studies in jurisprudence and philosophy had not adequately prepared him to make informed comments on these theories.

> On the other hand, at that time when good intentions 'to push forward' often took the place of factual knowledge, an echo of French socialism and communism, slightly tinged with philosophy, was noticeable in the *Rheinische Zeitung*. I objected to this dilettantism, but at the same time frankly admitted in a controversy with the Allgemeine Augsburger Zeitung that my previous studies did not allow me to express any opinion on the content of the French theories. (Marx, 1976, pp. 19–20)

This lacuna in his previous studies was the spur for his deep, and long term, engagement with French theories of socialism and communism, the second foci of his studies in the 1840s.

What about German philosophy? Why was that one of the foci of his studies in the 1840s? Of course, part of the reason was that he was a philosopher by training – recall that he had completed a PhD in philosophy – and he liked engaging in philosophical debates and discussions. But there was another, more political, reason. As a young radical in Berlin, Marx had been forced to engage with the writings of Hegel, the most important thinker in mid-nineteenth-century Germany. Even as he had already imbibed a 'left' interpretation of Hegelian philosophy developed by the 'Young Hegelians', he was dissatisfied with their exclusive focus on the realm of ideas. His encounter with issues of 'material interest' – as editor of the *Rheinische Zeitung* – had convinced him of the limited purchase of speculative philosophy. He had not worked out his ideas fully on how to locate philosophical enquiry within his overall project, but his political and journalistic engagements had generated enough doubts in his mind that called for his attention. Hence, he engaged with classical German philosophy once again.

These three strands of enquiry came together in his intellectual work when Marx moved away from the public stage in 1843. Under Marx's energetic editorship, the *Rheinische Zeitung* quickly gained readership and recognition, becoming the largest selling and most quoted daily in Germany. Its consistently democratic and radical tone and coverage soon ran afoul of the conservative and authoritarian Prussian monarchy. When middle-class shareholders of the *Rheinische Zeitung* pressurized Marx in 1843 to tone down the radical and democratic thrust of the paper – in the hope of escaping suppression by the Prussian government – Marx refused. Instead of changing the orientation of the newspaper, he tendered his resignation as editor and 'eagerly grasped the opportunity to withdraw from the public stage' to his study.

What emerged from this initial phase of studies, which was partly carried out in collaboration with his lifelong friend and comrade, Friedrich Engels, was a creative synthesis of three strands of European thought – English political economy, French socialism and German philosophy – into a coherent and integral world outlook. This coherent body of work became the kernel of what would later be called 'Marxism' (Lenin, 1913; Ollman, 1981).

This initial phase of his studies produced several important pieces of work (some discovered and published many years after Marx's death):

- *Economic and Philosophic Manuscripts of 1844* (sometimes also referred to as the 'Paris Manuscripts' that was completed in 1844);
- *Theses on Feuerbach* (1845);
- *The Poverty of Philosophy* (1847);
- *The Communist Manifesto* (written jointly with Engels and published in 1848); and
- *Wage Labour and Capital* (1849).[1]

In these studies, Marx developed two important ideas that would deeply inform his later work on political economy: the 'dialectical method' and the 'materialist conception of history' (or historical materialism).

2.1.2 Dialectical Method

There is lot of unnecessary mystery surrounding the notion of the dialectic or dialectical method. In this section, we will briefly discuss the concept of the dialectic to dispel the aura of mystery that surrounds it. We will first understand the dialectic as it was developed in the writings of Hegel. We will, then, understand how Marx used the dialectic in his own work and how his dialectic differs from the dialectic in Hegel.[2]

---

[1] The text of this pamphlet was delivered as a lecture in Brussels in 1847 and published in 1849 (Marx, 1993a, Preface by Engels, p. 90).
[2] I draw heavily on Wood (2004, Chapters 13–15) for the discussion of the dialectic.

The Dialectic in Hegel

In Hegel's work, the dialectic refers to two things simultaneously: the structure of 'ultimate reality', and the process of comprehension of that reality. Hegel's vision of reality comes from his speculative metaphysics, that is, his theory of ultimate reality. For Hegel, ultimate reality is a self-actualizing thinking principle or form-giving principle, which he calls the *geist* or the spirit. The self-actualization of the spirit is visualized by Hegel as consisting of two distinct steps. In the first step, the spirit objectifies itself, alienates itself; and in the second step, the spirit comprehends itself in and through the objects created in the first step. The comprehension, therefore, ends the alienation of the first step and re-establishes the unity of the spirit with itself.

The first step of the process, that is, objectification, itself has two aspects. First of all, the thinking principle objectifies itself in the form of universal 'concepts' that can be comprehended by speculative thought, that is, by the intellectual activity of the philosopher. But, according to Hegel, this comprehension will remain 'abstract' and incomplete unless the concepts are properly exemplified. Therefore, comprehension requires a second process: concepts need to be exemplified in the phenomenal world through particular entities. In other words, the process of objectification moves from concepts to the real world. In the real world, there are finite minds, which are endowed with the ability to think and comprehend. It is through these finite minds, that is, the activity of the philosophers (and Hegel was the philosopher *par excellence*), that the spirit finally comprehends itself. Through this comprehension, the spirit re-establishes its unity as a self-knowing entity.

This heavy dose of metaphysics is not of much use to us. What is important for our purpose, that is, for the study of political economy, are two Hegelian ideas: (*a*) the structure of reality is to be conceptualized as an organized or self-organizing whole and (*b*) a pronounced tendency for development or change is a defining characteristic of this reality. Hegel's understanding of the structure of reality, which he takes from Kant, is best seen as a model of a self-conscious living organism. The different parts of the organism are connected to each other in a determinate way. Each part derives its meaning from being part of the whole, that is, the organism, and from being connected to and dependent on the other parts. But the organism is also self-conscious. Hence, it can comprehend itself. In its comprehension of itself, the organism understands the limitations of its specific structure. Hence, comprehension propels a movement of change in its structure as a way to overcome the perceived limitation. This is what imparts a pronounced developmental tendency to reality understood as a self-conscious living organism. In the Hegelian vision, the development of reality proceeds through a series of stages, each of which is limited and inadequate, and leads to a new and higher stage of development as a way to overcome the limitations of the previous stage.

It is this process of organic, self-directed, inner development that Hegel refers to as the 'dialectic'. It has a parallel with the older use of that word 'dialectic' in Greek philosophy where it meant the emergence of truth through the confrontation of incorrect or incomplete ideas (and opinions) in the process of debates and discussions. For Hegel, therefore, the process of organic development of reality is akin to a cosmic dialogue, where each stage is marked by the confrontation of incomplete or inadequate forms, and leads to the emergence of a new stage or structure as an advance over the previous stage. Hegel specifies this movement through stages with the idea of a 'contradiction'.

In each stage of its development, reality (or the spiritual being) contains opposing tendencies or aspects. These aspects are not only mutually dependent on each other but are also opposed to each other. These mutually opposed and codependent aspects define the very essence of the structure of reality and propels its development and change. As long as the structure manages to contain them through a balancing of the opposed tendencies, the structure is stable. But when the conflict of the opposed aspects can no longer be contained in the given structure, it leads to change. A new structure emerges. Thus, the movement or development of the spiritual being is conceived by Hegel as a dialectical series of structures, each evolving out of the previous step through the working out of the inner logic, that is, contradiction, of each stage.

The implication of this vision of reality for the process of comprehension is also important to note. If we are to comprehend an organic totality with such a pronounced developmental tendency, then our conceptual apparatus must also have the same structure as the reality it is trying to comprehend. The conceptual apparatus must be an organized set of concepts that form a dialectical series in the same way that reality, according to Hegel, forms in its development.

The Dialectic in Marx

Marx takes what he finds useful in Hegel's dialectic and discards what is not of use. Specifically, Marx refers to his relationship with the Hegelian dialectic through two metaphors. In the first metaphor, Marx separates out the 'rational kernel' from the 'mystical shell' of the Hegelian dialectic. He takes the former and discards the latter. In the second metaphor, Marx 'inverts' Hegel's dialectic. In Hegel, the dialectic is by standing on its head; it needs to be inverted and stood on its feet, claims Marx. Both these metaphors can be interpreted to mean that Marx takes the vision of reality expounded by Hegel but rejects his speculative metaphysics.

Marx's vision of social reality is similar to Hegel's vision of ultimate reality. For Marx, society should be understood as *a self-organizing structure with a pronounced developmental tendency.* Hence, society's development through historical time should be conceptualized as a dialectical series of socio-economic forms. The developmental tendency driving this evolution or progression of socio-economic forms comes from the contradictions inherent in each form. So far, Marx is very much in agreement with Hegel. But then he radically departs from the Hegelian dialectic by discarding the latter's speculative metaphysics. For Marx, the development tendency in society does not come from the process of self-actualization of any spiritual being or *Geist,* as in Hegel. Rather, that the structure of reality is dialectical, that human societies evolve in historical time as a dialectical series is a philosophical postulate of Marx. He does not posit any extra-material entity, like the spirit, to justify this postulate.

Since Marx accepts Hegel's vision of reality (without the speculative metaphysics), he also accepts the implication of that vision for the process of comprehension of reality. To be adequate to its task, the set of concepts must form a dialectical series – to reflect in thought the reality it is trying to comprehend. In more specific terms, Marx's theoretical project, therefore, includes both an understanding of the structure and stability of any socio-economic form and an understanding of the contradictions that could lead to its dissolution and replacement by a higher socio-economic form. Description, analysis and critique are therefore fused into one in Marx's theoretical project.

2.1.3 Materialist Conception of History

Through his studies into philosophy, law, history and politics, Marx developed a novel way to understand the *structure of society* and *large-scale social change*. While previous thinkers had tried to explain the structure of society and historical change by focusing on political institutions or on legal relations or on the domain of ideas, Marx pointed out that this approach left unanswered the questions as to what determines political structures and legal relations or what determines the contours of dominant ideas of a society. Marx's studies in the early 1840s, especially his critical engagement with Hegelian philosophy, had convinced him that explanations about legal and political structures could only be found by relating them to the way society organized the production of material life.

> My inquiry led me to the conclusion that neither legal relations nor political forms could be comprehended whether by themselves or on the basis of a so-called general development of the human mind, but that on the contrary they originate in the material conditions of life, the totality of which Hegel, following the example of English and French thinkers of the eighteenth century embraces within the term 'civil society'; that the anatomy of this civil society, however, has to be sought in political economy. (Marx, 1976, p. 20)

Marx went on to make more specific claims about the structure of society, and large-scale historical change of societies using the notions of productive forces (or productive power), the economic structure and the political and legal superstructure. Together, these explanatory claims about the structure and epochal changes of society are known as the materialist conception of history or historical materialism. The main ideas that comprise historical materialism were independently arrived at by Marx and Engels and often jointly elaborated. Some of the more important pieces of work where the materialist conception of history is outlined or explained are the following: *The German Ideology* (Marx and Engels, 1845–46); Marx's letter to P. V. Annenkov (28 December 1846); Preface to *The Contribution to the Critique of Political Economy* (Marx, 1859); *Socialism: Utopian and Scientific* (Engels, 1880); Engels' letter to Joseph Bloch (21–22 September 1890).

One of the most quoted passages from Marx's writings that is given below summarizes the key claims of historical materialism regarding both structure and change. First, Marx offers explanatory claims about structure.

> In the social production of their life, men inevitably enter into definite relations, which are independent of their will, namely relations of production *appropriate to* a given stage in the development of their material forces of production. The totality of these relations of production constitute the economic structure of society, the real *foundation*, on which arises a legal and political superstructure and to which *correspond* definite forms of social consciousness. The mode of production of material life *conditions* the general process of social, political and intellectual life. It is not the consciousness of men that determines their existence, but their social existence that *determines* their consciousness. (Marx, 1976, emphasis added)

Next, Marx lays out his claims about large-scale social change.

> At a certain stage of development, the material productive forces of society come into conflict with the existing relations of production or – this merely expresses the same thing in a legal framework – with the property relations within the framework of which they have operated hitherto. From forms of development of the productive forces these relations turn into their fetters. Then begins an era of social revolution. *The changes in the economic foundation leads sooner or later to the transformation of the whole immense superstructure.* In studying such transformations it is always necessary to distinguish between the material transformation of the economic conditions of production, which can be determined with the precision of natural science, and the legal, political, religious, artistic, or philosophic – in short, ideological forms in which men become conscious of this conflict and fight it out. (Marx, 1976, emphasis added)

The italicized phrases and sentences in the above quotes direct our attention to the key explanatory claims of historical materialism, and we will now try to understand them in greater detail.[3]

---

[3] This section draws on Cohen (1986a,b). For a more detailed analysis see Cohen (2001), and also

Defining Terms

The *productive power* (or productive forces) refer to the means of production and the labour-power (capacity to do useful work) available in any society. The means of production are the non-labour inputs into production – the tools and implements, the structures and equipment, the raw materials and other auxiliary materials. Labour-power is the labour input into production and refers to the labouring capacity of the direct producers.

When considering the means of production and labour-power available to any society, we need to consider both quantitative and qualitative aspects. At any point in time, the means of production, especially the structures and equipment, embody the current state of knowledge about production. Thus, the means of production not only refers to the quantity of the non-labour inputs but also incorporates information about its quality. In a similar manner, labour-power refers not only to the labour force, that is, the number of direct producers potentially available for working, but also their average level of skills, which, in turn, reflects the current state of knowledge about production.

The *economic structure* of any society is composed of the relations of production. By relations of production, we mean the relationships of economic power that human beings have over the means of production and labour-power – the two elements of the productive power of society. By economic power over means of production or labour-power, we mean the ability to access and use, or dispose of, the means of production or labour-power. Relations of production define and distinguish large groups of people that comprise the *fundamental social classes* of any society.

In a slave society, slaves and slave owners form the two fundamental social classes. The slaves do not have economic power over the means of production or the labour-power; slave owners have economic power over both means of production and labour-power. In a feudal society, serfs and lords comprise the two fundamental social classes. Serfs have partial economic power over the means of production and labour-power. The partial economic power over means of production comes from access to some land that the serf has, and the partial power over labour-power comes from the ability to work on her land in any way she pleases. In a capitalist society, the workers and the capitalists define the fundamental social classes. The worker

---

Wood (2004, Chapters 5–8).

has no economic power over the means of production, but has full economic power over labour-power.[4]

The *superstructure* can be understood as being comprised of some of the key non-economic institutions of society. While there is agreement that the superstructure consists of non-economic institutions, there is controversy with regard to the specific institutions that could or should be included. For instance, while the legal and political institutions are largely understood to be part of the superstructure, and artistic activities and institutions for regulating artistic production are understood to *not* be part of the superstructure, there is less agreement about, for instance, scientific activities and institutions of science.

Claims about Structure

Historical materialism makes two explanatory claims about the structure of society at any point in time.

- Claim 1: The productive power of a society determines the nature of its economic structure.

- Claim 2: The economic structure of society determines the nature of its legal and political superstructure.

The first claim here is that productive power determines the economic structure of society, that is, the quality and quantity of means of production and labour-power determine the economic relations of power over the means of production and labour-power. The claim about 'determination' should be understood as an explanatory claim and not as a causal claim. When we say that the productive power determines the economic structure of society, we are asserting that the latter can be explained by the former in the following way: The specific economic structure occurs because of the effect it has on the productive power. What effect? The effect that it facilitates the development of the productive power. To summarize: the economic structure is explained by (or determined by) the productive power in the sense that it occurs because of the (beneficial) effect it has on the productive power.

---

[4]This is the meaning of the 'double freedom' of labour under capitalism that we will encounter in Chapter 3 – workers are free of any kind of bondage to the class of owners of means of production *and* are also free from, that is, without direct access to, the means of production. Here, the second, admittedly ironical, sense in which the word 'freedom' is used highlights Marx's way of deflating claims about the freedom that capitalism supposedly creates.

Before we look at the second claim, it is important to be clear about certain aspects of the explanation that has been offered here. Such explanations are known as *functional explanations* or teleological explanations because they explain the *explanandum* (what needs to be explained) in terms of its effect on the *explanans* (what is supposed to be doing the explaining). Here, 'economic structure' is the explanandum and 'productive power' is the explanans. The effect in question is the facilitation of the development of the 'productive power'. The 'economic structure' is explained by the effect it has on the productive power.

Why does historical materialism require functional explanations? While historical materialism claims that 'productive power' explains the nature of the 'economic structure', it also makes another, equally important, claim: the economic structure has a causal effect on the development (or retardation) of the productive power. Since the economic structure has a causal effect on the productive power of society, the only way in which we can sustain the claim that the latter *explains* the former is by claiming that the explanation in question is a functional explanation and not a causal explanation. In fact, the causal effect of the economic structure on the productive power of society is essential for the conceptual coherence of historical materialism. While certain economic structures facilitate the development of the productive powers, other economic structures impede its development. It is only because of this causal impact of the economic structure on the productive power of society that we can ascertain whether, and if at all, the former is functional to the latter.

Since it has been a source of common misunderstanding, let us reiterate this point. We are saying:

- (A): the productive power of society *explains* its economic structure, and
- (B): the economic structure of society *has a causal impact on* the development of the productive power of society.

There is no contradiction between (A) and (B) because the explanation involved in (A) is a functional explanation. This has an important implication. Since the key claims of historical materialism are functional explanations, it is a serious misunderstanding to claim that historical materialism is an example of economic (or any other kind of) *determinism*. The fact that historical materialism allows for, in fact needs, the causal impact of the economic structure on the productive power, captured in proposition (B), means that it cannot be *determinist* in the sense of asserting the unidirectional causal impact of the productive power on economic structure.[5] Because historical materialism uses a functional explanation, it also maintains the *explanatory primacy* of the productive power of society over the economic structure – as captured by (A). But this explanatory primacy does not rule out, but in fact needs, the causal impact of the economic structure on the productive power of society – as captured in (B).

Let us now look at the second claim of historical materialism so far as it is related to the structure of society. The claim is that the superstructure is determined by the economic structure. Once again, the claim about determination should be understood as a claim about explanatory primacy and not about causality. Historical materialism is claiming that the superstructure is explained by the economic structure in the sense that a specific superstructure occurs because of the effect it has on the economic structure. The effect in question relates to stability, that is, a specific superstructure occurs because it stabilizes the economic structure of a society.

Let us take an example to understand the important point that the above claim about determination does not exclude, but in fact needs, the causal impact of the superstructure on the economic structure. In a capitalist society, a capitalist has economic power over the means of production. From where does the capitalist derive this power? The power comes from the legal institutions of capitalist society, which allows the capitalist to exclude others from using or accessing the means of production she owns. This power of the capitalist is guaranteed by the legal structure of capitalist society and enforced by the State. Here, then, we have a case where an element of the superstructure (the legal institutions) has a causal impact on the economic structure (the power over means of production) even though the economic structure has explanatory primacy over the superstructure.

Claims about Large-Scale Social Change
Historical materialism makes three claims to explain large-scale social change.

- Claim 1: There is an inexorable tendency for society's productive power to increase over time.

---

[5] An influential strand of Marxist thinking accepts the charge of determinism and then tries to overcome that problem (Resnick and Wolff, 1987). An alternative approach, which I have presented in this section, builds on the work of the philosopher G. A. Cohen (Cohen, 2001). In this alternative approach, the key claims of historical materialism are understood as involving functional explanations. This means that historical materialism does not adhere to any form of determinism. Hence, there is no reason to accept the charge of determinism or to build an alternative non-determinist Marxism.

- Claim 2: Changes in the productive power determine changes in the economic structure of society.

- Claim 3: Changes in the economic structure determine changes in the superstructure of society.

The first claim identifies the pronounced development tendency that is characteristic of any organic totality. Recall from our discussion in the previous section that this is an important component of Marx's dialectical understanding of reality. Since Marx, unlike Hegel, does not posit any non-material entity to justify this claim, it should rather be understood as a philosophical postulate. We can convert it into an empirical claim and see if we can gather evidence to either support or refute it. It is a well-established empirical fact that the amount of social labour time that is needed to produce goods and services to satisfy basic subsistence needs of the direct producers has secularly declined over time. This is a most direct empirical support of the claim about the pronounced developmental tendency in society. It should be noted that here we are using a fixed subsistence consumption, rather than actual consumption, of the direct producers to assess the claim. This is meaningful because actual consumption is determined by social, historical and cultural factors, but the claim we are assessing relates to the technological capability of society, so far as its productive power (capacity) goes. And to assess the technological claim, we need to use a fixed bundle of consumption.

The second and third claims are explanatory claims, that is, in these claims the word 'determines' should be understood as 'can explain'. The second claim can be restated as follows. In a stable social system, the economic structure corresponds to the productive powers of that society, that is, it facilitates the development of society's productive powers. At a certain point, the economics structure no longer facilitates the development of the productive power of society; it becomes an impediment to its further development. At this point, which can be thought of as a period of transition between two stable social systems, the productive powers of society and its economic structure are no longer in correspondence, they are in conflict. In such a situation, the economic structure of society must change to bring itself, once more, in correspondence with the changed (or developed) productive powers.

Why must the economic structure change and not the productive powers of society? Two underlying assumptions give this result. First, from a *long run perspective*, productive powers of society are not destroyed, productive powers develop and do not regress. In a deep sense, it is the continuous progress of the productive powers of human beings that provide intelligibility and coherence to history.

> Because of [the] simple fact that every succeeding generation finds itself in possession of the productive powers acquired by the previous generation, which serve it as the raw material for new production, a coherence arises in human history, a history of humanity takes shape which is all the more a history of humanity as the productive forces of man and therefore his social relations have been more developed. (Tucker, 1978, p. 137; *Marx's 1846 letter to P. V. Annenkov*)

Second, no economic structure has infinite flexibility, that is, no economic structure can allow for an infinite development of the productive powers of society. At some point in time, the economic structure will no longer be able to facilitate the development of productive forces. At that point, the economic structure is in conflict with the productive forces. Since productive powers cannot regress, it is the economic structure that has to change to allow further development of the productive powers of society. It is important to note that if any economic structure had infinite flexibility, the point of decisive conflict would never arise. It would always be able to accommodate further development of the productive forces. It is a postulate of historical materialism that that is not possible.

The third claim about large-scale social change is analogous to the second. It asserts that during or after the transitional period, the existing superstructure is no longer able to stabilize the economic structure. A lack of correspondence develops between the economic structure and the legal and political superstructure. The superstructure is in conflict with the economic structure. Correspondence is once again established through changes in the superstructure. That is the sense in which changes in the economic structure has explanatory primacy over changes in the superstructure.[6]

---

[6]Many scholars do not use a full-blown functional explanation in their exposition of historical materialism. Instead they use opaque notions like 'structural causality' or unexplained phrases like 'determination in the last instance' or give up the notion of causality or replace the explanatory primacy of the productive powers and the economic structure with heuristic claims (Cohen, 1986b, p. 222). The exposition offered in this chapter, which borrows from the work that the philosopher G. A. Cohen carried out in the 1970s, is probably the only rigorous way to make sense of historical materialism. In

What about Class Struggle?

The account of historical materialism presented in the previous sections did not even mention class struggle. Readers might find this surprising because Marx and Engels had asserted in the *Communist Manifesto* that all history is the history of class struggle.

> The history of all hitherto existing society is the history of class struggles. Freeman and slave, patrician and plebeian, lord and serf, guild-master and journeyman, in a word, oppressor and oppressed, stood in constant opposition to one another, carried on an uninterrupted, now hidden, now open fight, a fight that each time ended, either in a revolutionary reconstitution of society at large, or in the common ruin of the contending classes. (Marx and Engels, 1998)

Does Marx, then, have two different theories of history? If not, how do we reconcile the productive power and relations of production theory with the theory of class struggle?

Marx did *not* have two different theories of history. The account of historical materialism that we have seen above is his theory of history. Class struggle fits into that picture at the level of actions by groups of human beings to bring about social change. But, why such collective, political action leads to one outcome rather than another is explained by the productive power – relations of production theory. Another way to state this is to note that the fundamental, or underlying, factor driving large-scale historical change is the contradiction, or lack of correspondence, between the productive power and relations of production of a society. This contradiction is reflected in, and fought out through, the conflict in the interest of fundamental social classes, for example, serfs and lords, or workers and capitalists. The collective political action of human beings, in this case classes, then bring about a change in the economic structure of society, that is, the relations of production, that is necessary to resolve the contradiction that gave rise to the conflict of class interests in the first place. Thus, class struggle is the *mechanism* through which historical change is effected, but the

---

a curious turn of events, Cohen himself seems to have fallen prey to the rational choice explanatory framework that he had so effectively argued against (when arguing against the political theorist Jon Elster) in the 1970s and 1980s (Callinicos, 2006).

shape of that change can only be explained with reference to the contradiction between the productive power and the relations of production.

Summing Up

At this point, it would be useful to summarize two key points for future reference. Through his studies in philosophy, law and history, Marx had reached two crucial conclusions that would guide his future studies: (*a*) to understand the complex entity called society one needs to understand, first and foremost, the economic structure of society; and to do the latter, one need to use the tools of political economy and (*b*) to understand large-scale historical change in society, one needs to identify the contradictions between fundamental social classes (which is itself a reflection of the deeper contradiction between the productive powers and relations of production). While the first conclusion was facilitated by classical political economy, the second was helped by Marx's engagement with dialectics, especially of the Hegelian variety.

Here, then, we have an understanding of both the motivations for and the future trajectory of Marx's studies in political economy. Marx took up the study of political economy because that would allow him to understand the 'anatomy of civil society'. He oriented his studies in political economy towards an investigation of 'the categories which make up the inner structure of bourgeois society and on which the fundamental classes rest' because the contradictions between the 'fundamental classes' held the key to the understanding of large-scale historical change.

2.1.4   *Interruption of Studies*

Before Marx could continue with the study of political economy using these insights as guiding principles, the revolutionary movement flared up across Europe in 1848. Marx and Engels interrupted their studies and plunged headlong into day-to-day political work of propaganda and agitation.

> The tidal wave of revolution pushed all scientific pursuits into the background; what mattered now was to become involved in the movement. (Engels, 1869)

When the revolutionary movements of 1848 failed in one country after the other, Marx, one of the most vocal and articulate defenders of the revolution, was chased across the continent by the secret and not-so-secret police. He was expelled, in quick succession, from Belgium, Germany and France. He finally moved to England in 1849, and settled down in London to an alienated and difficult life common among mid-nineteenth-century émigré intellectuals. When the insurrection of the Paris workers was defeated in 1850, Marx (and his comrade, Engels) reached the conclusion that revolution was no longer on the cards in the immediate future. They envisaged their primary work during this period of reaction as one of education, study and development of revolutionary theory and withdrew from day-to-day organizational politics.

2.1.5   Second Phase of Studies

Marx resumed his studies on political economy in 1850, using the insights he had reached in the 1840s as his guiding principles. When he received a reader's ticket for the reading room of the British Museum in 1850, he was overjoyed. He not only had a place for quiet study but could also access the wealth of information available in the British Museum and use them as invaluable source material for developing and testing his theories. Despite serious financial difficulties and health problems, and occasionally being drawn into political struggles, Marx spent most of his time now in studying various aspects of economics and the evolution of capitalism.[7] This phase of his studies continued until his death in 1883, but it was the onset of the economic crisis of 1857 which forced Marx to try to work out his ideas into a publishable format. This was not easy and Marx struggled to conclude his studies and find the proper form to present his analysis of capitalism for many more years.

The first text where he tried to present some of his key ideas was the *Grundrisse: Foundations of the Critique of Political Economy (Rough Draft)*. The *Grundrisse* was written as a series of seven notebooks in 1857–58, and mainly served the purpose of self-clarification. It is not clear whether the *Grundrisse* was meant for publication, and it was certainly not published during his lifetime. Over the next decade, Marx worked his way through the intricacies

---

[7]The period between 1864 and 1872 was the second period of intense political activity for Marx – the first being the period during 1848–49. During this eight year period, he was heavily involved with, and the *de facto* leader of, the International Working Men's Association. The key difference with the first period of political activity during 1848–49 was that Marx was able to keep working on his book on political economy during this eight year period of 1864–72.

of political economy, and left the result of his studies in the following published and unpublished work:

- *A Contribution to the Critique of Political Economy* (published in 1859, this is primarily a re-draft of the first chapter of the *Grundrisse* and remained incomplete);

- The 1861–63 manuscripts comprising 23 notebooks, parts of which were published as *Theories of Surplus Value* (first published by Kautsky in 1905–10), portions of Volume I of Capital (published in 1867), and some portions of Volume III of *Capital* (published by Engels in 1895);[8]

- A manuscript of 1864–65, most of which was incorporated in Volume III of *Capital*;

- Four manuscripts written in 1865 or 1867, numbered as MS I to IV, which went into Volume II of Capital;

- The first German edition of Volume I of Capital that was published in 1867;

- Four manuscripts written in 1878, numbered as MS V to VIII, which was used for Volume II of Capital;

- Russian translation of Volume I of Capital in 1872;

- The second German edition of Volume I of Capital that was published in 1873;

- The French edition of Volume I of Capital that was published between 1872 and 1875. Marx was not satisfied with the French translation by Mr. J. Roy and made many changes to the text to 'make it more intelligible to the reader'. Moreover, while doing so, he also added additional historical and statistical material, and provided critical suggestions to the second German edition (Marx, 1992, Postface to the French edition). *Marx saw the second French edition as the definitive edition of Capital* and the third German edition, published by Engels in 1883, was based on this. The first English edition was a translation of the third German edition. The work of translation was carried out by Samuel Moore and Edward Aveling and the whole edition was

---

[8]The 1861–63 manuscripts, entitled 'Zur Kritik der politischen Ökonomie', were a continuation of the manuscript of the same title published in 1859 (Marx, 1993a, Preface by Engels, p. 84).

published under the supervision of Engels in 1886.[9]

In approaching the three volumes of *Capital*, we need to keep two things in mind. First, as Engels indicated in the introduction to the edited version of Marx's 1849 *Wage Labour and Capital* that he published in 1891, Marx could complete his study of political economy only by the end of the 1850s. Hence, his earlier work on economics (produced in the 1840s) should be considered incomplete and even incorrect, to some extent. It is the body of work that emerges from 1857–58 onwards that is the relatively complete part of Marx's writings on political economy.

Second, while Marx was working out his ideas and experimenting with the best form to present them, he put them down in many notebooks (as we have seen earlier). We will see in detail in section 2.2 that, after some experimentation, Marx *finally* conceived of the presentation of his work on political economy in terms of three books, which were published as the three volumes of *Capital*. But Marx could complete the work only on Volume I of *Capital*. Ill health prevented him from concluding the work for Volume II and III, and so they should be considered relatively incomplete. I say *relatively* incomplete because he had worked out much of the details of Volume II and III and left the results in the unpublished notebooks.

It was left to Engels to work through the manuscripts, organize the material in a proper format and publish the other volumes of *Capital*: Volume II and III were published in 1884 and 1895, respectively.[10] Marx's work on the history of economic thought, which was a detailed engagement with almost all important classical economists that came before him, was first published in 1905–10 by Karl Kautsky as the *Theories of Surplus Value*.[11] Following a suggestion by Engels (Marx, 1993a, Preface by Engels, p. 84), most scholars consider this as Volume IV of Capital.

Thus, while it is true that only Volume I of *Capital* could be completed by Marx, the above two considerations – that Marx conceived of the

---

[9]For the discussion in this book, I am using the English translation by Ben Fowkes of the third German edition that was published in 1976 as part of the Marx Pelican Library.

[10]Engels managed to publish two German editions of Volume II, the first in 1884 and the second in 1893. The English edition is a translation of the second German edition. I am using the English edition that was published in 1976 as part of the Pelican Marx Library, with the work of translation being done by David Fernbach. Engels published the first German edition of Volume III in 1895. I am using the 1981 English translation of this work by David Fernbach – published as part of the Pelican Marx Library.

[11]The edition published by Kautsky was not accurate. It has been superseded by the edition published by the Institute for Marxism-Leninism, Berlin, in 1956–62.

presentation of his work on political economy in terms of the three volumes of *Capital*, and that he had substantially worked through the *whole argument* presented in the three volumes together before he devoted himself to giving final shape to Volume I of *Capital* – suggest that we study all the three volumes together and that these three volumes give us a relatively complete picture of Marx's economics. That is why, in this book, we will study the main argument developed by Marx in the three volumes of *Capital* taken together. But before we delve into the content of *Capital*, we must first understand its structure.

Further Readings

- For informative accounts of the life and times of Karl Marx, see Wheen (2001) and Gabriel (2011).

- Introductions to Marxism, which emphasize how it is a creative synthesis of three key strands of European thought, can be found in Lenin (1913) and Ollman (1981).

- The classic but brief statement of the materialist conception of history can be found in Marx (1976, Preface). Early expositions are available in Marx and Engels (1998) and Engels (1877). The most sophisticated and clear account of the materialist conception of history can be found in Cohen ([1978] 2001), and a shorter version of the same argument can also be found in Wood (2004, Chapters 5–8).

- The political theorist, Jon Elster, has been a fierce and consistent critic of historical materialism and functional explanations. For a critical review of Cohen's book, see Elster (1980); for a response by Cohen, see Cohen (1980). In Elster (1982), Jon Elster made a case for the use of game theory and methodological individualism; for a critique, see Cohen (1982). Elster's position was elaborated further in Elster (1985); for a critical review of Elster's treatment of functional explanation in that book, see Wood (1986b).

- For a clear and philosophically sophisticated exposition of the dialectical method and the relationship of Marx and Hegel, see Wood (2004, Chapters 13–15). Classic accounts of the dialectical method can also be found in Lenin (1915) and Tse-tung (1937).

2.2 The Structure of *Capital*

In the 1857–58 manuscript, which was later published as the *Grundrisse* (Marx, 1993c), we find the first outline of Marx's plans for a comprehensive study of the whole capitalist system; in a 1865 letter to Engels, we find the final outline of his plans. Over this 7–8 year period, Marx experimented with the plan of the outline as he worked out the material and thought about the best form in which to present the result of his research.[12] The first outline shows Marx working with a six-book plan, with a book each on: capital, wage-labour, landed property, the state, foreign trade, and the world market and crisis.[13] By the time of the final outline in 1865, Marx had changed his plan in two specific ways.

First, in the 1857–58 plan, Marx thought of devoting only one of the six books to a study of capital, while the other books were meant to deal with other categories like wage labour, landed property, and so on. But in the 1865 plan, the whole work is conceived as a study of capital. This change came from Marx's understanding that the concept of capital was not one of many concepts needed to understanding capitalism, it was the key concept.

> The exact development of the concept of capital [is] necessary, since it [is] the fundamental concept of modern economics, just as capital itself, whose abstract, reflected image [is] its concept [*dessen abstraktes Gegenbild sein Begriff*], [is] the foundation of bourgeois society. The sharp formulation of the basic presuppositions of the relation must bring out all the contradictions of bourgeois production, as well as the boundary where it drives beyond itself. (Marx, 1993c, p. 331)

Second, while the 1857–58 outline had a plan for a six-book work, the 1865 outline showed a plan for a three-book presentation of the study of capital: the first book would be devoted to the production process of capital, the second book would deal with the circulation process of capital and the final book would look at the process of capitalist production as a whole.

In moving from the first outline of 1857–58 to the final outline of 1865,

---

[12]For a detailed discussion of the frequent but small changes that Marx made to the original outline as he worked out his ideas, and for the logic underlying the continuity and change between the first and the final outline, see Rosdolsky (1977, pp. 10–56).

[13]This outline is most clearly seen in a letter written by Marx at the end of February and before the completion of the manuscripts of 1857–58 (Marx, 1993c, Foreword by Martin Nicolaus, p. 54).

Marx was guided by his understanding of the correct method of political economy and his attempt to be faithful to that understanding in his presentation of the results of his research. In the 'Introduction' to the *Grundrisse*, Marx set out a fairly detailed account of his understanding of the correct method of political economy.

> It seems to be correct to begin with the real and the concrete, with the real precondition, thus to begin, in economics, with e.g. the population, which is the foundation and the subject of the entire social act of production. However, on closer examination this proves false. (Marx, 1993c, p. 100)

Why is this false?

> The population is an abstraction if I leave out, for example, the classes of which it is composed. These classes in turn are an empty phrase if I am not familiar with the elements on which they rest. E.g., wage labour, capital, etc. These latter in turn presuppose exchange, division of labour, prices, etc. For example, capital is nothing without wage labour, without value, money, price, etc. Thus, if I were to begin with the population, this would be a chaotic conception of the whole, and I would then, by means of further determination, move analytically towards ever more simple concepts, from the imagined concrete towards ever thinner abstractions until I had arrived at the simplest determinations. From there the journey would have to be retraced until I had finally arrived at the population again, but this time not as the chaotic conception of a whole, but as a rich totality of many determinations and relations. (Marx, 1993c, pp. 100–01)

Marx sees this double movement playing out in the evolution of the discipline of economics itself.

> The former is the path historically followed by economics at the time of its origins. The economists of the seventeenth century, e.g., always begin with the living whole, with population, nation, state, several states, etc.; but they always conclude by discovering through analysis a small number of determinant, abstract, general

relations such as division of labour, money, value, etc. As soon as these individual moments had been more or less firmly established and abstracted, there began the economic systems, which ascended from the simple relations, such as labour, division of labour, need, exchange value, to the level of the state, exchange between nations and the world market. The latter is obviously the scientifically correct method. (Marx, 1993c, pp. 100–01)

In this passage, Marx argues that 'ascending from the abstract to the concrete' is the only scientific way to understand a concrete reality like a capitalist society. Since concrete reality is a structured synthesis of numerous aspects, or what Marx calls 'determinations', it is necessary to start with the simplest economic categories – those that capture key aspects of the concrete reality – and build up a picture of that reality as a synthesis, that is, internally related whole, of those simple categories by gradually incorporating newer determinations.

Initial perception of the real world – what we can call real-concrete – gives a 'chaotic conception' of that world in our minds. Next comes the work of 'analysis', which breaks up the chaotic conception into its parts and finally gives us simple or abstract concepts. From there, the reverse movement of 'synthesis' begins. Starting from the simplest economic categories is the stage of the 'abstract' and gradual incorporation of newer determinations is the ascent towards the 'concrete'. This movement ends with a structured synthesis of determinations, which is how Marx visualized the reproduction in thought of the concrete reality he was studying – which we can call thought-concrete.[14] A schematic representation of this method of producing knowledge about the real world is given in the box below:

Real-concrete	$\Rightarrow$	Chaotic conception	$\Rightarrow$	ANALYSIS
				$\Downarrow$
Thought-conrete	$\Leftarrow$	SYNTHESIS	$\Leftarrow$	Abstract concepts

The original outline seems to have been motivated by the desire to understand the economic condition of the three fundamental social classes in capitalist society: the capitalists, the landowners and the workers. That is why the original outline has separate books on capital, landed property and

---

[14]For a rich discussion of the Introduction to the *Grundrisse*, see Carver (1975).

wage labour. The book on capital, in turn, includes separate sections on 'capital in general', 'competition', 'credit system' and 'share-capital'. Thus, the outline of 1857–58 already shows an understanding of two important issues: first, that 'capital in general' must be dealt with separately from what Marx would later call 'many capitals', that is, the analysis of capital at the aggregate level must be completed prior to studying issues that arise due to the competition between capitals; and second, that the processes of generation, realization and distribution of surplus value must be studied separately from each other, as processes that are analytically separate.

As his research progressed and he assimilated the material, Marx not only retained his key insights but also sharpened his methodological understanding. He might have realized that having separate books on capital, landed property and wage labour was not completely compatible with organizing the presentation according to different levels of abstraction. Thus, to adhere to his methodological understanding of the correct method of political economy as an ascent from the abstract to the concrete, he reorganized the original outline of six books into three. The analysis, according to the final outline, is organized at two levels of abstraction, one at the level of 'capital in general' and the other at the level of 'many capitals'. The former refers to the study of the totality of the capitalist system by abstracting from competition between capitals, that is, studying the relationship between capital and labour at the aggregate level; the latter refers to taking the analysis to a lower level of abstraction by bringing in the competition between capitals and relations of credit.

Organizing the material in this way, that is, with a strict adherence to, and separation of, levels of abstraction, meant that separate books on landed property and wage labour no longer made sense. Since an analysis of the global relationship between capital and labour required an understanding of wage labour, the book on wage labour was incorporated into the first book in the final outline (which dealt with the process of production of capital). Similarly, since the income of landowners, that is, rent, arose from the redistribution of surplus value, the book on landed property was absorbed in the third book in the final outline (which dealt with the totality of capitalist production from the perspective of the distribution of surplus value). The section of the book on capital in the original outline that dealt with the circulation of capital was converted into the second book in the final outline and dealt with exactly the same issue – the circulation of capital and the realization of surplus value.[15]

This gives us the final structure of *Capital*, a three volume/book work that operates at two primary levels of abstraction, 'capital in general' and 'many capitals'. The analysis at the level of 'capital in general' is divided into two volumes. The first volume deals with the process of production of capital; and the second volume deals with the process of circulation of capital. The analysis at the level of 'many capitals' is presented in one volume (Volume III) and deals with the totality of the process of capitalist production. Using surplus value, one of the key concepts of *Capital*, as the central organizing principle of Marx's analysis of capitalism, we can think of the three volumes of *Capital* as dealing with, respectively,[16]

- the generation and accumulation of surplus value (Volume I);
- the realization of surplus value (Volume II);
- the distribution of surplus value (Volume III).

I will use this framework in this book because that is, how Marx conceived of the relationship between the three volumes of *Capital*. At the beginning of section 7 in Volume I of *Capital*, Marx makes explicit his understanding of the relationship between the three volumes of *Capital*. Anticipating some discussion that we will take up in the next chapter, let us note that the circulation of capital is a movement through three successive phases – conversion of money into means of production and labour-power (first phase), production of the commodity (second phase), and conversion of the finished output into money (third phase). Volume I is essentially devoted to a detailed study of the second phase – the production process, which

> is complete as soon as the means of production have been converted into commodities whose value exceeds that of their component parts, and therefore contains the capital originally advanced plus a surplus-value. (Marx, 1992, p. 709)

---

[15] Marx could not get to the other three books in the original outline – the books on the state, foreign trade and the world market. But even in the original outline, all the six books did not have the same importance. 'It is by no means my intention to work evenly all six of the books into which I divide the whole, but rather, in the last three, to give mostly only the basic strokes; whereas in the first three, which contains the basic developments proper, elaboration of detail is not always avoidable' (Marx, 1993c, Foreword by Martin Nicolaus, p. 55).

[16] For an illuminating discussion of the centrality of 'surplus value' to Marx's economic analysis, see Marx (1993a, Preface by Engels, pp. 97–102).

After describing the three-phase process of circulation of capital, Marx indicates the relationship of Volume II and Volume I.

> The first condition of accumulation is that the capitalist must have contrived to sell his commodities, and to reconvert into capital the greater part of the money received from their sale. In the following pages [of Volume I], we shall assume that capital passes through its process of circulation in the normal way. The detailed analysis of the process will be found in Volume II. (Marx, 1992, p. 709)

Thus, in Volume I Marx abstracts away from the issue of what we would today call the problem of aggregate demand, that is how commodities are sold at prices necessary to realize their value. Marx returns to this issue in Volume II so that the main content of Volume II is an analysis of the questions related to the sale of commodities and the realization of the surplus value embedded in them.

Once the generation and realization of surplus value has been investigated in Volumes I and II, Marx moves to analysing the distribution of surplus value in Volume III. The analysis of the distribution of surplus value will allow us to grasp the different forms that surplus value assumes in capitalist society. It will also allow us to understand the important distinction between production and realization of surplus value. Looked at from the perspective of individual capitals, we will see that the location of production of surplus value might be different from the location of its realization.

> The capitalist who produces surplus-value, i.e. who extracts unpaid labour directly from the workers and fixes it in commodities, is admittedly the first appropriator of his surplus-value, but he is by no means its ultimate proprietor. He has to share it afterwards with capitalists who fulfill other functions in social reproduction taken as a whole, with the owner of the land, and with yet other people. Surplus-value is therefore split up into various parts. Its fragments fall to various categories of person, and take on various mutually independent forms, such as profit, interest, gains made through trade, ground-rent, etc. We shall be able to deal with these modified forms of surplus-value only in Volume III. (Marx, 1992, p. 709)

Further Readings
- The classic account of the logic underlying the structure of *Capital* is Rosdolsky (1977).

- Marx's account of the method of his presentation that moves from the abstract to the concrete can be found in Marx (1993c, Introduction, pp. 100–10). Some important clarifications about Marx's method of analysis and presentation is available in Carver (1975), Foley (1986b, Chapter 1) and Wood (2004).

3

The Generation and Accumulation of Surplus Value

In the previous chapter, we familiarized ourselves with some introductory methodological issues that will help us in understanding Marx's economic theory. We understood how Marx came to the study of political economy via his engagement, as a journalist, with issues of what he called 'material interest'. We saw how his lifelong study of economics could be divided into two phases: 1843–47 and 1850–83. In the first phase of his studies, he engaged not only with political economy but also with classical German philosophy and French socialist ideas. From this engagement emerged a coherent and integral worldview – a critical synthesis of British political economy, classical German philosophy and French socialism – that later came to be called Marxism. Two key ideas developed by Marx during the first phase of his studies were the dialectical method and historical materialism. When Marx was able to resume his studies in 1850, these two ideas remained his guiding posts. But during this second phase of his studies, the focus was almost singular – his intellectual energies were devoted to the study of only political economy.

By the late 1850s, Marx had more or less completed his studies of political economy and his mature ideas about economics had taken concrete shape. In the backdrop of the economic crisis of 1857, Marx started experimenting with the best form to present his ideas to the wider public. It would take him almost another decade to finalize the structure and content of his work on economics in terms of the three volumes of *Capital*, as we have seen in the previous chapter. While Marx managed to finalize and publish the first volume – not one but several editions – he only left notes for the other two volumes. It was left to his lifelong friend and comrade, Frederich Engels, to work through the notes and publish them. It is the body of work available in the three volumes of *Capital* which will be the object of study in this and the following two chapters.

In this chapter, we begin the study of Marx's political economy of capitalism by working through the details of the argument in Volume 1 of *Capital* (Marx, 1992). We know from the discussion in the previous chapter that Volume 1 of Capital (Marx, 1992) is devoted to a study of the process of production of capital. Using the key concept of surplus value, we can restate the object of investigation in Volume 1 as the *generation* and *accumulation* of surplus value. To understand capital, one needs to understand surplus value – because capital generates and is generated by surplus value.   But, to understand surplus value, one needs to first understand value; and to understand value, one needs to understand the commodity.   That is the reason why the analysis in Volume 1 of *Capital* begins with the commodity, which Marx identifies as the 'elementary form' of wealth in capitalist societies.

3.1   The Commodity

A commodity is any good or service that is produced for exchange rather than for use. The difference between a good and service is not important as far as its property of being a commodity is concerned. For a 'service is nothing other than the useful effect of a use-value' (Marx, 1992, p. 299). What is important is whether the use-value or its useful effect is produced for exchange. If it is produced for exchange, rather than for direct use, then it is a commodity. Let us look at some examples of commodities and non-commodities.

- Rice grown by a farmer to be sold on the market is a commodity.
- An orange grown by a family on its kitchen garden for consumption by family members is not a commodity because the orange was not produced for sale but for use (by the members of the family).
- A car produced in a Toyota factory is a commodity because it is produced to be sold in the market.
- A haircut produced by a barber for sale is a commodity – note that the haircut is a service and not a good but it is a commodity nonetheless because it was produced for sale.

- Taking care of the elderly, the young (especially infants) and the sick within a household by members of the household is an example of a service that is not a commodity. If that care service was instead purchased from the market, it would become a commodity.

To begin investigation of the properties of a commodity in greater detail, it is important to clarify two preliminary issues – the relationship of exchange to capitalism and the proper domain of applicability of a study of commodity production. By a commodity-producing society, we will mean a society where most of production (of goods and services) is organized through exchange, that is, where most objects of social use are produced for exchange and not for direct use. Thus, almost tautologically, the product of labour – what Marx calls the labour-product – takes the form of a commodity in a commodity-producing society. How does a commodity-producing society relate to capitalism? While the existence and dominant role of production for exchange is a necessary condition for capitalism, it is not sufficient – an additional condition will be needed to convert a commodity-producing society into a capitalist society. We will take up this additional condition later, but at this point, it is important to keep in mind that conceptually, commodity production is not coterminous with capitalism, and that, historically, exchange predates capitalism by many centuries.

We know from numerous historical studies that the process of exchange existed not only in feudalism but also in pre-feudal times. But such exchange as existed in these societies occurred at the boundaries of tribes or kinship networks, and were not fundamental to those societies. Most of what was produced and consumed in these societies were not mediated by the process of exchange. In a similar manner, exchange existed in feudal times in Europe in even greater magnitudes. But again, the process of exchange was peripheral in these societies – which were largely self-sufficient village economies (Huberman, 1936). The predominant part of production and consumption, for the vast majority of the population, was not mediated through the process of exchange.[1] Hence, we should not consider these societies as examples of commodity-producing systems.

With the concept of a commodity-producing society, we move beyond these historical examples, that is, we move beyond the logic of pre-feudal and

---

[1] Marx gives the following examples of societies where the labour-product is not a commodity: a rural patriarchal family, an ancient Indian community and the Inca State (Marx, 1992, Chapter 2).

feudal societies, and come, instead, to consider a society where the *preponderant part of social production is organized through and mediated by exchange*. Whether such a society ever existed in history before the emergence of capitalism is a matter of debate among historians, but that does not concern us. For us, as for Marx in the early chapters of Volume I of *Capital*, a commodity-producing society is a conceptual construct, which is useful for understanding properties of the commodity and key aspects of exchange – initial steps in the understanding of capital.

But what does it mean to say that social production is organized through exchange? In a commodity-producing system, most production is carried out by private entities (individuals, families, firms, and so on) acting independently of other producer entities. Because they are independent of each other, there is no conscious coordination of their production plans and decisions. But, to survive and reproduce over time, any society needs social coordination. It needs to ensure that, at the aggregate level, requisite amounts of food, clothing, shelter are produced; it must ensure that worn out means of production are replaced with new means of production; it must ensure that supply and demand are not constantly out of balance. Since conscious social coordination is absent in commodity-producing societies, its place has to be taken by some other mechanism. The process of exchange (of the labour-products of the independent and private producers) is the mechanism of social coordination of production. Since society would unravel without social coordination of production, the process of exchange, as the social coordination mechansim, is central in any commodity-producing society. By saying that production is organized through exchange in a commodity-producing system, it is the centrality of exchange that is sought to be highlighted.

While the concept of a commodity-producing society allows us to focus on essential aspects of exchange, it is equally important to keep in mind that the concepts that are developed to study a commodity-producing society will not be of much use to study societies where exchange is peripheral or accidental. Only where exchange has become a regular feature of economic life and where most of the production is mediated through exchange will these concepts be applicable. This immediately allows us to demarcate the domain of applicability of the key concept of *value* that will be developed through an investigation of the commodity. On the one hand, the concept of value cannot be used when studying pre-feudal, feudal or even socialist societies – because in these societies, production is not organized through exchange. On the other hand, the concept of value cannot be applied to production that is *not* for exchange, even when that process of production is located within a commodity-producing society. Let me repeat two examples given earlier to underline this point. In a rural patriarchal family, in late-Medieval Europe for instance, which itself produces all the things that it needs – corn, cotton, yarn, linen, and so on – the labour-products are not commodities; hence the concept of value is not useful to study this society. In a capitalist society, goods or services produced for own consumption – for instance, vegetable grown in a kitchen garden for consumption by family members or care produced by one family member for another – are not commodities because the goods and services were not produced for sale; hence the concept of value will not be applicable to these vegetables. The concepts relevant to studying a commodity-producing system will only be of use in studying societies and instances where production is organized through exchange.

Let me summarize: at this stage of the development of the argument, we are studying a commodity-producing society, that is, a society where all production is organized through exchange.[2] In such a society, the product of labour is known as a commodity. With these initial comments, we are now ready to investigate properties of commodities in detail and to see how that investigation will lead to the development of the key concept of value.

3.1.1   Use Value, Exchange Value and Value

A commodity has two aspects: *usefulness* and *exchangeability*. The first aspect of the commodity – its usefulness – is known as 'use value'. It refers to the fact that a commodity is of use to someone. If it were not useful to anyone, it would not be accepted in an act of voluntary exchange.[3] The second aspect

---

[2]For the moment, let us ignore the fact that even in commodity-producing societies, some production is not organized through the logic of exchange. We will return to this important issue at many places in the further development of the argument, for example, when we discuss the value of labour-power.

[3]The term 'use value' is used in two senses by Marx, firstly to refer to a useful object, that is, as a noun, and secondly, to refer to the property of being useful, that is, as an adjective. Here is an example of the first use: 'Value is independent of the particular use-value by which it is borne, but a use-value of some kind has to act as its bearer' (Marx, 1992, p. 295). Here is an example of the second use: 'In that case the labour of the spinner was specifically different from other kinds of productive labour, and this difference revealed itself both subjectively in the particular purpose of spinning, and objectively in the special character of its operations, the special nature of its means of production, and the special

of a commodity – its exchangeability – is known as 'exchange value'. This refers to the fact that a commodity can be exchanged with other commodities. This is of course definitionally true because a commodity is something that is produced for exchange. The aspect of exchangeability has to be present if the labour-product is to be a commodity.

Use-value is easy to grasp. It comes from the physical properties of the commodity. A commodity is useful when it satisfies some human need. It can do so because of the physical properties it has. A chair is useful for sitting because of its physical properties; a shirt is useful for covering our bodies because of the physical properties of the shirt, among other things; a haircut is useful because of the physical effect, that is, change in the shape and size of hair, that it brings about. Exchange value is radically different. It cannot derive from the physical properties of the commodity because commodities with vastly different physical properties – a chair, a shirt, a haircut – all have exchange value, that is, they can be exchanged for other commodities.

To understand the source of exchange value, to understand where the exchangeability of commodities comes from, it is useful to distinguish its qualitative and quantitative aspects. The qualitative aspect of exchangeability is that one commodity can be exchanged with every other commodity. The quantitative aspect of exchangeability is that commodities exchange with one another in definite ratios, for example, 1 chair for 10 shirts. The question we need to address, following Marx in the first chapter of *Capital* is, therefore, this: What can account for the exchangeability of commodities, that is, both the qualitative and the quantitative aspects of exchange value?

Marx argues that the process of exchange of commodities is made possible by the fact that the commodities participating in exchange have something in common; it is this commonality that makes the process of exchange possible. Marx takes this idea from the Greek philosopher Aristotle, who had argued that exchange is only possible on the basis on *commensurability*, the presence of a common standard in the objects participating in the relationship of exchange. Hence the question, what can account for the exchangeability of commodities, can be reformulated as follows: What is it that is common to all commodities in as much as it relates to their exchangeability?

The history of political economy offers two broad answers to this question. The classical tradition that developed through the work of thinkers

---

use-value of its product' (Marx, 1992, p. 295). I will follow Marx in using the term 'use value' in both ways.

like Adam Smith, David Ricardo and Karl Marx argues that the key commonality of all commodities that can account for their exchangeability is the fact that they are all products of human labour. An alternative answer is provided by the neoclassical tradition that developed in the later part of the nineteenth century in the writings of thinkers like Leon Walras, Stanley Jevons and Alfred Marshall. The neoclassical tradition identifies the usefulness of commodities – and calls it 'utility' – as the key commonality that underlies exchange. There is an important difference between the answers provided by the two traditions. Usefulness is a subjective aspect of a commodity and varies from person to person, especially its quantitative aspect. The same commodity will offer different magnitudes of 'usefulness', if at all we are able to define such magnitudes meaningfully, to different persons, and even to the same person in different situations. Hence, the neoclassical theory of value – deriving from 'utility' of commodities – is a subjective theory of value. In this approach, exchangeability of commodities come from the usefulness derived from their consumption. On the other hand, the labour involved in the production of any commodity is an objective fact that derives from the process of production. It might be difficult to measure, but it is an objective fact nonetheless. Hence, the classical theory of value – deriving from the labour that goes into producing a commodity – is an objective theory of value.

We will follow the classical thinkers and Marx and use the classical theory of value which understands the labour that goes into producing (and reproducing) commodities as the crucial commonality that underlies their exchangeability. Using this classical-Marxian perspective, we can then consider the totality of labour that goes into producing all the commodities over a given period of time in a society. Since all commodities are products of human labour, it means that each commodity absorbs some portion of the total productive labour of society.[4] For the classical tradition, this then is the genesis of the concept of 'value': a commodity has value because, and to the extent that, it has absorbed a part of the total productive labour of society that is involved in *commodity production*. The magnitude of *value* of any

---

[4]In Volume I of *Capital*, Marx assumes, for the most part, that is other than in Chapter 16, that the labour that is being discussed is productive labour. He discusses the distinction between productive and unproductive labour in greater detail in Volume III. I will explain this important distinction when we come to discuss Volume III in Chapter 5.

commodity is proportional to the total labour-time required to produce, and reproduce, it.

This definition pins down both the qualitative and quantitative aspects of exchange value, and gives us the rudiments of a 'labour theory of value'. Using the labour theory of value, we get a way to understand the qualitative aspect of exchange: commodities exchange with one another because each commodity has value, that is, each commodity has absorbed some portion of the productive labour of society involved in commodity production. Another way of putting this is to state that the commonality among commodities of being the product of human labour makes exchange possible. With the labour theory of value, we also have a way to approach the quantitative aspect of exchange value: commodities exchange with one another in the specific ratio that preserves equality of value in exchange. Since each commodity has absorbed some labour, what is preserved in exchange is the amount of labour that went into producing commodities. This also means that we can measure the magnitude of value of commodities in units of labour-time, for instance, labour hours.

With this understanding, we will need to slightly modify the claim with which we began this section, namely that a commodity has two aspects, use-value and exchange value. By probing the concept of exchange value we arrived at the concept of value – the labour that is needed to produce (and reproduce) a commodity at any point in time. Thus, exchange value of commodities arise from their underlying values. Hence, exchange value is a form of expression of value – value is the content and exchange value its form of appearance. Thus, it is more accurate to state that *a commodity has two aspects, use-value and value.*[5]

These initial concepts of the labour theory of value is more or less what Marx took from Ricardo. The further development of these concepts in Volume I of *Capital* led to two crucial differences with previous classical thinkers. The first difference related to the level of aggregation at which the labour theory of value should be understood. Marx was clear that the labour theory of value applied to the aggregate production of commodities, not to individual commodities. Why? Because the level of abstraction in Volume I of *Capital* was 'capital in general'. This means that the analysis abstracts from

---

[5]'When, at the beginning of this chapter, we said in the customary manner that a commodity is both a use-value and an exchange-value, this was, strictly speaking, wrong. A commodity is a use-value or object of utility, and a 'value'. It appears as the twofold thing it really is as soon as its value possesses its own particular form of manifestation, which is distinct from its natural form' (Marx, 1992, p. 153).

the competition between many capitals and treats all of capital as one block and, on the other side, abstracts from divisions within labour and treats all of labour as one block. The analysis, therefore, investigates the contradictory interaction between capital and labour at the aggregate level. Since individual fragments of capital are abstracted from, we also abstract from the individual commodities produced by different fragments of capital. Hence, the theory of value pertains to the whole aggregate production of commodities. Moreover, as we move to Volume III of *Capital*, we will see that with the introduction of competition between capitals, long run prices of individual commodities – prices of production – will systematically differ from their values. But the equivalence between long run prices and value *can* continue to hold at the aggregate level – so far as it pertains to the value of the aggregate of newly produced commodities, what modern economics refers to as net national product. Hence, it is important to keep in mind that the key claims of the Marxist labour theory of value applies, first and foremost, at the aggregate level, and only later at the level of individual commodities.

The second difference relates to the link between labour and value. While we have seen earlier that the initial argument relates the labour used in production to the value of commodities, we need to probe deeper. We need to specify what kind of labour creates value. We need to develop a way to compare the magnitude of value created by different types of labour. To address these issues, Marx introduced some key clarifications and worked out some significant extensions of the labour theory of value that he took from classical thinkers like Adam Smith and David Ricardo. These important qualifications that help us better conceptualize the link between labour and value can be divided into two groups, those that relate to qualitative aspects of value and those that relate to its quantitative aspects.

3.1.2 Qualitative Aspects of Value

The qualitative aspect of Marx's clarification relates to the following question: What type of labour creates value? Or, how do we distinguish labour that creates value from labour that does not? To answer this question, Marx introduced the distinction between *concrete labour* and *abstract labour* and asserted that value is created by abstract labour. The concept of abstract labour has created enormous, and to my mind unnecessary, confusion among

Marxists and non-Marxists alike. Hence, it is important to develop the idea of abstract labour carefully.

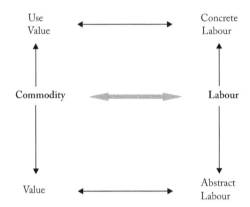

Figure 3.1   Concrete and abstract labour
Source: Author.

Abstract Labour

Concrete labour is the specific *form* of human labour that creates a specific use-value. For instance, the labour of a tailor, the labour of a worker in a car manufacturing factory, the labour of a computer programmer who writes code for an IT firm which is then sold to a banking firm are all examples of concrete labour. Each of these forms of human productive labour is geared towards producing a specific, and different, use-value. The labour of a tailor produces a coat, the labour of the manufacturing worker produces a car, the labour of the computer programmer produces code to automate certain tasks by a computer in a bank.

Recall that our domain of investigation is a commodity-producing society. In such a society, the products of labour are commodities. Thus, the shirt, the car and the computer code are all commodities, that is, they possess the aspect of exchangeability. Since they can be exchanged with other commodities, each of the products of labour (produced for exchange) have value. Thus, the shirt has value, the car has value and the computer code has value. It follows that each form of labour that went into producing those specific use-values (destined for exchange) – the labour of the tailor, the labour of the assembly line worker, the labour of the programmer – has the ability to create value, to impart the aspect of exchangeability to its labour-product. But this must mean that the aspect of exchangeability possessed by any commodity cannot derive from the specific form of labour that created it, that is, it cannot arise from concrete labour. The aspect of exchangeability can only arise from what is common to all concrete forms of labour, namely that they are all expenditures of human labour in general (within the context of a commodity-producing system).

Returning to the examples we have been working with, it is worth noting that all forms of labour involved in commodity production create value. For instance, it would make no sense to assert that the labour of a tailor creates value but the labour of a factory worker does not. The products of both forms of labour possess the aspect of exchangeability, that is, both have value. Hence, the value-creating ability of productive labour can only be understood by *abstracting from* its concrete form. Marx refers to this as abstract labour or 'human labour in the abstract', that is, human labour once we have abstracted from its concrete form, and notes that value is created by abstract labour. Following Marx we can emphasize that labour that creates value should be understood as abstract labour, that is, *all human labour involved in commodity production no matter what its concrete form, no matter what specific use-value it creates.*

One way to understand the concept of abstract labour is to recall that a commodity has two aspects: use-value and value. Since a commodity is a product of labour that is produced with the intention of sale, the labour that produced the commodity can also be understood as having two aspects. The first aspect of the labour that produces the commodity, which Marx calls concrete labour, is the aspect that imparts the commodity its specific usefulness, its use-value. On the other hand, when we look at various types of concrete labour, we can also abstract from their specific features. If we did so, we would be left with human labour in general (in a commodity-producing system), and this second aspect of labour is what Marx calls abstract labour. The relationship between the two aspects of a commodity and the corresponding two aspects of the labour that produces the commodity is depicted in Figure 6.2.

> If then we disregard the use-value of commodities, only one property remains, that of being products of human labour. But even the product of labour has been transformed in our hands. If we make the abstraction from its use-value, we abstract also from the material constituents and forms which make it a use-value. It

is no longer a table, a house, a piece of yarn or any other useful thing. All its sensuous characteristics are extinguished. Nor is it any longer the product of labour of the joiner, the mason or the spinner, or of any other kind of productive labour. With the disappearance of the useful character of the products of labour, the useful character of the kinds of labour embodied in them also disappears; this in turn entails the disappearance of the different concrete forms of labour. They can no longer be distinguished, but are all together reduced to the same kind of labour, human labour in the abstract. (Marx, 1992, p. 128)

A natural question arises: Is abstract labour a physiological concept? By using abstract labour as the value-creating laobur, was Marx advancing a physiological theory of value? The answer is a resounding no. When we use the concept of abstract labour, it is not a physiological property that we are after, rather we want to point towards its peculiar *social* character.[6] One way to emphasize this is to note that human labour in general is *not* abstract labour. For instance, human labour in a rural patriarchal family set-up in late Medieval Europe was not abstract labour; in general, human labour in feudal society is not abstract labour; human labour in a socialist society is not abstract labour. Only human labour involved in *producing for exchange* in a commodity-producing society – after we have abstracted from the specific form it takes in producing specific use-values – is abstract labour. The social substance that Marx refers to is human labour within a particular social context – a commodity-producing society. Hence, the domain of applicability of the whole analysis should always be kept in mind – we are studying a commodity-producing society – and that would prevent any misunderstanding of the concept of abstract labour as a physiological concept.[7]

How does valuation of commodities according to magnitudes of *abstract* labour actually come about? Marx emphasized that in a commodity-producing system, the process of exchange forces 'real' abstraction from concrete labours – the specific forms of labour that creates specific use-values

---

[6]'... let us remember that commodities possess an objective character as values only in so far as they are all expressions of an identical *social substance*, human labour, that their objective character as values is therefore purely social' (Marx, 1992, p. 138, emphasis added).

[7]There are other, to my mind less transparent, ways of making this point. For a rendering, see Rubin (1978, Chapter 14) and Heinrich (2012, Chapter 3).

– and makes society value 'abstract' labour, that is, the predominance and stability of exchange forces society to use 'abstract' labour as the measure of value. As we have already seen, in a commodity-producing society the process of exchange is not peripheral or accidental, it is fundamental in that it mediates the process of all (or most) production. Regularization of the process of exchange means that the ability of all commodities to exchange with all other commodities is well established. Through the perpetual repetition of such exchanges, concrete labour is abstracted from in a very real sense – in each and every act of exchange. Thus, the centrality of the process of exchange in commodity-producing systems establishes abstract labour, that is, human labour in general, as value-creating labour.

The interpretation of abstract labour I am arguing for would cut through unnecessary and complicated debates on the philosophical subtleties involved in the concept of abstract labour. I am suggesting that *all conrete labour that is involved in producing commodities in a commodity-producing society be understood as abstract labour.* This is because all such labour participates in commodity production and is regulated through the process of exchange of its labour-products. In a commodity-producing system, the process of exchange is not peripheral; it is central to social coordination. Hence, all concrete labour that produces commodities, in any commodity-producing society, is regulated by the process of exchange. Thus, it should be understood as abstract labour.

A caveat is immediately in order. The interpretation I am offering only relates to the *qualitative* aspect of value. Thus, what I am suggesting is that in a qualitative sense, all concrete labour involved in commodity production should be considered abstract labour, that is, all such labour should be understood as having the capacity to create value. But this does not yet address the quantitative aspect of the question, that is how much value? Hence, the interpretation I am offering is provisional and incomplete. Only when we have investigated the quantitative aspect of value, which we will do in the next section, will we get a complete picture.

The advantage of this interpretation will become clear only when the quantitative aspect of value-creating labour is analysed. For, when we move to actually measuring the value created in any society during a period of time, we will not be burdened with the almost impossible task of separating abstract from concrete labour. All concrete labour involved in commodity production is qualitatively abstract labour, by my interpretation, and hence it will not be necessary to try to identify concrete labour that should not be included in value calculations. Of course, we will need to carry out some conceptual demarcations. For instance, we will need to demarcate labour that is involved in commodity production from that which is not involved in producing commodities. But this is a far more manageable task than the philosophically charged task of identifying abstract from concrete labour in any actual economy.

Does this reduce the weight of the concept of abstract labour in Marxist political economy? I do not think so. The concept is useful because it forces us to make two important distinctions that are necessary for Marxist value theory. The first is the distinction between concrete labour in a non-commodity-producing society and concrete labour in a commodity-producing society. Only the latter has the potential to become abstract labour; the former cannot ever become abstract labour. With the first distinction in place, let us now focus on concrete labour in a commodity-producing society. All such labour is not involved in producing commodities, that is, all such labour is not regulated through exchange. Only concrete labour that is regulated through exchange in a commodity-producing society is abstract labour. This two-step process of conceptual demarcation foregrounds the centrality of exchange. It allows us to retain the importance of the concept of abstract labour *and* to make it operational in actually computing value in a real commodity-producing society.

3.1.3   Quantitative Aspects of Value

To complete the analysis of value-creating labour, we must now turn to the quantitative aspect of Marx's clarifications. In working out these clarifications, Marx offered an answer to the following question: How do we compare the quantum of value created by expenditures of different types of concrete labour that is involved in producing commodities in a commodity-producing system? Note that here I have posed the question as explicitly referring to *concrete labour* because I have already argued, in the previous section, that all concrete labour involved in commodity production in a commodity-producing society can be understood as abstract labour, that is, as value-creating labour. To understand the quantitative aspect of this question relating to Marx's clarifications, we need to pay attention to three distinctions – between complex and simple labour, between socially necessary and socially wasted labour, and between social and private labour. After these clarifications, we will turn to discussing two additional concepts that are needed to complete the analysis of the quantitative aspects of the labour theory of value: productivity of labour and intensity of labour.

Complex Labour

To understand the motivation for the first distinction, let us start with a specific question. How should we compare the value-creating capacities of one hour of labour of a farmer who grows wheat and an artisan who makes special types of tools? To answer this question, let us assume that the set of tasks necessary for growing wheat can be accomplished by basic skills of literacy and numeracy acquired by all adult persons in the commodity-producing society we are studying. Let us call this type of labour as 'simple labour' and note that it denotes the lack of any special types of skills or experience, that is, simple labour involves the presence of skills and experience that are, or can be, acquired by almost all members of a given society in a routine manner. In the commodity-producing society we are studying, many workers would have acquired skills and experience that go beyond the level associated with simple labour, for example, the artisan who makes specialized tools for agriculture, or the artisan who makes silk shirts. It is this difference that is sought to be highlighted by Marx with the concept of 'complex labour'.

Marx calls labour that has acquired special skills and has gained experience as 'complex labour' and argues that value created by the expenditure of one hour of complex labour (the labour of the artisan, for instance) is a multiple of the value created by an hour of simple labour (the labour of the farmer who grows wheat, for instance). The exact multiple is determined by the magnitude of labour-time needed to acquire the specific skills and experience that creates complex labour – in comparison to what has been designated as simple labour. For instance, if simple labour is denoted as that labour which has acquired one year of experience, presumably available to all workers in the society we are studying, and complex labour involves an additional 10 years of training, then the value created by this complex labour in an hour will be several times the value created by an hour of simple labour. This method of computing equivalences of simple and complex labour is known as the process of *reduction of complex to simple labour* and we will call the associated multiple as the *reduction coefficient*.

> More complex labour counts only as intensified, or rather multiplied simple labour, so that a smaller quantity of complex labour is considered equal to a larger quantity of simple labour. Experience shows that this reduction is constantly being made ... The various proportions in which different kinds of labour are reduced to simple labour as their unit of measurement are established by a social process that goes on behind the backs of producers ... (Marx, 1992, p. 135)

Marx did not spell out the details of the 'social process that goes on behind the back of producers' that reduce complex to multiples of simple labour. But his general intuitions about this process have been developed by later Marxist scholars. Here, I will draw on Laibman (1992) to present a possible way to conceptualize the reduction of complex to simple labour.[8] The basic idea behind the reduction is that the creation of complex labour-power is the process of skill acquisition by producers. The process of skill acquisition can be thought of as storing up socially necessary labour in the form of the complex labour-power.[9] When complex labour-power is used, we get complex labour. Hence, complex labour releases, during the process of production, the stored up labour, which is then embodied in the commodities that are produced. In every hour of work of a skilled producer, that is, the bearer of complex labour-power, more than an hour of simple labour is released because some of what is released is stored labour. The ratio between stored labour and simple labour involved in production gives us an estimate of the reduction coefficient, that is, how many units of simple labour each unit of complex labour is equivalent to.

To be more precise, consider a skilled producer, say a master crafts person. Let the total working life of the master crafts person – the bearer of complex labour-power – be given by 35 years, where 10 years is spent on apprenticeship (training, skill acquisition) and 25 years count as productive life. Of the total of 25 years of productive life, the master crafts person has to devote a fraction, let us say 0.3, in training the next generation of artisans, that is, imparting

---

[8]For more details of how the reduction of complex to simple labour can be conceptualized, see Appendix 3.A.

[9]Labour-power is the capacity to do useful work. When labour-power is used, we get labour. We will study this concept in greater detail in section 3.3.

skills to apprentices. Thus, he can work on producing commodities for 17.5 (= 0.7 * 25) years, and has to devote 7.5 years to training the next generation of crafts persons. This is the way in which the system takes account of the cost of creating complex labour. This can also be thought of as the manner in which the trainee pays for skill acquisition to the master craftsman.

What is the reduction coefficient in this case? We know that the reduction coefficient is the ratio of the total amount of labour hours stored in the skilled labour-power of the master crafts person and the total hours of labour that she will devote to producing commodities. The master crafts person had to go through 10 years of apprenticeship, and she can can devote 17.5 (= 0.7 * 25) years to production of commodities. Hence, at the beginning of her productive life, the master crafts person has stored labour hours worth of 27.5 years. On the other hand, as we just saw, she will devote 17.5 years in producing commodities. Hence, each hour of her labour spent in production will create 1.57 (= 27.5/17.5) times the value created by an hour of simple labour.

Let us point out two immediate issues that need to be kept in mind when thinking about the reduction of complex to simple labour. First, the difference between complex and simple labour does not involve any normative judgments. The difference is only meant to make possible the comparison of the magnitudes of value created by the myriad forms of labour found in any given commodity-producing society. It does not involve any normative judgments about the different types of labour, that is, whether complex labour is superior to, or better than, simple labour; it is only meant to facilitate quantitative comparison and aggregation by taking account of the labour-time cost of producing complex labour. Thus, for instance, when we compare the value-creating capacity of labour from different countries, the average degree of complexity across countries will be important to keep in mind for meaningful comparison. If we try to equate 1 hour of social labour across countries at very different level of capitalist development, we are liable to make an error – because we are comparing labour of very different degrees of complexity.

Second, income differentials observed in actual commodity-producing societies are probably much higher than what would be implied by the reduction of complex to simple labour that has been outlined earlier. We will return to this issue when we discuss the peculiar commodity labour-power in capitalist societies. In that context, what will be important to engage with is the observed wage differentials of different types of complex labour-power. In that discussion, we will see that there will be two routes to explaining the large observed wage differentials. First, we could allow for the presence of various types of monopolies and barriers associated with access to schooling and skill acquisition (Wright, 2015). If such barriers are important and strong, then they might explain the divergence of wage differentials from the true cost, in terms of total labour-time, of producing complex labour-power. An alternative route will be to use what is known as the classical *long-period method of analysis* (see Appendix 3.A).

Socially Necessary Labour

To understand the second distinction, let us, again, begin with an example. Suppose, given the current state of technology and intensity of work, it takes 10 hours of labour to produce a tweed suit. Now consider two tailors, the first using the currently prevalent technology and working at the average intensity of work, and the second using the same technology as the first tailor but working at lower-than-average intensity. As a result, the first tailor makes suits in 10 hours each, but the second tailor takes 15 hours to make each of the same suit. Would the Marxist labour theory of value imply that the suit created by the second tailor has more value than the one created by the first tailor because the second tailor took more time to make the suit? We know the answer as soon as we pose the question: No. It would be absurd to assert that the suit created by the second tailor (who worked at lower-than-average intensity) has more value because it was created in 15 hours, whereas the suit produced by the first tailor (who worked at average intensity) has lower value because it was created in 10 hours. To rule out such absurdities, Marx introduced the notion of 'socially necessary labour'.

Socially necessary labour-time is the amount of labour-time needed to produce a given commodity under the average conditions of production, that is, using the average technology and working at the average intensity of work.

> Socially necessary labour-time is the labour-time required to produce any use-value under the conditions of production normal for a given society and with the average degree of skill and intensity of labour prevalent in that society. (Marx, 1992, p. 129)

In our example, the socially necessary labour-time needed to produce the tweed suit is 10 hours. Labour-time expended in producing a commodity that is over and above what is socially necessary is socially wasted and does not create value. In our example, the 5 extra hours of labour that the second tailor expends in making the suit is wasted – this labour does not create value. Hence, the value of the suit created by the second tailor is also proportional to 10 hours, and not 15 hours, of labour-time.

The concept of socially necessary labour puts forward a social benchmark to use whenever we wish to compute the value of any commodity. The fact that it is a *social* benchmark, and not an individual benchmark, is important to note. It means that irreducibly social considerations go into the determination of the value of commodities – value is determined socially and not individually. The idea of the social benchmark underlying the value of a commodity will also be important in our discussion of technological change in capitalist economies – but in a way that will be exactly opposite of the situation discussed in the earlier example. To anticipate some discussion in later sections of the book, we will see that when an innovator capitalist implements a cheaper way to produce a commodity, that is, using less labour-time than that currently required on average (because of a more productive technology, perhaps), the value of the commodity does not change. It is still determined by the average conditions of production prevailing in the economy, which have not changed. Hence, if commodities sell at their values, the innovator capitalist will be able to earn super-profits until the time that the new technology diffuses through the economy and determines the new social average. Here then we have a strong incentive for technological innovation – a point highlighted by Marx in Chapter 12 of Volume I (Marx, 1992).

Social Labour

The final distinction relates to what we have already seen: the domain of applicability of value-theoretic analysis. Recall, once more, that we are studying a commodity-producing system. This is a system of social production where all production is for exchange, that is, all products of labour are produced with the intention of sale. Marx refers to all such labour as 'social labour', that is, labour involved in commodity production, and contrasts this with all labour that is not involved in producing commodities. The latter is referred to as 'private labour'. Marx argues that only social labour creates value, which is true by definition because only social labour produces commodities, and only commodities have value. Private labour, on the other hand, does not create value because it does not produce commodities.

Just like the other distinctions we have studied here, the distinction between private and social labour does not involve any normative judgment. The distinction is not coterminous with distinctions like useful-useless labour, necessary-superfluous labour, rational-irrational labour, and so on. It is merely meant to be a way to carefully stick to the domain of applicability of value-theoretic analysis. By asserting that labour that is not involved in commodity production, like household labour or community labour, does not create value, one is not suggesting that that labour is not useful, or that it is not necessary, and so on. It is only pointing out that it does not participate in producing commodities, that it does not participate in the system of production mediated by and organized through exchange. It is merely saying that private labour does not impart the property of exchangeability to its labour-products.

Productivity of Labour

There are two different notions of labour productivity in Volume I of *Capital*. The first notion can be called use-value productivity of concrete labour; the second notion can be called the value productivity of abstract labour. Let us look at both.

In Chapter 1, Volume I of *Capital*, Marx gives us a clear definition of use-value productivity.

> By 'productivity' of course, we always mean the productivity of concrete useful labour; in reality this determines only the effectiveness of productive activity directed towards a given purpose within a given period of time. Useful labour becomes, therefore, a more or less abundant source of products in direct proportion as its productivity rises or falls. As against this, however, variations in productivity have no impact whatever on the labour itself represented in value. (Marx, 1992, p. 137)

In this definition, it is clear that Marx wants to restrict the notion of labour productivity to concrete labour. Labour productivity is just a measure of the quantity of use-values produced in a fixed period of time by concrete labour. It has no bearing on its value – because the latter arises from abstract labour and not from concrete labour. In the very next sentence, Marx makes this clear.

> As productivity is an attribute of its concrete useful form, it naturally ceases to have any bearing on that labour as soon as we

abstract from its concrete useful form. The same labour, therefore, performed for the same length of time, always yields the same amount of value, independently of any variations in productivity. (Marx, 1992, p. 137)

We encounter a different notion of labour productivity in Chapter 15, where Marx discusses machinery and large-scale production. When discussing the idea of value transferred by machines to the output, Marx offers the second notion of labour productivity, which I would like to call value productivity.

It is evident that whenever it costs as much labour to produce a machine as is saved by the employment of that machine, all that has taken place is a displacement of labour. Consequently, the total labour required to produce a commodity has not been lessened, in other words, the productivity of labour has not been increased. (Marx, 1992, p. 513)

In the discussion surrounding this paragraph, Marx seems to be using the definition of value productivity of abstract labour, that is, the productivity of labour is understood as the reciprocal of the total amount of labour needed to produce a commodity. Since the total amount of socially necessary abstract labour required to produce a commodity is its value, here we have a definition of labour productivity as the reciprocal of value. That is why I call the second definition the value productivity of abstract labour.

There are important differences between the two notions of labour productivity. Use-value labour productivity would refer only to living labour because it only concerns concrete, useful labour. Thus, in a production process which uses both nonlabour inputs and labour, the use-value productivity would be the physical quantity of output per unit of living labour. This definition would not take account of the value (that is, abstract labour) transferred by the non-labour inputs to the output. It would not concern itself with the value of a unit of the output. Being a ratio of a quantity of a specific use-value and labour input, the use-value productivity of labour cannot be compared across commodities, industries or sectors (unless we use prices to deflate the money value added and thereby compute some 'real' index of value added or net output). For instance, if a tailor produces 1 shirt in 12 hours while a carpenter produces 1 chair in 4 hours, how can we compare the labour productivity of these two types of concrete labour? After all, there is no way to compare 1/12 shirt and 1/4 chair, which are respectively the quantity of use-value produced in one hour by the tailor and the carpenter.

Value productivity would refer to the total labour required to produce a commodity. Hence, it would refer to both living and dead labour. In a production process involving non-labour inputs and labour, the value productivity would refer to the total abstract labour embodied in a unit of the output. If we use this notion of labour productivity, we would be easily able to compare its magnitude across industries and sectors. But the disadvantage of this measure is that it would no longer refer to any particular, concrete labour. It would only refer to abstract, homogeneous labour.

There is also a technical issue to consider because the second measure would potentially create some difficulties of comparing productivity over time unless we use replacement cost valuation of long-lived fixed assets. Since the value of any commodity at any point in time is the sum of value added by living labour and value transferred by the use of the non-labour inputs, including the depreciation of fixed productive assets, we need to value the fixed assets using replacement cost (or current cost) valuation. This means that we consider the value of the fixed asset as the total labour required to produce it in the current period (replacement cost), and not the total labour that was expended to produce it in the past (historical cost). If we used historical cost valuation, instead of replacement cost valuation, we would be adding up units of living labour (value added) and past labour (depreciation). In that case, we would not be able to use the reciprocal of the value of a commodity to estimate the productivity of labour in the current period.

The first measure, that is, use-value productivity of concrete labour, is closely related to the definition of labour productivity used in national income accounts. In a recent paper, Flaschel et al. (2013) have argued that the second measure, that is, value productivity of abstract labour, is a better way to capture labour productivity and its macroeconomic aspects. In this book, I will follow Marx's discussion in Chapter 1, Volume I of *Capital* and define 'productivity of labour' to mean the use-value productivity of labour. Using this definition, we can see that when the productivity of labour rises, a larger magnitude of use-values is produced with a given labour. Hence, the total value created by labour is distributed over a larger quantity of use-values. Hence, the value of each unit of the the use-value falls.

Intensity of Labour

When the intensity of labour increases that entails 'an increased expenditure of labour within a time which remains constant, a heightened tension of labour-power, and a closer filling up of the pores of the working day, i.e. a condensation of labour' (Marx, 1992, p. 534). Thus, increased 'intensity of labour means increased expenditure of labour in a given time' (Marx, 1992, p. 660). One way to understand the intensity of labour is to think of the time it takes to complete a fixed set of tasks related to production. When a given set of tasks is completed in less time, then we can say that the intensity of labour has increased. Hence, with an increase in the intensity of labour, each hour of work accomplishes a larger set of tasks. Thus, an increase in the intensity of labour is associated with two different effects. On the one hand, each hour of more intense labour converts a larger magnitude of inputs into output, that is, its use-value handling capacity rises. On the other hand, each hour of more intense labour creates more value, that is, its value-creating capacity increases. It will be important to keep both these aspects in mind when we analyse the impact of intensification of labour on value, surplus value and exploitation.

3.1.4 Labour Theory of Value: Summary and Implementation

We can summarize this discussion of the Marxist labour theory of value with the following proposition: a commodity has value only if and to the extent that it has absorbed a part of the total *socially necessary abstract labour* involved in commodity production; in the aggregate, the total labour expended in the production of commodities (with complex labour counted as relevant multiples of simple labour) during a given period represents the total value added to the newly created bundle of commodities. The substance of value is socially necessary abstract labour and its measure is labour-time.[10] It is also important to emphasize once again a point I discussed earlier: the concept of 'value' is only relevant for studying a historically specific system of social production, that is, a commodity-production system.

> The product of labour is an object of utility in all states of society; but it is only a historically specific epoch of development which presents the labour expended in the production of a useful article as

---

[10]From this point on, whenever I use the term 'labour' I will mean socially necessary abstract simple labour, unless the context suggests otherwise.

THE LOGIC OF CAPITAL

an 'objective' property of that article, i.e. as its value. It is only then that the product of labour becomes transformed into a commodity. (Marx, 1992, pp. 153–54)

How would a researcher implement this definition of value and compute it in a commodity-producing society at any point in time?

- The researcher would collect information on the technology used in the production of commodities – this will provide information about the 'socially necessary' part of the definition.

- Then the researcher would collect information on different types of complex labour and use some method to reduce complex labour to multiples of simple labour – this will take care of the heterogeneity of concrete labour.

- Then the researcher would collect information on the intensity of labour, and use it to weight the different types of complex labour. A higher weight will be attached to labour of higher intensity.

- The final task will be to make sure that the researcher is only counting 'abstract labour'. We have argued in this chapter that all concrete labour involved in producing commodities in a commodity-producing society can be qualitatively understood as abstract labour. Hence, the researcher will only need to make sure that she is including in her computation concrete labour that produces commodities in the commodity-producing society she is studying. That will take care of the 'abstract labour' part of the definition of value.

Hence, by adding up the socially necessary, simple concrete labour involved in commodity production, the researcher will arrive at a quantitative estimate of the 'value' created during any period of time. The unit of this 'value' will be hours of social labour-time.

While this section has developed the main contours of Marx's labour theory of value and has provided a clear route to implement it in any real commodity-producing society, it certainly calls for further investigation of many issues. For instance, a reader might ask several questions: Why is labour the substance of value and not something else? Can we rule out all other possible candidates for a substance of value? What are some of the common points of criticism of conceiving of labour as the substance of value? How does the Marxist tradition respond to such criticism? For a discussion on some of these questions, please turn to Appendix 3.C. The discussion in Appendix 3.C can be most easily followed if read after completing the whole of this chapter. Hence, my suggestion is to return to Appendix 3.C only after covering the whole of this chapter.

3.1.5 A Simple Model of Production

We will use a simple model of production to convert our intuitions about value into more concrete quantitative claims. The key actors in the simple model economy are commodity producers who own their means of production. Each commodity producer produces the identically same commodity called 'corn'. This commodity can be consumed, and it can also be saved and invested. Production of corn requires both a non-labour input, corn itself that has been saved from before, and labour. To be more specific, suppose it takes a units of corn and l hours of simple labour to produce 1 unit of corn, which we can represent as follows:

a units of corn + l units of simple labour $\Rightarrow$ 1 unit of corn

Given the above technological relationships, we can now write the value equation for corn. The value of the output is the sum of the *value transferred* by the non-labour input, that is, corn, used up in production and the *value added* by labour. If we denote by λ the value of 1 unit of corn, we will have $\lambda = \lambda a + l$, where λa is the value transferred by corn and l is the value added by labour. Hence,

$$\lambda = \frac{l}{1 - a} \qquad (3.1)$$

Note that for the value of a unit of corn to be positive, we need $a < 1$. This makes intuitive sense. If more corn is needed as input than what will be produced as output, then that technology is not a feasible one. Hence, let us assume that $a < 1$ because this is necessary to ensure that technology is feasible. This assumption then ensures that the value of each unit of corn is positive.

Let us work through an example to understand these points. Suppose a = 0.5 and l = 1. Thus, 0.5 units of corn and 1 unit of simple labour is used to produce 1 unit of corn. Then the value of each unit of corn is given by $1/(1 - 0.5) = 2$.

Complex Labour

We can use this model to see how complexity, productivity and intensity of labour will impact the value of a commodity. If it took a units of corn and l hours of complex labour to produce 1 unit of corn, then we would have

a units of corn + l units of complex labour $\Rightarrow$ 1 unit of corn.

If we knew that each hour of complex labour is equivalent to k hours of simple labour, where $k > 1$, then the value equation for corn would be written as $\lambda = \lambda a + kl$, where λa is the value transferred and kl is the value added. Hence,

$$\lambda = \frac{kl}{1-a} \qquad (3.2)$$

and we see that the value of a unit of corn is k times the value of corn when it was produced with simple labour. Thus, an increase in the complexity of labour, holding technology of production constant, increases the value of each unit of the commodity.

Let us return to the above example and assume that $k = 1.25$. This means that 1 hour of complex labour adds 25 per cent more value than 1 hour of simple labour. If the technology of production remains unchanged, that is, 0.5 units of corn and 1 unit of labour is needed to produce each unit of corn, then with the use of complex labour, the value of a unit of corn would become 1.25 * 1/(1 - 0.5) = 2.5. Thus, the value of a unit of corn is now 25 per cent higher than before.

Productivity of Labour

Let us now investigate the impact of an increase in the productivity of labour on value creation. An increase in the productivity of labour means that each hour of labour converts a larger quantity of inputs into a larger quantity of output.

Using the simple model we are working with, we can capture an increase in the productivity of labour as follows. If the productivity of labour increases μ_1 times holding intensity constant, where $\mu_1 > 1$, then l hours of simple labour can convert $\mu_1 a$ units of corn (input) into μ_1 units of corn (output). This can be represented as follows:

$\mu_1 a$ units of corn + l units of labour $\Rightarrow \mu_1$ unit of corn

It is worth noting that an increase in the productivity of labour leads to a *proportional increase* in the quantity of inputs used up *and* the quantity of output produced in a given period of time. Why proportional? When the productivity of labour increases by μ_1 times, workers handle μ_1 times more inputs every hour. To simplify the exposition, we assume that the technical relationship between non-labour inputs and output remains unchanged, that is, the ratio of the quantity of non-labour inputs and the quantity of output remain unchanged.[11] Hence, output also increases by μ_1 times. That is why an increase in the productivity of labour increases the quantity of inputs and output by the same factor by which the productivity of labour rises.

To understand the impact of a change in the productivity of labour, let us hold the intensity of labour fixed. This means that the value added by each hour of labour remains unchanged. If λ' denotes the value of 1 unit of corn in the new situation (when the productivity of labour has increased), the value equation can be written as, $\lambda'\mu_1 = \lambda'\mu_1 a + l$, where the first term on the right-hand side is value transferred from corn, and the second term is the value added by labour. Hence,

$$\lambda' = \frac{l}{\mu_1\left(1 - a\right)}$$

Using (3.1), we can see that $\lambda'/\lambda = 1/\mu_1 < 1$. Hence, when the productivity of labour rises, the value of each unit of the commodity (corn) falls.

Continuing with the above example, suppose $\mu_1 = 1.5$, that is when the productivity of labour rises, 1 hour of labour can covert 0.75 (= 1.5 * 0.5) units of corn into 1.5 units of corn. Hence, the value of each unit of corn becomes 1/(1.5 * (1 − 0.5)) = 1.33. Compared to the initial situation, when the value of a unit of corn was 2, we see that the value of corn has fallen.

Intensity of Labour

An increase in the intensity of labour has a technological aspect and a value aspect. The former is related to the use-value handling capacity of labour, and we will capture it with the constant μ_1; the latter is related to the value-creating capacity of labour, and we will capture it with the constant μ_2.

---

[11] This is a specific type of technology, that is, fixed coefficient technology. This assumption will not hold in more general specifications of technology.

The technological relationships in the case of an intensification of labour is the same as when the productivity of labour increases:

$$\mu_1 a \text{ units of corn} + l \text{ units of labour} \Rightarrow \mu_1 \text{ units of corn}$$

To write the value relationships in this case, let us note that l hours of simple labour now adds μ_2 units of value, where μ_2 is some constant with the property that $\mu_2 > 1$. This is precisely how we capture the fact that the value-creating capacity of labour has increased. If λ' denotes the value of 1 unit of corn in the new situation, we have, $\lambda'\mu_1 = \lambda'\mu_1 a + \mu_2 l$, where, like before, the first term, $\lambda'\mu_1 a$, captures value transferred by corn and the second term, $\mu_2 l$, captures value added by labour. Hence, $\lambda' = \mu_2 l / [\mu_1 (1 - a)]$. Using (3.1), we get

$$\frac{\lambda'}{\lambda} = \frac{\mu_2}{\mu_1} \tag{3.3}$$

Thus, we see that the ratio of the value of each unit of corn is exactly equal to the ratio of the two constants μ_2 and μ_1, both of which are larger than unity. What do these constants represent? The constant μ_1 captures the use-value handling capacity of labour. The fact that $\mu_1 > 1$ means that when the intensity of labour rises, each hour of labour is able to convert a larger quantity of inputs into output. The constant μ_2 captures the value-creating capacity of labour. When the intensity of labour rises, each hour of labour creates more value than before. The fact that μ_2 is greater than unity captures this fact. Thus, there are two different aspects of an increase in the intensity of labour. On the one hand, it increases the use-value handling capacity of labour (captured by μ_1); on the other, it increases the value-creating capacity of labour (captured by μ_2).

The expression in (3.3) shows that we need to consider three cases. First, consider the case in which $\mu_1 = \mu_2$. This condition means that an increase in the intensity of labour leads to an equal increase in its value-creating capacity, μ_2, as in its capacity to convert physical quantities of inputs into outputs, μ_1. From (3.3), we see that if $\mu_1 = \mu_2$, then $\lambda' = \lambda$. Thus, the value of each unit of corn remains unchanged. Second, consider the case when $\mu_1 < \mu_2$. This condition means that an increase in the intensity of labour leads to a lower increase in its capacity to convert physical quantities of inputs into outputs (μ_1) than in its value-creating capacity (μ_2). From (3.3), we see if $\mu_1 < \mu_2$, then $\lambda' > \lambda$. Thus, the value of each unit of corn rises. Finally, consider the third case when $\mu_1 > \mu_2$. This condition means that an increase in the intensity of labour leads to a higher increase in its capacity to convert physical quantities of inputs into outputs (μ_1) than in its value-creating capacity (μ_2). From (3.3), we see that if $\mu_1 > \mu_2$, then $\lambda' < \lambda$. Hence, the value of corn falls.

Let us return to the example discussed above and consider three cases associated with an increase in the intensity of labour. Case 1: If the use-value handling and value-creating capacity of labour rises by 10 per cent each, then the value of each unit of corn will not change. Case 2: If the use-value handling capacity of labour rises by 5 per cent and value-creating capacity of labour rises by 10 per cent each, then the value of each unit of corn will rise by 4.76 per cent $(= (1.1/1.05) - 1)$. Case 3: If the use-value handling capacity of labour rises by 10 per cent and value-creating capacity of labour rises by 5 per cent each, then the value of each unit of corn will fall by 4.54 per cent $(= (1.05/1.1) - 1)$.

Let me summarize what we have found: an increase in the complexity of labour increases the value of each unit of the commodity; an increase in the productivity of labour leads to a fall in the value of each unit of the commodity. An increase in the intensity of labour has an ambiguous impact on the value of each unit of the commodity. Depending on the relative magnitudes of changes in the value-creating and use-value handling capacity of intensified labour, the value of each unit of the commodity can either increase, decrease or remain unchanged.

3.1.6 Comparing Value over Time and across Countries

It is often of interest to researchers to compare the magnitude of value over time and across countries. While such questions were not investigated in any systematic manner by Marx, the Marxist labour theory of value that we have studied in this section will allow us to carry out such comparisons in a consistent manner. There are two key issues that we have to deal with in carrying out such comparisons in a consistent manner – the first relates to complex labour, that is, to the change in the degree of complexity of concrete labour over time and across countries, and the second relates to the intensity of labour.

To consistently compare the magnitude of value created by one hour of socially necessary abstract labour in a given country at two different points in time or across two countries at a given point in time, we have to make sure that we limit ourselves to commodity-producing labour working under the average conditions of production, that is, using the average technology, at the two points in time in the same country or across the two countries at the same point in time. Once we have done so, we will be confident that the only difference between the value created by an hour of labour will arise from differences in their degree of complexity *and* their intensity. Whether the labour is more or less productive, in the use-value sense of the term, is not relevant.

If the country under investigation is growing over time in such a way that the degree of complexity of labour, on average, is increasing over time, then each hour of labour at a later date will create more value than each hour of labour at the earlier point in time – holding the intensity of labour constant. The exact multiple can be determined by comparing the reduction coefficients of labour at the two points in time. In a similar way, if one country is more 'developed' than another, in the precise sense that the degree of complexity of labour, on average, is higher in the first than in the second, then each hour of labour in the first country will create more value than in the second – holding the intensity of labour constant. The exact multiple can, once again, be determined by comparing the reduction coefficients of labour in the two countries. In a similar manner, if the intensity of labour increases over time in a country, then the value created by each hour of labour would also increase over time. Similarly, if one country has, on average, a higher intensity of labour, then one hour of labour in that country will create more value than in another country with a lower intensity of labour. The implication of this discussion is important for comparative analyses: comparing hours of social labour over time or across countries without taking account of differences in the complexity or intensity of labour is bound to give misleading results.

Further Readings
- Sections 1 and 2 in Chapter 1 of Volume I of *Capital* (Marx, 1992) are essential reading for understanding Marx's labour theory of value.
- Useful introductions and clarifications of the labour theory of value can be found in Sweezy (1942, Chapters II, III), Eaton (1963, Chapter II) and Foley (1986a, Chapter 2, pp. 12–18). For discussions of abstract labour, see Rubin (1978) and Heinrich (2012).

3.2 Money-Form of Value

How is the value of commodities expressed? First and foremost, the value of commodities is expressed in exchange value, that is, in ratios in which a given commodity will exchange with other commodities.[12] Thus, we might say that exchange value is a form of expression of value. That is why Marx calls exchange value as the value-form of commodities. Of course, in a society where commodity production has taken hold, value is not expressed through exchange values of commodities – which would be the case in barter economies – but *money* emerges as the social device to express the value of commodities. Marx calls this the money-form of value and develops the concept of money from *within* the very logic of commodity production.

> Now, however, we have to perform a task never even attempted by bourgeois economics. That is, we have to show the origin of the money-form, we have to trace the development of the expression of value contained in the value-relation of commodities from its simplest, almost imperceptible outline to the dazzling money-form. (Marx, 1992, p. 139)

3.2.1 Money as Universal Equivalent

Marx develops his argument about money, or the money-form of value, in three steps. He starts with the simplest value-relation, the one that obtains between two commodities, and moves all the way to the most complicated value-relation, the one that obtains between commodities and money. Since Marx was dealing with a commodity money system, what he will show is how one particular commodity becomes identified as, and starts functioning as, the money commodity, that is, as money.

To begin with, consider the exchange between two commodities, say A and B, which is the simplest value-relation. Suppose 2 units of A exchange for 1 unit of B, that is, 2A = 1B. In this relationship of equivalence, which Marx refers to as the *simple form of value*, commodity A occupies the relative position and commodity B occupies the equivalent position, that is, the value contained in 2 units of A (the commodity in the relative position) is expressed in 1 unit of B (the commodity in the equivalent position). But the universe

---

[12]The exchange value of any commodity will be a vector with as many elements as there are commodities, excluding the one whose exchange value is being ascertained.

of commodities is not limited to these two commodities, A and B. In fact, A can exchange with not only B, but with all other commodities, C, D, E, and so on, with each exchange occurring in a specific ratio. For instance, $2A = 1B = (1/2)C = 3D = (1/4)E = \cdots$, or equivalently, $A = (1/2) B = (1/4) C = (3/2) D = (1/8) E \cdots$

The recognition of the openended-ness of the series of exchanges possible for any commodity immediately takes us to the second step of the argument, to a form of equivalence that Marx calls the *expanded form of value*. Now, the value contained in 1 unit of A (the commodity in the relative position) is expressed by definite quantities of all other commodities. Since the equivalent position can now be occupied by all other commodities, and not just B, this is an expanded form of value. But the chain of equivalences which captures the expanded form of value can lead to a qualitative change. It can be flipped around as $(1/2) B = (1/4) C = (3/2) D = (1/8) E = \cdots = A$, so that now commodity A occupies the equivalent position, with all other commodities occupying the relative position. With this we come to the third step of the argument, to an equivalence that Marx calls the *general form of value*, where commodity A has become the 'universal equivalent' (or the general equivalent) because it expresses the value contained in all other commodities.

The transition from the general form of value to the money form is completed when the universal equivalent becomes 'socially validated'. For future reference, let us put down the definition that emerges from the above argument. *Money is a socially validated universal equivalent.* Once the concept of money has been established, we can define price of any commodity as follows: the price of a commodity is the amount of money for which one unit of that commodity can be exchanged.[13]

3.2.2 Functions of Money

Money fulfills three different but essential functions. It is a measure of value, it functions as a medium of circulation, and it operates as a means of payment.

Measure of Values
The first function of money is to act as a *measure of value* (Marx, 1992, pp. 188–98). Since money is a social device to express value, specific amounts of money represent specific quantums of value. A person who possesses a

---

[13]Marx interchangeably refers to price as the *money-form* or *price-form* of value.

definite amount of money, in effect, possesses the quantum of value represented by the amount of money. Hence, money becomes a way in which value – definite amounts of socially necessary abstract labour – can be measured and stored. For instance, for a commodity producer who sells commodity A and wishes to purchase commodity B, money is the way in which the definite quantum of value is stored between the two acts of exchange.

Medium of Circulation

The second function of money is to act as a *medium of circulation* or *medium of exchange* (Marx, 1992, pp. 198–227). By circulation, Marx means the process of exchange of commodities. In any commodity-producing system, other than the most rudimentary, the exchange of commodities is conducted via money, that is, commodities are not exchanged one for the other, as in barter. Rather, a commodity is first exchanged for money, and then money is exchanged for another commodity. This process of exchange, or the process of simple circulation of commodities, to use Marx's terminology, can be represented as $C - M - C'$. In the first step of the process, the commodity C is exchanged for money M, that is, it is sold. In the next and final step of the process, the money M is exchanged for a different commodity, C', that is, C' is purchased. Here, money, represented by M, has functioned as the means by which the circulation of commodities was completed.

In discussing the function of money as a means of circulation, Marx poses an important question. What quantity of money is needed on average to facilitate the circulation of commodities? Marx's answer is what we would today call the equation of exchange.

> The total quantity of money functioning during a given period as the circulating medium is determined on the one hand by the sum of the prices of commodities in circulation, and on the other hand by the rapidity of alternation of the antithetical process of circulation. (Marx, 1992, pp. 217–18)

In discussions around the passage quoted above, Marx explains that the amount of money needed on average to facilitate the circulation of commodities is determined by the ratio of two magnitudes: (*a*) the product of the price of commodities and their volume of sale/purchase and (*b*) the velocity of circulation of each unit of money (the number of times, on average, that each unit of money changes hands). If M is the quantity of money, V the velocity of its circulation, P the general price level, and Q the volume of commodities circulating over a given period of time, then $MV = PQ$, so that $M = (PQ)/V$. This is what is known as the *equation of exchange*. It just tells us that the total value of transactions involved in the circulation of commodities, which is the product of the price of each commodity, P, and the volume of commodities sold or purchased, Q, has to be equal to the product of the quantity of money, M, and the velocity of circulation, V. For instance, in 2020, the nominal gross domestic product for the US economy was 20.93 trillion dollars, that is, $P * Q$ was 20.93 trillion dollars. In January 2021, the stock of money, as measured by what economists refer to as M2, was 19.41 trillion dollars. Hence, V was 1.08 (= 20.93/19.41). This shows that the velocity of circulation was about 1, that is, each dollar changed hands roughly once every year.

It is important to note that the equation of exchange is very different from a quantity theory of money. The equation of exchange is an *ex post* equality which will always hold. It will give us a theory of price determination only when we impose more structure. For instance, if we were to assume that the velocity of circulation, V, and the volume of commodities in circulation, Q, were fixed magnitudes, then we could assert that a change in the quantity of money in circulation, M, for instance by the Central Bank, would change the price level, P, in the same direction. This would be a monetarist reading of the equation of exchange, of which Marx was explicitly critical.

> A one-sided observation of the events which followed the discovery of fresh supplies of gold and silver led some people in the eighteenth century to the false conclusion that the prices of commodities has risen because there was more gold and silver acting as the means of circulation. (Marx, 1992, p. 214)

Marx's views on the quantity of money in circulation is closer to what we today know as the theory of endogenous money supply. Marx emphasized that the quantity of money in circulation is determined by the needs of circulation, and not the other way round. With the development of commodity exchange and a money commodity, for example, gold, the process of circulation leads to the building up of hoards of the money commodity. The existence of such hoards, which is a stock of the money commodity sitting idle outside the sphere of circulation, allows the process of circulation to proceed smoothly. If the need of circulation increases, for instance during the upswing phase of a business cycle, the hoards are drawn down to meet the need for the extra amount of money; if the need of circulation falls, the money commodity leaves the sphere of circulation and increases the size of hoards (Marx, 1992, pp. 231–32).

Discussions in Volume III of *Capital* suggest clearly that Marx was well aware of the fact, later discovered by John Maynard Keynes, that an increase in the quantity of money in circulation would have an impact on the velocity of its circulation, and might even impact the volume of commodities in circulation through changes in the interest rate. Hence, Marx concluded, there was no direct link between changes in the quantity of money in circulation and the price of commodities. There is no doubt that Marx was thoroughly opposed to what is now called a quantity theory of money, that is, the assertion that changes in the supply of money leads to a one-for-one change in the prices of commodities (Friedman, 1970). It is important to note that there is scant empirical evidence in support of the quantity theory of money. Not only is there no one-for-one relationship between the quantity of money and the price level in the short run, careful empirical analyses show that, even in the long run, changes in the money supply account for only a tiny fraction of the variation in the price level. Most of the variation is accounted for by non-monetary shocks (Wen, 2006). Hence, both on theoretical and empirical grounds, there is no basis for accepting the quantity theory of money, that is, a monetarist reading of the equation of exchange.

Means of Payment

The third function of money is that it acts as a *means of payment* (Marx, 1992, pp. 232–40). This relates to the use of money in settling of debts and emerges as soon as acts of exchange come with a contractual deferral of payment (for instance, in forward transactions.) For instance, suppose commodity A is sold with a contract to make payment for the sale in a month's time. In this transaction, the buyer of the commodity incurs debts to the seller, and the seller accumulates credit vis-a-vis the buyer. The contract will be fulfilled and the debt extinguished only when the buyer transfers the agreed upon amount of money to the seller. Here, money functions as a means of payment (of outstanding debts).

3.2.3 Forms of Money

In Marx's writings on money, we find discussion of three primary forms of money: commodity money, inconvertible paper money and credit money. In Volume I, Marx discusses the first two forms in detail, and mentions credit money briefly. This is because a proper discussion of credit money will have to wait until the concept of credit is developed in detail in Volume III of *Capital*. Competition between capitals and credit has been abstracted from in Volume I because it operates at the level of abstraction given by 'capital in general'.

Commodity Money

When Marx was writing, economies used commodities like gold or silver as money, and hence his emphasis was on the commodity form of money. 'The specific kind of commodity with whose natural form the equivalent form is socially interwoven now becomes the money commodity, or serves as money' (Marx, 1992, p. 162). In a commodity money system, the state fixes a *standard of price*, which is a fixed amount of the money commodity that is referred to by the name of the national currency, for instance the $. Recall that in Volume I of *Capital*, the level of abstraction is 'capital in general'. This means that we are abstracting from competition between capitals and conceptually consider the whole capitalist system in aggregate terms. In such a context, which we will call as 'equal exchange', the value of a commodity will be equal to its price. Thus, in a commodity money system, the price of a commodity in units of the money commodity, when there is equal exchange, is the ratio of the value of the commodity and the value of the money commodity. To convert the price in terms of the national currency, we just need to divide it by the standard of price.

Let us work through an example. Suppose the state decides that the standard of price is 0.1 grams of gold. This means that the national currency, 1$, is equivalent to 0.1 grams of gold. Suppose it takes 100 hours of socially necessary labour-time to produce 1 gram of gold. Thus, the value of 1 gram of gold is 100 hours. Suppose it take 20 hours of socially necessary labour-time to make a shoe. What would its price be, in the setting we are working with? The gold price of the shoe would be 0.2 (= 20/100) grams of gold. Since the standard of price is 0.1 grams of gold, the price of the shoe in units of the national currency is 2$.

For completeness, let me express this discussion in algebraic terms. If the value of gold (the money commodity) is λ_g hours of labour-time, the value of commodity A is λ_A hours of labour-time and the standard of price is s grams of gold per \$ (the national currency), then the price of commodity A in units of the national currency is given by $P_A = \lambda_A / (s * \lambda_g)$. In the previous example, $\lambda_A = 20$, $\lambda_g = 100$ and $s = 0.1$. Hence, $P_A = 2\$$.[14]

Inconvertible Paper Money
Paper money issued by the state that is no longer convertible to gold, the money commodity, is what Marx calls inconvertible paper money. This form of money is forced into circulation by the state, often to finance wars or pay off accumulated stocks of debt. Two prominent historical examples are the *assignat* issued by the French National Assembly during the French Revolution, and the *greenback* issued by the US government during the Civil War. Inconvertible paper money is a *symbol of money*, the latter still being gold, the commodity money. Thus, when Marx discusses inconvertible paper money, the universal equivalent is still gold, and hence it is still a commodity money system that we are dealing with.

> Paper money is a symbol of gold, a symbol of money. Its relation to the value of commodities consists only in this: they find imaginary expression in certain quantities of gold, and the same quantities are symbolically and physically represented by the paper. Only in so far as paper money represents gold, which like all other commodities has value, is it a symbol of value. (Marx, 1992, p. 235)

With gold (commodity money) and (incovertible) paper money circulating in the same economy, a market develops where gold and inconvertible paper currency is exchanged.[15] Moreover, there will be two prices of each commodity – a price expressed in gold (or the standard of price) and a price expressed in the paper money. As long as the quantity of inconvertible paper money is not 'too large', it will trade at par with gold, that is, 1 unit of paper money will be equal to 1 unit of gold. In such a situation, the two prices of commodities will coincide. When the issuance of paper money is too large, it sells at a discount with respect to gold, that is, 1 unit of paper money will exchange for less than

---

[14]When 'equal exchange' does not hold, the price of a commodity may deviate from the monetary expression of its value (socially necessary abstract labour-time).
[15]'A law peculiar to the circulation of paper money can only spring up from the proportion in which that paper money represents gold' (Marx, 1992, p. 224).

1 unit of gold. In that case, the paper money price will be larger than the gold price of commodities. This will show up as inflation in the paper money prices of commodities. Note that this inflation is not caused by an excess supply of money chasing a given supply of goods (the monetarist understanding of inflation), but by the process of discounting of paper money for gold money (Foley, 1986b).

How much paper money is too large for an economy? We have already seen that Marx had a very firm grasp of the equation of exchange: $MV = PQ$. The adequate amount of paper money can be defined, on average, using this equation as $M = (PQ)/V$. This defines the total quantity of money that fulfills the needs of circulation. Since both gold and paper currency meet the needs of circulation, we will have $M = M_g + M_p$, where M_g and M_p refer to gold and inconvertible paper money in circulation. Over any period of time, the needs of circulation can be ascertained with a large degree of certainty. Hence, given M_g, we will be able to arrive at the correct amount of M_p, the amount of paper money that is needed for circulation. Any issuance of inconvertible paper money in excess of this need of circulation will force the paper money to start selling at a discount with respect to gold money, leading to an inflation in the paper money price of commodities.

Credit Money

In the contemporary world, we do not have a commodity money system. From around the middle of the twentieth century, capitalist economies have moved away from the use of commodity money altogether. The primary form of money in contemporary capitalist economies is *credit money*. While Marx briefly discusses credit money in Volume I, the full analysis is presented in Volume III in the context of the distribution of surplus value. Marx followed this procedure to stick to his plan about presenting the material at the correct level of abstraction. Credit money presupposes credit, which is a relationship between different fragments of capital. Since Volume I is pitched at the level of 'capital in general', credit, and therefore, credit money cannot be discussed in Volume I. We will discuss some aspects of credit money in section 5.5, but it is possible to explain its origins and form right away using the concept of 'means of payment'.[16]

---

[16]The discussion in this section draws on Marx (1993b, Chapter 25) and Lapavitsas (2013).

As soon as money functions as a means of payment, there emerges relationships of credit – in fact, the two go together. Suppose commodity owner A sells her commodity, also called A, to commodity owner B on a certain date but agrees to receive payment 3 months later. The contract between the two commodity owners is specified in a 'bill of exchange' that B gives to A. The contract specifies the amount of money that its holder will get on a certain date (which is exactly 3 months from the date when B receives the commodity from A). Initially, the contract is held by A – with the intention of presenting it to B on the specified date and receiving the payment noted on the bill of exchange.

The bill of exchange is an asset for A and a liability for B because B has a payment commitment, and A has the right to receive the payment. If before the date on which the bill of exchange matures, that is, the date specified on it, A were in need of some commodity, she could use the bill of exchange to pay for the purchase. If the bill of exchange – liability of B – is accepted for purchase of commodities, it starts functioning as credit money. On the other hand, A might even take the bill of exchange, before its date of maturity, to a bank and exchange it for a sum of money. The bank will pay A a slightly lower amount than what is specified on the bill of exchange – a process known as 'discounting' of bills.

The transaction between A and the bank is interesting and worth considering in some detail. The bank has accepted the bill of exchange, and it now becomes its asset. In turn, it has issued its own liability to A. That money can now be used by A to purchase commodities or settle other debts. Hence, it is credit money. If an economy has an active market for discounting of bills of exchange, it starts developing a robust credit money system. Of course, the social validity or acceptance of either the original bill of exchange or the liabilities of the banks is crucial. If there is lack of social acceptance, then credit money can collapse. And this is where the state steps in, via the Central Bank, taking us to the final step of the process of creating a stable credit money system.

Every capitalist country has a Central Bank, a 'bank of banks', which is closely tied to the capitatist state. Commercial banks hold accounts with the Central Bank, where they deposit their reserves, and the liabilities of the Central Bank are used to settle debts between commercial banks. The state makes liabilities of the Central Bank legal tender, that is, it can be used for settlement of debt by decree of the state. This step finally ends the need of a commodity to function as money – and we are in a full-fledged credit money system. Moreover, the backing of the state ensures social validity for credit money – so long as there is acceptance of the power of the state. No wonder, periods of hyperinflation are periods when the power of the state is severely eroded for political or economic reasons.

It is important to recognize that the basic logic of money as a socially validated universal equivalent remains operational even in the case of contemporary credit money systems. The only difference is that the form of money has changed. Instead of a commodity, for example, gold, the liabilities of a country's Central Bank (currency) and liabilities of the commercial banking system (deposits) together function as the universal equivalent. The function of money as the social device to express the value contained in commodities that is separate from their physical (or natural) form remains unchanged.

3.2.4 Monetary Expression of Value

Definition and Measurement
The monetary expression of value (MEV) is a conversion factor that Marx frequently, and implicitly, used to move back and forth between value magnitudes (measured in units of labour hours) and monetary magnitudes (measured in units of the monetary unit of account, the rupee or the dollar, for instance). Here are some examples.

> If 1 hour of work is embodied in 6 pence, and the value of a day's labour-power is 5 shillings . . . (Marx, 1992, p. 430). Let the value of labour-power be 3 shillings, and let the necessary labour-time amount to 6 hours (Marx, 1992, p. 659) If we suppose that the value produced by one worker in an average social working day is expressed in a sum of money to the value of 6 shillings . . . (Marx, 1993b, p. 119)

The concept of the MEV was possibly first highlighted in Foley (1982b) and is now used widely in Marxist economics. The MEV is defined as the ratio of the total monetary value added in the production of all newly produced commodities over some time period (which is what contemporary economists call the gross domestic product), measured in monetary units of the national currency, and the total amount of productive labour involved in the production of those commodities, measured in hours of labour:

$$MEV = \frac{\text{monetary value added}}{\text{productive labour hours}}$$

Intuitively, the MEV is the monetary expression of one hour of socially necessary abstract labour-time and its unit of measurement is the monetary unit per hours of labour-time. For instance, in India the MEV would be expressed in terms of rupees per hour of social labour; in the US, it would be expressed in units of USD per hour of social labour.

Three important issues related to the MEV need to be highlighted at this point. First, once we have computed the MEV for a particular economy for a given year, we can easily convert between value and monetary magnitudes. To move from value magnitudes to monetary magnitudes, we need to multiply with the MEV; to convert monetary magnitudes to value magnitudes, we need to divide with the MEV. The second point to keep in mind is that the MEV is an aggregate concept and can only be defined meaningfully at the level of a whole capitalist economy. Of course, once defined, it can be used to convert value magnitudes into monetary magnitudes and vice versa at lower levels of aggregation. But the MEV itself cannot be defined at lower levels of aggregation. For instance, it would not be meaningful to define the MEV for an individual industry or firm. Third, in the actual computation of the MEV, the numerator is relatively easily available. It is the gross domestic product (GDP), that is, money value added, of the productive sectors of the economy.[17] On the other hand, the denominator is the challenging part. It is the total socially necessary abstract labour-time. To arrive at this magnitude, a researcher must aggregate concrete labour, involved in commodity production in a commodity-producing society, because that is what is observed, and we know that concrete labour involved in commodity production is abstract labour in qualitative terms. Hence, the main task for the researcher in carrying out the aggregation is to reduce complex labour to relevant multiples of simple labour and consistently use the benchmark of 'socially necessary labour' by identifying average conditions of production – including technology and intensity of labour.

---

[17] Of course, some important distinctions need to be made to make this computation consistent with Marxist understanding of productive and unproductive labour. The relevant discussion can be found in section 5.4.

One concern with the definition of the MEV might be that, instead of focusing on produced value, the measure is looking at realized value (value realized through sale of commodities). On closer inspection, this concern seems misplaced. In National Income and Product Account, the gross domestic product is a measure of an economy's output (and not sales). One way of measuring output is to sum up value added across all industries. Here, 'value added' is defined as follows: value added = total output – intermediate purchases, where total output = sales + change in inventories arising from production. If some approximation of market prices are used for valuing inventories, then 'value added' captures production rather than sales (because inventories are included in the computation of value added). Hence, when we use GDP – for a suitably defined sub-sector of the economy to focus only on productive activities – to compute the MEV, we are using 'produced value' and not only 'realized value'.

Since the MEV is the ratio of aggregate money value added to the newly produced commodities and the total productive labour involved in its production, it depends on both an aggregate price level and the aggregate productivity of labour.[18] Hence, if we compare the MEV across countries, we should expect it to vary because of both the price level and the productivity of labour. Similarly, if we track the movement of the MEV over time for any country, we would expect changes in the MEV over time to depend on the rate of inflation and changes in the labour productivity.[19]

An Example

Let us work through an example to clarify the concept of MEV. From the U.S. Bureau of Economic Analysis, we know that the total monetary value added by businesses in the US in 2018 was 15,680.8 billions USD. According to the U.S. Bureau of Labour Statistics, the total number of workers employed in all private industries was 122,615,800 in 2018. On average, they worked for 33.74 hours per week; and they worked on average for 52 weeks in a year. Hence, total number of hours worked by all workers was 304.22 billion hours. Hence, the MEV in US economy in 2018 was 70.58 USD per hour, which is the ratio of monetary value added and total hours worked. Note that in

---

[18]We have already encountered the concept of labour productivity in section 3.1.6 and will discuss it again in section 5.2.
[19]For a more detailed analysis of comparison of MEVs over time and across countries, see Appendix 3.B.

this calculation, we have not reduced complex to simple labour; we have just added up all the hours of labour. Hence, our estimate of the MEV is only approximately correct. In fact, we know that the magnitude we have computed is an overestimate of the true MEV – because when we convert complex labour to simple labour, the denominator in the definition of the MEV will increase.

Now that we have computed the MEV for the US economy in 2018, we can convert labour-time magnitudes into monetary magnitudes and vice versa. Suppose we wish to find the monetary expression of 100 hours of social labour. Since the MEV is 70.58 USD per hour, 100 hours of social labour will be expressed in 7,058 USD (70.58 * 100). Now, let us work out the reverse conversion: suppose we wish to find the social labour-time equivalent of 1,000 USD. To do so, we would divide 1,000 by the MEV, 70.58, to get 14.17. Thus, for the US economy in 2018, 1,000 USD would be equivalent to 14.17 hours of social labour.

3.2.5   Price–Value Deviation

When prices are proportional to value, the price of a commodity is the amount of money needed to express the value contained in one unit of the commodity. But price and value need not always be proportional to each other, and, in fact, we can easily understand why they might diverge.

The price of a commodity, being a quantity of money, can be converted into its social labour-time equivalent by dividing the price with the MEV, as we did earlier. This would give us the social labour-time equivalent *realized* by the sale of the commodity, that is, the value realized in sale. On the other hand, the value of the commodity is the socially necessary labour-time needed for its *production*. Is there any reason for the social labour-time equivalent of the price of a commodity to coincide with the socially necessary labour-time needed for its production? As long as we abstract from 'many capitals', that is, as long as we operate at the level of abstraction proper to Volume I and II, the two labour-time magnitudes will coincide. Once we introduce competition between capitals, that is when we move to the setting of Volume III, we will see that there are sound theoretical reasons to believe why they will not coincide. It is worth noting, also, that instances of such exchanges, that is where the value realized in sale is different from the value of the commodity, are instances of *unequal exchange*, because one party to the exchange gets a different quantum of value than the other. An important insight of Marx's analysis is that unequal exchanges are pervasive in competitive capitalism, that is, unequal exchange can and does arise even in the absence of monopolies and different barriers to mobility of capital and labour. Of course, when monopolies are erected and maintained that brings in additional mechanisms for supporting unequal exchange.

> The possibility, therefore, of a quantitative incongruity between price and magnitude of value, i.e. the possibility that the price may diverge from the magnitude of value, is inherent in the price-form itself. This is not a defect, but, on the contrary, it makes this form the adequate one for a mode of production whose laws can only assert themselves as blindly operating averages between constant irregularities. (Marx, 1992, p. 196)

We will discuss this issue in greater detail in two subsequent chapters, in non-technical terms in Chapter 5 and in more technical terms in Chapter 7.

3.2.6   Comparing Monetary Magnitudes over Time and across Countries

Many important questions of political economy involve comparisons of monetary magnitudes over time and across countries. We would now like to understand how to carry out such comparisons in a consistent and meaningful manner from a Marxist perspective. While this is an issue that Marx did not study systematically in *Capital*, the analysis we have developed so far will allow us to carry out such comparisons in a consistent manner.

A first issue that we need to clarify is the objective of the comparisons. For instance, we could be interested in comparing monetary magnitudes over time with the intention of identifying the 'real' magnitudes it represents, that is, its purchasing power. Such a comparison could be done over time and across countries. For instance, we might be interested in understanding the purchasing power of 100 USD in 1960 and in 2010. This question can be answered by taking account of the change in the general price level in the US economy between 1960 and 2010. Similarly, if we are interested in comparing the purchasing power of 100 USD and 100 rupees (Indian currency) in 2010, we would need to take account of the differences in the price levels in the US and India in 2010.

When we are comparing monetary magnitudes from a Marxist perspective, these are not the questions that motivate us. We are instead interested in understanding the social labour-time equivalent of monetary magnitudes over time and across countries. Thus, for instance, we might be interested in understanding how many hours of social labour is represented by 100 USD in 1960 and how that compares with the social labour-time equivalent of 100 USD in 2010. We know how to carry out such a comparison. We need to divide the 100 USD by the MEV in 1960 and compare that with the ratio of 100 USD and the MEV in 2010. Thus, the social labour-time equivalent of every USD will change over time as the MEV changes over time. If the MEV rises rapidly, then the social labour-time equivalent of every USD will fall rapidly, and vice versa. We know that the MEV changes over time proportionately to changes in the price level, that is, inflation rate, and to changes in labour productivity.[20] Hence, if labour productivity rises rapidly, it will increase the MEV, and will lead to a fall in the social labour-time equivalent of every USD, other things remaining constant.

To facilitate comparison across countries, let us identify two countries, US and India. If we want to compare the social labour-time equivalent of a USD and an Indian rupee, we need to first convert them into their respective social labour-time equivalents. The social labour-time equivalent of 1 USD is the reciprocal of the MEV in the US; the social labour-time equivalent of 1 Indian rupee is the reciprocal of the Indian MEV. Hence, the relative 'social labour time power', instead of purchasing power, of the two currencies is given by the reciprocal of the ratio of the two MEVs. Of course, for this comparison to be consistent and meaningful, the MEVs in the two countries need to be computed properly – and the main challenge there is to properly add up units of complex labour, with the correct reduction coefficient, and to take account of the intensity of labour. This discussion leads me to propose a Marxian exchange rate.

3.2.7   *A Marxian Exchange Rate for International Exchange*

Let us define the *Marxian exchange rate* between two national currencies as the exchange ratio that preserves social labour-time in exchange. Hence, the Marxian exchange rate between two national currencies is the ratio of their MEV. To be precise, let $e_M^{A,B}$ denote the Marxian exchange rate between

---

[20] See Appendix 3.B.

countries A and B, let m_A and m_B denote the MEV in country A and B, respectively. Then

$$e_M{}^{A,B} = \frac{m_A}{m_B} \tag{3.4}$$

Let us look at an example to make sense of this definition. Suppose country A is the US, and country B is Brazil. Further, suppose that the MEV in the US is 50 USD per hour of social labour, and the MEV in Brazil is 25 Real per hour of social labour. Then, the Marxian exhange rate between the USD and the Real is

$$e_M{}^{USA,BRA} = \frac{m_{USA}}{m_{BRA}} = \frac{25}{50} = 0.5RE/USD$$

What does the Marxian exchange of 0.5 *RE/USD* rate mean? It means that 0.5 units of the Brazilian national currency (the Real) represents the same amount of social labour-time as 1 unit of the US national currency (the USD). Why? From the MEV in the US, we know that 1 USD is equivalent to 1/50 hours of social labour. We also know from the MEV in Brazil that 1 Real is equivalent to 1/25 hours of social labour. Hence, 0.5 Real is equivalent to 1/50 hours of social labour.

To see the import of the Marxian exchange rate, let us contrast it with the market exchange rate of the two currencies. The market or nominal exchange rate between two currencies is the price of one in terms of the other. For instance, in July 2020, the nominal exchange rate between the USD and the Brazilian Real was 5 *RE/USD*, that is, the price of a USD was 5 Brazilian Real. Hence, to purchase every USD, one has to give up 5 Real. If the Marxian exchange rate is 0.5 RE/USD, this means that through the market transaction of the currencies, 10 hours (= 5/0.5) of social labour is given up by the Brazilian economy in exchange for every hour of social labour of the US economy. If the MEV has been computed properly, that is, by properly taking account of the *complexity* and *intensity* of labour in both economies, then we have here a situation of unequal exchange of social labour in the market-based transactions between the US and Brazilian economy.[21]

---

[21] A researcher will have to properly compare a unit of 'simple labour' in the two economies. For instance, it is possible that the average level of skills, for example, captured by average years of formal schooling, in the US is higher than in Brazil. Hence, 1 unit of 'simple labour' in the US would create a multiple of the value created by each unit of 'simple labour' in Brazil. Hence, after the reduction

To illustrate this further, let us suppose a Ford car costs 15,000 USD in the US. When it is exported to Brazil, its price, ignoring transportation and other costs, will be 75,000 Real, using the market exchange rate. If the Marxian exchange rate had been used, the Ford car should have been sold at 7,500 Real in Brazil. This price would have ensured that the sale and purchase of the car preserved social labour equivalence. Transaction at the market exchange rate means that the US economy gets back 10 times more social labour in the price of the car than was needed to produce the car.

This is precisely the usefulness of the Marxian exchange rate. It will allow us to investigate possible unequal exchanges of social labour in international market transactions between nation states. This is an issue of long-standing interest to Marxian and World Systems theorists. But existing approaches are flawed either because they do not use flows of labour or when they do, they do not properly account for differences in the complexity and intensity of labour across countries (Emmanuel, 1972; Wallerstein, 1974; Chase-Dunn, 1998). Using the Marxian exchange rate proposed here, a researcher can consistently investigate the possibilities of unequal exchange in international trade.

3.2.8   Commodity Fetishism

Let me end this section by pointing to some very interesting discussion about a peculiar distortion in thought that emerges in commodity-producing societies, which Marx calls the 'fetishism of commodities' (Marx, 1992, section 4, Chapter 1). The key idea seems to be that in a commodity-producing society, the essential interdependence between commodity producers is no longer transparent. The fact that each commodity producer is part of a social division of labour is systematically obscured from view because each commodity producer's labour is conducted privately and independently of other commodity producers. The relationship between the labours of different commodity producers – which Marx refers to as the conversion of private labour into social labour – is only established through the process of exchange, when the products of their labour are brought into relationship with each other. Thus, not only is it obscured from view that, for instance, the tailor depends on the farmer and vice versa, but the social

---

coefficient is computed for each country, a further reduction of US labour to Brazilian labour would need to be carried out with the ratio of the value of simple labour in the two countries. '*Simple average labour* ... varies in character in different countries and at different cultural epochs, but in a particular society it is given' (Marx, 1992, p. 135, emphasis in original).

relationship between them is read onto the relationship between the shirt and the wheat. Value, which derives from the labour of the commodity producer, now attaches to the product of her labour, the commodity. It is thus that commodities start attaining fantastic powers of their own, that is, being converted into festishes.

3.2.9   Long-period Method of Analysis

Distribution of Labour and Exchange Value

In his analysis of commodity production and capitalism, Marx uses the classical long-period method of analysis developed by Adam Smith (1991, Book I, II).[22] According to Adam Smith, the prime source of the increase in the wealth of nations is the rise in the productivity of labour. A complex social division of labour promotes specialization and leads to an increase in the average productivity of labour. While a complex social division of labour increases labour productivity, at the same time it creates a problem of *social coordination*. This is because the social division of labour creates a system of independent commodity production, where production is carried on by independent commodity producers who make production decisions privately and independently of each other. How does such a system coordinate the production decisions of the independent commodity producers to, on average and over the long run, balance out supply and demand?

The system of commodity production lacks any central authority that can coordinate the production decisions of independent, private commodity producers. An alternative, decentralized coordination mechanism must be in place to solve the problem of social coordination. Adam Smith's key insight is that the process of exchange is that decentralized social coordination mechanism. What is important for our purpose is to note that social coordination through the process of exchange has two important aspects. On the one hand, it leads to a distribution of the total labour of society into different lines of production; on the other, labour involved in the production of commodities acquires a dual character – concrete labour and abstract labour – and abstract labour is expressed in the form of 'value' of commodities (which, in turn, underlies exchange value).

---

[22]In developing the ideas presented in this section, I have benefitted from extended conversations with Duncan Foley.

> Every child knows that a nation which ceased to work, I will not say for a year, but even for a few weeks, would perish. Every child knows too that the masses of products corresponding to the different needs require different and quantitatively determined masses of the total labour of society. That this necessity of the *distribution of social labour* in definite proportions cannot possibly be done away with by a particular form of social production but can only change the form in which it appears, is self-evident. No natural laws can be done away with. What can change, in historically different circumstances, is only the form in which these laws operate. And the form in which this proportional distribution of labour operates, in a state of society where the interconnection of social labour is manifested in the private exchange of the individual products of labour, is precisely the *exchange value of these products*. (Marx's letter to L. Kugelmann, July 11, 1868. Quoted in Rubin [1990, p. 77])

What does Marx mean by the 'distribution of social labour' and why does this lead to the expression of productive labour in the form of 'value'? Consider a thought experiment. At the beginning of a production period, sufficiently long to allow for supply and demand adjustments to work themselves out, a commodity-production system has a total supply of human labour. This society has a definite structure of social and individual needs, fulfilment of which requires a definite quantity of use-values. Given the state of technology, the production of use-values to satisfy the social structure of needs requires a definite distribution of the total labour into different lines of production. This is just another way of saying that homogeneous human labour, that is, abstract labour, in a commodity-producing system, needs to take the form of concrete labour (involved in the production of specific use-values) and that there must be a determinate distribution of concrete labour across lines of production.

How is the specific distribution of total labour into its concrete forms accomplished? What is the mechanism that leads to the distribution of total labour that is necessitated by social needs and technology? Adam Smith's key insight is that, over the long run, commodity producers choose to locate themselves in specific lines of production by balancing the 'advantages' and 'disadvantages' of labour in different lines of production. Here, 'advantage' refers to income earned and 'disadvantage' denotes the cost of producing the specific type of labour-power, where cost of production should be understood broadly to include the cost of training, the reproduction of labour-power within the household, and so on.

If there is a line of production, where the ratio of income earned and cost of producing that type of labour-power is lower than the social average, commodity producers will leave this line and move to others where the ratio is higher than the average. For lines of production where the ratio is higher than the social average, there will be a reverse movement of commodity producers into that line of production. Over the long run, if there are no impediments to the mobility of labour across lines of production, the ratio of income earned and cost of producing that type of labour-power will tend towards equality. The tendency towards equalization of the ratio of 'advantages' and 'disadvantages' will lead to the specific distribution of labour across lines of production that is needed to meet social demand, given technology. It will also give rise to exchange value, that is, ratios in which commodities exchange, that will reflect the quantity of socially necessary abstract labour that has gone into the production of commodities. Hence, we will have the labour theory of value, exactly as it has been outlined in the previous few sections of this book.[23]

An Example

I would now like to work through a simple example and show how in a commodity-producing system, where producers own their means of production, exchange ratios will be proportional labour values. The simplest model of a commodity-producing economy where we can investigate the issue of exchange value (or exchange ratios) is one with two commodities – and we will work with such a model. This is an extension of the one commodity (corn) model we worked with in previous sections, and the logic of production and exchange are very similar.

Suppose the economy produces two commodities. Instead of giving them names, we will just identify the two commodities with the numbers 1 and 2. Production of each commodity requires non-labour inputs of both commodities and a labour input. We can specify these technological

---

[23]The centrality of exchange in the theory of value and the dual manifestation of the regulation of social production by exchange in a distribution of total social labour across lines of production and definite ratios in which the products of labour exchange with each other has been highlighted in Rubin (1990) and Sweezy (1942).

relationships of production with a 2×2 matrix of non-labour input coefficients,

$$\boldsymbol{A}^{24} = \begin{bmatrix} a_{11} & a_{12} \\ a_{21} & a_{22} \end{bmatrix}$$

and a 1×2 row vector of labour input coefficients

$$\boldsymbol{l} = \begin{bmatrix} l_1 & l_2 \end{bmatrix}$$

The columns of the matrix $\boldsymbol{A}$ give the physical quantities of each of the two commodities needed to produce 1 unit of the commodity represented by each column. For instance, the first column gives the inputs of commodity 1 and 2 required to produce each unit of commodity 1; and the second column gives the inputs of commodity 1 and 2 needed to produce 1 unit of commodity 2. Thus, the entries of the matrix $\boldsymbol{A}$ should be read as follows: a_{ij} is the physical quantity of commodity i required to produce 1 unit of commodity j. The entries of the vector $\boldsymbol{l}$ should be read in an analogous manner: l_j is the hours of labour needed to produce 1 unit of commodity j.

Let the following row vector give labour values of the two commodities,

$$\boldsymbol{\lambda} = \begin{bmatrix} \lambda_1 & \lambda_2 \end{bmatrix}$$

and let the following row vector give prices of the two commodities,

$$\boldsymbol{p} = \begin{bmatrix} p_1 & p_2 \end{bmatrix}$$

Using the technological relationships given earlier, we can write equations for the value system. For commodity 1, we have

$$\lambda_1 = \lambda_1 a_{11} + \lambda_2 a_{21} + l_1$$

where $\lambda_1 a_{11} + \lambda_2 a_{21}$ is value transferred from non-labour inputs and l_1 is value added by labour. In a similar manner, for commodity 2, we have

$$\lambda_2 = \lambda_1 a_{12} + \lambda_2 a_{22} + l_2$$

Using matrix notation, we can write the above two equations more compactly as

$$\boldsymbol{\lambda} = \boldsymbol{\lambda} \boldsymbol{A} + \boldsymbol{l}$$

[24]In this book, vectors and matrices are denoted in boldface text.

Under plausible conditions, the matrix $(I - A)$ is invertible.[25] Hence, we can solve the above equation to get the vector of values as

$$\lambda = l\,(I - A)^{-1}$$

In a similar manner, we can also write the price equations. In the production of commodity 1, let us denote the ratio of income earned and labour input by w_1; then we have

$$\frac{p_1 - (p_1 a_{11} + p_2 a_{21})}{l_1} = w_1$$

because the numerator on the left-hand side is the income earned per unit of commodity 1, and the denominator is the labour input per unit of commodity 1. We can think of w_1 as the income earned per hour of labour input in the production of commodity 1.

Turning to commodity 2, let the ratio of income earned and labour input in its production be denoted by w_2; then, we have

$$\frac{p_2 - (p_1 a_{12} + p_2 a_{22})}{l_2} = w_2$$

We can, again, interpret w_2 as income earned per hour of labour input in the production of commodity 2. Over the long run, the mobility of labour will ensure that income earned per hour of labour input is the same in the two lines of production, that is, $w_1 = w_2 = w$. Hence, the price equation for commodity 1 will become

$$p_1 = p_1 a_{11} + p_2 a_{21} + w l_1$$

and the price equation for the second commodity will become

$$p_2 = p_1 a_{12} + p_2 a_{22} + w l_2$$

Using matrix notation, we can write the price system as

$$p = pA + wl$$

Upon solving this, we get

$$p = wl\,(I - A)^{-1} = w\lambda$$

---

[25] For details, see Chapter 7.A.

On the left-hand side we have the price vector, p; on the right-hand side we have the vector of labour values, λ multiplied by a scalar, w. Hence, prices are proportional to labour values, that is, $p_1 / p_2 = \lambda_1 / \lambda_2$.

While we have worked with a system that produces only two commodities, the argument holds for a general case where the system produces n commodities. The main claim demonstrated by the example discussed here is well known: if the means of production are owned by the direct producers, in which case there is no profit income, prices of commodities are proportional to labour values. Thus, in a simple commodity-production economy, that is, the model discussed by Marx in Chapters 1 through 3 of Volume I of *Capital*, exchange ratios will be proportional to the ratio of values – as shown by the long-period method of analysis.

An important implication of the long-period method should be noted: in every line of production, the ratio of income earned and the cost of labour input, the latter broadly understood, is equal. In computing such ratios, we need to evaluate the labour input taking account of the complexity and intensity of labour. That is how we take account of the difference in the cost of producing the labour input. Turning this around, we can then claim that the ratio of incomes earned across different lines of production give us a correct estimate of the cost of producing different types of complex labour and the cost of using labour-power more intensively. While incomes earned are easily observed, the true cost of producing different types of complex labour-power are not. Hence, the long-period method of analysis suggests that the former can be used as good estimates of the latter.

One important and difficult issue will need to be addressed while properly conceptualizing the cost of producing complex labour-power. Labour-power, that is, the ability to do useful work, is produced in a complex social process that straddles the spheres of commodity production and direct production of use-values (that is, non-commodities). How should we deal with labour involved in the production of labour-power that falls outside the domain of commodity production? We will return to this issue in section 3.3.3 when we focus on a context in which labour-power has become a commodity.

Further Readings

- The following sections from Volume I of *Capital* should be read to understand Marx's theory of money: whole of Chapter 2, sections 2 and 3(b) of Chapter 3 and section 4 of Chapter 1.

- Marx develops his argument about money as the universal equivalent in section 3 in Chapter 1 of Volume I of *Capital*. Further elaboration are presented in Marx (1992, Chapters 2, 3), the former discussing the process of exchange and the latter dealing with the functions and forms of money.

- Clear expositions can be found in Eaton (1963, Chapter II) and Foley (1986b, Chapter 2, pp. 18–30). The concept of MEV, and its reciprocal, the value of money, can be found in Foley (1982b) and in (Foley, 1986b, Chapter 2).

3.3 Capital, or Self-Valorizing Value

Now that we have understood the concept of money and seen how it emerges from within the logic of commodity production itself, we are ready to begin the study of capital, and with it, a capitalist economy. It is useful to recall that a commodity-producing system, whose properties we have studied in detailed in the previous two sections, is not by itself a capitalist economy. The widespread prevalence of commodity production, whereby production is regulated through exchange, is a necessary but not a sufficient condition for a society to be characterized as capitalist. The additional, and crucial, condition that is needed to turn a commodity-producing society into a capitalist society is that labour-power becomes a commodity. We will study this issue in great detail in this section. We will see that labour-power is a peculiar commodity. It is different from all other commodities, and on it hinges the whole value, and surplus value, creation process of a capitalist economy. To understand the logic of capital, that is, the intrinsic logic of a capitalist system, we need to pay close attention to the commodity labour-power.

> The historical conditions of its [i.e. capital's] existence are by no means given with the mere circulation of money and commodities. It arises only when the owner of means of production and subsistence finds the free worker available, on the market, as the seller of his own labour-power. And this one historical pre-condition comprises a world's history. Capital, therefore, announces from the outset a new epoch in the process of social production. (Marx, 1992, p. 274)

3.3.1 Two Forms of Circulation

Let us begin our study of capital by considering two typical forms of circulation, that is, exchange of commodities, observed in capitalist societies: (*a*) selling in order to buy (sale followed by purchase) and (*b*) buying in order to sell (purchase followed by sale). The first can be represented as $C - M - C'$ and, as we have seen earlier, is called the 'simple circulation of commodities' by Marx; the second can be represented as $M - C - M'$ and is called the 'circulation of money' by Marx. What is the difference between these two forms of circulation?[26]

In the first form of commodity circulation, $C - M - C'$, an economic agent with some commodity, C, comes to the market, sells it for the sum of money, M, and purchases some other commodity, C', with the proceeds of the previous sale. The aim of this form of commodity circulation is qualitative transformation of one commodity into another, that is, of C into C', which is effected through exchange, and ultimately points towards an aim in consumption, that is, outside production. Hence, the simple circulation of commodities ends with C'.

The second form of commodity circulation, $M - C - M'$, is very different from the first. Here, a commodity producer comes to the market with a sum of money, M, purchases some commodity, C, and then returns to the market to sell that (or another) commodity for a sum of money, M'. The starting and end points of the circulation process, being sums of money, are qualitatively identical. Hence, the only possible motive for engaging in this process of circulation can be a quantitative increase in the sum of money. The very logic of the process dictates that M' must be larger than M; otherwise the process becomes meaningless. Moreover, by its internal logic, the process of circulation represented by $M - C - M'$ recreates its beginning at the end of each cycle. This is because the endpoint is a sum of money (possibly larger in magnitude), just like the beginning, so that it can potentially function as the beginning of a new cycle, $M' - C' - M''$.

Let us use some examples to make these abstract formulas more concrete. Consider an artisan who bakes bread in his house and sells them on the market. She uses the proceeds of the sale to purchase vegetables and rice for her family. This is an example of the simple circulation of commodities,

---

[26]In these abstract representations, C stands for a commodity, M stands for a sum of money, C' stands for a different commodity and M' stands for a sum of money that is different from M.

where C represents bread, M represents the proceeds of sale of bread and C' represents the vegetable and rice that the artisan purchases. Let us now contrast the artisan with a capitalist who owns a bread-making factory. The capitalist uses a sum of money M to purchase wheat, machines and other inputs, and then hires workers. When the bread is produced, the capitalist then sells it on the market for a sum of money M'.

Recall that money is a social device to express the value (of commodities). Hence, $M - C - M'$ represents a process whereby value moves through a circular process in terms of its form, that is, it starts in monetary form, M, coverts itself to a commodity form, C, and then returns to its monetary form, M'. This movement of forms of value can therefore be conceived as a 'circuit', that is, a circular movement (where the beginning and end are the same forms of value). Along with this change in the forms attained by value, there is also a quantitative aspect. The magnitude of value is not only preserved through the circuit, but it increases in size. In Marx's terminology, value has valorized itself. The increment in value, $\Delta M = M' - M$, is known as surplus value and $M - C - M'$ is called the 'general formula for capital'. An investigation of the two forms of circulation, therefore, leads to the following definition: capital is value in motion that also increases itself in size, that is, to use Marx's terminology, *capital is self-valorizing value*. In terms of the previous example, the bread-making capitalist ends up with more money than she started with, and the difference between the two, $M' - M$, is the surplus value.

3.3.2 Surplus Value

How does value in motion valorize itself? What is the source of surplus value? Where does the surplus value come from? These questions attain significance when we realize that, in Marx's analysis in Volume I of *Capital*, every act of exchange is an exchange of equivalent magnitudes (of value). Even if there were cases of unequal exchange, since the gain of one party would be exactly equal to the loss of the other party in that exchange, they would not be able to explain the emergence of surplus value at the level of the aggregate capitalist economy – one party's gain would be cancelled out by another party's loss when we aggregate across all transactions.[27] That is why Marx sets himself

---

[27]If the interaction of a capitalist system with a non-capitalist system results in unequal exchange, then it is possible for the magnitude of value recorded in the capitalist system to increase by the transfer of value from outside the system. But even in this case, if we take a global perspective and consider

the challenge of explaining the origin of surplus value when all exchanges are instances of equal exchange.

The Circuit of Capital

Let us return to the general formula for capital: $M - C - M'$. The first phase of the formula is an act of exchange, where money is used to purchase a commodity: $M - C$. Since we are only considering cases of equal exchange, surplus value cannot arise in this phase. Similarly, the second phase is also an act of (equal) exchange, where a commodity is sold for a sum of money: $C - M'$. Hence, surplus value cannot arise in this phase too. The inescapable conclusion is that surplus value must arise in between the two phases of circulation of the general formula for capital. What happens in between the two phases of circulation? Between the two phases of circulation is located the process of production. Thus, to understand the origin of surplus value, we need to leave the sphere of circulation, where commodities are exchanged, and enter the sphere of production, where the commodity is produced.

We can begin our study by expanding the general formula for capital in two steps. In the first step, we represent capital as $M - C - C' - M'$. Here, we make explicit the fact that the commodity purchased in the first phase, C, is different from the commodity sold in the second phase, C'. Without this qualitative difference between C and C', surplus value cannot be generated in the context of equal exchange. This is because the same commodity, C, cannot have two different magnitudes of value, one when it is purchased and another (higher value) when it is sold. But with C and C' recognized as two different commodities, we can have equal exchange at the two ends of $M - C - C' - M'$ and yet allow for the possibility of generation of surplus value. This is simply because the value of C' can be greater than the value of C. To see how the value of C' can be greater than the value of C, we expand the formula further, in a second step, by making explicit the process of production hidden within $M - C - C' - M'$ as follows: $M - C\{LP, MP\} \cdots (P) \cdots C' - M'$. Here (P), the new element in the formula, refers to the process of production, with the letter P referring to the actual production of commodities and the parentheses highlighting the fact that the process of circulation is interrupted during the production process.

---

the capitalist and non-capitalist system as part of a larger social formation, then no surplus value can be generated by unequal exchange.

To go back to the example of the capitalist bread maker, M will represent the initial sum of money with which the whole process is started, C will represent the inputs purchased and the labour hired, C' will represent the bread and M' will represent the revenue earned by the capitalist upon sale of the bread. Thus, we can see how C and C' are different commodity bundles, and also understand that, under normal circumstances, M' will be larger than M. Otherwise, there will be no reason for the capitalist to keep producing and selling bread.

The expanded general formula of capital, $M - C\{LP, MP\} \cdots (P) \cdots C' - M'$, also referred to as the 'circuit of capital', represents the operation of a typical unit of industrial capital (organized as a capitalist firm), or equally well, the aggregate of industrial capital (the whole capitalist economy involved in commodity production).[28] Our main aim is to explain how the value of C' can be greater than the value of C. But what does C and C' represent? C represents the initial bundle of commodities that the capitalist firm purchases, which is comprised of labour-power, LP, and means of production, MP, and C' represents the finished commodities that the same firm sells. To see how the value of C' can be greater than the value of C, we need to trace the flow of value through the circuit of capital with a focus on the process of production of the commodity.

The process of production of the commodity can be looked at from two different perspectives that mirror the two aspects of the commodity as a use-value and as value. Looking at the process of production from the perspective of the production of use-value leads us to the study of what Marx calls the 'labour process', and looking at the process of production from the perspective of the creation of value, and surplus value, leads us to investigate what Marx calls the 'valorization process'.

Labour Process
While our main interest is in the valorization process – so far as we are trying to discover the sources of surplus value – let us nonetheless briefly look at the *labour process*.

---

[28]The term 'industrial capital' should be understood broadly as referring to capital that is involved in the production of commodities, which can be goods or services. It does not refer to industrial production only. Marx uses this term to distinguish capital involved in production from 'merchant capital', which is involved in the purchase and sale of commodities and 'usurious capital', which is involved in lending and borrowing of money. Both these forms of 'capital' predate 'industrial capital' and are characterized by the fact that they appropriate value through unequal exchange but do not organize the production of commodities and the concomitant generation of surplus value.

> Labour is ... a process by which man, through his actions, mediates, regulates and controls the metabolism between himself and nature. (Marx, 1992, p. 283)

This definition makes clear that the labour process consists of three elements: (*a*) purposeful human activity, (*b*) object of labour and (*c*) instrument of labour. While the second and third elements are together called the 'means of production', the first element is called 'productive labour'. In the labour process, human beings use the instrument of labour to work on the object of labour to fashion a product according to some preconceived plan – the plan reflecting the purpose of the whole activity.

> The product of the process is a use-value, a piece of natural material adapted to human needs by means of a change in its form. Labour has become bound up in its object: labour has been objectified, the object has been worked on. (Marx, 1992, p. 287)

Every process of production can be ultimately traced back to nature. Either the object of labour and/or the instrument of labour is taken by human beings from nature. Of course, as societies become more complex, the link with nature is lost sight of because the immediate objects and/or instruments of labour themselves arise as results of previous labour processes. But the link to nature can always, in principle, be worked out, and hence, Marx views the labour process as a process of metabolism between human beings and nature.

Without the metabolism with nature represented by the labour process, a society of human beings cannot survive materially. Hence, the labour process is universal and common to all forms of society – hunter-gatherer societies, slave societies, feudal societies, capitalist societies and post-capitalist societies must all organize the metabolism with nature. But what is interesting from a historical materialist perspective is that in every form of society, the universal labour process gets additional features coming from that specific form of social and political organization. Under capitalism, the labour process attains the following additional features that stamp it as a specifically capitalist labour process: (*a*) the capitalist controls the labour process and the worker must work according to the dictates of the former (or her representative) and (*b*) the product of the labour process no longer belongs to the worker (the direct producer) who creates it; it belongs to the capitalist as her private property. Since the capitalist controls the labour process and owns its product, we must ask: What is the aim of the capitalist?

The capitalist has two specific aims. First, she wants the labour process to produce a use-value which also has exchange value. In fact, she is much less concerned about the former than the latter. Second, not only does she want to produce a use-value that has exchange value, that is, not only does she wish to produce a commodity, she also wants the commodity to have more value than the 'sum of values of the commodities used to produce it'. If the end result has more value than the value of the inputs used up, then there will be surplus value. Thus, the aim of the capitalist is to produce a use-value which has exchange value and generates surplus value. To see how the capitalist can fulfil her aim, we need to turn to a study of the process of production as a *valorization process*.

Valorization Process

The capitalist starts with a sum of money, M, enters the marketplace to purchase the commodity bundle, C. If we peer closely into the commodity bundle, we see that the capitalist has purchased two very different types of commodities. The first, which we will denote as MP, is the means of production – the raw materials, the machinery, the power, the fuel, in brief, all the non-labour inputs to production – and the second, which we will denote as LP, is labour-power (the commodity that will provide the labour input into production). The value of C is equal to sum of the value of the MP and LP. When we turn to the bundle of finished commodities, C', we see that its value can come from two sources: the value transferred by MP used up during production, and the value added by the expenditure of labour. Since MP can at most transfer its own value to the finished product, we reach the important conclusion that the only source of increment in value, that is, surplus value, can be the commodity LP.

What is LP? LP refers to the commodity 'labour-power' or labour-capacity. It is the human ability to do useful work. What is sold by workers in the marketplace, and bought by the capitalist, is this capacity to do useful work. Just like any other commodity, its owner, the capitalist can use it for whatever purpose she chooses. The important point is that when this commodity is used by the capitalist, it means that workers work according to the plan of the capitalist; when labour-power is used, workers exercise their ability to do useful work. Hence, the result of using labour-power is labour, the actual expenditure of human energy in carrying out some specific tasks, in this case dictated by the capitalist or her representative. We know from the previous sections that labour used in the production of commodities creates value. Hence, the usefulness of the commodity labour-power to the capitalist is that it is the source of value, the value added to the objects of labour. This immediately points to the secret of the origin of surplus value.

The capitalist purchases labour-power at its value – this is important to emphasize because in all transactions, value is preserved, there is equal exchange. When labour-power is put to use in the process of production, that is, when workers work on the objects of labour (using instruments of labour), value is added by their labour. This immediately tells us that the only way that surplus value can be generated is if the *value added by the use of labour-power* is greater than the *value of labour-power*. But, what does it mean to say that the value added by the use of labour-power in production is greater than the value of labour-power? To answer this question, we need to think carefully about this unique commodity, labour-power, and understand how its value is determined.

3.3.3   Labour-Power as a Commodity

How Is Labour-Power Reproduced?

Labour-power, the commodity that is sold by workers to the capitalists, is the ability or capacity to do useful work. This capacity exists in the body of workers. As an individual worker traverses her life from infancy to adulthood, she develops her physical and mental capacities, her labour-power. As an adult worker, the capacity is developed further or is reproduced at a given level, on a regular basis, until the worker becomes old and leaves the workforce, or, being mortal, dies. At retirement or death, she leaves the labour force, either by choice or because her labour-power has declined to a point where it is no longer useful to the capitalist system, or because the worker is no longer alive. For the capitalist system to continue to operate, new workers must replace those that have exited the labour market, that is, the class of workers must be continuously available to capital. To think about the reproduction of labour-power, therefore, it will be useful to use two different perspectives, the perspective of the individual worker and the perspective of the whole working class.

The individual worker's labour-power develops through the years of her life. Part of her abilities to do useful work is developed within the family, as the worker grows up learning language skills, basic skills of numeracy and other social skills necessary to function as part of groups or to carry out tasks on one's own. These skills are further developed when the worker participates in the schooling system, formal or informal, in which more systematic training is imparted about basic science, history, geography, mathematics, and so on. The final site where labour-power is further developed is often the work place – this refers to various forms of on-the-job training or other types of training provided by the capitalist firm where the worker works. Therefore, at any point of this process of the development (or production) of labour-power, the worker would have a stock of capacities (to do useful work). This is what we are referring to as labour-power.

When labour-power is used, we get labour. When the worker uses the accumulated stock of her ability to do useful work in the production process, it generates a flow of labour. The flow of labour reduces the stock of labour-power, and hence it needs to be replenished on a regular, daily basis. Hence, when the worker, upon the completion of the working day, returns home, she has to regenerate her abilities so that she can return to work the next day with those capacities in place. Within the working-class household, the family members cook and clean and provide love and emotional support, all of which, through a complex human process regenerates the worker's labour-power. Hence, within the household (of whatever form), not only is the initial stage of production of labour-power accomplished but its daily regeneration is also carried out. Moreover, this *daily regeneration* is carried out until the worker retires from the work force. After retirement, and all through old age, the worker is taken care of primarily within the household.

The process of capitalist production is a continuous process. It does not brook interruption – unless forced on it by economic or political crises. Hence, once the worker leaves the workforce, either because of death or retirement (forced or voluntary), she has to be replaced – if capitalist production is to continue uninterrupted. Thus, from the perspective of the whole working class, the production and reproduction of labour-power also means the *generational replacement* of members of the working class (Vogel, 2013). The working class must have the capacity to reproduce biologically and ensure a steady stream of new entrants into the capitalist workforce that can replace the flow of workers leaving the workforce.

If we bring together the above discussion about the production and reproduction of labour-power, we see an important point: some of the labour-power is produced within the domain of capitalist commodity production and some of the labour-power is produced outside the logic of capitalist commodity production. This suggests that we can split up these two parts explicitly: a non-market component of labur-power and a market component of labour-power.

The *non-market component of labour-power* refers to the fraction of the labour-power that is produced and reproduced outside the framework of commodity production, either within the working-class household or in non-capitalist institutions, for example, state or non-profit institutions. Within working-class households, we see the generational replacement of the working class through biological reproduction, caring of the infant worker, imparting basic language and numeracy skills, the daily regeneration of the stock of depleted labour-power, and caring for the sick and old worker. If the worker has received formal education in state or non-profit institutions, then another fraction of her ability to do useful work is produced in these institutions that fall outside the logic of commodity production.

Within the non-market component of labour-power, we can make a further distinction between two sub-parts. One part of the non-market component of labour-power is 'paid for' by the logic of capitalist commodity production and another part is 'unpaid'. The paid part refers to the non-market component of labour-power that is produced and reproduced in state and non-profit institutions. This sub-part can be designated as 'paid' because state and non-profit institutions are financed by tax and non-tax revenues, which come out of wage and profit incomes generated in capitalist commodity production. On the other hand, we can also identify an unpaid part of the non-market component of labour-power. This refers to the part of labour-power that is produced within the working-class household. This labour is unpaid and is largely undertaken by women. Capitalist commodity production does not have any identifiable income stream for this category of labour. That is why, following Marxist–feminist scholarship, I call this part 'unpaid'.

The *market component of labour-power* refers to the fraction of the labour-power that is produced and reproduced within the capitalist commodity-production system itself. This refers to the part of labour-power produced within the system of private schooling, private colleges, private diploma institutions and would also include the training provided to the workers in the workplace. This component must also include the commodities that are purchased for the reproduction and maintenance of the working-class family and would include, food, clothing, housing, durables, medical care, transportation, entertainment and other services purchased from the market.

The important conceptual point in distinguishing these two components of the production and reproduction of labour-power is to think carefully about the different sites where labour-power is produced and also to clearly demarcate the part that is not 'paid for' according to the accounting system of capitalist commodity production from the part that is. To emphasize this once again, note that, for instance, training provided by private schools, colleges, diploma institutions have to be purchased by the workers. On-the-job training is paid for either by deductions from workers' wages or from the profit income of the capitalist firm. Commodities purchased by the working-class household is paid from their wage income. In all these cases, it is accounted for, but the part of labour-power that is produced and reproduced outside the logic of capitalist commodity production is not accounted for in that way.

Which Labour to Count in Valuation?

The value of labour-power is conventionally defined as the socially necessary labour-time needed to produce, and reproduce, the commodity labour-power, that is, the value of labour-power is the (labour-time) cost of producing this commodity. While this definition captures the fact that labour-power is a commodity in capitalist societies, it misses the uniqueness of that commodity. Unlike all other commodities, labour-power is not produced by any capitalist firm. It is produced and reproduced through a complex social process that reproduces the working class. Since labour-power is the human ability to do useful work, its process of production straddles the domains of production for exchange and production for use, as we have seen earlier. This is the unique feature of this key commodity, labour-power. The fact that the production of labour-power straddles the domains of commodity and non-commodity production raises a difficult question about its valuation. How can we define the socially necessary labour-time needed to produce labour-power when some of the labour involved in its production falls outside the domain of commodity production? Trying to answer this question forces us to face a dilemma.

On the one hand, it is abundantly clear, as emphasized in the previous section, that the production of labour-power involves significant amounts of concrete labour that falls outside the domain of commodity production. If we leave out this labour when we consider the socially necessary labour to produce labour-power, we are leaving out an important part of society's labour that is necessary to produce and reproduce the human ability to do useful work. On the other hand, theoretical consistency demands that we limit ourselves to the labour involved in commodity production, that is, abstract labour, to value labour-power just like we do for any other commodity. Since the value of a commodity is the socially necessary *abstract* labour required to produce it, we cannot count the concrete labour involved in the production of labour-power that falls outside the domain of commodity production.

Marxist–feminist scholarship is divided on this issue. One strand argues that we need to include the concrete labour carried out in working-class households in our definition of the socially necessary labour that produces labour-power. If we accept this argument, then we face a second task. How should household labour be valued? Since this labour does not participate in the process of commodity production and exchange, like labour that produces commodities, researchers have typically used wages earned by similarly located domestic workers to impute value to domestic, household labour. An alternative strand argues that we should only count that labour as socially necessary for the production of labour-power that is mediated through the process of commodity exchange. In this book, I will adopt the second approach while at the same time recognizing and emphasizing that production of labour-power involves a larger magnitude of labour than is captured by nonhousehold labour.

The first reason why I choose to leave out household labour from a definition of the value of labour-power is that I want to keep intact the distinction between concrete and abstract labour. This conceptual distinction is important for the labour theory of value, and I would like to use it consistently for all commodities, including labour-power. The attempt to impute value to household labour by using the wages earned by domestic workers amounts to erasing the conceptual distinction between concrete and abstract labour. There is the additional problem that much of market-organized domestic work does not produce surplus value because this labour is exchanged for revenue and not for capital. When a family hires a domestic worker to do, for instance, cleaning and cooking, the money that is used to purchase the labour-power of the domestic worker is not participating in any circuit of capital. This is because the household that hires the domestic worker from the labour market is not advancing money to make more money. It is just purchasing a commodity for its own use. This additional factor complicates attempts to impute value to household labour using the wage income of domestic workers.

The second reason for leaving out household labour from a definition of the value of labour-power can be made clear by recalling the long-period method of analysis (see section 3.2.9). The key insight of this method of analysis is that concrete labour acquires the characteristic of abstract labour only when it is regulated, in the long run, by the process of exchange. The quality of abstract, value-creating capacity of labour requires an underlying process whereby the possesors of that labour-power move between alternative employments to balance advantages and disadvantages of labour. Looked at from this perspective, it is not at all clear that the *social allocation* of household labour responds to market pressures. While it is true that the allocation of household labour to different tasks within a family might respond to cost-benefit calculation broadly conceived, it is difficult to maintain that the allocation of domestic labour across families would respond to the differences in relative advantages of one type of labour to another. In view of both these reasons, I will exclude household labour from the definition of the value of labour-power.

Two Definitions of the Value of Labour-Power

There are two different ways to implement the above intuition about the value of labour-power. The first, conventional way, following Marx (1992, p. 274), is to define the value of labour-power as the value of the commodities consumed by the average worker, that is, the value of the real wage bundle. The second, unconventional way, following Foley (1982a), is to define the value of labour-power as the ratio of the money wage rate and the MEV.[29] I will explain the unconventional definition first, then come to the conventional definition and finally compare the two.

To understand the logic of the unconventional definition of the value of labour-power, let us think about the typical transaction in the labour market. The worker sells each unit of labour-power, say each hour, in the market, for a price known as the wage rate. Therefore, the wage rate is the amount of money needed to purchase one unit of labour-power. If we divide the wage rate by the MEV, we get the social labour-time equivalent of each hour of

---

[29]For a definition of the MEV, see section 3.2.4.

labour-power. For instance, if the working day is 8 hours long and the daily wage is \$40, the wage rate is \$5 per hour of labour-power. If the MEV is \$10 per hour of social labour, then the value of labour-power is $1/2$ hour of social labour per hour of labour-power, that is, for each hour of labour-power sold (and therefore one unit of labour performed), workers get back $1/2$ hour of social labour in return, in the form of the hourly wage rate.[30] Recall that the MEV is the monetary expression of each hour of social labour-time involved in commodity production. Thus, the ratio of the money wage rate and the MEV provides an estimate of the fraction of the total social labour-time of society (involved in commodity production) that the working class has a claim over – through their wage income.

The conventional way to define the value of labour-power is through the value of the 'means of subsistence' that is consumed by the average worker.

> ... the value of labour-power is the value of the means of subsistence necessary for the maintenance of its owner. (Marx, 1992, p. 274)

The logic of this approach is also straightforward. Labour-power is the ability to do useful work. Since the ability to work inheres in the body of the worker, the production of labour-power is equivalent to the reproduction of the worker. The reproduction of the worker requires a bundle of commodities: food, clothing, housing, health care, entertainment, and so on. This is purchased by the worker with the nominal wage – 'the equivalent of labour-power expressed in money' – that she earns by selling her labour-power. Hence, in this traditional approach, the value of one unit, say one hour, of labour-power is the value of the commodity bundle consumed by the average worker per hour of labour-power sold. Of course, what is actually consumed is understood as that which is *necessary* to maintain the worker. But, what is 'necessary'?

Marx points out three important dimensions of the determination of the 'necessary' means of subsistence (Marx, 1992, pp. 274–76). First, that which is necessary is determined historically, politically and morally, rather than biologically. The necessary means of subsistence is not to be understood as a biological minimum but instead should be understood as being determined

---

[30] Here we use the implicit assumption that each hour of labour-power sold by an average worker is converted, on average, into one hour of labour. The fact that the extraction of labour from labour-power is not trivial and requires a whole technology of supervision and surveillance is quite true. We ignore these issues at this point for ease of exposition.

by the 'level of civilization attained by a country'. The value of labour-power will, therefore, vary across countries according to their level of economic and social development. There are unmistakable moral and political elements in the determination of the value of labour-power. Second, what is deemed necessary must be adequate to maintain not only the individual worker at any point in time but also workers as a class and over time, that is, the necessary means of subsistence must ensure the generational continuity of the working class. This means that the necessary means of subsistence must maintain and reproduce the whole family of the worker. Third, the necessary means of subsistence must include the cost of education, training and development of skills adequate for the given stage of capitalism.

> In order to modify the general nature of the human organism in such a way that it acquires skill and dexterity in a given branch of industry, and becomes labour-power of a developed and specific kind, a special education or training is needed, and this in turn costs an equivalent in commodities of a greater or lesser amount. The costs of education vary according to the degree of complexity of the labour-power required. (Marx, 1992, pp. 275–76)

Let us now compare the two definitions. On the one hand, the conventional definition focuses our attention on a bundle of commodities because the value of labour-power is defined as the value of the bundle that is consumed by the average worker. It is additionally assumed that, on average, the amount of commodities that is to be considered 'necessary' must be adequate to reproduce labour-power of the individual worker, of the working class family and of the whole working class over time. On the other hand, the unconventional definition focuses our attention on the *wage share* in national income. To see this, note that the unconventional definition of the value of labour-power is the ratio of the money wage rate and the MEV. If we multiply both the numerator and the denominator with the total productive labour (measured in hours of labour-time), then the ratio will remain unchanged. Moreover, now the numerator is the total wage bill and the denominator is the total money value added, that is, the national income. Hence, the value of labour-power, according to the unconventional definition, is always equal to the share of wages in national income.[31]

---

[31]If we denote the money wage rate as w, the value of labour-power as vlp and the MEV as m, then

If we conceive of the money wage rate as being determined by class struggle, then the conventional definition implies that workers are able to struggle for and obtain a money wage rate that, given the existing price level, converts into a bundle of commodities, that is, a real wage rate, that covers their necessary consumption. The unconventional definition, on the other hand, suggests that workers are able to struggle for and obtain a money wage rate that, given the existing level of labour productivity, converts into a specific share of the national income. A further step is then needed, in the unconventional approach, to convert the share of national income into the basket of commodities that is adequate to cover the necessary consumption of the working class.

The first, conventional definition is straightforward and direct in that it asks us to think about the material standard of living as a determinant of the value of labour-power. The second, unconventional definition, while not so direct does have the advantage that it asks us to consider labour productivity, as well as the real wage bundle, as a determinant of the value of labour-power.[32] Perhaps, the unconventional definition is better able to capture Marx's intuition that the value of labour-power is determined historically, politically and culturally, by explicitly allowing for the role of labour productivity. But then, it also has the disadvantage that the same value of labour-power in two different countries can mean very different material standards of living of the working class if the labour productivity is very different. For instance, the same wage share in the US and in Bangladesh will mean very different levels of real consumption. Hence, the link between the value of labour-power and the material standard of living of the working class is much more tenuous in the unconventional definition.

There is an additional point to consider regarding the comparison of the two definitions. The two definitions are identical when prices are proportional to values of commodities, which is precisely what holds at the level of abstraction at which Volume I and II of *Capital* operate, and workers spend all their income. But when prices deviate from values, which is what holds when we move to the context of the discussions in Volume III of *Capital*, then the two definitions no longer coincide. Why? The reason is

---

we have $vlp = w/m = wL/mL = W/Y$, where W and Y are the total wage income and the total monetary value added, so that W/Y is the wage share.

[32]The wage share, W/Y, is also the ratio of the real wage rate and the real labour productivity: divide the numerator and denominator by the total labour input and then by the general price level.

that when prices deviate from values, the price of each commodity in the typical worker's commodity bundle no longer reflect its value (embodied labour-time). Thus, the social labour-time equivalent of the price of a commodity does not coincide with the embodied labour-time of the commodity. Hence, the value (embodied labour-time) of the whole bundle of commodities purchased by the wage income no longer coincides with the social labour-time equivalent of the wage income. Thus, if we use the traditional approach, then the value of labour-power and the social labour-time equivalent of the wage no longer coincide when we move to the context of Volume III of *Capital*. This creates some tricky issues of interpretation with relation to the so-called transformation problem (more details can be found in section 7.5). To avoid these problems, I will use the unconventional definition even as I recognize the intuitive appeal of the conventional one.

Surplus Value and Exploitation

Let us now return to the discussion of the origin of surplus value. We have seen earlier that surplus value can only arise at the aggregate level of the capitalist economy when the value added by each unit of labour-power is higher than the value of each unit of labour-power. Another way to capture this is to note that the condition that ensures the generation of surplus value is that the value of labour-power is less than unity. This simply follows from the fact that we define the value created by the use of one unit of labour-power, say one hour of labour-power, as unity. Yet another way of seeing this is to note that the value of labour-power is the ratio of: (*a*) the social labour-time equivalent of the wage rate (the numerator) and (*b*) value created by the use of one hour of social labour (the denominator). The difference between the denominator and the numerator of this ratio is precisely surplus value. Thus, the only way that surplus value can be generated is if the ratio representing the value of labour-power is less than 1, in which case the value added by one hour of social labour will be greater than what the worker gets back for each hour of labour-power sold (as the social labour-time equivalent of the wage rate). Since the value represented by the wage income is lower than the value added to the product by the use of labour-power, this leads to an important conclusion: surplus value arises from the exploitation of the working class.

The existence of surplus value, the one and only source of income of the capitalist class (and its various factions), can also be illustrated through a

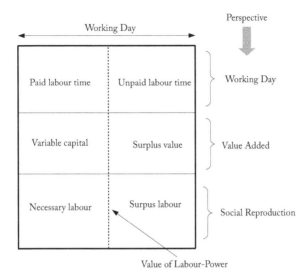

Figure 3.2 Visual representation of Marx's metaphor of the working day that is divided
between necessary and surplus labour
Source: Adapted from Foley (1986b).

metaphor that Marx used in Volume I of *Capital* (see Figure 3.2 for an
illustration). Here, the total labour-time of productive workers in a capitalist
society is viewed as one working day. Marx notes that we can divide up the
working day into two parts using the value of labour-power. From the
perspective of the working day, the first part is the 'paid labour time' and the
second part the 'unpaid labour time'; from the perspective of the value added
in production, the first part represents variable capital (wages) and the second
part represents surplus value (profits broadly construed); from the perspective
of social reproduction, the first part represents 'necessary labour' and the
second part represents 'surplus labour'.

The first part represents the portion of the working day that the working
class gets back in the form of the money wage. If commodities exchange at
their values, which is the setting of the analysis in Volume I of *Capital*, then
this is also equal to the time that the working class needs to produce the
commodities it will consume with its wage income. Hence, we can call this
portion of the working day as the 'paid labour time' and the labour
corresponding to this time period as the 'necessary labour'. It is necessary in
the sense that this is the amount of social labour that is needed to produce

the means of subsistence necessary to fulfill the needs of the working class at any given point in time – which, as we have seen, is determined socially and not biologically.

The other part represents the portion of the working day during which the working class works not for itself, but for the capitalist class. During this part of the working day, the working class works to create the primary source of the income stream of the capitalist class: surplus value. Hence, we can call this portion of the working day the 'unpaid labour time' and the labour corresponding to this time period, the 'surplus labour'.

It is a key insight of Marx that the division of the working day into paid and unpaid labour time, or of total labour into necessary and surplus labour is concealed by the voluntary transaction between the worker and the capitalist on the labour market, what Marx calls the wage-form. It is one of the primary goals of his analysis, of his critique of the received wisdom of classical political economy, to bring this division to light.

> The wage-form thus extinguishes every trace of the division of the working day into necessary labour and surplus labour, into paid labour and unpaid labour. All labour appears as paid labour. Under the *corvee* system it is different. There the labour of the serf for himself, and his compulsory labour for the lord of the land, are demarcated very clearly both in space and time. In slave labour, even the part of the working day in which the slave is only replacing the value of his means of subsistence, in which he therefore actually works for himself alone, appears as labour for his master. All his labour appears as unpaid labour. In wage-labour, on the contrary, even surplus labour, or unpaid labour, appears as paid. In the one case, the property-relation conceals the slave's labour for himself; in the other case the money-relation conceals the uncompensated labour of the wage-labourer. (Marx, 1992, p. 680)

The existence of surplus labour makes it abundantly clear that capitalism rests on the exploitation of the working class, on what Marx refers to as the 'tribute annually extracted from the working class by the capitalist class', and thereby makes capitalism similar to other class-based societies like feudalism, which rested on the exploitation of serfs, and slave society, which rested on the exploitation of slaves.

A question arises immediately. What ensures that the value of labour-power is always less than 1? What ensures the continued existence of surplus labour? We will return to this question soon but a quick answer, anticipating some discussions further on, is the following: the existence of what Marx called the 'reserve army of labour' or 'relative surplus population' ensures the continued existence of surplus labour in capitalism.

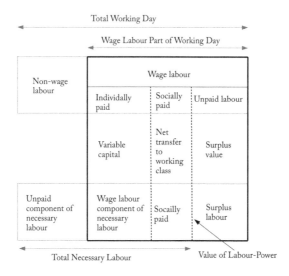

Figure 3.3 Visual representation of Marx's metaphor of the working day expanded to take explicit account of the non-market component of labour-power
Source: Adapted from Foley (1986b).

To complete our discussion of surplus value and exploitation, we need to return to the depiction of the working day in Figure 3.2 and note that it is incomplete. This is because it does not take account of the non-market component of labour-power. Our discussion above has explicitly noted the non-market component of labour-power, that is, the component of labour-power that is produced and reproduced with labour that is *not* regulated by the logic of commodity production. We can incorporate this important perspective and expand Marx's metaphor of the working day (for an illustration, see Figure 3.3). From Figure 3.3, we see clearly that the total working day is larger than the wage labour component of the working day. The latter had been the sole focus in Figure 3.2, but a complete analysis would require us to take account of the non-market component of labour-power as well.

In the expanded picture depicted in Figure 3.3, the total working day is the sum of the wage labour and non-wage labour parts of the working day. The wage labour component is paid for by capitalist firms, and some of the non-wage labour that is carried out in state and non-profit institutions are paid for by tax and non-tax revenues (which themselves come out of wage and profit incomes). Looked at from the perspective of social reproduction, we see that the labour of social reproduction, that is, total necessary labour, is larger than what is captured by the accounting system of capitalist commodity production.

While the 'unpaid' part of the non-market component of labour-power cannot be accounted for in the calculus of value and surplus value, the 'paid' part can be accounted if we are willing to expand the value of labour-power to what is commonly referred to as the social wage. In our expanded definition of the value of labour-power, we can consider the social wage to be the sum of the market wage and the part of social labour-time that is a representation of the 'paid' component of the non-market component of labour-power. The paid component would include things like paid leave, paid childcare services, public health care, public housing, public education, and so on, in short, the social cost of the part of reproduction of labour-power that is provided to the working-class households by the state financed by taxes on surplus value. In this broader definition, the value of labour-power would be measured by the ratio of the social wage rate and the monetary expression of value.

3.3.4   Some Terminology and Three Ratios

At this point, we can introduce some terminology that Marx uses. Returning to the typical industrial capitalist firm at the beginning of the circuit of capital, we can divide the sum of money that starts off the circuit into two parts. One part is used to purchase means of production. Marx refers to this as 'constant capital'. This value is transferred to the finished commodity as is, that is, without any increment; hence, the prefix 'constant' in constant capital.[33] The other part is used to purchase labour-power. Marx refers to

---

[33]To be more precise, constant capital refers to the value of the means of production *used up* during production. Marx often works with the simplifying assumption that all means of production are used up in one cycle of production. Under this assumption, constant capital is also the sum of money used to purchase the means of production. When some portion of the means of production, for instance machinery, lasts for many cycles of production, constant capital is less than the total sum of money

this as 'variable capital', also known as the wage bill, because the value represented by this sum of money increases when added to the value of the finished commodity; hence, the prefix 'variable' in variable capital. To see this, recall that the use of labour-power in the process of production adds value to the finished commodity. Hence, the value of the finished commodity is the sum of constant capital (value transferred from the means of production used up) and the 'value added' (by the use of labour-power). We know that the value added by the use of labour-power is greater than the value represented by the wage bill, the difference being the surplus value. Hence, the value added by the use of labour-power is the sum of variable capital and surplus value. We can summarize this with the following well-known formula: the value of a commodity is the sum of constant capital, variable capital and surplus value. We are now ready to define three important ratios.

The first is the 'rate of exploitation', which is defined as the ratio of surplus value generated (that is, additional value created by workers that is not returned to them in their wage) and variable capital (the wage bill). In terms of labour hours, the rate of exploitation is the ratio of surplus labour-time to necessary labour-time. Thus, it is the ratio of the value that is extracted from workers for each unit of the wage bill, or, to put it in another way, it is the amount of surplus labour that the working class has to perform per hour of necessary labour. Thus, it represents the degree of exploitation of the working class by the class of capitalists.

The second is the 'organic composition of capital' (OCC), which is defined as the ratio of constant capital and variable capital. It represents the ratio in which the capital outlay – the sum of money that is advanced in the circuit of capital – is divided between purchasing non-labour and labour inputs to production. Hence, it a value-theoretic representation of what contemporary economists call the capital intensity of production, that is, how much non-labour inputs are used by each unit of labour-power.

The third ratio is the 'rate of profit', which is, defined as the ratio of (*a*) surplus value and (*b*) the sum of constant and variable capital, that is total capital outlay. The rate of profit represents the income of the whole capitalist class as a proportion of its total capital outlay. From the perspective of the

---

used to purchase the means of production. For the purposes of exposition, I will assume that all means of production is used up in one cycle of production. Using more technical terminology, we can say that we are working with a pure circulating capital model, that is, we are ignoring fixed capital.

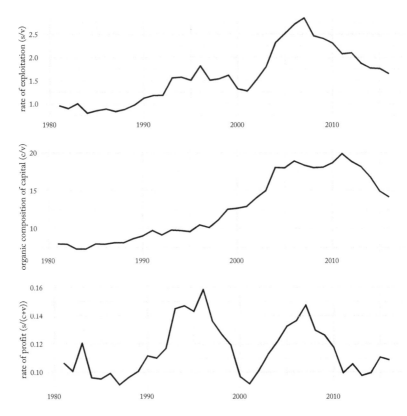

Figure 3.4 Time series plots of the rate of exploitation, the OCC and the rate of profit
for India's organized manufacturing sector, 1981–82 to 2016–17

Source: Created by author using data from Table 1, Annual Survey of Industries 2016–17,
Ministry of Statistics and Program Implementation, Government of India.

capitalist class, there is no difference between the two components of capital
outlay, constant capital and variable capital, as far as the return on capital
outlay (investment) goes. The capitalist is only concerned about the return on
the total investment, the sum of constant and variable capital. This is the
structural reason for the inability of capitalists to recognize profit income as
the unpaid labour-time of workers or to accept the existence of exploitation
in capitalist economies. To highlight these aspects in the rate of profit, Marx
divides both the numerator and denominator in the expression for the rate of

profit with variable capital, to get a useful expression for the rate of profit: it is the ratio of (*a*) the rate of exploitation (numerator) and (*b*) one plus the OCC (denominator).[34] Written in this form, it is easy to see that the rate of profit derives from the rate of exploitation of the working class. This simple analytical device lays bare the real source of profit in capitalism: the unpaid labour of the working class.

3.3.5   Estimates for India's Organized Manufacturing Sector

In Figure 3.4, I illustrate the evolution of these three important ratios from the 1980s onward in India's organized manufacturing sector.[35] To measure the three ratios, I need data on surplus value, variable capital and constant capital. I measure variable capital as total compensation of workers (wages, salaries and employment contributions to social security) and constant capital as the sum of non-labour input costs and depreciation of fixed capital. I subtract total compensation from net value added to get an estimate of surplus value. All these quantities are measured in monetary units (lakh rupees), so that dividing them with the MEV would give us the magnitudes in terms of labour-time units. But our quantities of interest are ratios. Hence, we do not need to convert the variables into labour-time magnitudes, but can work with ratios of monetary magnitudes.

In the top panel of Figure 3.4, we see that the rate of exploitation in the early 1980s was around 1, that is, for every rupee used to purchase labour power, 1 rupee was extracted as surplus value. For the next 25 years, the rate of exploitation kept increasing, other than a small reversal in the late 1990s. It reached a peak value of more than 4 in 2007 and has been declining since. In the middle panel, we see that the OCC has increased continuously from the early 1980s to the mid-2000s; since then, it has been mostly flat, with some decline seen since 2011. Putting these two variables together gives us the rate of profit – seen in the bottom panel. We see two periods of increase and two periods of decline in the rate of profit. The first period of increasing

---

[34]If we use r, s, v and c to represent, respectively, the rate of profit, surplus value, variable capital and constant capital, then $r = s/(c + v) = (s/v)/(1 + c/v)$, where s/v is the rate of exploitation and c/v is OCC.

[35]Data on key variables come from the 2016–17 Annual Survey of Industries, published by the Ministry of Statistics and Programme Implementation, Government of India. Summary tables from the ASI of various years can be downloaded from the following website: `http://mospi.nic.in/asi-summary-results`.

profitability ran from the early 1980s to the mid-1990s; the profit rate fell sharply from the mid-1990s to the early 2000s, and then began an ascent for the next couple of years, before the rate of profit started to decline again from 2007 onwards. Visual inspection suggests that movements in the rate of profit are largely driven by movements in the rate of exploitation.

Further Readings

- Suggested reading: Chapters 4, 5, 6 of Volume I of *Capital* (Marx, 1992).

- Marx develops his argument about surplus value and capital in Chapters 4, 5 of Volume I (Marx, 1992), and clear expositions can be found in Sweezy (1942, Chapter IV), Eaton (1963, Chapter IV) and Foley (1986b, Chapter 3, pp. 31–33).

- Marx's argument about surplus value and the commodity labour-power can be found in Marx (1992, Chapters 6, 7, 9). A useful elaboration of Marx's ideas is available in Eaton (1963, Chapter IV). The unconventional definition of the value of labour-power was developed in Foley (1982b). For an insightful Marxist–feminist analysis of labour-power, from which I have benefitted, see Smith (1978), Vogel (2000) and Vogel (2013, Chapters 9, 10, 11).

- The existence of surplus value and its appropriation by the class of capitalists implies exploitation of the working class by the capitalist class. While this might seem obvious, establishing a rigorous definition of exploitation and working out its political and philosophical implication is not straightforward. A large literature has emerged around the analysis of exploitation. For a discussion, see Chapter 8 in this book.

- For discussion of constant and variable capital and the three ratios, see Marx (1992, Chapter 8), Sweezy (1942, Chapter IV) and Foley (1986b, Chapter 3, pp. 44–48). These or analogous ratios appear in Marxist profitability analyses. The classic reference is Weisskpof (1979). For a Marxist profitability analysis of the US economy and its relationship to the 2008 crisis, see Basu and Vasudevan (2013); for a Marxist analysis of profitability in India's organized manufacturing sector, see Basu and Das (2018).

3.4 Production under Capitalism

3.4.1 Absolute and Relative Surplus Value

Since surplus value is the ultimate source of income of capitalist class – the ruling class in capitalist societies – there is a structural pressure in capitalism to increase both the *mass* and *rate* of surplus value over time. The total mass of surplus value is the product of the rate of surplus value and the variable capital. The latter increases, if the value of labour-power is fixed, by the increase in the supply of labour-power to the capitalist production process. The supply of labour-power increases both because of demographic factors that impact the growth rate of population and fluctuations of the reserve army of labour. We will study the reserve army of labour in the next section (section 3.5.1). Here we want to focus on the other component, that is, the rate of surplus value.

How does the rate of surplus value increase over time? Capitalism has at its disposal two very different ways of increasing the rate of surplus value. If the necessary labour-time is fixed, the rate of surplus value can be increased by increasing the length of the working day. This is known as the production of 'absolute surplus value'. On the other hand, if the length of the working day is fixed, the rate of surplus value can be increased by reducing necessary labour-time. This is known as the production of 'relative surplus value'.

> I call the surplus-value which is produced by the lengthening of the working day, *absolute surplus-value*. In contrast to this, I call that surplus-value which arises from the curtailment of the necessary labour-time, and from the corresponding alteration in the respective lengths of the two components of the working day, *relative surplus-value*. (Marx, 1992, p. 432)

Figure 3.2 can help us distinguish between the production of absolute and relative surplus value. When the width of the box increases, holding the value of labour-power fixed, we have the production of absolute surplus value; when the value of labour-power falls, holding the width of the box fixed, we have the production of relative surplus value.

Under the assumption that labour-power is purchased by the capitalist class at its value, the interaction of three variables helps us clearly see the difference between absolute and relative surplus value: productivity of labour, intensity of labour and length of the working day (Marx, 1992, p. 646). When the length of the working day is increased holding the productivity and intensity of labour fixed, we have production of absolute surplus value; when the productivity of labour increases, holding the intensity of labour and the length of the working day fixed, we have production of relative surplus value. When the intensity of labour rises, holding the length of the working day fixed, we can have the production of either or both absolute and relative surplus value, though in realistic scenarios, an increase in the intensity of labour is likely to be associated with the production of only absolute surplus value.

To understand these cases, let us refer back to the simple model of production discussed in section 3.1.5. The one commodity (corn) model captured the dynamics of a simple commodity-producing system. But now we are studying a capitalist economy. Hence, we need to make explicit the key feature of capitalism: that labour-power is a commodity. Labour-power is bought on the labour market for a money wage and given prices, the money wage is converted into a real bundle of commodities. To keep the analysis simple, let us directly assume that the real wage bundle is given by d units of corn *per hour of labour*. Once we add this assumption to the model of section 3.1.5, we have a simple model of production of a capitalist economy. We can now use this model to investigate the generation of absolute and relative surplus value.

To facilitate this discussion, let us use the corn model to define the rate of exploitation, e. We know that the rate of exploitation is the ratio of surplus value and the value of labour-power. If λ denotes the value of a unit of corn, then the value of labour-power for each hour of labour is given by λd. The value added in an hour of labour is, by definition, 1. Hence, surplus value generated in each hour of labour is given by $1 - \lambda d$. This gives us the expression for the rate of exploitation as

$$e = \frac{1 - \lambda d}{\lambda d} = \frac{1}{\lambda d} - 1 \tag{3.5}$$

Length of Working Day
To see how lengthening of the working day can lead to the production of absolute surplus value, let us assume, as does Marx, that the productivity and intensity of labour, as also the real wage bundle is fixed. In terms of the corn model of capitalist production, this means that the non-labour and labour coefficients, a, l, and the real wage bundle, d, are fixed. This implies, from (3.1), that the value of a unit of corn remains unchanged. Hence, the value of labour-power per hour of labour, λd, remains unchanged (because the real

wage bundle is fixed at d units of corn). Lengthening of the working day means that workers work $1 + \delta$ hours now, with $\delta > 0$, for every hour that they worked earlier. Using the same reasoning that underlies (3.5), the rate of exploitation is now given by

$$e' = \frac{1 + \delta - \lambda d}{\lambda d}$$

which shows that $e' > e$, that is, the rate of exploitation rises. Since the value of labour-power has not changed, the increase in the rate of surplus value comes from an increase in the length of the working day, captured by $\delta > 0$. Clearly, this is a case of the production of *absolute surplus value*.

Productivity of Labour

Let us now investigate the situation when there is an increase in the productivity of labour, holding fixed the length of the working day, the intensity of labour and the real wage bundle per hour of labour. From section 3.1.5, we know that when the productivity of labour rises, the value of each unit of the commodity (corn) falls. Since the real wage bundle is fixed at d, the value of labour-power per hour of labour falls, that is, $\lambda' d < \lambda d$, where λ' is the unit value of corn after the increase in labour productivity. The value added by each hour of labour has not changed and remains constant at 1. Hence, using (3.5), we see that the fall in the value of labour-power leads to an increase in the rate of surplus value. Therefore, this is a case of the production of *relative surplus value*.

Intensity of Labour

What happens when the intensity of labour increases, holding the length of the working day and the value of labour-power fixed?[36] From section 3.1.5, we know that the result will depend on the relative impact of the increase in the intensity of labour on its value-creating capacity, μ_2, and its use-value handling capacity, μ_1. Suppose λ' denotes the value of each unit of corn after the increase in intensity of labour. Then, the rate of exploitation can be written as

$$e' = \frac{\mu_2 - \lambda' d}{\lambda' d} = \frac{\mu_2}{\lambda' d} - 1 \qquad (3.6)$$

---

[36] For a more detailed analysis of the intensification of labour on the rate and form of surplus value, see Basu, Haas and Moraitis (2021).

There are two differences in this expression from (3.5). First, the value of each unit of corn is now λ', instead of λ, and second, each hour of labour now adds μ_2 units of value, instead of 1, due to the increase in the intensity of labour.

Consider the case in which $\mu_1 = \mu_2$. This condition means that an increase in the intensity of labour leads to an equal increase in its value-creating capacity, μ_2, as in its capacity to convert physical quantities of inputs into outputs, μ_1. From (3.3), we see that if $\mu_1 = \mu_2$, then $\lambda' = \lambda$. Thus, the value of each unit of corn remains unchanged. Since the real wage bundle is fixed at d units of corn, the value of labour-power per hour of labour does not change. Moreover, value added per hour of labour has increased to μ_2 from 1, because $\mu_2 > 1$. This leads to the increase in the rate of exploitation, as can be seen from a comparison of (3.5) and (3.6). Since the value of labour-power has not changed, this is clearly a case of the production of *absolute surplus value*.

Now consider the case when $\mu_1 < \mu_2$. This condition means that an increase in the intensity of labour leads to a lower increase in its capacity to convert physical quantities of inputs into outputs (μ_1) than in its value-creating capacity (μ_2). From (3.3), we see if $\mu_1 < \mu_2$, then $\lambda' > \lambda$. Thus, the value of each unit of corn rises. Since the real wage bundle is fixed at d units of corn, this leads to an increase in the value of labour-power per hour of labour. What happens to value added? Since value added per hour of labour is μ_2, where $\mu_2 > 1$, the value added increases in comparison to the original situation when it was 1. What happens to the rate of exploitation? Using (3.5) and (3.6), we can see that $(1 + e') / (1 + e) = \mu_2 / (\lambda'/\lambda)$. Now, using (3.3), we see that this expression reduces to μ_1. Since $\mu_1 > 1$, we can conclude that $e' > e$, that is, the rate of exploitation increases. Is this production of absolute surplus value or relative surplus value? Recall that in this case, the value of labour-power has increased. That rules out the production of relative surplus value. We are left with the conclusion that here too we have a case of the production of *absolute surplus value*.

Finally, consider the case when $\mu_1 > \mu_2$. This condition means that an increase in the intensity of labour leads to a higher increase in its capacity to convert physical quantities of inputs into outputs, μ_1, than in its value-creating capacity, μ_2. From (3.3), we see that if $\mu_1 > \mu_2$, then $\lambda' < \lambda$. Hence, the value of corn falls. Since the real wage bundle is fixed at d units of corn, this leads to a fall in the value of labour-power per hour of labour. What happens to value added? Since value added per hour of labour is μ_2, where $\mu_2 > 1$, the value added increases from its original magnitude of 1. Hence, surplus value increases. Is this production of absolute or relative surplus value?

Let e and e' denote the rate of surplus value in the original and new situations, respectively. Then, a little algebra shows that

$$e' - e = \frac{1}{d} \left[\frac{1}{\lambda'} (\mu_2 - 1) + \left(\frac{1}{\lambda'} - \frac{1}{\lambda} \right) \right]$$

This shows that the change in the rate of surplus value comes from a combination of both absolute surplus value (the first term on the right-hand side) and relative surplus value (the second term on the right-hand side). The first term represents absolute surplus value because it captures the increase in the value-creating capacity of labour, that is, $\mu_2 > 1$. It is as if workers work μ_2 hours in place of every 1 hour, *keeping intensity fixed*. That is why the first term can be associated with the production of *absolute surplus value*. The second term represents relative surplus value because it comes from the fall in the value of a unit of corn, that is, $\lambda' < \lambda$. With a fall in the value of corn and the real wage bundle fixed at d units of corn, there is a fall in the value of labour-power per hour of labour. Hence, the second term indicates the production of *relative surplus value*.

In normal situations of work, intensification of labour can be expected to have an equal effect on its use-value handling capacity and its value-creating capacity ($\mu_1 = \mu_2$). If intensification of labour is pushed beyond normal levels and leads to exhaustion of workers, it is possible for the use-value handling capacity of labour to increase by a smaller magnitude than its value-creating capacity ($\mu_1 < \mu_2$). The opposite scenario seems unrealistic. It is difficult to see how intensification of labour, on its own, can ever increase the use-value handling capacity of labour by a larger magnitude than its value-creating capacity ($\mu_1 > \mu_2$). Thus, even though I have analysed this last case for the sake of completeness, it should be noted that on grounds of realism it is only the first two cases that are relevant.

Examples

During the early phase of capitalist development, when the productivity of labour is low, absolute surplus value is the main method by which the rate of surplus value is increased. With the productivity of labour low, because the techniques of production are still relatively less capital intensive, the capitalist class pushes to increase the length of the working day to absurd limits, even as the real wage – 'the means of subsistence placed at the disposal of the worker', that is, the necessary labour-time – remains fixed (due to the abundant supply of labour). As the reserves of labour gradually dry up and the working class gets organized, it fights back to limit the length of the working day to a 'normal' duration. The epic struggles of the working class in mid-nineteenth-century England that resulted in the Factory Act becomes intelligible once we look at them through the lens of absolute surplus value.

Once the struggle of the working class has forced the length of the working day to be reduced to and then fixed at a normal duration, it becomes a structural necessity of the capitalist system to increase the productivity of labour and the intensity of labour.[37] If the productivity of labour increases, a smaller fraction of total social labour-time would be enough to produce the bundle of commodities consumed by the average worker, that is, necessary labour-time would fall. This would free up a larger portion of total labour-time during which the working class would work for capital, that is, would perform surplus labour. Thus, once capitalism has developed beyond the stage when the length of the working day can still be increased, its technological progressivity comes to the fore. The structural need to increase surplus value by reducing necessary labour-time accounts for one of the most important and striking features of capitalism: the constant revolutionizing of the methods and organization of production. The structural need to increase the productivity of labour goes hand in hand with the effort to increase the intensity of labour. In fact, the induction of machinery in large-scale production, changes in methods of management and adoption of newer techniques of production often facilitate, at the same time, an increase in the productivity and intensity of labour. When the intensity of labour is increased, we have the production of absolute surplus value, as we have seen earlier. Hence, in advanced capitalism, we have both forms of surplus value in play, the production of relative and the production of absolute surplus

---

[37] Discussing machinery and large-scale industry, Marx notes: 'As soon as the gradual upsurge of working-class revolt compelled Parliament compulsorily to shorten the hours of labour, and begin by imposing a normal working day on factories properly so called, i.e. from the moment that it was made impossible once and for all to increase the production of surplus-value by prolonging the working-day, capital threw itself with all its might, and in full awareness of the situation, into the production of relative surplus-value, by speeding up the development of the machine system' (Marx, 1992, pp. 533–34). Marx's ideas on the effect of intensification of labour were not completely correct. In this passage, he seems to be suggesting that an intensification of labour leads to the production of relative surplus value. As we have seen earlier, that is not correct.

value. It is important to keep in mind that the production of absolute surplus value has not been surpassed in advanced capitalism.

Let us look at some contemporary examples of absolute and relative surplus value. In a typical worker's contract, implicit or explicit, the working day is assumed to include time for breaks from work – for eating, for using the bathroom, for relaxing, and so on. In recent years, there have been fierce struggles over the time allotted to workers for breaks. For instance, if the time for using bathrooms can be reduced, or if the duration of the lunch break can be shortened, the length of working time, for a fixed working day of say 8 hours, increases, leading to the production of absolute surplus value. An important example of intensification of labour is the much commented *speed-up* of work, that is, when reorganization of work leads workers to work at a faster pace, completing a given set of tasks in less time. The introduction of the assembly line in the early twentieth century was a major organizational innovation by the capitalist system that instituted speed-up in the production process. As we have seen earlier, this will lead to the production of absolute surplus value. Adoption of a labour-saving technique of production at the aggregate level can lead to an increase in the productivity of labour. In this case, the rate of surplus value increases because of an increase in the productivity of labour even as the working day (and possibly intensity of labour) remains unchanged. Hence, this would be a case of production of relative surplus value.

3.4.2 Evolution of Production

Capitalism's structural need to generate relative surplus value has led to an interesting pattern of historical evolution of the organization and form of production. The first change that capitalism brought about when it took over non-agriculutural production from the stage of *handicrafts* was to bring together a large number of workers under one roof. This phase of development of capitalist production, called *cooperation*, witnesses increases in the productivity of labour not due to changes in techniques of production but due to savings arising from bringing together many erstwhile producers under one roof.

The next stage in the development of capitalist production, called *manufacture*, witnesses a real leap in the productivity of labour due to specialization within the firm (something missing from the earlier phase of cooperation). The process of production is broken up into many parts – Adam Smith's division of labour – and workers are assigned to one or a few specific tasks. The extreme specialization leads to huge increases in the productivity of labour but at the enormous cost of deskilling of individual workers. From the perspective of capital, there is an unwanted development too: it increases the bargaining power of some of the workers associated with key steps of the whole production process.

The development of *machine production* and large-scale industry, the next stage in the development of capitalist production, solves the problem of bargaining power and control from the perspective of capital. Key tasks are now performed by machines, which not only gives another enormous boost to labour productivity by making huge mechanical power available to labour-power but also takes deskilling of workers to the extreme: workers are converted into mere appendages of machines, where tending machines becomes their primary responsibility. All steps become routine and with it the bargaining power of groups of workers located in key stages of the production process fades away. In several insightful chapters in Volume I (especially Chapters 10 to 15), Marx highlights the profound ambiguity of capitalist production: while the social productivity of labour increases rapidly through cooperation, manufacture and machine production, at the same time, it dehumanizes workers, and we might now add, despoils nature.

3.4.3 Formal and Real Subsumption

In an appendix to Volume I of *Capital*, Marx introduces the interesting concepts of the formal and real subsumption of labour under capital that are directly related to the concepts of absolute and relative surplus value.[38] As capitalism develops out of the womb of earlier modes of production, the production process changes along with changes in the relations of production. But the former change takes place in two steps.

In the first step, capitalism takes over the production process handed down by previous modes of production and incorporates it into the circuit of capital, that is, the labour process gets the additional feature of a valorization process as well. But during this phase, the details of the labour process, the actual mode

---

[38] This text was part of the 1864–65 manuscript, the majority of which went into the making of Volume III of *Capital*. It has been published under the title 'Results of the Immediate Process of Production'. Marx discusses the concepts briefly in Chapter 16 of Volume I also.

of labour, the techniques of production, and so on are left relatively unchanged. Thus, the relations of production are changed, that is, the capital-relation is established, but the actual labour process, from a technological point of view, is left untouched. Marx calls this the *formal subsumption of labour by capital*.

> The labour process becomes the instrument of the valorisation process, the process of the self-valorisation of capital – the manufacture of surplus value. The labour process is subsumed under capital (it is its *own* process) and the capitalist intervenes in the process as its director, manager. For him it also represents the direct exploitation of the labour of others. I call this the *formal subsumption of labour under capital*. (Marx, 1992, p. 1019)

In the second step, capitalism starts changing the details of the labour process too. The mode of labour and the technology and organization of production is changed according to the needs of capital. Marx calls this the *real subsumption of labour by capital*.

> ... the *real* subsumption of labour under capital, i.e. *capitalist production proper*, begins only when capital sums of a certain magnitude have directly taken over control of production, either because the merchant turns into an industrial capitalist, or because larger industrial capitalists have established themselves on the basis of the *formal subsumption*. (Marx, 1992, p. 1027)

It is important to keep in mind that both formal and real subsumption of labour are forms of the capital-relation. Hence, both generate surplus value through the exploitation of labour. But there is a key difference between the two. In the formal subsumption of labour by capital, surplus value is generated by a prolongation of the working day. This is because the labour process remains unchanged, that is, there is no technological change as regards the details of the production process. Hence, the only way capital can increase the rate of surplus value is as the production of absolute surplus value. On the other hand, in the real subsumption of labour under capital, the labour process is transformed – moving through the stages of cooperation, manufacture and machine production. There is continuous technological change, and the main form of increase of the rate of surplus value is as the production of relative surplus value.

133

If the production of absolute surplus value was the material expression of the formal subsumption of labour under capital, then the production of relative surplus value may be viewed as its real subsumption ... To these two forms of surplus-value there correspond two separate forms of the subsumption of labour under capital, or two distinct forms of capitalist production. And here too, one form always precedes the other, although the second form, the more highly developed one, can provide the foundations for the introduction of the first in new branches of industry. (Marx, 1992, p. 1025)

The interplay of formal and real subsumption, and the corresponding interplay of absolute and relative surplus value, is important to note. Once capitalism has conquered all branches of production and the methods of production have evolved into large-scale industrial production, absolute surplus value makes a comeback. Now capital increases the rate of surplus value using a combination of absolute and relative surplus value. All manner of increasing the length of the actual working day and increasing the intensity of labour are now intertwined with pure technological advance.

... we have seen how methods of producing relative surplus value are, at the same time, methods of producing absolute surplus value. Indeed, the unrestricted prolongation of the working day turned out to be a very characteristic product of large-scale industry. The specifically capitalist mode of production ceases in general to be a means of producing relative surplus value as soon as it has conquered an entire branch of production; this tendency is still more powerful when it has conquered all the important branches of production. (Marx, 1992, p. 646)

The pure technological progressivity, that is, each hour of labour producing a higher quantity of use-values, that we had noted above as one of the most striking features of capitalist production is muted to the extent that the weight of absolute surplus value increases in capital's strategies for increasing the rate of surplus value.

Further Readings
- Marx's analysis of the struggle over the length of the working day is contained in Marx (1992, Chapter 10), and his analysis of the evolution

of the organization of production are presented in Marx (1992, Chapters 12–15). An analytically useful summary can be found in Foley (1986b, Chapter 4, pp. 49–61).

- One of the key themes that emerge from Marx's discussion of the evolution of technology under capitalism is the sheer indifference of capitalism to the effect of technological change on both the worker and nature – the two original sources of wealth. Hence, the issues discussed in this section can be a useful entry point into analyses of the degradation of work and alienation of workers under capitalism. A good place to start engaging with the large literature on the evolution of the labour process and its effects on the worker is the classic account in Braverman (1998). The effect of capitalist relations on nature has been studied by a very large literature. For a balanced and informed account of the ecological crisis, that steers clear of both the triumphalism of market mechanisms and the pessimism of deep ecology, see Boyce (2002, especially Chapter 1).

- Does the recent development of information technology and its increasing use in the production process render the labour theory of value obsolete? A recent literature has emerged that engages with such questions. A good account of the issues involved in this debate can be found in Starosta (2012).

3.5 Accumulation of Capital

So far the focus of the analysis has been to explain how surplus value is produced by capital. Now we turn to the complementary movement, the production of capital by surplus value, which is also known as the accumulation of capital. Once the capitalist firm has sold the finished commodities, it gets back the value of those commodities in monetary form. Since the value of the finished commodities is the sum of constant capital, variable capital and surplus value, the firm now has, in monetary form, not only the original capital outlay (the sum of constant and variable capital) but also the surplus value.

The capitalist firm has at least two options regarding how it disposes of the surplus value. First, it can use it all for consumption expenditure of the capitalist class. If this is the case, there will be no investment of the surplus and production will be carried out in the next period at the same scale as before. This is referred to by Marx as *simple reproduction* of capital. Second, it can use a part of the surplus value for capitalist consumption and reinvest the rest into the next cycle of production. The part of surplus value that is reinvested into production is thereby converted into capital because it becomes part of the pool of money that is used to start a fresh cycle of production of surplus value. The reconversion of surplus value into capital can be called the monetary aspect of accumulation of capital. It takes the concrete form of purchase of additional means of production (this part of the reconverted surplus value becomes part of constant capital) and/or additional labour-power (this part of the reconverted surplus value becomes part of variable capital). If the reinvested surplus value is divided between constant and variable capital in the currently prevailing ratio, and the techniques and organization of production remain unchanged, then we have what Marx calls *expanded reproduction* of capital. But in many cases, the reconversion of surplus value into capital goes hand in hand with changes in the techniques and organization of production. This more general form of the expansion of the scale of production through reinvestment of surplus value is referred to by Marx as the accumulation of capital.

Accumulation of capital increases the scale of production and the size of the capital value because of the reinvestment of a part or whole of the surplus value. The increase in the size of capital takes two different forms, concentration and centralization of capital. An increase in the scale of production due to reinvestment of surplus value in the same capitalist firm is known as *concentration of capital*. When part or whole of the surplus value or even borrowed money is used to facilitate mergers of two or more existing capitalist firms, this is known as *centralization of capital*. With the development of the banking and financial sector, huge pools of funds can be mobilized for mergers and acquisitions. Hence, with the growth of finance, centralization has become the main channel for the rapid increase in the size of capitals.

Three important questions arise in relation to the process of capital accumulation. First, how does the capitalist system ensure that the finished commodities are sold at their value so that the entire surplus value is realized through sale and comes back to the firm in monetary form? Second, how does the capitalist system ensure that the additional means of production (that will be needed to support the increase in the scale of production) and additional means of consumption (that will be needed for the consumption needs of the additional labour-power purchased, and possibly also increases in capitalist consumption) will be available to support the accumulation of capital? Third, what will be the impact of the accumulation of capital on the value of labour-power, and how do changes in the value of labour-power react back on the accumulation of capital? The first and second questions relate, respectively, to the problems of realization of surplus value and the problem of the correct product mix, that is, use-value composition, of the total output. Marx deals with both issues in Volume II of *Capital*, and we will discuss them in the next chapter. The third problem is dealt with in Volume I, and to that we now turn.

Further Readings
- Marx's analysis of the accumulation of capital is present in Marx (1992, Chapters 23–25). Useful discussions of the key issues are available in Eaton (1963, Chapter V) and Foley (1986b, Chapter 5, pp. 62–64).

3.5.1 Reserve Army of Labour

The Theoretical Question
The value of a commodity produced under capitalist conditions is, as we have seen earlier, the sum of three components: constant capital (value of means of production used up in the production process), variable capital (value of labour-power) and surplus value (value appropriated by the capitalist firm that is in excess of the variable capital). Capitalist firms are much less interested in the specific commodity they produce and sell than in the surplus value they appropriate. The central dynamic of capitalist economies arises from the behaviour of capitalist firms as they try to generate, realize and reinvest surplus value.[39]

Surplus value comes from unpaid labour time of workers, as we have seen in the previous sections of this chapter. It is the difference between the value added by the use of labour-power and the value of labour-power. The former is what the worker adds to means of production in each hour of work; the latter is what the capitalist pays to purchase each hour of labour-power (the ability to do useful work). If the difference between the two narrows, surplus value falls. Without adequate magnitudes of surplus value, capitalism would be under threat, and this brings us to an interesting question.

---

[39]The discussion in this section draws on Basu (2021).

137

Reinvestment of surplus value is largely driven by the structural imperatives arising from the perpetual competitive struggle between capitalist firms. Without reinvesting surplus value and enlarging their capital values, capitalist firms risk falling behind their competitors in the race to generate and appropriate ever more surplus value. At the aggregate level, the reinvestment of surplus value generates new demand for means of production and labour-power.

Elements of the means of production are largely produced by capitalist firms. Hence, their aggregate investment decisions generate demand for the output of capitalists who specialize in the production of means of production. The mismatch of demand and supply of means of production are dealt with by the market mechanism, by fluctuations in the pace of production.

It is a wholly different story with labour-power. Labour-power is the ability to do useful work. This ability inheres in the body of the worker. Labour-power is not produced in any capitalist firms. Labour-power is produced and reproduced daily with the living worker. At the aggregate level, the total supply of labour-power comes from the generational replenishment of the working class. Thus, there is no market mechanism to deal with the mismatch of demand for and supply of labour-power.

If the demand for labour-power increases with reinvestment of surplus value, the price of labour-power might increase to a point where surplus value begins to fall. If this process continues for extended periods of time, the whole capitalist system might be under threat. After all, the central dynamic of capitalism will grind to a halt if the aggregate surplus value falls to zero. What mechanism – and this has to be a non-market mechanism – is available to the capitalist system to avert this possibility? What mechanism keeps the value of labour-power from rising too much? What ensures the stability of the value of labour-power that is necessary to keep generating adequate amounts of surplus value?

Ricardo's Answer

Borrowing from the writings of Thomas Malthus, the prominent classical economist David Ricardo offered one answer to the above question. For Ricardo, a theory of population offers an explanation of why the value of labour-power does not rise so far as to threaten the production of surplus value. When capital accumulation picks up and the demand for labour-power rises, the result is an increase in real wage rates. Rising incomes lead to increasing prosperity of the working class, which, in turn, increases the fertility rate. As the population rises, it gradually increases the supply of labour-power. This increase in supply eventually overtakes the rising demand for labour-power. The excess supply of labour-power then pulls down the real wage rate (Sweezy, 1942).

Marx never accepted the validity of this theory of population, and he certainly did not use it for answering the above question. With the benefit of hindsight, we can see that the Malthusian population theory is grossly inadequate in addressing the above question. Over long periods of time, increasing prosperity has been accompanied by falling, and not rising, fertility rates. This is exactly opposite of the Malthusian claim. Resting on empirically dubious claims, the Malthusian–Ricardian explanation just does not appear convincing.

Marx's Answer

In Volume I of *Capital*, Marx offered a powerful alternative answer to the above question by developing the concept of the reserve army of labour (Marx, 1992). Marx's answer to the above question was this: the key mechanism that keeps the value of labour-power within necessary bounds, that is, necessary for the generation of surplus value, is the fluctuation in the size of the *reserve army of labour*.

> The industrial reserve army, during the periods of stagnation and average prosperity, weighs down the active army of workers; during the periods of over-production and feverish activity, it puts a curb on their pretensions. The relative surplus population is therefore the background against which the law of the demand and supply of labor does its work. It confines the field of action of this law to the limits absolutely convenient to capital's drive to exploit and dominate the workers. (Marx, 1992, p. 792)

Before we understand the reasons for the fluctuation in the size of the reserve army of labour, let us look carefully at its construction and its components. Figure 3.5 presents a schematic representation of the labour market of a typical capitalist economy. The representation of the labour market involves both stocks and flows.

The total labour force, a stock, is divided into two parts: the active army of labour (workers employed in capitalist enterprises) and the reserve army of

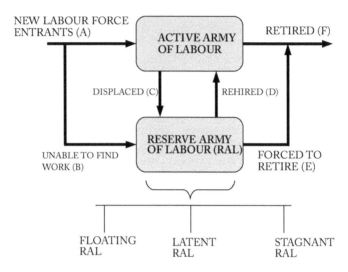

Figure 3.5 The labour market in a typical capitalist economy
Source: Basu (2013).

labour (workers not employed in capitalist enterprises but potentially available for employment). In Figure 3.5, the two rectangular boxes represent these two components of the labour force.

The two stock quantities, that is, the active and reserve armies of labour, are linked to the larger economy and to each other through various types of flows. Starting at the left end of Figure 3.5, we see the flow of new workers entering the labour force. This flow gets divided into two parts. The first part, labelled (A), represents the workers who find employment – of the new entrants to the labour force, they join the active army of labour. The second part, labelled (B), represents new workers who cannot find a job and are forced to join the reserve army of labour – at the very beginning of their working life.

The active and reserve armies of labour are connected to each other through two flows: some currently employed workers lose their jobs and move from the active to the the reserve army – this is represented by flow (C); there is also movement in the other direction, when some workers who are currently not employed find employment in a capitalist enterprise – this is represented by the flow (D). At the right end is the flow of labour-power out of the labour market. Some of the workers who are currently in the reserve army fall out of the labour force – represented by flow (E); and some workers who are currently employed retire and leave the labour force – represented by the flow (F).

Fluctuations in the Reserve Army of Labour

Fluctuations in the size of the reserve army of labour come from the flows represented in Figure 3.5 as (C) and (D). What are the causes of these flows? The flow labelled (C) represents workers losing their employment. This flow increases the size of the reserve army and is caused by three sets of factors.

The first, and most important, is labour saving technical change. When there is a sustained increase in the demand for labour-power, it leads to an increase in the price of labour-power. Since wage costs are an important and significant component of the total cost of production, capitalist firms have an incentive to reduce wage costs – in the context of rising prices of labour-power. The search for methods to reduce wage costs often leads to the search for and adoption of new techniques of production that reduce the use of labour-power relative to means of production. The new technique of production, thus, saves on labour – the costly input – and replaces it with the relatively less costly input – means of production. Such labour saving technical change leads to job loss for some currently employed workers. Hence, these workers move from the active to the reserve army of labour.

The second source of fluctuation is the regular cyclical movement of aggregate economic activity, what contemporary economists call business cycles. The cyclical fluctuations of aggregate activity are caused by fluctuations in various components of aggregate demand. Investment expenditure by capitalist firms can fluctuate due to movements in animal spirits; consumption expenditure by worker and capitalist households can fluctuate because of changes in consumer sentiments; government expenditure can fluctuate for fiscal policy reasons; and net exports can bounce around because of fluctuations in foreign economies. During the upswing phase of business cycles, jobs are created on a net basis. More workers move from the reserve to the active army than the other way round. During the downswing phase of business cycles, the opposite movement, that is, from the active to the reserve army, dominates.

The third source of fluctuation in the size of the reserve army of labour can be relocation of production across geographical regions. The relocation can be within or across national boundaries. In the location that loses economic activity, the flow from the active to the reserve army of labour is likely to be large; in locations that manage to attract new economic activity, the opposite flow is likely to be equally big. In either case, geographical relocation of production, which has become especially important since the last few decades of the twentieth century, will lead to a fluctuation in the size of the reserve army of labour.

Components of the Reserve Army of Labour
In Volume I of *Capital*, Marx distinguished between three components of the reserve army of labour (Marx, 1992, Chapter 25). The three components – floating, latent and stagnant – of the reserve army of labour are indicated at the bottom of Figure 3.5. Considering the three components separately allows us to think carefully about the short and long run forces governing the formation and reproduction of the reserve army of labour.

The floating reserve army of labour is the component that fluctuates most with the fluctuation of economic activity and capital accumulation. It is composed of workers who have lost jobs due to labour saving technical change, recessions or geographical relocation of production. When the pace of economic activity picks up, some, or most, of these workers will be rehired. Hence, they will move back into the active army of labour – once the recession is over. Thus, the floating reserve army of labour is the part whose formation is governed by short run economic forces.

The latent component of the reserve army of labour directs our attention to longer run forces responsible for its formation. It is the part of the reserve army of labour that is gradually formed, over many decades, with the evolution and expansion of capitalism. The two important sub-components of the latent reserve army of labour are household labour and labour involved in peasant farming and other forms of non-capitalist production.

Historically, the bulk of household labour, that is, work involved in raising children, caring for the elderly and sick, carrying out daily activities of household labour like cooking, washing and cleaning, have been done by women. Because of this unequal division of household labour between men and women, the latter have historically been largely confined within the household. This does not contradict the fact, highlighted by recent historical research, that women's labour was crucial during the Industrial Revolution (Burnette, 2008). While individual branches of production relied heavily on women's labour, there was an overall decline in the labour force participation of women in the 18th and 19th centuries in England (Horrell and Humphries, 1995, Table 1, last column). The declining labour force participation of women was driven largely by changes in demand arising from structural and institutional changes of an industrializing, capitalist economy.

Thus, it seems fair to assert that women's labour gradually became a potential source of the reserve army that was latent. Even though the capitalist system was not using it, it could draw on this labour as and when needed.

This movement of women's labour from the household and into the labour force was seen most forcefully in Europe and the United States in the decades after the end of the second world war. For instance, using data for the US from the Federal Reserve of St. Louis, we see that only 33 per cent of women were in the labour force in 1948. For the next five decades, the labour force participation rates of women increased secularly. In 2000, about 60 per cent of women were in the labour force. The pattern of steady increase in the labour force participation rates of women in the US has been halted since the early 2000s – perhaps indicating exhaustion of an important component of the latent reserve army of labour.

The second sub-component of the latent reserve army of labour consists of workers involved in non-capitalist production. The largest section of such workers have been involved in small-scale peasant farming and artisanal petty production. In western Europe, the process of 'primary accumulation of capital' led to their destitution and dispossession over a 300-year period (see section 3.6). Peasant producers losing access to land and petty non-agricultural producers ruined by competition from big business swelled the ranks of the working class that supported capitalist development. As the pace of capitalist production increased and industrialization proceeded, the second sub-component of the latent reserve army was drawn into the domain of capitalist production.

In much of what is today known as the developing world, the 'primary accumulation of capital' is incomplete. A large segment of the working population in these countries work in what the development economist W. A. Lewis called the 'traditional sector' (Lewis, 1954). Distinguished from the 'modern sector', which is characterized by capitalist relations of production and the use of reproducible capital, the 'traditional sector' is the domain of non-capitalist relations and labour intensive techniques of production – small-scale family farming in agriculture and petty non-agricultural commodity production. These workers form a large latent reserve army that is potentially available to capital, not only domestic capital in these countries but also global capital (Foster et al., 2011).

The third, and final, component of the reserve army is the stagnant component. This is composed of workers who live on the margins of society, who have fallen out of the labour force due to illness, loss of skills or psychological reasons. There is neither a stable short run nor a steady long run logic to its formation. The formation of the stagnant component of the reserve army seems to be related to the institutional setting of capitalism, to the existence, or its lack, of a strong social safety net and a social environment that can help workers come back to the labour force if they fall out of it.

The existence and reproduction of the reserve army of labour modulates movements of the value of labour-power in such a way that continued production of surplus value is not jeopardized. During periods of rapid capital accumulation, the demand for labour-power increases. As the reserve army is drawn down, there is upward pressure on real wages. When the reserve army is reduced substantially and comes close to being completely depleted, the upward movement of real wages start outpacing the growth of labour productivity. This can lead to a decline in the rate of surplus value. The rapid rise in the labour cost of production and the falling rates of surplus value might lead to declines in the rate of profit. When this happens, it prompts the capitalist class to start searching for ways to reduce labour costs. One way to do so is to increasingly mechanize the production process, that is, replace workers with machines. Mechanization reduces the demand for labour-power and increases its supply (by forcing unemployment on many currently employed workers) at the same time. The growth in the supply of labour-power relative to its demand starts replenishing the reserve army of labour. Once the reserve army has become large enough, it nullifies the upward movement of real wages, and eventually starts pulling it down relative to the growth of labour productivity (because a large number of unemployed workers now compete for the same job). The value of labour-power falls and the rate of surplus value starts rising again, providing a spur to capital accumulation and growth. The capitalist economy is now ready for another cycle of accumulation. Thus, this incessant fluctuation of the pace of capital accumulation and the size of the reserve army of labour is the 'normal' process of growth of capitalist economies.

We are now in a position to answer an important question that was raised earlier: what ensures that the value of labour-power is always less than one, or what is the same thing, what ensures that a positive amount of surplus value is continuously generated? It is the existence and reproduction of the reserve army of labour – through labour saving technical change and business cycle downturns – that ensure that wages move within a range that is necessary to generate positive amounts of surplus value. The implication of the continued existence of the reserve army of labour in capitalist economies is striking: these economies typically do not employ all of its potential labour force. A portion of the available labour force is almost always left unemployed, or is marked by different degrees of attachment to the labour force. Workers who are unemployed and underemployed not only bear the direct loss of forgone income but also a much larger non-monetary loss of subjective well-being. At the individual level the loss of subjective well-being increases with the duration of unemployment (Ochsen and Welsch, 2011). At the societal level, the indirect, non-monetary loss is several fold larger than the direct, monetary loss (Helliwell and Huang, 2014).

3.5.2 *Reserve Army of Labour in the US Economy*

Building on Basu (2013), now I present estimates of four measures of the reserve army of labour in the post-war US economy using data from the monthly survey conducted by the Bureau of Labour Statistics (BLS) of the U.S. Department of Labour called the Current Population Survey (CPS).[40] Initiated as the Work Projects Administration Project in 1940, the CPS has been conducted every month since then. The current sample size is about 60,000 households (which translates to about 110,000 individuals). Every month, a fourth of the sample is changed, that is, every household is surveyed for four consecutive months, followed by an eight-month period when it is not surveyed; the household is then surveyed again for four consecutive months before exiting the sample for good. This procedure reduces the burden on individual households while ensuring that 75 per cent of the sample remains same from month to month and 50 per cent of the sample remains constant from year to year. This allows researchers significant latitude in inferring time series patterns in the US labour market.

Data
The starting point for estimating the reserve army of labour is the civilian non-institutional population (CIV). CIV is an estimate of every person 16 years and above who is neither in an institution (prison or mental health institution) nor on active duty in the U.S. Armed Forces. Based on a detailed interview, the CPS assigns every person in CIV to either of three pools:

---

[40]For details, see http://www.bls.gov/cps/.

1. pool of employed workers (EMP): these are the persons who reported doing any wage or salary work (either full-time or part-time) at the time of the interview; or, they reported as having done self-employed work; or, reported that they had a job but were not at work currently due to vacation, illness, and so on; or, were doing unpaid family work;

2. pool of unemployed workers (UNEMP): these are the persons who reported as not having a job currently and who had actively looked for a job in the previous four weeks (with reference to the time of the interview), and are, therefore, currently available for work;

3. pool of those who are not in the labour force (NLF): these are the persons who fall neither into the category of employed workers nor can be counted as being unemployed.

The information gathered by the BLS through the CPS, and made publicly available, will allow us to construct estimates of increasingly comprehensive measures of the reserve army of labour. While it is obvious that all the unemployed workers would be part of the reserve army of labour, the question as to which part of the NLF should be included in the reserve army of labour requires little more analysis. Based on answers to questions in the CPS, the NLF can be divided into two broad groups: (a) those who reported that they want a job and (b) those that reported as not wanting a job, the latter being by far the largest component of NLF.[41]

There are, in turn, two big categories of persons who did not want a job: (a) those who were attending educational institutions and (b) those who had retired. Among those who did want a job, the CPS allows us to distinguish two important groups: (a) those workers who searched for jobs sometime in the past 12 months (but did not do so during the past four weeks) and (b) those workers who did not search for jobs anytime in the past 12 months. Of those who had actively searched for work sometime during the past 12 months, the workers who report as being currently available for work are referred to as the 'marginally attached workers'. An important subset of the marginally attached workers are those that have stopped looking for jobs because of discouragement, with the reason for discouragement being varied. Some believe that no work is available for them, or that they lack necessary schooling or training; some believe that their employer thinks them either too young or too old; some are discouraged because of other types of

---

[41] Data to break up the NLF into these groups are available only from 1994 onwards.

discrimination in the labour market; they are all referred to as the 'discouraged workers'.

These finer distinctions among workers that are all grouped together under the category of NLF will be useful in constructing various measures of the reserve army of labour. But before we do so, we must also look at another, often overlooked, category of workers: those undergoing incarceration. According to the International Center for Prison Studies, the US economy has, by far, the largest prison population in the world as a share of the total population.[42] This forms a small but significant part of the relative surplus population because this population is potentially available to capital; by removing them off the labour market, pressure on wages is reduced. Hence, one must include some measure of the population in prisons and jails to get a more accurate measure of the reserve army of labour. The Bureau of Justice Statistics (BJS) has made available annual data on the 'correctional population' for the period since 1980. Though there are some issues of comparability of the data over years, it gives us a usable number for the population in prisons and jails.[43]

Alternative Measures

In this book, following Basu (2013), I present four, increasingly comprehensive, measures of the reserve army of labour (RAL) in the US economy over the post-war period. The first measure, RAL1, is the total number of unemployed workers (that is, RAL1 = unemployed workers); this is the most conservative estimate of the reserve army of labour.[44]

The second measure, RAL2, adds the marginally attached and part-time workers to the unemployed workers (that is, RAL2 = unemployed workers + part-time workers + marginally attached workers).[45] This is more comprehensive than RAL1 because it includes (*a*) workers who are not counted as unemployed because they did not actively look for work anytime in the 4 weeks preceding the CPS and (*b*) part-time workers who wish to switch to a full-time job but are unable to do so because of economic reasons.[46]

---

[42] See http://www.prisonstudies.org/.

[43] For details, see http://bjs.ojp.usdoj.gov/.

[44] The number of unemployed is computed as the product of the civilian labour force and the unemployment rate. The civilian labour force is the series CLF16OV and the unemployment rate is the series UNRATE, both from FRED, Federal Reserve Bank of St. Louis.

[45] Part-time workers is from the BLS series LNU02026631; marginally attached workers is from the BLS series LNU05026642

[46] To construct estimates of RAL2 for the whole post-war period, we face some data issues because

The third measure, RAL3, adds all workers who are not in the labour force but wanted a job to the total number of unemployed and part-time workers (that is, RAL3 = unemployed workers + part-time workers + workers not in the labour force but wanting a job).[47] This measure is more comprehensive than RAL2 because there are many workers outside the labour force who are not part of the 'marginally attached worker' category.

The fourth and most comprehensive measure, RAL4, is the sum of people in prison and jail and RAL3 (that is, RAL4 = RAL3 + persons in prison and jail). Data on the number of persons in prison and jail is available at an annual frequency from 1980 to 2016. Hence, the RAL4 series starts in 1980 and runs up to 2016. Moreover, the figure for the prison and jail population for a particular year is added to the RAL3 figure for every month in that year. Note that even this measure, the most comprehensive so far, provides only a lower bound for the 'true' reserve army of labour. This is because the latent reserve army is almost certainly not properly estimated in RAL4. In a sense, the latent reserve army can only be estimated *post facto*, that is, after the latent labour force has actually joined the labour force. Hence, almost always, this portion of the reserve army will be underestimated.

To summarize, and for easy reference, we will use the following four measures of the RAL.

1. RAL1 = unemployed workers;
2. RAL2 = RAL1 + part-time workers + marginally attached workers;
3. RAL3 = RAL2 + all workers currently not in the labour force who did not search for work anytime during the past 12 months and those who searched but are not available for work currently;
4. RAL4 = RAL3 + persons in prison and jail.

Trends and Patterns

I present monthly time series plots of the four, increasingly comprehensive, measures of the stock of the reserve army of labour in the US economy in Figures 3.6 and 3.7 (the shaded regions refer to National Bureau of Economic Research [NBER] recessions); Table 3.1 presents summary statistics of these four measures for the whole post-war period and also

---

the number of marginally attached and part-time workers are available only from January 1994. For details, see Basu (2013).

[47] Workers not in the labour force but wanting a job is from BLS series LNU05026639.

separately for the regulated and the neoliberal period, using 1980 as the demarcation year.[48]

Why might it be useful to break up the whole post-war period, 1948–2016, into the regulated and neoliberal periods? Even though capitalism, as a mode of production, has characteristic features like wage labour to distinguish it from other modes of production like feudalism and socialism, global capitalism also develops temporally through a succession of stages defined by specific institutional features. Especially relevant in this respect is the set of institutions that impinge directly on the process of capital accumulation like state involvement in the process of production, the institutions that mediate class struggle between capital and labour and institutions that provide money and credit to different agents in the economy. Since the early 1980s, a group of influential Marxist scholars have popularized the term Social Structure of Accumulation (SSA) to refer to this set of institutions, and have argued that the history of capitalism can be understood as a succession of SSAs. Within this framework of historical materialist analysis, the whole post-war period can be divided into two distinct periods:

- the period of regulated capitalism that runs from 1948 to the mid to late 1970s: this period was characterized by at least three distinct features: (*a*) unchallenged US hegemony in the global capitalist system; (*b*) adoption of Keynesian demand management policies in most advanced capitalist countries backed by a strong welfare state and (*c*) strict regulation of the capitalist sector, especially the financial sector, by the state. While this period delivered unprecedented growth and prosperity in the advanced capitalist countries for about 25 years, maturing of its internal contradictions led to the structural crisis of capitalism in the early 1970s (Bowles et al., 1983).

- the period of neoliberal capitalism that runs from the early 1980s onwards: with neoliberalism emerging as the 'solution' to the structural crisis of regulated capitalism, it overturned several of the key features of the previous period; some of its key features, in turn, are: (*a*) deregulation of business and finance, and privatization of many state services; (*b*) renunciation of aggregate demand management policies and (*c*) globalization of production and finance (Kotz, 2009).

---

[48]For NBER business cycle recession dates, see http://www.nber.org/cycles.html.

Since the two SSAs, regulated and neoliberal, were marked by very different institutional features, it is interesting to study the differential evolution of the RAL in the two periods. Hence, in Table 3.1, I present disaggregated data for the regulated and neoliberal periods, the first running from 1948 to 1980, and the second from 1980 to 2016.

Reserve Army of Labour (Absolute Magnitude)

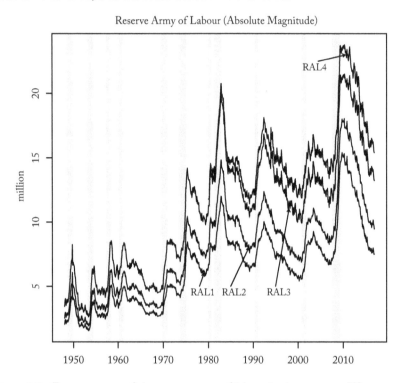

Figure 3.6   Four measures of the reserve army of labour in the post-war US economy, 1948–2016

Source: Bureau of Labour Statistics, US Department of Labour and US Bureau of Justice.

Several interesting patterns emerge from the information in Table 3.1 and Figure 3.6 and Figure 3.7. First, as depicted in the top panel of Table 3.1, the absolute magnitude of the RAL has grown about fivefold over this period, growing from about 5–6 million in the 1950s to about 25 million in 2011, before declining by about 5 million over the next few years. The growth in the magnitude of the RAL was especially rapid in the decade of the 1970s:

the RAL almost doubled in magnitude within that decade highlighting the consensus view among heterodox economists that the 1970s was a period of structural crisis of capitalism. Between 1980 and 2010, on the other hand, the size of the RAL remained relatively stable. It soared skywards once again during the current recession, again indicating that the 2007–08 period was another structural crisis of capitalism.

Second, as can be seen from Table 3.1, the mean and median values of the RAL more or less doubled between the regulated and neoliberal periods of post-war US capitalism. The mean value of RAL1 was 4.02 million in the regulated period; it increased to 8.64 million during the neoliberal period. RAL2 increased from a mean value of 4.97 million to 10.63 million; and RAL3 increased from a mean value of 6.75 million to 14.30 million. The median value shows a similar pattern. Interestingly, the standard deviation for every measure of the RAL is higher in the neoliberal period than in the regulated period, indicating higher monthly fluctuations in the size of the RAL. Among other things, this increase in the volatility of employment would certainly increase the uncertainty and precariousness of wage income (and the corresponding consumption expenditure) flows unless cushioned by credit markets.

Since part of the growth of the RAL comes about due to population growth, we need to normalize the size of the RAL with respect to some measure of the population of the country to get a better appreciation of the true trends. We choose to normalize stock measures of the RAL by the labour force (the sum of the employed and the unemployed) to arrive at pictures of trend movement of the RAL with respect to the relatively more mobile portion of the labour force. This normalization brings us to the third pattern that we wish to highlight. As depicted in Figure 3.7, the RAL as a proportion of the labour force has also grown over time. While there was rapid growth during the decade of the 1970s, the proportion of the RAL with respect to the labour force has remained relatively stable (at a high value) since the early 1980s. It is interesting to note that RAL2, RAL3 and RAL4 were bigger as a share of the labour force during the recession of the 1980s than they are now.

As can be seen from Table 3.1, the mean and median values of RAL1, RAL2 and RAL3 as a share of the labour force are significantly higher in the neoliberal period (in comparison to the regulated period). The mean value of RAL1, as proportion of the labour force, was 5.15 per cent in the regulated period; it increased to 6.38 per cent during the neoliberal period, an increase

Table 3.1 Reserve army of labour in the post-war US economy

	RAL1	RAL2	RAL3	RAL4
Post-war Period, 1948–2016				
Magnitude (millions)				
Mean	6.50	8.00	10.80	15.92
Median	6.66	8.22	11.40	15.07
Standard Deviation	3.04	3.67	4.68	3.07
Share of Lab Force (%)				
Mean	5.81	7.16	9.69	11.74
Median	5.60	6.91	9.40	11.23
Standard Deviation	1.64	1.97	2.51	2.15
Regulated Period, 1948–1980				
Magnitude (millions)				
Mean	4.02	4.97	6.75	
Median	3.79	4.67	6.36	
Standard Deviation	1.57	1.94	2.64	
Share of Lab Force (%)				
Mean	5.15	6.36	8.65	
Median	5.20	6.42	8.73	
Std.Dev	1.39	1.72	2.34	
Neoliberal Period, 1980–2016				
Magnitude (millions)				
Mean	8.64	10.63	14.30	15.92
Median	8.13	10.02	13.64	15.07
Standard Deviation	2.27	2.63	2.90	3.07
Share of Lab Force (%)				
Mean	6.38	7.85	10.60	11.74
Median	5.90	7.27	9.99	11.23
Standard Deviation	1.62	1.91	2.30	2.15

Source: Data for this table comes from the Bureau of Labour Statistics, US Department of Labour and US Department of Justice. For definitions of the different measures of the reserve army of labour, see the sub-section 'Alternative Measures'. The sample stops in 2016 because data on the incarcerated population, which enters in the most comprehensive measure, is available until 2016.

Reserve Army of Labour (Proportion of Labour Force)

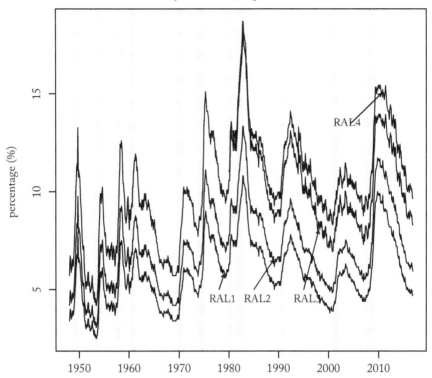

Figure 3.7 Four measures of the reserve army of labour, as a proportion of the labour force, in the post-war US economy, 1948–2016

Source: Bureau of Labour Statistics, US Department of Labour and US Bureau of Justice.

of more than a percentage point. RAL2, as a proportion of the labour force, increased from a mean value of 6.36 per cent to 7.85 per cent, an increase of more than 1 percentage point; and RAL3, also as a share of the labour force, increased from a mean value of 8.65 per cent to 10.60 per cent, an increase of close to 2 percentage points. As can be seen from Table 3.1, the median values of the three measures of the RAL also show a similar pattern. Interestingly, the standard deviation for every measure of the RAL as a proportion of the labour force continues to be higher in the neoliberal period than in the regulated period. This might reflect the higher turnover in the labour market in the neoliberal period which increases, as already indicated, the uncertainty associated with employment and thus increases the precariousness of jobs.

This brings us to the fourth and, in a sense, the most interesting pattern observed in Figures 3.6 and 3.7. All measures of the RAL, both in absolute magnitude and as a proportion of the labour force, show marked cyclical fluctuations at business cycle frequencies; this is immediately obvious in Figures 3.6 and 3.7. Along the lines of Marx's intuition in Chapter 25 of Volume I of *Capital*, the RAL grows during recessions and is depleted during the recovery and boom phase of the business cycle. This fluctuation is driven by fluctuations in the demand for labour power which is, in turn, derived from fluctuations in the pace of capital accumulation. This remarkable and completely intuitive pattern is true for every business cycle in the post-war period.

But there is an interesting shift, within this overall pattern of cyclical fluctuations, from the regulated to the neoliberal period. In the business cycles of the regulated period, the phase of depletion of the reserve army would start immediately after the business cycle trough and would run all the way to the next peak. In the neoliberal period, this has gradually changed and the new pattern is most clearly visible in the business cycles since 1990. In the neoliberal period, the phase of depletion of the RAL starts later (starting several quarters after the trough) and ends early (ending several quarters before the next peak). While this seems to be an important issue for in-depth future study, a hypothesis suggests itself immediately: neoliberal globalization and the relocation of production in the periphery of the global capitalist system (for instance, see [Basu and Foley, 2013]).

Marx's understanding about the dynamic evolution of the capitalist economic system highlighted the important impact of capital accumulation on the lives of workers. One aspect of this impact was the continuous growth of the reserve army of labour with capital accumulation. Mechanization and the adoption of labour saving technologies, which are an intrinsic part of the process of capital accumulation, constantly replenishes the floating reserve army of labour. The extension, often with the use of force, of capitalist relations of production into the periphery of the global capitalist system destroys subsistence agricultural production systems and draws an increasingly large population into the capitalist labour market as a latent reserve army of labour. Deskilling of workers that comes with capital accumulation and discouragement of workers at fading employment prospects that arise from long periods of unemployment swells the ranks of the stagnant reserve army of labour. All these mechanisms ensure a continual, though fluctuating, growth of the reserve army of labour (Foley, 1986b). Time series plots in Figures 3.6 and 3.7 emphasize that this view is remarkably in accord with the facts of post-war US capitalism, both during the regulated and the neoliberal periods.

Within this overall pattern of fluctuations of the RAL, the data also suggests some possibly important new developments. As Edward Wolff has argued, the recovery of profitability in the US economy during the 1980s and 1990s was marked by a slowdown in the growth of the capital-labour ratio (Wolff, 2003). While this pattern might partly be the result of technological stagnation, it is almost certainly also related to neoliberal globalization and the relocation of production to the low wage and minimally regulated periphery of the global economy. The systematic dismantling of barriers to the flow of goods, services and capital across national boundaries under neoliberalism has facilitated the development and deepening of the world market and a global reserve army of labour. This lies behind the structure of contemporary global capitalism where corporate control and profits are concentrated at the top with workers at the bottom working for abysmally low wages (Foster et al., 2011). Movement of production to the low cost periphery (or even the threat of that movement) is, at the same time, used by capital to keep the RAL from depleting too soon in the centre. Thus, the pattern in the data noted earlier, whereby the phase of depletion of the RAL has been considerably shortened under neoliberalism, suggests that the relative importance of labour saving technical change (in the form of mechanization) and relocation of production as alternative mechanisms for disciplining labour (and pushing down wages) in the advanced capitalist countries might be gradually changing.

Further Readings

- Marx's discussion of accumulation and the reserve army of labour is present in Marx (1992, Chapters 19, 25.3). Good expositions are available in Sweezy (1942, Chapter V) and Foley (1986b, Chapter 5, pp. 64–66). For empirical estimates of the reserve army of labour in the post-war US economy, see Basu (2013).

3.6   The Primary Accumulation of Capital

The analysis in the first 25 chapters of Volume I of *Capital*, the material that we have covered so far in this chapter, took us right into the heart of the process of production of capital. We have not only understood how surplus value is produced by capital but also how capital is produced by surplus value. Once capitalism establishes itself as the dominant mode of production, these twin processes repeat themselves endlessly, and in the process it reproduces the basic class relation of capitalism, what Marx calls the 'capital-relation'. This is the relationship between, on the one hand, owners of means of production and consumption and, on the other, the proletariat – those who have no way to survive other than by selling their labour-power. This relationship becomes the basis for the endless generation and realization of surplus value.

But how did this relationship come into being? How were the conditions for its emergence created? How did the capital-relation emerge in the first place? The answers to these questions are provided by Marx through the concept of the 'primary accumulation of capital' (which has been mistakenly translated as 'primitive' accumulation of capital).

To understand the primary accumulation of capital, it is useful to begin with the circuit of capital (the expanded general formula for capital):

$$M - C\{LP, MP\} \cdots (P) \cdots C - M'$$

Using the circuit of capital to represent the basic structure of capitalist production enables us to inquire into the three conditions that need to be met to ensure the emergence of the capital-relation.

The first condition is that there must be accumulation of money in the hands of the class of capitalists; this condition corresponds to the beginning point of the circuit, represented by M. If the capitalist class does not have sufficiently large sums of money at their disposal, they cannot advance the capital value, represented by M, that can start the circuit of capital. The second condition is that means of production, means of consumption and labour-power must be available for purchase on the market as commodities; this condition corresponds to the second step of the circuit, $M - C\{LP, MP\}$. Without the availability of LP and MP on the market, the capital value advanced cannot be converted into the factors needed to carry out production. The third and final condition is that there must be a market – the 'home market' – for the output of capitalist firms to be sold; this condition will ensure the completion of the last step of the circuit, $C' - M'$, and realize the value of, and the surplus value embedded in, the finished commodities through sale. The whole series of complex historical processes that created these three conditions for the emergence of capitalism is referred to by Marx as the *primary accumulation of capital*.

Before looking at the details of the process of primary accumulation in Britain, it is important to note that Marx's analysis does not have any implication about the way primary accumulation will take place in any particular country or area of the global economy. In fact, it is likely that the exact set of processes that can be identified as the primary accumulation of capital will have large variation across the globe. What is important is the result of the process, not its form or shape, in that it must ensure: (*a*) accumulation of money in the hands of capitalists, (*b*) availability of LP and MP as commodities and (*c*) a market for the sale of the output of capitalist firms.

Marx's description of primary accumulation in Britain – and he emphasizes that the description is only about Britain – shows that the first condition, accumulation of money in the hands of capitalists, was fulfilled via two separate routes: (*a*) by the gradual accumulation of revenue in agricultural petty commodity production, which is nothing but the 'slow process evolving through many centuries' of the development of the capitalist farmer and (*b*) by the much more abrupt and sudden emergence of the industrial capitalist through the accumulation of money as usurious and merchant capital through commercial wars, monopoly trade, the slave trade and open loot and plunder in the colonies.

Even if money has accumulated in the hands of merchants, it cannot lead to the emergence of capitalist relations of production unless that money can be used to purchase labour-power and means of production as commodities on the market. Marx is quite emphatic that the emergence of labour-power and means of production as commodities – the second condition of primary accumulation – is the *key condition* for the emergence of capitalism. He is also clear that in the fulfilling of this condition, there is an essential role for the use of extra economic force. This is because the essence of the second condition is the *forcible* separation of direct producers, mainly peasants, from their means of labour, mainly land. The second condition – availability of labour-power, means of production and means of consumption as commodities – was primarily met, notes Marx, through the brutal expropriation of the agricultural population through the Enclosure Movement.[49]

The third condition – development of a home market – was satisfied through the gradual destruction of handicraft production. With the decline of handicrafts, the erstwhile demand for non-agricultural products could be met by the output of capitalist industry. At the same time, the forcible separation of the peasants from the land and their employment in capitalist industry meant that their means of consumption, which was earlier produced by themselves, would now be produced by capitalist producers. This was another part of the home market. While all the three conditions together comprise the primary accumulation of capital, Marx was clear that the second condition, the 'expropriation of the agricultural producer, of the peasant from the soil, is the basis of the whole process'.

Further Readings

- Marx's analysis of the primary accumulation of capital is present in Marx (1992, Chapters 26–33). A good exposition is available in Sanyal (2007, Chapter 3, pp. 113–19).

- Contemporary discussions that use the concept of primary accumulation can be found in Harvey (2004), Sanyal (2007) and Levien (2011).

3.7 Conclusion

In this chapter, we have studied the argument developed by Marx in Volume I of *Capital*. The argument in this chapter revolved around the question of the generation of surplus value in capitalist economies. To develop this argument, Marx first built up the labour theory of value, borrowing ideas from classical economists but also extending and amending them in several ways. We understood that the notion of value should be, first and foremost, applied at the aggregate level of a commodity-producing system, and that by value we mean the socially necessary abstract labour needed to (re)produce a commodity.

---

[49]It is important to note that the general accumulation of capital can also lead to the separation of direct producers from their means of labour. This can happen, for instance, through pauperization of petty commodity producers through the operation of market forces. In this case, the separation of direct producers from their means of labour does not rely on the use of extra economic force. Hence, it cannot be understood as an instance of primary accumulation.

The labour theory of value led to a straightforward understanding of money as the social device to express the value of commodities in a form that is different from the commodity's own physical form. That set the stage for our analysis of capitalism, a form of social organization of production that is based on commodity production and where the capacity to do useful work, labour-power, has itself become a commodity. In such an economic system, the source of surplus value – the income of the class of capitalists – is the exploitation of workers. The value of labour-power is smaller than the value added by labour-power in production. Hence, even when there is equal exchange, that is, all commodities are bought at their values, surplus value can be generated at the aggregate level in a capitalist economy. Money used to beget more money, that is, to generate surplus value through the exploitation of workers, is capital.

Capitalist relations of production have a profound impact on the evolution of the methods and organization of production. The need to increase the rate of surplus value either as absolute surplus value or as relative surplus value can throw light on the struggle of the working class over the length of the working day, the regulation of conditions of work and the evolution of capitalist technology over the centuries.

Once the commodities have been sold and surplus value realized in monetary form, the capitalist system is ready for the next cycle of investment, production and sale. The conversion of surplus value into capital leads to the process of general accumulation of capital. Since accumulation of capital will lead to an increase in the demand for labour-power, we were led to ask the question: What mechanism is available to capitalism to ensure that the price of labour-power does not rise to such an extent that surplus value is pushed down to zero? Marx offered the concept of the reserve army of labour or the relative surplus population as the definitive answer to that important question. Once the issue of general accumulation of capital had been analysed in detail, Marx posed an interesting question: What conditions are necessary for the emergence and consolidation of the capitalist system? Marx developed the notion of primary accumulation of capital to answer this question.

The analysis in Volume I of *Capital* made two important assumptions: (1) that commodities were sold at their value – in modern terminology, Marx abstracted from problems of aggregate demand – and (2) that the use-value composition of the output is such as to meet all the needs for the smooth reproduction of capital. In Volume II of *Capital*, Marx returns to analyse these assumptions with a study of the process of circulation of capital, and to that we turn in the next chapter.

3.A   Appendix A: Reduction of Complex to Simple Labour

3.A.1   *The Intuition*

The most consistent approach to deal with the reduction of complex (skilled) to simple (unskilled) labour was enunciated by Hilferding (1949), as a response to Böhm-Bawerk's critique of Marx, and has been nicely formalized by Rowthorn (1974). In this appendix, I present a brief account of how the reduction of complex to simple labour can be rigorously theorized and used to inform the labour theory of value. The basic idea of this approach is captured by this remark of Marx:

> All labour of a higher, or more complicated, character than average labour is expenditure of labour power of a more costly kind, labour-power whose production has cost more time and labour than unskilled or simple labour-power, and which therefore has a higher value. This power being of higher value, it expresses itself in labour of a higher sort, and therefore becomes objectified, during an equal amount of time, in proportionately higher values. (Marx, 1992, p. 305)

In the above passage, Marx is arguing that differences in the value-creating capacity of different types of complex labour derive from the differences in their *cost of production*, where cost is to be reckoned in terms of labour-time. In this section, I present two ways to formalize this idea. The first presentation of this intuition is based on Laibman (1992) and works out the reduction in a simple setting, where no explicit account is taken of means of production. The second presentation is based on Rowthorn (1974) and discusses the reduction in a multisectoral framework where explicit account is taken of means of production. The latter presentation uses some formalism that I discuss only in the appendix to Chapter 7. Therefore, my suggestion for the reader is to return to this second presentation after going through

Chapter 7. For those familiar with the input–output formalism, the whole discussion can be read right away.[50]

3.A.2 Simple Model

Let the total working life of a master craftsman – the bearer of complex labour – be given by $t + p$ years, where t years are spent on apprenticeship (training, skill acquisition) and p years count as productive life. Of the total of p years of productive life, the master craftsman has to devote a fraction, α, in training the next generation of workers, that is, imparting skills to apprentices.

Given the above division of the total productive lifetime of the master craftsman into training and producing, the total hours of labour-time that the master craftsman can devote to production proper is $(1 - \alpha)\, p$. Hence, this is the amount of labour that is released during the production and embodied in the commodity that the master craftsman produces. On the other hand, the total hours of labour-time that are 'stored' up by the master craftsman is the sum of the time spent in apprenticeship and the time spent working, $t + (1 - \alpha)\, p$.[51] If x denotes the reduction coefficient, then it will be given by the ratio of the total labour-time stored and total labour-time released. Hence, in this case, we will have

$$x = \frac{t + (1 - \alpha)\, p}{(1 - \alpha)\, p} = 1 + \frac{t}{(1 - \alpha)\, p} \tag{3.7}$$

Since $t \geq 0$, $p > 0$ and $0 < \alpha < 1$, we can see that $x \geq 1$. Thus, each hour of complex labour (of the master craftsman) will create x times the amount of value created by each hour of simple (unskilled labour).

From the expression in (3.7), we can see immediately that the magnitude of x, the reduction coefficient, is an increasing function of t, the time spent in acquiring the necessary skills (during apprenticeship). If no time is spent in apprenticeship, $t = 0$; in this case, $x = 1$, and we are back to simple labour. As the time spent in skill acquisition is increased, the value-creating capacity of the resulting complex labour increases.

---

[50] The extant literature offers other ways to carry out the reduction of complex to simple labour: for an approach that specifies a separate real wage bundle for each type of complex labour-power, see Bowles and Gintis (1977) and Krause (1981); for an approach that uses different nominal wage rates for each type of complex labour to implicitly carry out this reduction, see Veneziani and Yoshihara (2017) and Cogliano et al. (2018).

[51] Each hour spent working is stored and released at the same time.

3.A.3 General Model

When we make the analysis more realistic by explicitly allowing for means of production, we need to think of a worker with complex labour-power, a skilled worker, as a worker with simple labour power, an unskilled worker, who also happens to have acquired a skill, much in the same way as an unskilled worker might have acquired a machine. Hence, we should think of complex labour-power as simple labour-power plus a stock of skill:

skilled labour-power = unskilled labour-power + stock of skills

In a broad sense, we can say that the creation of skills is a social process of production that uses labour and commodities to produce complex labour-power from simple labour-power. Hence, just like in the case of a commodity, skill can be thought of as an embodiment of socially necessary labour, which is then released gradually, and becomes embodied in commodities, when the complex labour-power is used in production, that is, when complex labour is performed.

Using this understanding of the production of skills means that skilled workers contribute to the value of the commodities they create in two ways: first, by adding unskilled (that is, simple) labour during the duration of their work and, second, by (gradually) releasing the socially necessary labour embodied in skills (they have acquired). Thus, every hour of skilled labour (coming from the expenditure of an hour of complex labour-power) is equal to the sum of an hour of unskilled (that is, simple) labour *and* the labour embodied in one hour of complex labour-power or skill. Of course, the labour embodied in skills can itself be skilled, whose production, in turn, can involve skilled labour, and so on. In that case, we just need to extend the decomposition indefinitely back to arrive at an expression for skilled labour as a sum of past unskilled (that is, simple) labours.

Let us visualize an economy which produces $i = 1, 2, \ldots, n$ commodities and has $m + 1$ types of complex labour-power, which we identify with the index r, where $r = 0, 1, 2, \ldots, m$. Labour-power of type 0 is unskilled or simple (that is, it gives simple labour on being used in production), and all the other m types of labour-power are skilled or complex labour-power. We will need to consider two distinct sectors of production – the production of commodities and the production of skills. We can think of the commodities as being produced in capitalist firms, and skills being produced in the household, in educational institutions and in the workplace. To allow for general interdependence across sectors, we will assume that both commodities and skills are produced with commodities and different types of complex labour, the latter coming from the use of different types of labour-power.

Commodity Production

Suppose a_{ij} units of commodity i and l_{rj} units of labour r are needed to produce 1 unit of commodity j. Let ϕ_r denote the *reduction coefficient* of labour of type r, that is, one hour of type r labour is equal to ϕ_r hours of unskilled labour (with $\phi_0 = 1$). Since skilled labour is involved in the production of commodities, we will need to *reduce* units of skilled labour to relevant units of unskilled labour before adding them up to arrive at an expression for the value of any commodity.

If σ_j denotes the total amount of unskilled labour embodied in a unit of commodity i, that is, the value of commodity i, then we have, for $j = 1, 2, \ldots, n$,

$$\sigma_j = \sum_{i=1}^{n} \sigma_i a_{ij} + \sum_{r=0}^{m} \phi_r l_{rj}$$

In matrix notation, this becomes

$$\boldsymbol{\sigma} = \boldsymbol{\sigma} \boldsymbol{A} + \boldsymbol{\phi} \boldsymbol{l} \tag{3.8}$$

where $\boldsymbol{\sigma}$ is the $1 \times n$ vector of values, $\boldsymbol{\phi}$ is the $1 \times (m+1)$ vector of reduction coefficients (with the first element being 1), $\boldsymbol{l}$ is the $(m+1) \times n$ matrix of labour requirements, and $\boldsymbol{A}$ is the $n \times n$ matrix of input–output coefficients.

Skill Production

Our next task is to write expressions for the reduction coefficients. Consider labour of type s. Since it is skilled labour, a unit of labour of type s is equal to the sum of 1 unit of unskilled labour and the labour emodied in 1 unit of skill (of type s). Hence,

$$\phi_s = 1 + \phi_s^*$$

where ϕ_s^* is the labour embodied in 1 unit of skill (of type s).

We conceptualize skills as produced through the educational system, which requires inputs of commodities and different types of labour (of the educators). To produce 1 unit of skill of type s, the following inputs are needed: (a) t_s^* units of unskilled labour, (b) l_{rs}^* units of labour of type r and (c) a_{is}^* units of commodity i. Hence,

$$\phi_s^* = t_s^* + \sum_{i=1}^n \sigma_i a_{is}^* + \sum_{r=0}^m \phi_r l_{rs}^*$$

so that, plugging into the equation for the reduction coefficient, we get

$$\phi_s = 1 + t_s^* + \sum_{i=1}^n \sigma_i a_{is}^* + \sum_{r=0}^m \phi_r l_{rs}^*$$

In matrix form, this becomes

$$\phi = (u + t^*) + \sigma A^* + \phi l^* \tag{3.9}$$

where u is a $1 \times (m+1)$ vector of 1s, t^* is a $1 \times (m+1)$ vector of unskilled labour requirements for producing skills, l^* is the $(m+1) \times (m+1)$ matrix of complex labour requirements for producing complex labour and A^* is the $n \times (m+1)$ matrix of input–output coefficients required for producing skills.

Solving for Values and Reduction Coefficients
Using (3.8) and (3.9), we get

$$(\sigma \quad \phi)(I - B) = (0 \quad u + t^*)$$

where I is a $(n + m + 1)$-dimensional identity matrix, and

$$B = \begin{bmatrix} A & A^* \\ l & l^* \end{bmatrix}$$

Hence, under conditions that ensure invertibility of $(I - B)$, we will have determined both the reduction coefficients for the m types of skilled labour and the values of the n commodities as,

$$(\sigma \quad \phi) = (0 \quad u + t^*)(I - B)^{-1}$$

3.A.4   Implications about Income and Wage

Conceptualizing complex labour (or skilled labour) as having been produced has important implications about distributions of incomes and wages. Recall from our discussion of the long-period method of analysis in section 3.2.9 that producers are understood as choosing lines of production to balance the long run 'advantage' and 'disadvantage' of employing their labour-power. Mobility of labour would therefore impart a tendency for the ratio of advantage and disadvantage to equalize across lines of production. If we understand the 'advantage' of employing labour as the income earned, and the 'disadvantage' as the cost of producing that labour-power, with cost conceived broadly to include cost of training, daily reproduction and generational replacement, then the long-period method of analysis leads to some interesting implications.

In a simple commodity-producing society, that is, a commodity-producing system where producers own their means of production, the advantage of employing labour is the income earned, that is, monetary value added per unit of the commodity; the disadvantage of employing labour is the cost, broadly understood, of producing that type of labour-power. Mobility of labour implies that the ratio of monetary value added and the cost of producing each unit of labour-power will be equalized across different lines of production. Hence, the ratio of monetary value added earned per unit of the commodity across different commodity pairs will be a reflection of the ratio of cost of producing those types of labour-power.

In a capitalist society, direct producers are separated from the means of production. In fact, the direct producers are the workers, who own and sell their labour-power; on the other hand, capitalists own the means of production and buy labour-power in the labour market. If we apply the long-period method of analysis in this setting, we will arrive at two important conclusions. On the one hand, capitalists will move their capital across sectors in search of higher profit rates. This will give rise to a tendency for the profit rate to equalize across sectors (or lines of production). We will study this when we discuss Volume III of *Capital*. On the other hand, workers (the direct producers in capitalism) will move across sectors to balance out the ratio of 'advantage' and 'disadvantage' of employing their labour-power – just like commodity producers did in a simple commodity-producing society. In a capitalist economy, the 'advantage' of employing labour is the hourly wage rate and the 'disadvantage' is the cost of producing that type of labour-power. Mobility of workers across sectors will lead to a tendency for this ratio to equalize across sectors. This means that wage differentials will reflect and mirror the differentials in the cost of producing labour-power of different degrees of complexity. In fact, this idea can be traced back to Adam Smith:

> When any expensive machine is erected, the extraordinary work to be performed by it before it is worn out, it must be expected, will replace the capital laid out upon it, with at least the ordinary profits. A man educated at the expense of much labour and time to any of these employments which require extraordinary dexterity and skill, may be compared to one of those expensive machines. The work which he learns to perform, it must be expected, over and above the usual wages of common labour, will replace to him the whole expense of his education, with at least the ordinary profits of an equally valuable capital. It must do this too in a reasonable time, regard being had to the very uncertain duration of human life, in the same manner as to the more certain duration of the machine. The difference between the wage of skilled labour and those of common labour, is founded upon this principle. (Smith, 1991, p. 107, Chapter X, Book I)

The implication is that we can use relative hourly wage rates to aggregate different types of complex (heterogeneous) labour in a capitalist society – as has been done by Veneziani and Yoshihara (2017) and Cogliano et al. (2018). This is a reasonable, and much more straightforward, alternative to the approach discussed in the previous section of this appendix. Instead of explicitly looking at the process of production of skills, we can simply use the relative wage rates of different types of skilled labour to reduce complex labour to simple labour.

3.B   Appendix B: Comparison of MEV over Time and Space

Recall that the MEV is defined as the ratio of aggregate money value added and the total productive labour involved in producing the new aggregate of commodities. Hence, we can express the MEV as follows: $m = Y/H$, where

m is MEV, Y is nominal GDP and H denotes total hours. The nominal GDP can be expressed as the product of 'real' GDP, that is, price-adjusted GDP, and the aggregate price level, that is, $Y = Py$, where y denotes real GDP and P denotes the price level. If we denote real, that is, price-adjusted, labour productivity as $x = y/H$, then we see that the MEV is the product of the general price level and the real productivity of labour: $m = P * x$. This gives us a way to compare the MEV over time and across countries.

Time series plot of the MEV in the US economy is given in Figure 3.8. In computing the MEV for the US economy, I use three series: (a) the nominal GDP created by the private business sector, which comes from line 2 of Table 1.3.5 of the National Income and Product Accounts; (b) average hours worked per week by all production and nonsupervisory employees in the private sector, which comes from the AWHNONAG series from the website of the Federal Reserve Bank (FRB) of St. Louis and (c) total number of production and nonsupervisory employees in the private sector, which is the USPRIV series from the FRB of St. Louis. Assuming that workers work for 52 weeks, we get the total hours worked in the US private sector as: $52 \times AWHNONAG \times USPRIV$. The MEV is then computed as the ratio of nominal GDP and total hours. It should be immediately noted that in computing total labour hours, complex labour has not been reduced to simple labour. Hence, the MEV plotted in Figure 3.8 is an overestimate of the true MEV in the US.

Changes in the magnitude of the MEV over time in any country come from changes in the price level, that is, the inflation rate, and changes in the real productivity of labour. We can be more precise. Since $m = Px$, we have $g_m = \pi + g_x$, where g_m is the growth rate of the MEV over any period of time, $\pi = g_P$ is the growth rate of the price level, that is, inflation rate according to the GDP deflator over that same period of time, and g_x is the growth rate of real labour productivity, again, over the same period of time. Hence, if we were to plot the magnitude of the MEV for any country over time, we could decompose its change over time into the inflation rate and the growth rate of real labour productivity.

Comparison of the level of the MEV across countries at any point in time is slightly more complicated. This is because each country's price level is expressed in terms of its own national currency. Hence, we will need a nominal exchange rate to convert prices to the same unit before comparison.[52] Let us say, we wish to compare the MEV in the US and

---

[52]Marx discusses the nominal exchange rate in Volume III of *Capital* (Marx, 1993b, Chapter 35).

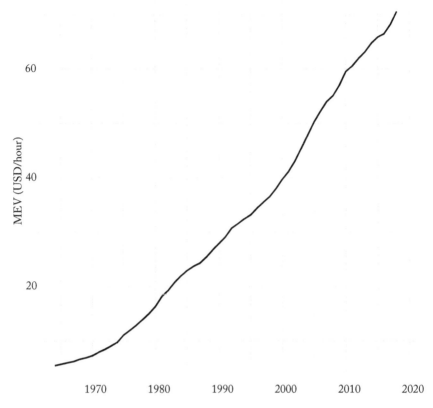

Figure 3.8 Time series plots of the monetary expression of value (MEV) for the US economy, 1964–2018

Source: Constructed with data from the Federal Reserve Bank of St. Louis.

Brazil. Prices in the US are expressed in units of the USD and prices in Brazil are expressed in terms of the BR (Brazilian Real). Suppose the nominal exchange rate between the two currencies is given by e, that is, e units of BR is needed to purchase 1 USD.[53] The levels of the MEV in the US and Brazil in their respective national currencies can be written as $m^{US} = P^{US}x^{US}$, and $m^{BRA} = P^{BRA}x^{BRA}$, where superscripts are used to identify countries.

---

[53] On 10 July 2020, the nominal exchange rate was $e = 5.34$, that is, 5.34 BR was needed to purchase 1 USD.

To compare the levels of the MEVs in the two countries, we can multiply the price level in US with the nominal exchange rate to express it in units of BR. Hence, a ratio of the MEVs in the two countries *expressed in the same units* would be given by

$$rm^{US,BRA} = \frac{eP^{US}x^{US}}{P^{BRA}x^{BRA}} = \frac{eP^{US}}{P^{BRA}} \times \frac{x^{US}}{x^{BRA}}$$

Since the MEV in any country is the monetary expression of 1 hour of social labour-time in that country, the ratio of MEVs for any two capitalist countries gives us a comparative magnitude of the monetary expression of an hour of social labour in the two countries.[54] Let us probe further.

The ratio of the price levels in the two countries expressed in the same units, $eP^{US}/(P^{BRA})$, is what economists call the 'real' exchange rate and denote it as η. It gives us the units of US commodities that can exchange for each unit of Brazilian commodities. Hence, the ratio of the MEVs in the two countries is the product of the real exchange rate (which is the ratio of price levels expressed in the same units) and the ratio of their real labour productivities. Thus, not only will different price levels matter, even the relative magnitudes of labour productivity across the countries will determine the comparative magnitude of the monetary expression of an hour of social labour in the two countries.

Change in this ratio will, therefore, be driven by changes in the real exchange rate and the relative changes in labour productivities, that is, the difference in the growth rates of the MEVs is given by,

$$g_m^{US} - g_m^{BRA} = g_\eta + \left(g_x^{US} - g_x^{BRA}\right)$$

where g_η is the growth rate of the real exchange rate, $\eta = eP^{US}/(P^{BRA})$, g_x^{US} is the growth rate of labour productivity in the US and g_x^{BRA} is the growth rate of labour productivity in Brazil. Thus, over any period of time, difference in the growth rate of MEVs between two capitalist countries will be the sum of the growth rate of the real exchange rate and the relative growth rates of their labour productivities. The growth rate of the real exchange rate can itself be broken down further,

$$g_\eta = g_e + \left(\pi^{US} - \pi^{BRA}\right)$$

---

[54] In section 3.1.6, we have defined the ratio of the MEVs in two countries, expressed in their national currency units, as the Marxian exchange rate for international exchange. By multiplying it with the nominal exchange rate, we express it as a pure ratio. If the nominal exchange rate is exactly the reciprocal of the Marxian exchange rate, then the ratio will be unity.

where π^{US} and π^{US} are rates of inflation in the US and Brazil, respectively, and g_e is the growth rate of the nominal exchange rate. Hence, we see that the difference in the growth rates of MEVs,

$$g_m^{US} - g_m^{BRA} = g_e + \left(\pi^{US} - \pi^{BRA}\right) + \left(g_x^{US} - g_x^{BRA}\right)$$

derive from three sources: difference in the inflation rates, difference in growth rates of labour productivity and growth rate of the nominal exchange rate between the two countries.

In closing our discussion of the MEV for now, let us note two interesting points. The first point relates to the choice of the exchange rate. One might wonder whether the nominal exchange rate is the correct conversion factor between national currencies. After all, the nominal exchange rate is the price of one national currency in terms of another in the global foreign exchange market. Market prices can be distorted in various ways. If one were to use a different exchange rate, for example, PPP exchange rates, one would arrive at a different picture of the relative magnitudes of MEV across countries.

The second point is that there is bound to be large differences in MEVs across countries because of the existence of large differences in labour productivities. Unless the real exchange perfectly mirrors the relative magnitude of labour productivities across countries, their MEVs will differ. Labour productivity will differ across countries both because of differences in the average degree of complexity of labour-power and because of differences in the means of production used by the average worker. It would therefore be a mistake to equate 1 hour of social labour-time across countries without making adjustments for relative labour productivities and the real exchange rate.

3.C   Appendix C: Labour as the Substance of Value

In this section, let us further probe the classical-Marxian position that labour is the substance of value. A question might arise in the mind of the reader: Why labour? What is so special about labour that classical thinkers, including Marx, singled it out as the element that could provide a foundation for a consistent theory of value? Drawing on Laibman (1992), I will provide two sets of answers to this important question, the first based on negative arguments and the second based on positive arguments. I will also discuss some common critiques of the Marxist labour theory of value and offer Marxist responses to the critiques.

3.C.1 The Negative Argument

The negative argument in support of the claim that labour *is* the substance of value comes from a careful reading of Chapter 1 of Volume I of *Capital*. According to Marx, the *social* substance of value must possess three properties:

1. it must be *omnipresent*, that is, it must be present in all commodities;

2. it must be *quantitatively homogeneous* so that we can compare different quantities of the substance in comparing values of different commodities;

3. it must be *socially objective* rather than subjective so that, in principle, different persons can reach an agreement about the magnitude of the substance contained in different commodities.

When we consider a commodity, we see that it has two important characteristics. First, a commodity is a product of labour, that is, labour has been used in its production. Second, every commodity is of use to someone, that is, it has utility. Thus, labour and utility are the two main candidates for a foundation of a theory of value.[55] We will arrive at labour as the substance of value by a process of elimination.

Let us start with utility, the property of commodities of being useful. It satisfies one of the three properties – utility is omnipresent. Every commodity will be accepted in voluntary exchange only if it is of some use to the purchaser. Hence, all commodities have utility. But utility does not satisfy the other two properties. Utility is a subjective factor because the usefulness of the same commodity can vary across persons. It can even vary for the same person depending on other factors like time of day, previous levels of consumption, state of health, and so on. Moreover, it is not clear how utility can be made quantitatively homogeneous – there is no natural and socially accepted unit to measure usefulness.

---

[55]The utility of commodities comes from their physical attributes. When the commodity is a good, it has physical attributes like weight, colour, volume, and so on. And when the commodity is a service, the physical attributes attached to it are the useful effects it creates. For instance, when we think of the service of transportation, the useful physical effect is a change of location of a person or an object. But it is obvious that these physical attributes vary across commodities and cannot be a commonality that can account for the value of commodities.

What about labour? It is omnipresent because all production requires labour – no commodity can be produced without labour. Can labour be made quantitatively homogeneous? While there are different types and qualities of labour, it can be potentially made quantitatively homogenous, as we have argued earlier, with the concept of socially necessary abstract simple labour (with an implicit reduction of complex to simple labour). Finally, the amount of labour that is required for producing a commodity is a socially objective fact, it does not depend on the subjective wishes of any person. Hence, labour satisfies all the three properties that Marx thought any substance of value should possess. Since neither utility nor physical qualities satisfy all three properties, by the process of elimination, we arrive at the claim that labour is the substance of value.

3.C.2 Neoclassical Critique and Response

From a neoclassical perspective, there are at least three objections that could be raised against the negative argument, and let us take them up in turn. The first objection that is often raised against the negative argument for the labour theory of value is that there are many objects that have value without being a product of labour, that is, labour as a substance of value is not omnipresent. The primary example of such an object is land – which is not a product of labour but has value. We can dispense with this objection quickly. The problem with this argument is that it rests on a confusion of the concepts of 'value' and 'price'. Plots of land, or titles of ownership to plots of land, can be bought and sold. Hence, land has price but it does not have value because it is not the product of human labour. The labour theory of value can easily explain such cases, as we will see when we discuss Marx's theory of rent in Chapter 5.

> The price-form ... may also harbour a qualitative contradiction, with the result that price ceases altogether to express value, despite the fact that money is nothing but the value-form of commodities. Things which in and of themselves are not commodities, things such as conscience, honor, etc., can be offered for sale by their holders, and thus acquire the form of commodities through their price. Hence a thing can, formally speaking, have a price without having a value. The expression of price is in this case imaginary ... On the other hand, the imaginary price-form may also conceal a real value-relation or one derived from it, as for instance the price

of uncultivated land, which is without value because no human labour is objectified in it. (Marx, 1992, p. 197)

The second objection relates to the question of quantitative homogeneity. If we can conceive of abstract labour, then why can we also not conceive of abstract utility? Just like the process of exchange forces us to abstract from concrete labour, is it not possible to understand the process of exchange as also abstracting from concrete utilities derived by different individuals from different commodities? Can we not posit something like 'abstract utility' as the substance of value? If we accept the neoclassical perspective, then we can.

The third objection is related to the third property – social objectivity. A neoclassical economist would question the claim that social objectivity is a necessary property that any substance of value must possess. It is true that, under a set of assumptions, neoclassical general equilibrium theory can demonstrate the existence of exchange ratios – exchange value in Marxist terminology – for a competitive economy on the basis of subjective preferences of individuals (Debreu, 1959). Hence, one cannot logically dispute the objection that social objectivity is not a necessary property of the substance of value. If all we are after is exchange value, then we can construct such a theory in a consistent manner on the basis of subjective utility or the more primitive notion of subjective preferences – the notion of a socially objective substance of value can be dispensed with.

It should be mentioned that such a theory rest on rather restrictive and unrealistic assumptions. Some of the key assumptions that are needed to construct such a theory of price formation are as follows: (*a*) preferences of one individual are not allowed to take account of other individuals, (*b*) there are no externalities of decisions related to production, (*c*) there is complete information about all relevant aspects of the economy and (*d*) there are no public goods. Such assumptions undermine the realism and applicability of the whole analysis and convert the whole exercise of theory building into an intensely ideological exercise.

3.C.3 Sraffian Critique and Response

The Sraffian, or post-Ricardian, critique of the negative argument for labour as the substance of value mainly consists of what can be called a redundancy argument. In the Sraffian tradition, the economy is viewed as being composed of n sectors. In the most common version of this theory, each sector produces a single commodity using a unique method of production which uses only circulating capital, that is, there is no fixed capital. The method of production for any commodity is described in terms of the magnitudes of the n commodities and the amount of labour required to produce one unit of that commodity. The real wage rate is specified in terms of a basket of commodities. In such a set-up, it is possible to solve for a set of relative prices, that is, exchange values, of the n commodities and the uniform rate of profit.

The redundancy argument was advanced most forcefully by Steedman (1977). The gist of the argument is that value magnitudes are redundant because a set of long run relative prices – prices of production – can be consistently computed without reference to any labour-time magnitudes. Moreover, analyses of all important phenomena in capitalism, like technological change, class struggle over distribution of income, and so on can be conducted on the basis of these prices. Thus, neither for description nor for analysis are value magnitudes necessary. The whole search for the source of value in labour-time magnitudes is a useless and unnecessary theoretical detour. This is a powerful argument and I consider it in detail, and offer a Marxist response, in Chapter 7. In brief, the Marxist response that I present asserts that there is a consistent way to define values and to calculate prices of production and the uniform rate of profit *without* making value magnitudes redundant.

3.C.4   Analytical Marxist Critique and Response

The Analytical Marxist (AM) critique of the labour theory of value can be called a multiplicity argument. It is part of a broader argument that is known in the literature as the generalized commodity exploitation theorem, or GCET (Yoshihara, 2017). Clear expositions of this argument can be found in Gintis and Bowles (1981) and Roemer (1982, Appendix 6.1). The crux of the argument is the claim that there is nothing special in labour that can make it the sole candidate for the substance of value. Other commodities can as well function as the substance of value. Moreover, we can also show that when we choose some other commodity as the candidate substance of value, it is bound to be exploited in a capitalist economy. This is an important argument and I will discuss this in detail in Chapter 8. Let me note here in brief that the AM critique rests on two conceptual problems: (*a*) the inability to distinguish between labour-power and labour and (*b*) the inability to distinguish between labour-power and all other commodities.

3.C.5   *The Positive Argument*

While the Sraffian tradition differs radically from the neoclassical tradition in the use of certain foundational concepts related to a description of a capitalist economy, it shares one feature with the neoclassical tradition – the centrality of relative prices. Therefore, it is not surprising that both the neoclassical and Sraffian critiques of the labour theory of value relate, in one way or another, to relative prices. But it cannot be denied that, on their own terms, both the neoclassical and Sraffian critiques are powerful. If the focus of our analysis was *only* on relative prices, then we would probably have to abandon the labour theory of value. But for Marxist political economy, relative prices are not of fundamental importance. It is concerned, in a much more serious manner, with questions of social classes, their location in capitalist society, the sources of their incomes, the exploitative relationships that link them together and the contradictions of the system that arise because of these features. The positive argument in support of the claim that labour is the substance of value is an elaboration of this aspect of Marxist political economy. The argument is developed in two steps. In the first step, we will consider a general class-divided society and establish the link between power and labour. In the second step, we will consider capitalism, a special form of class-divided society, where we will then establish the link between power and value.

Class Power and Labour

Let us consider a class-divided society and ask the following question: What is the key mechanism through which the ruling class maintains its power over the exploited class? One answer might be that the ruling class can maintain its power through the use of force, where the state is the instrument for the deployment of force in the interest of the ruling class. The second and related answer might be that not only the state but a host of other institutions generate legitimacy for the exercise of ruling-class power – and this is how the ruling class maintains its power over the exploited class. Both these answers need to confront the question: What is the material basis of the exercise of state power or the legitimizing functions of ruling-class institutions? For instance, how are the functionaries of the state, the judiciary, the police, the army and the bureaucracy materially supported, how are the 'worldly goods' that they need provided for?

The ruling class can materially support the state, and related institutions for generating legitimacy for its class rule, if it has control over the *surplus product*, that is the part of the physical output over and above what is needed for replacing the used-up tools and implements and providing the subsistence needs of the exploited, labouring class. The surplus product, apart from supporting the consumption needs of the ruling class, can also be used to provide for the 'worldly goods' of the functionaries of the state, the judiciary and the army – who, then, deploy force to maintain the power of the ruling class. Is control over the surplus product enough, or is it necessary for the ruling class to control the surplus labour-time of the exploited class?

Control over surplus labour-time, that is, the part of the working time during which the exploited, labouring class produces the surplus product, implies control over the surplus product, but not the other way round. It is theoretically possible to conceive of scenarios where the ruling class has only control over the surplus product, but not the actual labour process or the way the total working time of the exploited class is divided between necessary and surplus labour-time. But history seems to suggest otherwise. In all class-divided societies, including slavery and feudalism, the ruling class has, first and foremost, control over the surplus labour time of the exploited class. Control over the surplus product is an outcome of the control of surplus labour-time. Control of surplus labour-time goes hand in hand with control over the labour process. This latter control is important because only then can the ruling class modulate the degree of exploitation, that is, the ratio of surplus and necessary labour, according to its needs. All these considerations suggest that conceptually and historically, the most secure foundation for the exercise of ruling-class power is the control over the surplus labour-time of the exploited class.

Capitalist-Class Power and Value
Capitalism is a form of class-divided society. Hence, the above argument holds for capitalism. But capitalism has unique features not shared by any other class-divided society – and these unique features will bring the additional dimension of value into the analysis of power. The key characteristics of capitalism as a class-divided society are, first, that it is a

form of commodity-producing society, and second, that the exploited class has to sell its ability to work, that is, labour-power, as a commodity on the market. Like in any class-divided society, the ruling class of capitalists control the surplus labour-time of the exploited, working class by controlling the labour process. But this control, this exercise of class power, is irreducibly mediated through exchange – and that is how power and value are inextricably linked in capitalist society.

All the material inputs required by capitalists in the production process have to be purchased in the market. The inputs are produced as commodities by other capitalists. Hence, the relationship within the capitalist class, that is, different elements and fragments of the capitalist class, is mediated through the market. In a similar manner, the relationship between the capitalist and the working class is established through the market, specifically the labour market, where the worker sells her ability to do useful work. Thus, relationships within and between fundamental social classes are mediated through the market – the domain of exchange.

To the direct control of the labour process by the ruling class is added the operation of the impersonal power of exchange relations. The direct control of the labour process, the struggle over the division of working time between necessary and surplus labour-time, remains salient in capitalism, as in previous forms of class-divided society (Gintis and Bowles, 1981). To the direct control of the labour process is added the social domination that is impersonal in nature and that is enforced through relations of exchange (Postone, 1993; Heinrich, 2012). Workers and capitalists alike have to submit to the impersonal power of market relations, and capitalist-class power has to be expressed in and through exchange relations, in addition to the direct exercise of power in the workplace.

As a class-divided society, capitalism must ensure direct control of the labour process (and hence, surplus labour-time) by the ruling class. This is what can potentially explain the evolution of management techniques used by capitalists to control the labour process, starting from the assembly line to Taylorist management methods. But as a special type of class-divided society, where production is organized through exchange, the power of the ruling class must also be expressed through, and validated by, impersonal exchange relations. It is this centrality of exchange relations in capitalism that is sought to be captured by the notion of value. And the claim that labour is the substance of value is the conceptual strategy to establish the link between power and surplus labour-time that respects its trans-historical character (for all class-divided societies) while, at the same time, making conceptual space for capitalism's specificity as a special type of commodity-producing system.

4

Realization of Surplus Value

In the previous chapter, we studied what Marx had termed the 'process of production of capital'. Using the key concept of surplus value, we saw that the process of production of capital involved two aspects (or steps): the generation of surplus value by capital in the first step, and, in the next, the accumulation of surplus value to create capital. This argument was developed by Marx in Volume 1 of *Capital*, and that had been the main object of our study in the previous chapter. We had also noted that in developing this argument, Marx had abstracted from two important issues: (*a*) how did the commodities find a market? and (*b*) how did the material underpinnings of the capital accumulation process get recreated over and over again?

> In Volume 1, the capitalist production process was analyzed both as an isolated event and as a process of reproduction: the production of surplus-value, and the production of capital itself. The formal and material changes undergone by capital in the circulation sphere were assumed, and no attempt was made to consider their details. It was therefore assumed both that *the capitalist sells the product at its value* and that *he finds in the circulation sphere the material means of production that he needs to begin the process anew* or to continue it without a break. (Marx, 1993a, pp. 428–29; emphasis added)

The fact that Marx had abstracted from these two questions was consistent with his method of presentation – of moving from the abstract to the concrete. Once the analysis of the process of production of capital was completed in

Volume I, Marx returned to these questions in Volume II and took up the issue of realization of surplus value. Since surplus value is realized only through sale of commodities, and since sale of commodities occur in what Marx calls the 'sphere of circulation', the analysis in Volume II begins with an investigation of 'formal and material changes undergone by capital in the circulation sphere'. Marx studies some general issues relating to the sphere of circulation and to the circulation of capital as a way to set-up the framework for the analysis of the problems of realization of surplus value – the main question investigated in Volume II of *Capital*. Parts 1 and 2 of Volume II deal with issues that are relevant for a general analysis of the circulation process of capital, and part 3 investigates the question of realization of surplus value.

In these analyses, Marx introduces two key analytical innovations: the *circuit of capital model* and the *reproduction schemas*. The analysis of the general circulation process of capital – in parts 1 and 2 of Volume II – is conducted with the conceptual apparatus of the circuit of capital, an abbreviated version of which we have already encountered in the previous chapter. The conceptual apparatus of the circuit of capital model allows Marx to clarify the meaning of circulation, analyse its key features, pose the problem of unproductive labour through an analysis of the 'costs of circulation', study the process of economic growth in capitalist economies and pose the question of aggregate demand in a transparent manner. The reproduction schemes allow Marx to study the question of the correct use-value composition of output needed for smooth reproduction of capital, and to highlight the problem of disproportionality as a possible source of crisis in capitalism.

4.1   Circulation of Capital

4.1.1   *The Circuit of Industrial Capital*

The conceptual apparatus used for an analysis of the circulation process of capital is the circuit of capital,

$$M - C \{MP, LP\} \cdots (P) \cdots C' - M' \tag{4.1}$$

which is an abstract representation of the flow of value through an individual capitalist enterprise or the whole capitalist economy. The circulation process for an individual industrial capital, as represented in the circuit of capital, has three stages.

The first stage is represented by $M - C$, and takes place in the *sphere of circulation*. In this stage, the capitalist enters the commodity and labour markets, as a buyer, with a sum of money, M, to purchase a bundle of commodities, C. The bundle of commodities purchased by the capitalist is comprised of two qualitatively different parts: the means of production, MP, and labour-power, LP. In the second stage of the circuit, which is represented by (P) and takes place in the *sphere of production*, the commodities purchased by the capitalist are brought together in the production process – labour-power works on and with the means of production to produce the output. The third stage of the circuit is represented by $C' - M'$ and takes place, once again, in the *sphere of circulation*. In this stage the capitalist returns to the commodity market, but now as seller of the finished product, C'. Under normal circumstances, the revenue from sales, M', not only recoups his cost of production, M, but also allows him to realize a surplus, $\Delta M = M' - M$.

4.1.2 *Production versus Circulation*

From the perspective of the labour theory of value, there is an important analytical difference between, on the one hand, the first and the third stages and, on the other, the second stage of the circuit. One way to highlight this distinction is to use the difference between content and form.

- Production refers to the set of processes in which the *content* of value (of commodities), so far as its magnitude is concerned, is changed.

- Circulation refers to processes in which only the *form* of value is changed. By definition, therefore, the process of circulation does not change the magnitude of value of commodities. All processes which change the magnitude of value would be included in the category of production.

With reference to the circuit of capital formula in (4.1), the first and third stages are processes of circulation of capital, and the second stage is a process of production of capital. The first stage is represented as $M - C$, so that we can see clearly that it only involves a change in the form of value – from the money form to the commodity form. Similarly, the third stage of the circuit is represented as $C' - M'$, where we see clearly, once again, that all that is involved is a change in the form of value – from the commodity form to the money form. In the second stage of the circuit, represented as (P), on the other hand, there is an increase in value – because the value of the finished output is higher than the value of the inputs. This is the case, as we have seen in the previous chapter, because of the generation of surplus value in the capitalist production process and derives from the fact that value *added by* the use of labour-power is higher than the value *of* labour-power.

In making the distinction between the production and circulation of capital, we need to understand the term 'production' broadly. The key point is that the physical location of production and consumption of many commodities, especially commodities that are referred to as goods, are different. Now, a commodity leaves the sphere of circulation only when it is consumed – either individually (which refers to personal consumption) or productively (which refers to the use of a commodity in the production process). Hence, the broader sense of the term 'production' should include not only the physical act of production but also the activities that are needed to change the physical location of the commodity from its site of production to its site of consumption. In more concrete terms, this means that, looked at from the perspective of the labour theory of value, the process of production comprises not only production proper but also transportation, storage, warehousing, and so on. Thus, labour involved in these activities create value, and also surplus value, if employed in capitalist enterprises.

But if we include transportation, storage, warehousing, and so on under the category of production, then what distinguishes this broader notion of production from circulation? The conceptual distinction rests on what we have indicated earlier: circulation involves only a change in the form of value, or, to use Marx's terminology, a 'metamorphosis of form' of value. Thus, it includes only the activities of *pure buying and selling* of commodities, that is, a transfer of ownership of commodities (which is accompanied by a change in the form of value). The clear implication is that labour involved in circulation does not create value, and so, nor does it create surplus value. Thus, the cost incurred for supporting the process of circulation are deductions from the surplus value created in production.

Even though circulation does not create value, it is, nevertheless, essential for the reproduction of capital. Without the process of circulation, the value (and, hence, surplus value) contained in commodities cannot be realized, that is, converted into its monetary form. And without realization of value and surplus value, the reproduction of capital would be interrupted. Hence, the costs of circulation are necessary costs of the reproduction of capital and are referred to by Marx as the *faux frais* of the reproduction process. We will return to these distinctions when we take up the issue of productive and unproductive labour in the next chapter.

4.1.3   Circular Movement of Forms of Value

In what sense is the circuit of capital a circuit, that is, a circular process? The circuit of capital is a representation of a circular process – hence, the term 'circuit' – insofar as *forms of value* are concerned. One can see that the flow of value through the circuit is accomplished by and through successive changes in forms of value – from money to commodities in the first stage, from commodities to productive capital in the second stage, and from commodities to money in the third and final stage.

> The two forms that the capital value assumes within its circulation stages are those of money capital and commodity capital; the form pertaining to the productive stage is that of productive capital. The capital that assumes these forms in the course of its total circuit, discards them again and fulfills in them its appropriate functions, is industrial capital - industrial here in the sense that it encompasses every branch of production that is pursued on a capitalist basis. (Marx, 1993b, p. 133)

In fact, there is not one but three circuits embedded in the circuit of industrial capital in (4.1) that becomes apparent once we expand the circuit and rewrite it to represent two consecutive circuits as

$$M - C \cdots (P) \cdots C' - M' - C'' \cdots (P') \cdots C''' - M'' \qquad (4.2)$$

If we start from capital value in the form of money, the circuit ends when capital returns to its monetary form. Hence, the circuit of money capital can be represented as $M \ldots M'$. If we start with the productive form of value, then the circuit completes itself when capital returns to its productive form, so that the circuit of productive capital can be represented as $(P) \ldots (P')$. On the other hand, if we use the commodity form of value as the starting point of our analysis, then the circuit completes itself when value returns to its commodity form. Hence, the circuit of commodity capital can be represented as $C' \ldots C'''$. Of course, from the perspective of the accumulation of capital, the circuit of money capital is the most important one. The circuit starts in a real sense only with a sum of money, M.

4.1.4   Flows and Stocks of Value

The circuit of capital model in (4.1) allows us to clearly see the relationship between *flows* and *stocks* of value in capitalist economies. We have seen earlier that the circuit of capital comprises three stages. Each stage represents a flow of value, as summarized in Table 4.1. In the first stage, there is a flow of value in the form of capital outlays to purchase means of production and labour-power. In the second stage, the flow of value takes the form of finished output – the commodities produced by labour. In the third and final stage, the flow of value manifests itself as the flow of revenue through sale of the finished commodities.

Each stage of the circuit can only complete itself in some positive amount of time. It takes time for the process of production to complete itself; the conversion of the raw materials into the finished product can only happen over a definite period of time. Similarly, the finished commodities do not find buyers instantaneously; the sale of the finished product takes positive amounts of time. In a similar fashion, the revenue that comes back to the capitalist enterprise is not immediately thrown back into circulation in the form of fresh capital outlays; the use of the money capital for capital outlays also takes time, depending on various factors relating to the state of aggregate demand, situation in the labour market, and so on.

The implication of each stage of the circuit of capital taking positive amounts of time to complete itself is that value has to remain in these different stages of the circuit for definite amounts of time in the form of stocks of value. Since each flow associated with the three stages of the circuit can only complete itself in definite periods of time, value accumulates within the circuit in the form of stocks. Corresponding to the three flows comprising the circuit of capital, we see three stocks of value.

Stocks of value in the sphere of production show up as stocks of *productive capital*. In concrete terms, productive capital consists of undepreciated plant and machinery, unused raw material, semi-finished output and unused labour-power. Stocks of value that show up as *commodity capital* are stocks of finished output awaiting sale; and stocks of *money capital* are the unspent revenue and the net worth (financial assets less financial liabilities) of the firms.

> It lies in the nature of the case, however, that the circuit itself determines that capital is tied up for certain intervals in the particular sections of the cycle. In each of its phases industrial

Table 4.1 Three stages of the circuit

Stage	Sphere	Flow
$M - C$	Circulation	Flow of Capital Outlays
(P)	Production	Flow of Finished Output
$C' - M'$	Circulation	Flow of Sales Revenue

Source: Author.

capital is tied to a specific form, as money capital, productive capital or commodity capital. Only after it has fulfilled the function corresponding to the particular form it is in does it receive the form in which it can enter a new phase of transformation. (Marx, 1993a, p. 133)

The circuit of capital model can, therefore, be conveniently represented as a circular flow of expanding value with three nodes (representing stocks of value) connected by three flows. Figure 4.1, inspired by Foley (1986b), is a graphical representation of the circuit. It represents the circular movement of value of the total aggregate social capital. Since each individual capital always exists in the three forms of value, aggregating across all units of capital allows us to construct the circuit of aggregate industrial capital.

> In so far as each of these circuits is considered as a particular form of the movement in which different individual industrial capitals are involved, this difference also exists throughout simply at the individual level. In reality, however, each individual industrial capital is involved in all the three [phases] at the same time. The three circuits, the forms of reproduction of the three varieties of capital, are continuously executed alongside one another. One part of the capital value, for example, is transformed into money capital, while at the same time another part passes out of the production process into circulation as new commodity capital ... The reproduction of the capital in each of its forms and at each of its stages is just as continuous as is the metamorphosis of these forms and their successive passage through the three stages. Here, therefore, the entire circuit is the real unity of its three forms. (Marx, 1993a, p. 181)

It is important to note that each element of the circuit of capital corresponds to observable quantities in real capitalist economies. While the flows of value in the circuit are recorded in the profit-loss statements of capitalist enterprises, the stocks are recorded in their balance sheets. This implies that a circuit of capital model can be empirically operationalized and used to study tendencies in 'actually existing capitalism'.

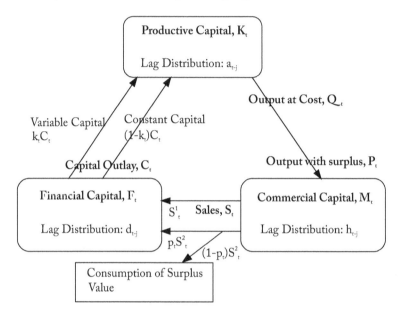

Figure 4.1 The circuit of capital
Source: Adapted from Foley (1986b) and Basu (2014). Arrows represent flows of value and boxes represent stocks of value. For a mathematical representation of the circuit of capital model, see Basu (2014).

4.1.5 *The Turnover of Capital*

Let us now consider the circuit of capital in Figure 4.1 from the perspective of the passage of time. Since the flow of value through each stage of the circuit takes positive amounts of time, the flow of value through one circuit takes a definite, non-zero amount of time. The total time taken by an atom of value to complete the circuit is known as the *turnover time* of industrial capital. The turnover time is the sum of *production time* and *circulation time*, the former referring to the period of time during which capital is in the sphere of production and the latter referring to the time capital spends in the sphere of circulation. The production time, in turn, is the sum of working time (the duration of the labour process) and waiting time (the period of time during which capital resides in the sphere of production to complete some natural process involved in the production of specific commodities).

> ... the movements of capital through the production sphere and the two phases of circulation sphere are accomplished successively in time. The duration of its stay in the production sphere forms its production time, that in the circulation sphere is circulation time. (Marx, 1993b, p. 200)

What does the turnover time measure?

> It ... measures the interval between one cyclical period of the total capital value and the next; the periodicity in capital's life-process, or, if you like, the time required for the renewal and repetition of the valorization and production process of the same capital value. (Marx, 1993b, pp. 235–36)

From the perspective of the aggregate social capital, positive amounts of turnover time imply that capital lies idle for some periods of time, that is, it is not involved directly in the valorization of capital. For instance, it might be lying idle as money capital awaiting to be recommitted to production, or it might be lying idle as finished commodities that need to be sold, or it might be lying idle as unused raw materials or semi-finished products. Since value lying idle is value not involved in the valorization process directly, there is a structural incentive for the capitalist system to reduce the turnover time of capital. Reduction of production time has come about through technological change in the production process; and reduction in the circulation time has been the result of technological change in transportation, communication and the financial sector. Once we use the circuit of capital framework to look at the capitalist economy, the structural logic of such technological changes becomes transparent.

4.1.6   Fixed and Circulating Capital

From the perspective of the circuit of capital, we can make sense of an important distinction that had befuddled many economists before Marx's time: the distinction between fixed capital and circulating capital. Recall that capital assumes three different forms within the circuit – money capital, productive capital and commodity capital (see Figure 4.1 for details). The distinction between fixed and circulating capital only relates to the second form, that is, productive capital. *Fixed capital* is that part of productive capital that transfers its value to the finished commodity over many production cycles. Examples of fixed capital are machinery, equipment and building. In contrast, *circulating capital* (which Marx also calls as fluid capital) is the part of productive capital that transfers its value to the finished commodity within one production cycle. Examples of circulating capital are raw materials and auxiliary materials (like power, oil).

It is important not to confuse the distinction between constant and variable capital, which we studied in the previous chapter, with the distinction between fixed and circulating capital. The former difference refers to the valorization process and the latter refers to the circulation process. Looked at from the perspective of valorization, the portion of money capital that is used to purchase means of production (the non-labour inputs into production) is the constant capital and the portion that is used to purchase labour-power is variable capital. Looked at from the perspective of circulation, the portion of productive capital that completes its circuit over many production cycles is known as fixed capital and the portion that completes its circuit within one production cycle is known as circulating capital.

4.1.7 The Process of Economic Growth in Capitalism

The picture of the aggregate capitalist economy captured through the circuit of capital model, depicted in Figure 4.1, allows us to pose the question of economic growth in capitalism. But what do we mean by growth of a capitalist economy? The growth of the capitalist economy is the growth in the size of the circuit of capital, that is, the size of the flow of value traversing the circuit. There are two independent sources of this growth.

The first source is the magnitude of surplus value that is generated in each cycle during the phase of production – which is nothing but the unpaid labour-time of the working class – and the second source is the speed with which the average unit of value traverses the whole circuit, starting in money form and returning to a money form. The first source is obvious because surplus value is the only source of capital; the second source arises because the sooner capital returns to a money form, after traversing the whole circuit, the sooner is it available to be recommitted to production of more surplus value.[1]

4.1.8 Formalization of the Circuit of Capital Model

An elegant continuous-time formalization of Marx's analysis of the circuits of capital was developed in Foley (1982a, 1986a). This model was empirically operationalized for the US manufacturing sector in Alemi and Foley (1997) and has been used recently in dos Santos (2011) to study the impact of consumption credit on economic growth. Matthews (2000) develops an econometric model of the circuit of capital model. A different, but related, strand of the literature emerged from Kotz (1991), who used a circuit of capital model to analyse crisis tendencies within capitalist economies. Loranger (1989) used the circuit of capital model to offer a new perspective on inflation.

Basu (2014) builds on and extends the approach in Foley (1982a, 1986a) by developing a discrete-time version of the circuit of capital model. In that paper, it is argued that the circuit of capital model offers a distinctive approach to analysing macroeconomic behaviour of capitalist economies, which is different from both the neoclassical and Keynesian approaches. The neoclassical approach focuses on supply-side issues to the virtual neglect of demand-side factors; hence, it is one-sided. The Keynesian approach restores the importance of demand-side issues within macroeconomics but, in turn, neglects the centrality of the profit-motive (the need for the generation and realization of surplus value) in driving the capitalist system. Hence, the Keynesian approach is one-sided too because it overlooks the constraints that are imposed on the capitalist system due to the blind drive for surplus value even in the absence of aggregate demand problems. By transcending both kinds of one-sidedness, the Marxist circuit of capital model offers a distinctive framework for macroeconomic analysis of capitalist economies which accords centrality to the generation and circulation of surplus-value.

There are many advantages of the Marxist circuit of capital model. First, it offers an extremely rigorous and realistic framework to address the knotty issue

---

[1]This explains the structural need for improvements in the means of communication, transportation and financial engineering in capitalism, which lead to an increase in the speed with which value can traverse the circuit of capital.

of time within macroeconomics. While it is recognized that the production and circulation of commodities take finite amounts of time, it has not been easy to incorporate this simple but profound fact in macroeconomics. Both neoclassical and Keynesian economics have opted for the abstraction of short and long runs as a way to deal with the passage of time. The most commonly used conceptual basis of separating the two 'runs' is the impact of investment expenditure, what we have called capital outlays, on the economy. Within this framework, the short run is defined by a fixed capital stock, that is, by a fixed productive capacity. Hence, in this framework, investment expenditure has only a demand-side effect in the short run. When we allow for changes in the capital stock due to investment expenditures, it is only then that we are assumed to be operating in the long run. But this distinction is clearly *ad hoc*. Investment expenditure includes the purchase of equipment and structures by capitalist enterprises and their incorporation into the production process; this increases the productive capacity of the economy. Hence, some forms of investment expenditure have, at the same time, both demand and supply-side effects. The typical neoclassical and Keynesian frameworks do not take this into account. The Marxist circuit of capital model, on the other hand, allows for this fact very naturally.

Second, the Marxist circuit of capital model, as developed by Foley (1982a, 1986a), is an accounting framework that carefully works out the relationships between flows and stocks of value. Thus, it is, by construction, a stock-flow consistent model. Since it is an accounting framework, it is potentially consistent with a wide range of behavioural assumptions about the economic agents populating the model. Hence, the Marxist circuit of capital model offers a rich set of choices to researchers in terms of specifying the behaviour of key sectors of the capitalist economy and developing and testing empirically meaningful and theoretically sophisticated macro models. This work of extending the existing version of the Marxist circuit of capital model can draw on behavioural economics, computational economics, agent-based simulation and other such emerging fields.[2]

---

[2]The main body of work in heterodox macroeconomics builds models by specifying behavioural assumptions about different agents in the economy. For instance, different savings behaviour is often assumed for workers and capitalists; behaviour of capitalist enterprises is modeled to give an investment function, and so on. The circuit of capital model does not contradict this stream of heterodox macroeconomics. Rather, it provides a larger stock-flow consistent, value-theoretic framework within which such behavioural assumptions can be fruitfully embedded.

Third, the Marxist circuit of capital model is firmly anchored in the labour theory of value tradition. Hence, unlike both neoclassical and Keynesian economics, the fact of exploitation of the working class by capitalists is never ignored. Since surplus value, at the aggregate level, is the monetary equivalent of unpaid labour-time of the working class, the dynamic of capital accumulation that is modeled by the circuit of capital model always has exploitation at the centre of the analytical framework.

The main challenge of using the Marxist circuit of capital approach to macroeconomics is the difficulty of empirically operationalizing the model due to lack of suitable data. Key parameters of the model, such as the production, realization and finance lags, are not observed and need to be estimated. Innovative approaches to empirical analysis of the Marxist circuit of model as developed, for instance, in Alemi and Foley (1997) and Matthews (2000), need to be extended in several directions. As more researchers come to adopt this framework, it can be hoped that some of these issues will be naturally addressed in the course of time.

Further Readings
- Basic ideas of the circuit of industrial capital are developed in Marx (1993a, Chapter 1).

- The distinction between production and circulation is discussed in Marx (1993a, Chapter 6).

- The discussion of the circuit of industrial capital as a circular movement of forms of value is developed in Marx (1993a, Chapters 1–4).

- The discussion about the emergence of stocks of value within the circuit of industrial capital and the relationship between flows and stocks is developed in Marx (1993a, Chapters 1–4).

- The discussion of the turnover of capital can be found in Marx (1993a, Chapter 7).

- Marx uses the circuit of capital to think of growth in capitalist economies at different places in Marx (1993a, Chapters 1–4, 7). An excellent summary of the key ideas on this issue can be found in Foley (1986b, Chapter 5, pp. 66–69).

- The discussion of fixed and circulating capital can be found in Marx (1993a, Chapter 8).

191

- Marx's ideas of the circuit of capital was formalized in a mathematical model by Foley (1982a, 1986a). Later work that has attempted to extend Foley's analysis in different directions or apply it to study different aspects of capitalist economies are dos Santos (2011), Basu (2014) and Vasudevan (2016).

4.2 The Problem of Aggregate Demand

The circuit of capital completes its final phase only when commodities are sold at their value. This is how the value, and more importantly the surplus value, created by the working class, is realized by the capitalist class in monetary form. However, the possible sale of finished commodities at their value creates a puzzle.

The capitalist class starts the circuit of capital with an initial sum of money, M. It uses this sum of money to purchase means of production and labour-power. In a capitalist economy, means of production and means of consumption are commodities produced by capitalists. Hence, the purchase of means of production is, at the same time, a transfer of money from one part to another part of the capitalist class. Similarly, when the wage income is used by workers to purchase their means of consumption, the corresponding sum of money returns back to a part of the capitalist class (the producers of the means of consumption). Hence, when capital outlays and purchase of means of consumption by workers is complete, the initial sum of money, M, returns to some part of the capitalist class. But here is the puzzle. The value of the finished commodities is M', and the viability of capitalism implies that M' is greater than M (because of the generation of positive amounts of surplus value). How, then, can the sum of money M realize the value of finished commodities, M', which is greater than M?

Towards the end of Volume II of *Capital*, Marx offers a solution to the puzzle that was taken up later by N. Bukharin in his critique of Rosa Luxemburg. Marx notes that the puzzle can be solved because there is one commodity that does not need to 'realize' its value through sale. This is the money commodity, which was gold during Marx's times. Thus, a part of the total value of finished commodities, M', does not need to be realized through sale; its value is realized through production itself. Hence, as long as there is a large and growing sector which produces the money commodity at the 'correct' rate, the capitalist system will be able to realize the full value created in production, that is, it will be able to solve the problem of aggregate demand.

What is the 'correct' rate of growth of the money commodity sector? During each period, the economy must produce an amount of the money commodity that is equal to the surplus value generated. As long as this is ensured, we will have the following: the initial sum of money will be used to realize its equivalent, M, and the rest, that is, the increment represented by the surplus value, will be realized by the fresh injection of the money commodity. Since there is growth in the mass of surplus value over time, this means that the sector producing the money commodity has to grow at the relevant rate. A fixed stock of the money commodity, no matter how large, will not suffice because it will eventually run out.

In contemporary capitalism, especially since the mid-twentieth century, money commodities are no longer used. So, how does the contemporary capitalist system solve the problem of aggregate demand and realize the full value of the finished commodities? The main mechanism used to solve the problem of aggregate demand in modern capitalist economies is credit, that is, borrowing and lending of sums of money. Suppose a part of the capitalist class lends sums of money to another part, through the financial system, to finance capital outlays. In that case, the gap in the amount of money needed to realize the full value of the finished commodities, that is, $M' - M$, can be closed. Hence, the problem of aggregate demand can be solved in every period, as long as the growth of credit keeps pace with the growth of surplus value.[3]

In fact, the growth rate of the economy will increase if the growth rate of credit is increased, as long as there is a sufficiently large reserve army of labour to keep wage pressures in check (so that the rate of surplus value does not fall). This is because larger amounts of credit will free up more money to function as capital and generate more surplus value; more credit will, at the same time, also solve the 'realization problem' by ensuring the sale of the finished output.[4]

---

[3]In contemporary economies, money is the credit extended by the Central Bank and the commercial banking system. Hence, an alternative way of making the same statement is the following: a sufficiently fast growth rate of the money supply would be able to solve the problem of aggregate demand that we have discussed here.

[4]The realization problem refers to the possible problem of selling finished commodities at a price that realizes the complete value of the commodity, that is, converts the full value of the commodity into monetary form.

Does this mean that there is no upper limit to the rate of growth of a capitalist economy? No. Marx's analysis of the circuit of capital in Volume II of *Capital* and its elegant mathematical representation in Foley (1982a) shows that there are internal limits to how fast a capitalist economy can grow. Given the rate of surplus value, the internal limit is determined by the minimum amount of time required for an average quantum of value to traverse the circuit of capital. This minimum amount of time is certainly much larger than zero, so that the maximum rate of growth has a finite upper bound.[5]

Readings
- The problem of aggregate demand and the role of money and credit in that context is discussed by Marx in Marx (1993a, Chapters 20–21). The basic ideas are explained clearly in Foley (1986b, Chapter 5, pp. 86–89).

4.3　Use-Value Basis of the Reproduction of Capital

The reproduction of capital requires a certain use-value composition of the total output of capitalist production. When the capitalist class is ready for a fresh round of production, that is, when the circuit of capital is to begin anew, industrial capitalists must find on the market means of production and means of consumption in the correct quantity and proportion, the former to start the process of production anew and the latter to meet the consumption needs of the workers it will employ (as also its own, possibly larger, consumption needs). Can the capitalist system produce means of production and means of consumption in the 'correct' quantity and proportion? Marx used the analytical device of the 'reproduction schemas' to think rigorously about this question in part 3 of Volume II of *Capital*.

Marx divides the whole of capitalist production analytically into two departments. Department I produces means of production, and Department II produces means of consumption. Now Marx asks the question: do the

---

[5]This analysis of the problem of aggregate demand is decidedly incomplete. What we have demonstrated is that a sufficiently fast growth of the availability of credit will create the conditions for solving the problems of aggregate demand. But the fact that they can be solved in this way does not yet explain if they actually will be. After all, the mere availability of credit will not lead to *expenditures* to purchase commodities. Hence, to complete the analysis, we will have to analyse the determinants of expenditures. And the key expenditure that drives the whole system is capital outlays. Hence, to complete the analysis, we will need to develop a theory of the determinants of the flow of capital outlays.

sizes of these departments – where we measure the size of each department, for instance, by the amount of labour-power employed – need to maintain certain proportions for a smooth reproduction of the aggregate social capital to be possible? Marx answers this question in the affirmative, for both simple and expanded reproduction.

4.3.1 Simple Reproduction

Consider simple reproduction, first, where the scale of production remains unchanged period after period, and note that this can happen only when all the surplus value is consumed. The scale of production can remain unchanged if the following two conditions are satisfied: (a) the value of output of Department I (means of production) is exactly equal to the sum of the value of means of production used up in both departments, so that means of production are replaced without any increment at the end of each production period and (b) the value of the production of Department II (means of consumption) is equal to the sum of the total wage income of the workers in both departments and the surplus value of the capitalists in both departments (recall that all surplus value must be consumed for the scale of production to remain unchanged). This immediately shows that the value of output in the two departments must bear a certain and definite relationship if both the conditions stated above are to be satisfied. If we then assume, as does Marx, that the process of production in both departments are characterized by certain fixed technical coefficients – the rate of surplus value, the OCC – then the proportionality of output, required by the above conditions, translates into the proportionality of variable capital (and, hence, the quantum of labour-power employed in the two departments). Marx reaches the following conclusion: if this proportion is maintained, simple reproduction will be ensured.

Let us work through the example that Marx used in Chapter 20 of Volume II of *Capital* to study simple reproduction, which is reproduced in Table 4.2. To understand why the economy represented in Table 4.2 is characterized by simple reproduction, let us investigate the demand and supply of the output of the two departments. Department I uses 4,000 units of constant capital and 1,000 units of variable capital. The rate of exploitation is 1. Hence, surplus value of 1,000 units is generated. Hence, the total value of output, that is, supply, in Department I is 6,000. What is the source of demand for the output of Department I? The demand comes from the need to replace means of production used up in the two departments. In Department I, 4,000 worth of constant capital has been used up; in Department II, 2,000 worth of constant capital has been used up. If the economy is to reproduce itself on the same scale as before, the used-up means of production will need to be replaced. Hence, the total demand for the output of Department I is 6,000 = 4,000 + 2,000. Thus, demand is equal to supply.

Table 4.2   Marx's example of simple reproduction

	C	V	S	W
Department I	4,000	1,000	1,000	6,000
Department II	2,000	500	500	3,000
Total	6,000	1,500	1,500	9,000

Source: This example is discussed in Marx (1993a, Chapter 20).

Let us next turn to Department II. Department II uses 2,000 constant capital and 500 variable capital. The rate of exploitation is the same across the departments (ensured by the mobility of labour). Hence, surplus value of 500 is generated, so that the total value of output in Department II is 3,000. What is the demand for the output of Department II? The demand for means of consumption comes from the workers and the capitalists. Workers spend all their wage income for consumption; hence, their demand for the output of Department II is 1,500. If an economy is to be characterized by simple reproduction, capitalists must use all the surplus value for consumption. Hence, the demand for the output of Department II from capitalists is 1,500. Hence, total demand for the output of Department II is 3,000, which is exactly equal to the total supply of the output of the department. Thus, demand and supply, in value terms, are exactly equal in both departments. There is neither excess supply nor excess demand. The economy will be able to reproduce itself smoothly over time. Thus, demand is equal to supply.

What is the key condition in the example of Table 4.2 that ensures smooth simple reproduction? Let us use simple algebra to answer this question by studying the equilibrium condition in Department I:

$$C_I + V_I + S_I = C_I + C_{II}$$

On the left-hand side of this equation, we have the total value of the output of Department I, where C_I, V_I and S_I denote the constant capital, the variable capital and the surplus value in Department I (which is indicated by the subscript). The right-hand side gives the demand for the output of Department I because it is the sum of the constant capital used up in Department I, C_I, and the constant capital used up in Department II, C_{II}. When the two are equal, we have equilibrium in the market for means of production. But equilibrium in the market for means of production will automatically ensure equilibrium in the market for means of consumption.[6] Hence, there will be equilibrium in the whole capitalist economy. Cancelling out C_I from both sides, we arrive at the equilibrium conditions:

$$V_I + S_I = C_{II}$$

If the value of constant capital used up in Department II is exactly equal to the sum of variable capital and surplus value in Department I, then there will be equilibrium in the whole capitalist economy.

One way to think of the equilibrium condition is to think of the exchange *between* the two departments. In Department I, the means of production that is used up, that is, C_I, can be replaced by exchanges within the department (when capitalists in Department I purchase means of production). Hence, $V_I + S_I$ represent the part of the total value of output of Department I that can be realized only through exchange with Department II. In a similar manner, $V_{II} + S_{II}$ of the total value of Department II's output, that is, $C_{II} + V_{II} + S_{II}$, can be realized through exchanges within the department (when workers and capitalists in the department purchase means of consumption). Hence, C_{II} represents the part of the total value of Department II's output that can be realized through exchange with Department I. The above equilibrium condition shows that there will be a balance of demand and supply in the economy only when the needs for interdepartmental exchange of the two departments coincide. In Marx's example in Table 4.2, we can see this condition being satisfied because $C_{II} = 2,000$, $V_I = 1,000$ and $S_I = 1,000$, so that $V_I + S_I = C_{II}$.

---

[6] If there are n markets in a capitalist economy, then equilibrium in $n - 1$ markets will automatically ensure equilibrium in all the n markets. This is known as Walras' Law.

We can also convert the equilibrium condition into a more explicit condition about proportionality between the department. To do so, let us define the *value composition of capital* as

$$k_I = \frac{V_I}{C_I + V_I} = \frac{1}{1 + q_I}$$

where q_I is what we have earlier encountered as the OCC, and

$$k_{II} = \frac{V_{II}}{C_{II} + V_{II}} = \frac{1}{1 + q_{II}}$$

The value composition of capital in the two departments, k_I and k_{II}, measures the fraction of capital outlays that go to purchasing labour-power. Thus, the composition of capital gives us a reflection of the capital intensity of production in value terms. Let us also define the rate of surplus value as, $e = S_I/V_I = S_{II}/V_{II}$, that is, both department have the same rate of exploitation. From

$$k_{II} = \frac{V_{II}}{C_{II} + V_{II}}$$

we can see that

$$C_{II} = \left(\frac{1 - k_{II}}{k_{II}}\right) V_{II}$$

Thus, using the above and the fact that $S_I = eV_I$, the equilibrium condition, $V_I + S_I = C_{II}$, becomes

$$\frac{V_{II}}{V_I} = \frac{1 + e}{\frac{1 - k_{II}}{k_{II}}} \tag{4.3}$$

which shows that a definite proportionality is needed between the two departments for simple reproduction. As long as this proportionality (in the sizes of variable capital) in the two departments hold, the economy will be characterized by simple reproduction.

4.3.2 Expanded Reproduction

Intuition and Marx's First Example
Of course, the natural state of capitalist economies is not simple reproduction, but the constant growth in scale of production. Hence, Marx

moves on to analyse the analogous relations of proportionality that would be required to ensure smooth reproduction on an expanded scale, that is, expanded reproduction. In Table 4.3, we give details of one example that Marx used to study expanded reproduction. The key thing to note is that now the output of Department I, 6,000, is larger than the sum of replacement needs of the two departments, 5,500. Similarly, total output of Department II, 3,000, is larger than the consumption demand of the workers, 1,750. Hence, to complete the analysis, Marx needs to show two things: (*a*) How the additional demand of 500 is generated to realize the value of the total output of Department I? and (*b*) How an additional demand for means of consumption, over and above the original consumption demand of workers, comes out to be exactly 1,250 (= 3,000 – 1,750)?

Table 4.3 Marx's first example of expanded reproduction

	C	V	S	W
Department I	4,000	1,000	1,000	6,000
Department II	1,500	750	750	3,000
Total	5,500	1,750	1,750	9,000

Source: This example is discussed in Marx (1993a, Chapter 21, p. 586).

While Marx was unable to work out the numerical example correctly in Volume II, the basic intuition is very much there. If a capitalist economy is to smoothly reproduce itself on an expanding scale, then the following conditions must be satisfied: (*a*) the value of output of Department I (means of production) must be exactly equal to the sum of the value of means of production used up in both departments and the additional means of production that will need to be purchased due to reinvestment of surplus value (the latter will ensure that the scale of production increases every period) and (*b*) the value of the production of Department II (means of consumption) is exactly equal to the sum of the following: the total wage income of the workers in both departments currently employed, the wage income of the workers who will be employed due to the reinvestment of surplus value, the portion of surplus value that is currently consumed by capitalists in both departments and the surplus value that will be consumed by capitalists in the future. A similar logic as before now gives us the proportionality of employment of labour-power in the two departments that would be consistent with the satisfaction of the above two conditions. The conclusion is exactly similar to what we saw in the case of simple reproduction: if the required proportion is maintained between the two departments, smooth reproduction will be ensured on an expanding scale.[7]

An Algebraic Treatment

Sale of the output comes from expenditures of capitalists and workers, the two classes in this economy. The capitalist class makes two types of expenditures: (*a*) capital outlays to carry out production, which is the sum of constant capital (the amount of money used to purchase means of production) and variable capital (the amount of money used to purchase labour-power) and (*b*) consumption expenditure. Variable capital, which is part of the capital outlays by capitalists, corresponds to the wage income of the working class, which is used for the consumption expenditure of workers. Hence, the total expenditure by the capitalist class is the primary source of all demand in the model of capitalist economies that we study here (the most important exclusions are the state and the rest of the world, which can be additional sources of autonomous expenditure).

We can re-group the expenditures in the economy to arrive at the sources of demand for the output of the two departments. The demand for the output of Department I come from two types of expenditures: (*a*) replacement of used-up means of production in Department I and II and (*b*) increments to the means of production in Department I and II. Note that both expenditures arise directly from the capital outlays in the two departments.

The demand for the output of Department II also comes from two types of expenditures: (*a*) consumption expenditure of workers in Department I and II and (*b*) consumption expenditure of capitalists in Department I and II. Consumption expenditure of workers comes from wage income, which is the variable capital component of capital outlays by capitalists. Thus, consumption expenditure of workers comes indirectly from the capital outlays of capitalists. On the other hand, consumption expenditure of capitalists comes from the surplus value realized through sale of the output.

---

[7] The fact that such a proportion will ensure smooth reproduction on an expanded scale does not imply that real capitalist economies can achieve that proportion. The unplanned nature of capitalism suggests that the problems of disproportionality will always be a serious issue, and under certain conditions can lead to crisis.

For a complete description of the model, we need to specify three parameters related, in turn, to the technology of production, the degree of exploitation of workers and the investment propensity of capitalists. To do so, we will continue to use subscripts I and II to identify the two departments. We have already encountered the first two parameters, k_I and k_{II}, the composition of capital in the two sectors, and e, the rate of exploitation (ratio of surplus value generated and variable capital advanced) that is common to both departments. The third and new parameter is what we can call the reinvestment rate. This is denoted by p_I and p_{II}, in the two departments, and refer to the share of surplus value that is reinvested into production. Note that p_I and p_{II} characterize the investment behaviour of capitalists in the two departments, with a higher value of p signifying a higher propensity to save and invest. Note also that if $p_I = p_{II} = 0$, then all the surplus value is consumed by capitalists and we get the special case of simple reproduction (which we have analysed in the previous section).

If this economy is to smoothly reproduce over time, it must be the case that there is neither excess demand nor excess supply in the market for the output of either department. Let us start by investigating the condition for equilibrium in the market for the output of Department I. Denoting constant capital by C, variable capital by V and surplus value by S, the total value of output in Department I is given by $C_I + V_I + S_I$. In equilibrium, this has to be equal to the total demand for the output of Department I. But what is the total demand for the output of Department I?

In Department I, the demand for means of production comes from the need to replace the means of production that has been used up, C_I, and the need for incrementing the means of production, ΔC_I. The increment to the means of production in Department I arises from the reinvestment of surplus value. In Department I, $p_I S_I$ is the amount of surplus value reinvested, of which the fraction $(1 - k_I)$ is used for purchasing means of production. Hence, the increment to the means of production in Department I is given by $\Delta C_I = (1 - k_I) p_I S_I$. In a similar manner, the demand for means of production in Department II comes from replacement needs, C_{II}, and from the need to expand the means of production, ΔC_{II}, where the latter is given by the expression: $\Delta C_{II} = (1 - k_{II}) p_{II} S_{II}$. Hence, the total demand for means of production is given by

$$C_I + \Delta C_I + C_{II} + \Delta C_{II}$$

which, using the expressions above, becomes

$$C_I + (1 - k_I)p_I S_I + C_{II} + (1 - k_{II})p_{II}S_{II}$$

There is equilibrium in the market for means of production if total supply (in value terms) is equal to total demand (in value terms), that is if

$$C_I + V_I + S_I = C_I + (1 - k_I)p_I S_I + C_{II} + (1 - k_{II})p_{II}S_{II}$$

where the left-hand side is the total supply of means of production (in value terms) and the right-hand side is the total demand for means of production (in value terms). The above condition can be manipulated to get the following:

$$\frac{V_{II}}{V_I} = \frac{1 + e - ep_I(1 - k_I)}{\frac{1 - k_{II}}{k_{II}} + ep_{II}(1 - k_{II})}$$

where we have used the following algebraic relationships

$$C_I = \frac{1 - k_I}{k_I} \times V_I,$$

$$C_{II} = \frac{1 - k_{II}}{k_{II}} \times V_{II}$$

and

$$e = \frac{S_I}{V_I} = \frac{S_{II}}{V_{II}}$$

Let us summarize this result as

Proposition 1. *Let V_I and V_{II} refer to the variable capital in Departments I and II, respectively. If the ratio of the sizes of the two departments is given by*

$$\frac{V_{II}}{V_I} = \frac{1 + e - ep_I(1 - k_I)}{\frac{1 - k_{II}}{k_{II}} + ep_{II}(1 - k_{II})} \tag{4.4}$$

then the capitalist economy can smoothly reproduce on an expanded scale. If, in addition, there is no capital mobility between sectors, and

$$k_I p_I = k_{II} p_{II} = \eta \tag{4.5}$$

then the two departments will grow at the same rate of growth given by $g = \eta e$.

The proof follows immediately from the above discussion. Note that the condition derived in (4.4) would also emerge if we investigated the condition for equilibrium in the market for the output of Department II. This is not surprising. Since total social production is broken up into two departments, equilibrium in the market for the output of one department will automatically imply equilibrium in the market for the output of the other. It is also interesting to note that when $p_I = p_I = 0$, then the condition in (4.4) becomes the condition in (4.3). This is because when there is no reinvestment of surplus value, that is, $p_I = p_I = 0$, then we have simple reproduction.

What is the intuition behind (4.4)? Given the parameters that capture technology, exploitation and investment behaviour in the two departments, the right-hand side of the expression in (4.4) is some positive number. Thus, Proposition 1 shows that if the sizes of the variable capitals in the two departments maintain the proportion given by the right-hand side of (4.4), then the capitalist economy can ensure smooth reproduction on an expanded scale. How do we know this? The condition comes from an algebraic manipulation of the condition for equilibrium – equality between demand and supply – in the market for the output of Department I. Hence, if this condition is satisfied, it will imply that the total demand for means of production will be exactly equal to its total supply, both expressed in terms of value. Moreover, since total social production is broken up into two departments, equilibrium in the market for means of production (the output of Department I) will automatically imply equilibrium in the market for means of consumption (the output of Department II). Thus, there will be neither excess demand nor excess supply in the market for means of production and the market for means of consumption, which means that there will be smooth reproduction of the whole system of production.

The fact that the condition about the proportional sizes of the two departments given in (4.4) ensures smooth reproduction also highlights a possible mechanism for the emergence of crisis: disproportionality between the two branches of production. If the two branches are not of sizes that satisfy the condition given in Proposition 1, then smooth reproduction of the system will not be possible. Either there will be excess supply for means of production, coupled with excess demand for consumer goods, or the economy will face an excess demand of means of production with also an excess supply of consumer goods. In either case, there will be an overproduction of commodities, and the economy will be plunged into a crisis – a crisis of disproportionality, as highlighted by Tugan-Baranowsky (see (see Sweezy [1942, Chapters X and XII]).[8]

Note that the analysis presented so far has implicitly ruled out an interesting possibility: the movement of capital between the two departments. This could happen, for instance, if some of the surplus value generated in Department I were invested in Department II in the next period, or vice versa. We have ruled this out by assuming that the investment to increase the scale of production in each department comes from surplus value generated within that department. This implicit assumption, captured by (4.5), simplifies the analysis. But how do we get this condition given in (4.5)? The intuition behind the condition is the following: if the two departments are to maintain the correct proportions over time without any interdepartmental transfer of capital, they will have to grow at the same rate on the basis of the surplus value generated within the department.

If growth in Department I comes from reinvestment of surplus value generated within the department only, then the rate of growth of variable capital in Department I is given by

$$g_I = \frac{\Delta V_I}{V_I} = \frac{k_I p_I S_I}{V_I} = k_I p_I e$$

Similarly, the rate of growth of gI, on the basis of reinvestment of surplus value generated within the department only, is given by

$$g_{II} = \frac{\Delta V_{II}}{V_{II}} = \frac{k_{II} p_{II} S_{II}}{V_{II}} = k_{II} p_{II} e$$

Hence, if $k_I p_I = k_{II} p_{II}$, then both departments grow at the same rate and the correct proportions are maintained over time, which is the condition in (4.5).

Completing Marx's First Example
Now we are ready to complete Marx's example that is given in Table 4.3. From the numbers given in the table, we see that $V_{II}/V_I = 3/4$, $e = 1$, $k_I = 1/5$ and $k_{II} = 1/3$. In the discussion surrounding this example, Marx was trying to find the correct rates at which surplus value in the two departments

---

[8]An alternative formalization of the circuit of capital model can be found in Foley (1982a). In that model, increases in production and realization lags can also open up a demand gap. The demand gap can either slow down the steady state growth rate of the economy or lead to a crisis.

need to be reinvested to facilitate expanded reproduction. He worked with various numbers, which brought him close to the solution. But he could not pin down the exact reinvestment rates because he did not use an algebraic treatment. Thus, all we need to do to complete Marx's analysis is to compute the reinvestment rates in the two departments using the equations written above. How do we get these? We can use (4.5) to get one equation relating the two unknown variables

$$p_I/5 = p_{II}/3$$

We can use (4.4) to get another equation relating the two unknowns

$$p_{II} = 1 - (8/5)p_I$$

Using these two equations, we can solve for the two unknowns: $p_I = 5/11$ and $p_{II} = 3/11$. With p_I and p_{II} known, now we can investigate the conditions for the balance of demand and supply.

What is the additional demand for means of production? It is given by $(1 - k_I)p_I S_I + (1 - k_{II})p_{II}S_{II}$. Plugging in the values of the variables, we see that this is equal to 500. Hence, the additional demand for the output of Department I is exactly what was needed by Marx to complete his analysis (see Table 4.3): 500. This is the difference between the value of the output of Department I, 6,000, and the replacement demand for means of production coming from the two departments, $4,000 + 1,500 = 5,500$. Hence, the additional demand is 500 ($= 6,000 - 5,500$). Now let us turn to Department II. What is the additional demand for means of consumption? This is given by $(1 - p_I)S_I + k_I p_I S_I + (1 - p_{II})S_{II} + k_{II}p_{II}S_{II}$. Using the values of the variables, we see that this is equal to 1,250. Once again, this is exactly equal to the demand for the output of Department II that is over and above the consumption demand of workers (see Table 4.3). Note that the output of Department II is 3,000 and the consumption demand of currently employed workers is 1,750 ($= 1,000 + 750$). That is why the additional demand for means of consumption is 1,250 ($= 3,000 - 1,750$). Hence, there is a balance of supply and demand in the market for the output of both departments. Thus, Marx's first example about expanded reproduction was correct in its essential details even though he was unable to find the correct reinvestment rates in the two departments.

205

Allowing for Capital Mobility

In the previous calculation, we had assumed that there is no capital mobility between the two departments. Thus, the two departments grew because of the reinvestment of surplus value generated within the department. Under this assumption, the growth rate would be the same in both departments only if (4.5) held. The assumption that there is no capital mobility between the departments was a simplifying assumption, and we can relax it now. Suppose fractions α and β of the surplus value generated in Department I and II, respectively, are invested in Department I. Hence, fractions $1 - \alpha$ and $1 - \beta$ of the surplus value generated in Department I and II, respectively, are invested in Department II.

The rate of growth of variable capital in Department I is given by

$$g_I = \frac{\Delta V_I}{V_I} = \frac{k_I \left[\alpha p_I S_I + \beta p_{II} S_{II} \right]}{V_I} = k_I e \left(\alpha p_I + \beta p_{II} \frac{V_{II}}{V_I} \right)$$

and the rate of growth in Department II is given by

$$g_{II} = \frac{\Delta V_{II}}{V_{II}} = \frac{k_{II} \left[(1 - \alpha) \, p_I S_I + (1 - \beta) \, p_{II} S_{II} \right]}{V_{II}}$$

which simplifies to

$$g_{II} = k_{II} e \left[(1 - \alpha) \, p_I \frac{V_I}{V_{II}} + (1 - \beta) \, p_{II} \right]$$

If the parameters are such as to ensure that $g_I = g_{II}$, then the two departments will grow at the same rate. Using this, we can now state the condition for balanced, expanded reproduction allowing for capital mobility between departments.

Proposition 2. *Let V_I and V_{II} refer to the variable capital in Departments I and II, respectively. If the ratio of the sizes of the two departments is given by*

$$\frac{V_{II}}{V_I} = \frac{1 + e - e p_I (1 - k_I)}{\frac{1 - k_{II}}{k_{II}} + e p_{II} (1 - k_{II})} \tag{4.6}$$

then the capitalist economy can smoothly reproduce on an expanded scale. If, in addition,

$$k_I \left(\alpha p_I + \beta p_{II} \frac{V_{II}}{V_I} \right) = k_{II} \left[(1 - \alpha) \, p_I \frac{V_I}{V_{II}} + (1 - \beta) \, p_{II} \right] \tag{4.7}$$

where fractions α and β of the surplus value generated in Department I and II, respectively, are invested in Department I, and the rest in Department II, then the two departments will grow at the same rate of growth.

The proof follows from the above discussion, and note that the first part of the proposition is exactly the same as the first part in Proposition 1. The second part follows from the fact that if (4.7) holds, then $g_I = g_{II}$ (as is shown by the discussion preceding the statement of this proposition). Hence, the two departments grow at the same rate. Note that if $\alpha = 1$ and $\beta = 0$, there will be no capital mobility between the departments because all of the surplus value generated in Department I will be invested in Department I, and the same will hold for Department II. Under these conditions, we will be back to the special case of Proposition 1 because (4.7) will become (4.5).

Readings
- Marx's discussion of the reproduction schemas are available in Marx (1993a, Chapters 20–21). Useful expositions are available in Sweezy (1942, Chapters V, X), Eaton (1963, Chapter VIII) and Foley (1986b, Chapter 5).
- Mathematical treatments of Marx's reproduction schemas can be found in Harris (1978), Foley (1986b) and Trigg (2006).
- The discussion of Marx's reproduction schemas in this chapter has emphasized the possibility of stable, balanced growth. But the model can be extended to generate instability and crisis tendencies. For this strand of the literature, see Morishima (1973, Chapter 10) and Okishio (1988).

4.4 Conclusion

We have now reached the end of the Volume II of *Capital* and it is useful to pause and summarize the argument we have studied so far. In terms of levels of abstraction, the analysis in the first two volumes of *Capital* operate at the level of 'capital in general', that is, in these two volumes, Marx studies the relationship between the whole of capital and the whole of labour. Whereas Volume I analysed the processes of production of capital, Volume II studied the process of circulation of capital. Using slightly different terminology, we can say that Volume I studied the process of generation and accumulation of surplus value, and Volume II analysed the realization of surplus value. This completes the analysis of the capitalist system at the level of the aggregate relationship between capital and labour. Now we are ready to move to a lower level of abstraction, to what Marx calls the level of 'many capitals', that is, the level of abstraction where the competition between capitals and credit is introduced in the analysis. This is precisely the domain of Volume III of *Capital*, where the totality of capitalist production is analysed from the perspective of the process of distribution of surplus value. The next chapter will present the details of the argument developed in Volume III of *Capital*.

5

Distribution of Surplus Value

In the previous two chapters, we have studied

- the processes of the generation and accumulation of surplus value that was analysed by Marx in Volume I of *Capital* (Chapter 3) and

- the processes surrounding the realization of surplus value in the sphere of circulation that was analysed by Marx in Volume II of *Capital* (Chapter 4).

To complete the analysis of the capitalist system, we now need to understand how the surplus value that is generated in production of commodities and realized through sale of commodities is distributed through various channels to finally emerge as the income stream of various fractions of the ruling class – the trading capitalists (the merchants), the industrial capitalists, the money capitalists and the resource owners. It is the purpose of this chapter to study the processes of distribution and redistribution of surplus value by discussing the main threads of the argument that were developed in Volume III of *Capital* (Marx, 1993b).

The first thing to note is that the argument in Volume III of *Capital* proceeds in two analytically separate steps. In the first step of the argument, we understand how the already produced surplus value is distributed across different sectors of industrial capital, that is, capital that is involved in the process of capitalist production of commodities. We will see that the key mechanism that brings about this redistribution of surplus value, in the first step of the argument, is the competition between industrial capitals, the latter manifested in the mobility of capitals across sectors in search of higher rates of profit. This process redistributes the already generated surplus value across different sectors of the economy, giving rise to a *uniform* (average) *rate of profit* and a corresponding set of prices of commodities known as *prices of production*. This argument about the emergence of prices of production will also move through two levels of abstraction. In the higher level of abstraction, we will abstract from commercial capital. After developing the argument in this simplified set-up, we will return to the argument and incorporate commercial capital – capital that is only involved in trade (pure buying and selling), but not in production (broadly understood) – into the analysis to see that the competitive process leads to the total surplus value being divided between industrial and commercial capital in the form of *industrial profit* and *commercial profit*, respectively.

In the second step of the argument in Volume III of *Capital*, we will see that some of the surplus value appropriated by industrial (or commercial) capital is further redistributed to other fractions of the ruling class that are not *directly* involved in either the production or circulation of commodities. One part of the industrial (or commercial) profit is appropriated by money capitalists as *interest*. The part of surplus value that remains with industrial capital after interest has been deducted is known as *profit of enterprise*. A part of the profit of enterprise is appropriated by owners of nonreproducible resources like land as *rent*. In both cases, the key mechanism that facilitates these latter appropriations of surplus value by money capitalists (as interest) and resource owners (as rent) is the process of bargaining between different fractions of capital.

Neither money capitalist nor natural resource owners are directly involved in the generation or realization of surplus value – the former is organized by industrial capital and the latter by commercial capital. Hence, we need to ask the question: Why do these fractions of the ruling class, that is, money capitalists and resource owners, get a share of the total surplus value even when they are not involved in its production or realization? The basic idea that Marx offers as an answer to this question is that some fractions of the ruling class are *functional* to the needs of the overall reproduction of the total capital even if they are not directly involved in its production or circulation. From the perspective of the total capitalist system, these functions are essential for the reproduction of the total social capital. It is because they perform these essential functions – essential from the perspective of the overall reproduction of capital – that these other fractions of the ruling class are able to appropriate fractions of the total surplus value as their income streams.

As we complete the argument about the distribution of surplus value by the end of this chapter, we will have understood the processes through which the income of all major fractions of the ruling class, in the forms of profit (of enterprise), interest and rent, arise. But more importantly, we will have understood that all these income streams are merely different *forms of surplus value*. This has an important implication that is worth pointing out. No matter what its form, the source of ruling-class income is the unpaid labour of productive workers.

5.1   Emergence of Prices of Production

In the classical tradition of political economy, competition between capitals occupies an extremely important analytical position. In fact, competition between capitals is the key mechanism through which the immanent laws of capitalism come to the fore, manifest themselves and impact the observable world. Marx shared this vision of competition with his classical predecessors. That is why he accords such an important role to competition in explaining the workings of a capitalist economy at lower levels of abstraction, the level where he deals with prices (of production), profit, rent and interest.

In the classical understanding, competition between capitals takes the form of the mobility of individual capitals across sectors of production in search of higher-than-average rates of profit. It is important to note that this is a long run description of the behaviour of capitalist economies, and the implicit understanding is that monopolistic or oligopolistic market structures cannot impede the mobility of capital across sectors over the long run. Hence, while the concentration and centralization of capital is very real, as analysed by Marx in Volume I of *Capital*, the development of large firms – firms with market power – does not generally annul the dynamics of competition between capitals that take the form of mobility of capitals across sectors in search of higher rates of profit.[1] For Marx, the mobility of capital across sectors is the key link between his analysis of value and surplus value in Volume I (where he

---

[1] For evidence on the tendency for the equalization of profit across sectors, see Duménil and Lévy (2002). Some special industries, like the utilities (water, electricity, telecommunication, and so on), might be partly exempt from this dynamic due to state regulation.

had abstracted from competition) and his analysis of prices of production in Volume III (where competition is introduced and plays the key role).

Thinking of the mobility of capital across sectors in search of higher rates of profit gives rise to an interesting problem. Recall that the value of a commodity, as analysed in Volume I of *Capital*, is the total socially necessary abstract labour needed for producing, and reproducing, the commodity. This value is the sum of indirect labour (the value transferred by the means of production used up in production) and direct labour (the value added to the means of production by the use of labour-power) used in producing the commodity. Now consider different branches of production, some producing consumer goods like clothing, food and footwear, and some producing machines, equipment and consumer durables. Since techniques of production would vary across different branches and commodities, the amount of means of production used per worker, that is, capital intensity, would also vary. The differences in the capital intensity would give rise to a difference of the OCC – the ratio of constant capital and variable capital – across branches of production. It seems safe to assert that the production of machines, consumer durables and luxury consumer items would certainly be more capital intensive than the production of food and many other essential items of consumption, so that the OCC would be higher in the former than in the latter sectors of production.

The difference of the OCC across branches of production has an important implication. Consider two commodities, A and B. Suppose that the mobility of workers across sectors give rise to a tendency for the rate of exploitation – the ratio of surplus value produced and variable capital advanced to purchase labour-power – to be equalized across all branches of production in the long run. Suppose that the OCC in the production of A is higher than the OCC in the production of B. This means that for every unit of capital invested (the sum of constant and variable capital), a larger proportion will be used to purchase labour-power, in the production of B than in A. Hence, for every unit of capital invested, the amount of surplus value generated will be higher in the production of B than in the production of A. Recall that the ratio of surplus value and the total capital invested is the rate of profit. Hence, if the commodities sell at their value, that is, if the sale of the commodities exactly realize the value (embodied labour) of commodities, then the rate of profit earned in the production of the commodities will be different. In the example we are considering, this means that the rate of profit in the production of B will be higher than in the production of A (because the production of B generates more surplus value for each unit of capital invested, than the production of A).

Different rates of profit in the production of different commodities cannot be a stable long run pattern. This is because fragments of capital in the lower-than-average rate of profit sectors will tend to move to higher-than-average sectors in the long run. This will reduce the output of commodities in lower-than-average rate of profit sectors and increase prices; this will, in turn, increase the rate of profit. On the other hand, the entry of capitals into higher-than-average rate of profit sectors will increase output and reduce prices in these sectors. This will push down profit rates in higher-than-average rate of profit industries. The long run equilibrium of this process of mobility of capital will be the emergence of a set of prices that will ensure equal rates of profit in all lines of production. These prices are what Marx calls *prices of production* (what some classical economists called 'natural prices').

The emergence of prices of production was referred to by Marx as the *transformation of values into prices of production*. There were several problems in how Marx carried out these computations in Volume III of *Capital*. A large literature has explored this issue, including solutions for Marx's errors, in great detail and is now known as the literature on the 'transformation problem'. Many scholars have incorrectly claimed that Marx's errors were fatal to his whole political economy. While it is true that some of Marx's claims cannot be supported, his key insights about the labour theory of value, surplus value and exploitation can be retained within an interpretation developed independently in the late 1970s by Marxist scholars Gérard Duménil and Duncan Foley. We will discuss the transformation problem in great detail in Chapter 7. In this section, we will work through Marx's procedure of transformation and locate the key problems in them. But before that, let us note two important theoretical implications of the emergence of prices of production.

5.1.1   Two Implications

When thinking of prices of production, the first point to keep in mind is that prices of production will necessarily diverge from values, that is, the ratio of prices of production of two commodities will not, in general, be equal to the ratio of the values of the commodities. In fact, this is the only way in which differences in the OCC across sectors of production can be consistent with an equalized, average, uniform rate of profit. For instance, going back to the example of the two commodities, A and B, we see that the same rate of profit in the production of both commodities will imply that the price of production of commodity A (with a higher OCC) will be higher than its value. On the other hand, the price of production of commodity B (with a lower OCC) will be lower than its value. This will become clear when we discuss Marx's example later.

Analysis of the prices of production is an application of the long-period method of analysis that we have encountered earlier in section 3.2.9. The long-period method of analysis in this context has two elements. First, the mobility of labour leads to, or gives rise to a tendency for, an equalization of the rate of exploitation across sectors. Hence, the surplus value generated in any sector will be proportional to the variable capital advanced to purchase labour-power. Second, the mobility of capital across sectors gives rise to a tendency for the rate of profit to be equalized across sectors. This means that the surplus value realized through sale of commodities will be proportional to the total value of capital advanced, not only the variable capital. Hence, prices at which commodities are sold, and which realize its value, will necessarily diverge from their values.

Does the divergence of prices of production from values invalidate the labour theory of value developed by Marx in Volume I of *Capital*? The answer is a resounding no. The level of abstraction at which the analysis in Volume I operates, it must be recalled, is 'capital in general'. Hence, the labour theory of value developed in Volume I operates at the aggregate level, that is, at the level of production of all commodities. This leaves open the possibility that there might be divergence of prices (of production) from values for individual commodities. Hence, we must always insist that the labour theory of value holds at the aggregate level, and negate the misleading impression that the labour theory of value claims convergence of prices (of production) and values for each commodity. The labour theory of value that Marx developed in the three volumes of *Capital* makes no such claims, and hence the divergence of prices of production from values does not invalidate Marx's labour theory of value.

The second point follows from the first. If prices of production diverge from values of commodities, there must necessarily be a redistribution of surplus value across sectors. Sectors with lower-than-average OCC produce relatively higher amounts of surplus value compared to sectors with higher-than-average OCC. Hence, in the process through which prices of production emerge in the long run, the former (low OCC sectors) will lose surplus value and the latter (high OCC sectors) will gain surplus value. This means that the *value realized in sale* will, in general, differ from the *value produced* for every commodity. This is an important point and takes us back to a discussion of the rate of exploitation.

So far in the text, we have used the concepts of rate of exploitation and rate of surplus value somewhat interchangeably. Both have been defined as the ratio of surplus value and variable capital. As long as prices and values of commodities do not diverge, the rate of exploitation and the rate of surplus value are the same. But once there is divergence between values and prices of commodities, the identity breaks down. The rate of exploitation refers to the sphere of production. It is to be understood as the ratio of the *surplus value generated* and the variable capital advanced to purchase labour-power. The rate of surplus value, on the other hand, refers to the sphere of exchange. It is to be understood as the ratio of *surplus value realized* and the variable capital advanced to purchase labour-power. In actual capitalist economies, we only observe the latter, but the long-period method of analysis suggests that mobility of labour imparts a tendency for equalization of the former.

The distribution of surplus value across sectors that arise with the emergence of prices of production is precisely the first analytical step of the distribution of the aggregate surplus value among fractions of capital discussed in Volume III of *Capital*. Marx uses an interesting metaphor to think of this form of redistribution.[2] He asks us to think of the total surplus value produced in a capitalist economy over a period as a pool of unpaid labour-time of the working class involved in production of commodities. Each fraction of 'industrial' capital contributes to this pool in proportion to the amount of labour-power it exploits and withdraws from the pool in proportion to the amount of capital it has invested in production, the latter ensuring that every sector of production earns the same rate of profit in the long run.

---

[2] Baumol (1974) highlighted the use of this metaphor by Marx and it has been subsequently used by Foley (1982b).

[T]he capitalists in the various spheres of production ... do not secure the surplus-value, and consequently the profit, created in their own sphere by the production of these commodities, but only as much surplus-value, and profit, as falls to the share of every aliquot part of the total social capital out of the total social surplus-value, or social profit produced by the total capital of society in all spheres of production ... The various capitalists, so far as profits are concerned, are so many stockholders in a stock company in which the shares of profit are uniformly divided for every 100 shares of capital, so that profits differ in the case of the individual capitalists only according to the amount of capital invested by each one of them in the social enterprise, according to his investment in social production as a whole, according to his shares. (Marx, 1993b, p. 258)

We can extend this metaphor further and think of rent, interest and commercial profit as further claims by different fractions of the ruling class – landlords, money capitalists and commercial capitalists – on this pool of surplus value created by the exploitation of labour in the production of commodities. To understand the concept of price of production and uniform rate of profit better, let us work through an example that Marx used in Volume III of Capital. Working through the example will also allow us to see clearly the mistakes Marx made while transforming values in prices of production.

Example

Consider an economy with five sectors.[3] Letting C and V denote constant and variable capital, S/V denote the rate of exploitation, W denote the value of the commodity and r denote the rate of profit, Table 5.1 summarizes key parameters of this economy. From the information provided in Table 5.1, we see that the sectors of the economy have different OCC, that is, ratio of constant capital and variable capital. Sector I has an OCC of 4, sector II 2.33, sector III 1.5, sector IV 5.67 and sector V has an OCC of 19. On the other hand, mobility of labour ensures that each sector face the same rate of exploitation of 100 per cent.

---

[3] This example was used by Marx in Chapter 9, Volume III of *Capital*.

Table 5.1   Unequal rates of profit

	C	V	e	W	r (%)
Sector I	80	20	1	120	20
Sector II	70	30	1	130	30
Sector III	60	40	1	140	40
Sector IV	85	15	1	115	15
Sector V	95	5	1	105	5

Source: This example is based on Marx (1993b, p. 255).

Note: C = constant capital; V = variable capital; S = surplus value; e = rate of exploitation; W = value; $r = S/(C + V)$ = rate of profit.

Let us compute the rate of profit that would be earned by capitalists in the five sectors *if every sector realized the surplus value it generated*. For sector I, the surplus value generated is 20 (because the rate of surplus value is 1 and the variable capital is 20). Since the constant capital used in sector I is 80, the value of the commodity of this sector is 120, which is the sum of constant capital (80), variable capital (20) and surplus value (20). Hence, the rate of profit in this sector, if it realized the total surplus value it generated, would be 20 per cent (= 20/100). In an analogous manner, we can compute the rate of profit in sector II as 30 per cent, in sector III as 40 per cent, in sector IV as 15 per cent and in sector V as 5 per cent. This is given in the last column in Table 5.1. Note that sectors with high OCC have low rates of profit and sectors with low OCC have high rates of profit.

The fact that different sectors have different rates of profit implies that this cannot be a situation of long run equilibrium. Capitalists in sectors with low rates of profit, and these are the sectors with high OCC, would move into sectors with high rates of profit. This movement would continue until capital invested in every sector earned the same average, uniform rate of profit. But how do we calculate the average rate of profit?

To calculate the average rate of profit, we divide the total surplus value generated by the total cost of production, that is, the sum of the total constant capital and the total variable capital. In the example given in Table 5.1, the total surplus value is 110, the total constant capital is 390 and the total variable capital is 110. Hence, the average rate of profit is 22 per cent (which is 110/(390 + 110)). Once we know the average or uniform rate of profit, we can go back to Table 5.1 and identify sectors as 'surplus profit' and 'deficit profit' sectors. A sector which has a higher than average rate of profit in Table 5.1 will be called a 'surplus profit' sector, that is, if this sector were to realize all the surplus value it generated it would end up with a rate of profit that was higher than the economy's average rate of profit of 22 per cent. In analogous manner and using the same intuition, a sector with lower-than-average rate of profit in Table 5.1 can be called a 'deficit profit' sector.

The average rate of profit will allow us to calculate the price of production for each sector. The price of production in any sector must be sum of the capital outlay, that is, the sum of constant and variable capital, and 22 per cent profit on the capital outlay. This is the only way each sector can earn the same, average, uniform rate of profit, which in this example is 22 per cent. This computation is shown in Table 5.2, where P refers to the price of production (all other symbols have the same meaning as in Table 5.1).

Table 5.2   Equalized rates of profit and prices of production

	C	V	e	W	P	P − W	S/V	r (%)
Sector I	80	20	1	120	122	2	1.1	22
Sector II	70	30	1	130	122	-8	0.73	22
Sector III	60	40	1	140	122	-18	0.55	22
Sector IV	85	15	1	115	122	7	1.47	22
Sector V	95	5	1	105	122	17	4.4	22

Source: This example is based on Marx (1993b, p. 256).

Note: C = constant capital; V = variable capital; S = surplus value; e = rate of exploitation; W = value; S/V = rate of surplus value; $r = S/(C + V)$ = rate of profit; P = price of production.

Note how the emergence of prices of production and the average rate of profit is a process of redistribution of the total surplus value created in production. For instance, sector V, which is the sector with the highest OCC, was a deficit profit sector, that is, a sector which would have earned a below-average rate of profit if it had realized the surplus value it generated (recall that the average rate of profit is 22 per cent and sector V's rate of profit in Table 5.1 is 5 per cent). After the emergence of prices of production, it gains 17 units of surplus value (as can be seen from the column $P − W$). On the other hand, sector III, which is the sector with the lowest OCC, was a surplus profit sector, that is, a sector which would have earned an above-average rate of profit if it had realized the surplus value it generated (recall that the average rate of profit is 22 per cent and sector III's rate of profit in Table 5.1 is 40 per cent). After prices of production have emerged, it loses 18 units of surplus value.

The complete sectoral redistribution of surplus value is shown in Table 5.2. We see clearly that the total surplus value is redistributed across sectors through the competitive process. Sectors with higher-than-average OCC gain surplus value, and sectors with lower-than-average OCC lose surplus value. The redistribution of surplus value is neatly reflected in the divergence between the rate of exploitation and the rate of surplus value in each sector. At one extreme, we have sector V, which gains surplus value in the process of redistribution. For sector V, while the rate of exploitation is 1, the rate of surplus value is 4.4. At the other extreme, we have sector III, which loses surplus value during the process of emergence of prices of production. While the rate of exploitation is 1 for sector III, its rate of surplus value is only 0.55.

For later use, let us use symbols to express the computations that underlies Table 5.2. If the constant and variable capital used per unit of a commodity is denoted by C and V, respectively, and the average rate of profit in the economy is denoted by α, then the price of production for the commodity, P, is given by: $P = (C + V)(1 + \alpha)$. How do we get this expression? Let us start from the cost of production: $C + V$. The price of production of the commodity is the price which gives the average rate of profit on the cost incurred, that is, $\alpha * (C + V)$. Thus, the price must recover the cost and on top of that must give the average rate of profit. Hence, the price must be $(C + V) + \alpha * (C + V)$, which is $(C + V)(1 + \alpha)$.

Before closing this discussion, let us quickly note two mistakes that Marx made while calculating prices of production (which I have reproduced and explained in the earlier paragraphs). First, Marx calculated the price of production of the output, but did not use price of production of inputs. This seems problematic because the same commodity that is sold as output by some capitalist firm will be bought as input by some other capitalist firm (or for consumption by workers of capitalists). Hence, the same commodity must have only one price, the price of production. Therefore, Marx's first mistake was that he did not consistently transform (from value to prices of production) both inputs and outputs. For instance, while computing the price of production for Section I earlier, we used the value of constant and variable capital as 80 and 20, respectively. These are value magnitudes. To be consistent, we should have used the price magnitudes of the constant and variable capital. Second, the rate of profit that Marx used for his calculation, and which I have reproduced earlier, is a ratio of value magnitudes. In actual capitalist economies, the rate of profit is a price magnitude. Hence, Marx's second error was that he did not use the correct definition of the rate of profit. For instance, we computed the uniform rate of profit as the ratio of 110 and 500. The former is the total surplus value and the latter is the total capital outlay. Both are value magnitudes. To be consistent, we need to compute the rate of profit using price magnitudes of both the profit income and the capital advanced. We will see in Chapter 7 that both errors can be relatively easily addressed.

Further Readings

- Marx's analysis of the emergence of prices of production and the average rate of profit are contained in Marx (1993b, Chapters 8–10). An excellent exposition is available in Foley (1986b, Chapter 6, pp. 91–104).

5.2   Detour: Technical Change

Following Marx's presentation in Volume III of *Capital*, I will take a detour to discuss the issue of technological change in capitalist economies, before resuming discussion of the distribution of surplus value in the form of commercial profit. The detour is important in its own right and holds a very special place in Marxist discussion of crisis tendencies in capitalism. Of course, the immediate context for this detour is Marx's discussion of the 'law of the tendential fall in the rate of profit' (LTFRP) in part III of Volume III of *Capital*. After discussing the emergence of the general (or average, or uniform) rate of profit in Section II, which we have discussed earlier, and before discussing the various forms that surplus value takes, Marx advanced the claim, in Section III, that the general rate of profit had a 'tendency' to fall over time. Marx seems to have attached lot of importance to this 'law', seeing it as the mystery that all of political economy had been trying to but failed to have solved, seeing it also as the expression of the deep contradictions of capitalism that highlighted the historical limitedness of that system of social production. Just like the literature surrounding the transformation problem,

Marxist and non-Marxist scholarship have produced an enormous literature around the LTFRP. In this section, we will get a quick introduction to the central issues discussed in this literature. A more detailed discussion of technical change and profitability can be found in Chapter 6.

5.2.1 Technical Change, Use-values and Value

Technological progress, in the Marxist framework, refers to changes in processes of production that increase the productivity of labour. The productivity of labour is always to be measured in terms of use-values. Productivity of labour relates to the following question: What magnitude of use-values does an hour of labour produce? When technological progress takes place and the productivity of labour increases, each hour of labour is able to produce a larger quantity of use-values; or, the same quantity of use-values can be produced in less time. For Marx, the sum total of use-values constitute the wealth of a society. Hence, an increase in the magnitude of use-values constitutes an increase in the wealth of a society. Marx highlights this with a simple example: two coats can clothe two persons; one coat only one (Marx, 1992, Chapter 1). Hence, when labour becomes more productive, the potential wealth of that society increases. That is the key importance of the concept of labour productivity.

What is the impact of technological progress on the value of commodities? If technological progress makes labour more productive, each hour of labour produces a larger quantity of use-values. Hence, the labour embodied in, or required to produce, each unit of the commodity falls. This implies that with technological progress, the value of commodities fall. Thus, technological progress has contradictory effects: it increases the quantity of use-values produced by labour and it leads to a fall in value of each unit of commodities.

We have discussed these issues in detail in section 3.1.5, and to refresh our memory, let us quickly look at an example. Suppose in 1980, it takes 4 hours of labour to produce a coat. In 1990, a new sewing machine becomes available that allows tailors to produce each coat in 2 hours. Hence, a tailor working for 8 hours a day would produce 2 coats every day in 1980; and in 1990, the same tailor would produce 4 coats in a day. The new sewing machine has made the labour of the tailor more productive, and this is reflected in the larger quantity of use-values, in this case coats, that tailors can produce in each hour. When we come to value calculations, we abstract from the concrete form of labour, in this case the labour of the tailors. Abstracting from the concrete form of labour means that one hour of labour of the tailor in 1980 is the same as one hour of labour of the tailor in 1990 – so far as its value-creating capacities are concerned. Thus, one hour of abstract labour of a *given complexity* is always expressed in the same magnitude of value, irrespective of its productivity.[4] This then implies that the value of each unit of the commodity declines. In this example, the labour-time necessary to produce a coat falls by half between 1980 and 1990. Hence, the value of a coat would also fall by half.

> However then productive power may vary, the same labour [i.e. labour of the same complexity], exercised during equal periods of time, always yields equal amounts of value. But it will yield, during equal periods of time, different quantities of value in use [use-values]; more, if the productive power rises, fewer, if it falls. The same change in productive power, which increases the fruitfulness of labour, and, in consequence the quantity of use-values produced by that labour, will diminish the total value of this increased quantity of use-values, provided such change shorten the total labour-time necessary for their production; and *vice versa*. (Marx, 1992, Chapter 1)

5.2.2   Process of Technical Change

Anticipating discussions in later volumes, Marx offers a picture of the process of technological progress in capitalist economies in Chapter 12 of Volume I. Consider the cotton textile industry. Suppose a silk shirt can be produced, using the currently prevailing technology and average intensity of work, in 10 hours. Now imagine an innovator capitalist firm inventing a new technology of production that would allow the same silk shirt to be produced in 8 hours. It is in the interest of the innovator firm to search for and adopt such new techniques of production. This is because the new technique would reduce the cost of producing the commodity – in terms of labour hours – and would thereby give its adopter an edge over its competitors. Why?

---

[4]We have seen earlier that degrees of complexity increase the value-creating capacity of labour. Hence, when Marx states that the exercise of the same labour during equal periods of time always creates the same magnitude of value, he must mean by 'same' labour of the same degree of complexity.

The value of the silk shirt is determined by the socially necessary abstract labour needed to produce it. The benchmark that defines the 'socially necessary' amount of labour is given by the average technology of production. Even when the innovator adopts the new technique of production, all other capitalist producers continue using the old technology. Hence, the old technology continues to define the social benchmark. Therefore, the value of the silk shirt remains unchanged even when the innovator capitalist adopts the new technique of production. The superior technique of production used by the innovator means that her commodities have lower labour embodied than the social average. To distinguish the innovator capitalist from the rest, Marx uses the concept of 'individual value' to refer to the labour embodied in the commodity of the innovator and 'social value' to refer to the socially necessary labour needed to produce the commodity. Hence, using Marx's terminology, the individual value of the silk shirt produced by the innovator capitalist is lower than the social value, and the difference between social and individual value is the *extra* surplus value earned by the innovator.

We can also express the same argument using the concept of price. If we adopt the level of abstraction that is proper for Volume I, then the price of the silk shirt would be proportional to its value. Hence, the price at which silk shirts are sold remains unchanged. But the innovator capitalist has, because of the new technology she has adopted, managed to produce shirts with 20 per cent less labour. So, by selling the silk shirt at the going price, the innovator is able to make extra profits, that is, profits over and above what her competitors are able to make. The lure of super-normal profits is a strong incentive for technological progress in capitalism.

5.2.3   *Technical Change and the Average Rate of Profit*

While it is easy to see that the rate of profit must increase for the innovator capitalist who introduces a better technique of production, it is not so easy to see the trajectory of the average (or uniform) rate of profit. Marx did not explore this issue in Chapter 12 of Volume I because the concept of the 'average' rate of profit had not yet been developed. After discussing the notion of the average rate of profit in part II of Volume III of *Capital*, he returns to this issue in part III of Volume III of *Capital* with a discussion of the LTFRP.[5]

---

[5] The discussion in this section draws on Basu (2019).

The primary relationship between different fragments of capital is one of intense and continuous competition. In the competitive struggle, those capitalists prosper who can earn higher rates of profit, and one of the surest ways of earning higher rates of profit is by reducing costs. Hence, the incessant competitive struggle at the very heart of capitalism enforces a constant search for cost-reducing methods of production. Since labour is a key, and costly, input into production – that capitalists get by purchasing labour-power and extracting labour from what they have purchased – there is every incentive to search for and adopt methods of production that use less labour. Capitalism, therefore, is systematically geared towards developing and adopting *labour-saving* technological changes.

The search for reducing cost by adopting labour-saving techniques of production often happens through the replacement of labour by machinery. Thus, the proportion between variable and constant capital shifts in favour of the latter, as capitalist firms adopt labour-saving technological change. But the adoption of labour-saving technological change is not limited to a few industries, it is witnessed across the whole capitalist economy. Hence, according to Marx, competitive pressures get reflected in the pronounced tendency for the economy-wide average OCC (the ratio of constant and variable capital) to increase. Since the average rate of profit, r, is given by

$$r = \frac{(s/v)}{1 + (c/v)}$$

where s/v is the average rate of surplus value and c/v is the average OCC, technological change imparts a downward trajectory to the average rate of profit, r.

This is Marx's celebrated LTFRP. If correct, it shows that capitalism undermines itself. After all, the main driver of the capitalist system is the search for surplus value. The average rate of profit is the total surplus value expressed as a ratio of the total capital outlay that generated it. If the average rate of profit has a long run tendency to fall, coming from within its own logic of competition and technological change, then capitalism's own dynamic would choke off the main element that drives the system. Looked at in another way, the main strength of the capitalist system, its technological progressivity, would, if Marx's argument was correct, also be the source of its greatest weakness – the long run tendency of the average rate of profit to fall.

Unfortunately, Marx's argument establishing the LTFRP is not watertight. There are several problems. First, the rate of profit would have a tendency to fall with an increase in the OCC only if the rate of surplus value did not rise as well. Marx has not given any argument as to why the rate of surplus value should not rise by itself or as a result of the same set of forces that increases the OCC. The second problem is that, even if we assume that the rate of surplus value remains unchanged, the result that Marx intends to establish does not follow. This is because the OCC is a value-concept and Marx's description has only established that there is a tendency for the physical replacement of workers by machines. But technological change in the machine-producing sector can lead to a fall in the value of machines. Thus, a larger quantity of machines used by each worker, which comes from labour-saving technological change, need not be reflected in a rise of the ratio of c (constant capital) and v (variable capital) because both terms in the ratio are denoted in terms of value and not in terms of physical magnitudes. The third problem is that Marx defines the rate of profit using value categories. In fact, he should define the rate of profit using price categories and then use this correctly defined rate of profit in his argument.

Even if we ignore the above three problems, there is an additional one we will have to confront. If technological change is bound to lead to a fall in the average rate of profit, then why would capitalists – who would surely know this – adopt labour-saving techniques of production in the first place? The celebrated contribution of Okishio (1961) demonstrated a stronger result: if capitalists behave as we expect them to behave, that is, to operate profit-maximizing firms, then the process of technological change will necessarily lead to a *rise* in the average rate of profit! Thus, not only does Marx's LTFRP not hold, in fact, the opposite is true – the average rate of profit has a long run tendency to rise because of profit-maximizing behaviour of firms.

5.2.4 *Marx or Okishio?*

There are two problems in the argument of Okishio (1961) about the tendency of the average profit rate to rise. First, there is an implicit suggestion that profit-maximizing behaviour of capitalist firms is incompatible with a decline in the *average* rate of profit. Second, the conclusion about the rise in the rate of profit rests on a specific, and questionable, assumption about the movement of the real wage rate.

Let us start with the first problem. Is it not possible for the adoption of a new technique of production to increase the rate of profit of the innovator (the first firm to adopt the new technique) and yet to lead to a fall in the average rate of profit? The answer is in the affirmative. The innovator capitalist, by searching for and adopting a new technique of production, is able to produce the relevant commodity at a cost that is lower than the social average. Since the value of the commodity is determined by the social conditions of production, it remains unchanged when one capitalist firm adopts a new technique of production. Hence, by selling the commodity at its ruling price (which is its value in the context of Volume I of *Capital*), the innovator firm is able to earn a super-normal rate of profit. This much we have seen earlier.

Now let us think as to how other capitalist firms react to the innovator capitalist. The fact that the innovator capitalist earns a rate of profit which is higher than what other capitalists in the industry earn is bound to create strong incentives to find out the details of the new technique of production, by hook or by crook. Hence, over time, there is bound to be a diffusion of the new technology across the industry (or the whole capitalist economy). When the new technique becomes widely used, it defines the new benchmark for the socially necessary labour needed to produce the commodity. Hence, the new benchmark determines the value of the commodity (which is now lower than before the widespread adoption of the new technique of production). Under certain conditions, it is possible for the average rate of profit to be lower after the new technique is adopted by all capitalist firms than what prevailed before the adoption of the new technique. Considering the conditions under which this might happen takes us to the second problem in the argument of Okishio (1961).

A key assumption of the analysis in Okishio (1961) is that the *real wage rate remains unchanged* before and after the adoption and diffusion of the new technique of production. This is the key assumption that drives the algebra of his result about the rise in the rate of profit, and it is easy to see why. Since the new technique of production reduces the overall cost of production, it leads to a fall in the value of the commodity. If the real wage rate remains unchanged, the total increase in the productivity of labour is appropriated by capitalists, and the rate of profit would rise. But is there any reason to assume that the real wage rate must remain constant during and after the process of technological change? No. The real wage rate is the result of class struggle between capitalists and workers and there are no economic arguments that can rule out the possibility of its increase during the process of technical change. If conditions of class struggle result in an increase in the real wage rate during periods of technological change, then Okishio's (1961) result will no longer obtain. In fact, it is possible, in a simple aggregate model of a capitalist economy, to compute a Marx-Okishio threshold for the rate of growth of the real wage rate that accompanies technological change. The Marx-Okishio threshold is a function of the rates of change of labour productivity and capital productivity, and if the actual real wage rate rises faster than the threshold, the average rate of profit will fall; if the growth rate of the actual real wage falls below the threshold, then the average rate of profit will rise.

We can conclude this discussion by noting that there are no theoretical grounds to claim that due to technological change, the rate of profit will have a tendency to always fall (as Marx claimed) or that it will have a tendency to always rise (as Okishio claimed). The impact of technological change on the average rate of profit depends crucially on labour-market dynamics. If the real wage rate rises sharply during the period of technological change, then the rate of profit tends to fall; on the other hand, if the real wage rate does not rise fast enough, then the rate of profit might rise. Hence, there is no necessary contradiction between the claims advanced by Marx and Okishio, as has been highlighted by Marxist scholars (Foley, 1986b; Laibman, 1992). We will discuss this issue in greater detail in Chapter 6.

Readings

- Marx's ideas on technological change can be found in Chapters 10 and 12 in Volume I and in part III in Volume III of *Capital*. The modern literature on the effect of technological change on the average of profit can be traced back to the path-breaking contributions in Okishio (1961, 1963). For an elaboration and extension of Okishio's argument, see Roemer (1978); for a critique of the Okishio argument, see Shaikh (1978); and for an account that allows for both a falling and a rising rate of profit, see Foley (1986b) and Laibman (1992).

5.3 Commercial Profit

With the important detour on technological progress completed, we can now return to our discussion of the distribution of surplus value. Once commodities are produced, they need to be sold to realize the value, and hence surplus value, generated in their production through the exploitation of labour. Consideration of the circuit of capital shows that the reproduction of capital requires the conversion of commodities into money, through sale of the finished product, $C' - M'$, as much as it requires the conversion of money into commodities, through the capital outlay of capitalist firms, $M - C$:

$$M - C\{MP, LP\} \cdots (P) \cdots C' - M'$$

It is only when the capital, in the form of money, laid out in the production of commodities has returned to its monetary form that the circuit of capital gets completed. Marx refers to these commodity-money and money-commodity conversions as 'metamorphosis of form' of capital, and notes that

> Capital is always involved in this movement of transition, this metamorphosis of form. In as much as this function acquires independent life as a special function of a special capital and is fixed by the division of labour as a function that falls to a particular species of capitalists ... [we have] commercial capital. (Marx, 1993b, p. 379)

Following Marx, we can therefore identify commercial profit as the part of surplus value that is appropriated by commercial capital.[6]

To understand the source of commercial profit, consider a vertically integrated capitalist firm, A, which not only produces commodities but also maintains a network of shops to sell the commodities to the ultimate consumer. This is the method of analysis that Marx suggests in the following passage:

---

[6]To be more precise, the fraction of capital that specializes in trading is referred to by Marx as *merchant or trading capital*. He divides merchant capital into two sub-types: *commercial capital* and *money-dealing capital*. The former carries out the more important functions of trade, that is, buying and selling of commodities, and the latter deals with the technical functions of circulation of money, for example, payment and receipt of money, settlement of balances, storage of money, and so on. We will absorb the latter function into the former and refer to the fraction of capital that specializes in both as commercial capital.

Since commercial capital is nothing at all but the form in which a part of the industrial capital functioning in the circulation process has become autonomous, all questions relating to it must be resolved in this way: the problem must at the outset be put in the form in which the phenomenon peculiar to commercial capital do not yet appear independently but are still in direct connection with industrial capital, of which commercial capital is a branch. (Marx, 1993b, p. 412)

Understanding 'production' broadly – as explained in the previous chapter – to include production proper, storage, warehousing and transportation, we can see that in the *pure act of selling*, nothing but a transfer of ownership of the commodity takes place, from the capitalist firm to the consumer. Hence, no value, and hence no surplus value, is created during the pure act of selling the commodity. With this understanding, we can divide up the set of activities of the capitalist firm into two parts. One part is involved in producing the commodity, where production is understood broadly. The other, complementary, set of activities are those that are involved in selling the commodity, that is, pure trade. From the fact that trade does not create any value follows the conclusion that the second set of activities is supported by the value, and hence surplus value, created in production and transportation. From the perspective of the firm, then, the whole set of activities involved in pure trade are *essential*, not because they produce surplus value, but because they *help in realizing surplus value*. After all, without selling the commodity, the firm cannot realize the value, and hence the surplus value, created during production.

Now suppose, firm A gets broken up into two smaller firms, B and C. The first firm, B, is involved in producing (including its storage, warehousing, and so on) and transporting the commodity to the location where it is sold; and the second firm, C, specializes in pure trade, that is, only in selling the commodity to the ultimate consumer. Comparing these two smaller firms to the vertically integrated firm discussed above, we see that firm C – the one specializing in trade – cannot create any value or surplus value. This is because its activity involves only a transfer of ownership of the commodity to the consumer, a mere 'metamorphosis of form' of capital – from a commodity form to a money form. While C creates no surplus value, nonetheless it is essential for the capitalist economy because it helps in *realizing the surplus value* created during production by B. The total income, and hence also the profit, of C comes out of the total surplus value generated in B (which is also the total surplus value realized by the vertically integrated firm A). How does the sharing of surplus value happen? Firm B sells the commodity to firm C at a price which is lower than the price of production of the commodity; firm C sells the commodity to the final consumer at its price of production. It is in this way that the two firms share the total surplus value contained in the output, which was realized, in total, by the vertically integrated firm. The first firm is willing to give up a part of the surplus to the second firm because the latter helps in realizing the surplus value generated by it. This is the source of 'commercial profit'.

In more concrete terms, commercial capital is functional to the overall reproduction of industrial capital in various ways. First, it shortens the overall circulation time of the aggregate social capital. Therefore, it reduces the turnover time of capital and increases the amount of surplus value generated by the system. Second, by using its expertise about marketing and trade, commercial capital extends the market and facilitates a division of labour among different fractions of capital. The division of labour, in turn, promotes the productivity of industrial capital. Third, by specializing in the functions of circulation, it reduces the magnitude of capital confined to the sphere of circulation, which, in turn, increases the magnitude of capital available in the sphere of production and increases the generation of surplus value (Marx, 1993b, pp. 392–93).

The splitting up of the surplus value between industrial capital (represented by firm B) and commercial capital (represented by firm C) can be made more precise by a more refined computation of prices of production. Whereas we had earlier included only industrial capital in the computation of prices of production, we now need to extend the analysis and include commercial capital. This is because commercial capital would need the same rate of profit as industrial capital to continue its operation. Moreover, the whole operation of trade requires capital to be laid out in the purchase of means of production – offices, stationary, equipment, and so on – and labour-power. The capital tied up in these trading activities will need to earn the same average rate of profit as the capital tied up as industrial capital. Hence, when we compute the average rate of profit, we need to use the sum total of industrial and commercial capital rather than industrial capital only. This principle allows us to see the division of surplus value between industrial and commercial capital in a transparent manner.

Example

To understand how the total surplus value is divided between industrial and commercial capital, let us go back to the example we worked with in the previous section (for details, see Tables 5.1 and 5.2). Instead of breaking up industrial capital into five sectors, let us club it all together into one so that for industrial capital, the constant capital is 390 and variable capital is 110. The new element that we now introduce is commercial capital. Let us assume that commercial capital that facilitates the sale of the commodities and helps in realizing the surplus value is of size 50 – with 40 laid out in means of production and 10 used to purchase labour-power.[7]

The first thing to note is that commercial capital does not create any value or surplus value. Hence, the total surplus value generated in this economy is exactly of the same magnitude as before. Assuming, as in the example of the previous section, a rate of surplus value of 1, the total surplus value generated in the economy is 110 (because the total variable capital is 110). The second thing to note relates to the details of the computation of the average rate of profit. Since industrial and commercial capital both participate in the formation of prices of production, the average rate of profit is obtained by dividing the total surplus value by the total capital advanced of 550. Note that this total is the sum of industrial capital advanced, 500, and commercial capital advanced, 50. Hence, the average rate of profit in this economy is 20 per cent once we take commercial capital into account (instead of 22 per cent that we had computed by ignoring commercial capital).

The output is now sold in two steps. In the first step, industrial capital sells the output to commercial capital at a price of p_1, say. In the next step, commercial capital sells the output to the final consumer at a price of p_2, say. To be consistent with Marx's analysis of the competitive process, p_2 must be equal to the price of production of the commodity, that is, the final price of the commodity has to be its price of production. What is the magnitude of p_2? Since the total capital advanced (industrial and commercial) is 550 and the average of profit is 20 per cent, the price of production is $550 * 1.2 = 660$. Hence, $p_2 = 660$. What is the magnitude of p_1, the price at which industrial capital sells the commodity to commercial capital? This price will

---

[7]This example is a variation on an example that Marx works with in Chapter 17, Volume III. It is conceptually important to note that the wage cost of the commercial capitalist does not function as variable capital. This is because it does not increment itself by generating surplus value (see discussion in Marx [1993b, p. 413]).

be such that it gives industrial capital a 20 per cent rate of profit on its capital advance of 500. Hence, $p_1 = 500 * 1.2 = 600$. Notice that in this two-step process of sale, two things happen: (*a*) the commodity is sold at its price of production to the consumer and (*b*) the total surplus value of 110 is divided between industrial and commercial capital in proportion to their magnitudes – the former gets 100 and the latter gets 10.[8]

Readings
  • Marx's discussion of commercial profit is contained in Marx (1993b, Chapters 16–19). Useful expositions are available in Sweezy (1942, Chapter XII) and Foley (1986b, Chapter 7, pp. 116–18).

5.4   Productive and Unproductive Labour

Commercial profit, as we have just seen, is a part of the surplus value created by industrial capital that is appropriated by commercial capital. Commercial capital does not produce surplus value; it helps in realizing surplus value. And for carrying out this essential function, it is able to appropriate a part of the surplus value created by industrial capital. This means that the workers employed by commercial capital do not create value or surplus value. This is an example of the category of unproductive workers that Marx takes over, with significant modification and clarification, from classical thinkers and discusses in some detail in Chapter 16 of Volume I, and again in Chapter 6 in Volume II and Chapter 17 of Volume III. Later Marxist scholars have clarified these issues and my presentation here draws heavily on the excellent treatment of this issue in Shaikh and Tonak (1994, Chapter 2).

5.4.1   Basic Activities of Social Reproduction

To understand the distinction between productive and unproductive labour, it will help to make an analytically prior distinction between production and non-production activities. The difference between the two is crucial and also transparent: while production results in the creation of new use-values

---

[8]In Chapter 7, we will discuss a more accurate way of computing prices of production. In such a framework, we can easily accommodate commercial capital by allowing for heterogenous types of labour and specifying some sectors and some types of labour as producing zero surplus value. For details, see section 7.A.5.

(wealth) on a net basis, non-production does not result in the creation of new use-values. Thus, *production is the creation of use-values and non-production is the using up of use-values.* Non-production activities can, in turn, be divided into three mutually exclusive and exhaustive groups: distribution, social maintenance and personal consumption.

- *Distribution* involves activities that transfer use-values, titles to use-values or sums of money from one set of economic agents to another. Using Marx's terminology that we saw in the previous chapter, distribution includes activities associated with the process of circulation of capital, that is, the metamorphosis of forms of value, either of the form $M - C$ or of the form $C' - M'$;

- *Social maintenance* refers to all activities that are geared towards the maintenance and reproduction of the social order, and include activities carried out by the police, army, judiciary and other arms of the state;

- *Personal consumption* includes all activities involved in the maintenance and reproduction of individuals within the social order.

All schools of economic thought distinguish between production and consumption. Moreover, they agree that production creates wealth and consumption uses up wealth. But there is a a key difference between the neoclassical and classical-Marxian traditions with regard to the characterization of the activities of distribution and social maintenance. For the neoclassical (and even Keynesian) tradition, these two activities – distribution and social maintenance – are understood as production as long they are marketable and some economic agent in the economy is willing to pay for the activity or the product arising from that activity. On the other hand, the classical-Marxian tradition differs sharply from this understanding and argues that distribution and social maintenance should not be understood as production; rather, they should be understood as social consumption. This is because they use up use-values (instead of creating them).

These alternative classifications of the basic activities of social reproduction by the neoclassical/Keynesian and classical-Marxian traditions are depicted in Figure 5.1 and can be summarized as follows:

- for the neoclassical/Keynesian tradition, personal consumption is coterminous with total consumption and total production is the sum of distribution, social maintenance and production proper;
- for the classical-Marxian tradition, distribution and social maintenance together make up social consumption, and the sum of social and personal consumption gives total consumption; total production, on the other hand, is just production proper.[9]

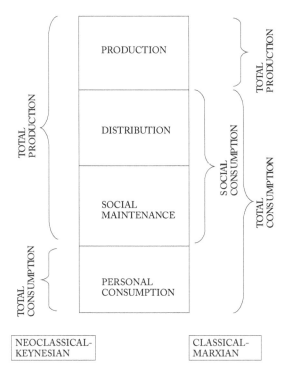

Figure 5.1   Categories of social activities
Source: Basu (2017).

The distinction between production and non-production activities allows us to separate out all labour that creates use-values, and hence value, from

---

[9]Production of use-values can, in turn, be broken up into two parts: (*a*) production of use-value not mediated by exchange, that is, use-values produced within households, within arms of the state, or in peasant communities and (*b*) production of commodities.

those that do not. Since a commodity can have exchange value only when it is a use-value, all labour that is not involved in production activities cannot create value (and, hence, also surplus value).[10] A use-value can either be a good or a service. When the use-value is a good, labour is materialized in a physical object. On the other hand, when the use-value is a service, the labour only creates a useful effect, without being materialized in any physical object. In the case of production of goods, there is an easily identifiable *physical* net output. Hence, there is no doubt that all labour involved in production of goods is located in the domain of production activities. On the other hand, in the case of services, there is no physical net output. Hence, only *some* types of services-production activities should be counted as falling within the domain of production and others should be excluded from that domain. We will return to this important issue in section 5.4.4.

5.4.2 Unproductive Labour in Capitalism

Within the domain of production activities, that is, activities that do create use-values, we need to distinguish three different *relations of production* under which the labour is performed:

- *Labour that creates use-values for direct use.* Here, the labour is performed outside the domain of commodity production because the product is for use and not for sale; hence, this labour does not create a commodity.

- *Labour that creates use-values for sale (to generate income) but not for profit.* Here, the reference it to petty commodity producers where there is no separation between labour-power and the means of labour. Thus, even though the product is a commodity, and hence, has value, there is no surplus value generated because there is no wage labour.

- *Labour that creates use-values for sale to generate profit (where labour takes the form of wage labour).* This is wage labour working in the service of capital to produce a commodity for sale. Hence, this labour creates value and also surplus value.

According to Marx, the first type of labour creates use-values, the second type creates use-values and value, and the third type creates use-values, value and surplus value.

---

[10]'Value is independent of the particular use-value by which it is borne, but a use-value of some kind has to act as its bearer' (Marx, 1992, p. 295).

Our capitalist has two objectives: in the first place, he wants to produce a use-value which has exchange value, i.e., an article destined to be sold, a commodity; and secondly he wants to produce a commodity greater in value than the sum of the values of the commodities used to produce it, namely the means of production and the labour-power he purchased with his good money on the open market. His aim is to produce not only a use-value, but a commodity; not only use-value, but value; and not just value, but also surplus-value. (Marx, 1992, p. 293)

On the basis of this understanding, *Marx defines productive labour in capitalist economies as all labour involved in production activities that generates surplus value*.[11] All other labour is defined to be unproductive because it does not generate surplus value (and hence, capital).[12]

While a detailed sectoral analysis of a mature capitalist economy to identify industries that would fall within the domain of 'production activities' is beyond the scope of this chapter – the interested reader should refer to (Shaikh and Tonak, 1994) – we can certainly identify two large sectors in all capitalist economies that fall outside the domain of production activities: trade and finance. While all activities that are involved in the production and transportation of commodities (from the site of production to the site of consumption) are part of 'production activities' broadly defined, trading activities, which transfer existing use-values or titles to existing use-values from one economic agent to another, and financial sector activities, which transfer sums of money or titles to financial assets from one economic agent to another, are non-production activities. Hence, these two sectors do not create value or surplus value. Thus, the total income – including wages and profit, if the sector is organized along capitalist lines – generated in these sectors comes from a redistribution of surplus value generated in capitalist

---

[11]When we use this definition to look at labour *within* capitalist enterprises involved in production activities, we need to further distinguish between, on the one hand, labour involved in production activities and, on the other, supervisory and managerial labour, with the understanding that only the former produces surplus value. The salary of the latter comes from the surplus value created by the workers involved in production.

[12]According to Marx, the way we understand the difference between productive and unproductive labour is specific to each mode of production. One cannot use transhistorical criteria to pin down the difference. Moreover, the difference between the two does not have anything to do with rationality, usefulness or necessity. For capitalism, it is a narrow and precise definition based on whether that labour creates surplus value, that is, whether it is productive of capital.

production. The income of the capitalists involved in trading, that is, pure buying and selling, is called 'commercial profit' (as we have seen in section 5.3); and the income of the capitalists involved in financial activities is broadly called 'interest'. We will discuss the category of interest in section 5.5, but before that we must address two important issues: Are unproductive workers exploited like productive workers? Are services unproductive activities?

5.4.3   Are Unproductive Workers Exploited?

Our discussion of the generation of surplus value in section 3.3.2 demonstrated that the working is exploited because it produces surplus value for the capitalist class. They add more value to the output than they get back in the form of their wage income. The difference is the surplus value, and its existence rests on the exploitation of the working class. This naturally raises the question: since workers who perform unproductive labour in capitalist firms do not produce value and surplus value, can they be exploited? The answer is in the affirmative. It is true that workers who perform unproductive labour do not produce value and surplus value. Hence, we cannot use the concept of surplus value to understand the exploitation of unproductive labour. But we can use the more primitive concept of surplus labour to address the issue.

With respect to the work done by a worker, we can define surplus labour as the difference between the labour she performs for the capitalist (who employs her) and the social labour-time equivalent of her wage. In a context where prices are proportional to values and workers consume all of their income (the classical savings assumption), the social labour-time equivalent of her wage would be equal to the labour embodied in her consumption bundle. But when prices diverge from values and/or workers save some fraction of their income, this latter definition cannot be used. Hence, we will use the more general definition: surplus labour = labour performed by a worker *less* the social labour-time equivalent of her wage income.

The notion of surplus labour can help us understand that any worker – productive or unproductive – is exploited in capitalism because she performs surplus labour for her employer. When the worker is involved in performing productive labour, her surplus labour takes the form of surplus value. When she performs unproductive labour, her labour does not take the form of surplus value – because the labour is not involved in the domain of production and is involved, for instance, in pure buying and selling, or in financial activities. Nonetheless, surplus labour still exists for unproductive workers, and hence, unproductive labour is also exploited, just like productive labour.

5.4.4 Are Services Unproductive?

There is a common misunderstanding that regards all or most services as examples of unproductive activities, and hence, thinks of the labour involved in services as unproductive. At several places in *Capital*, Marx cautions against making this mistake. For instance, in the chapter on absolute and relative surplus value in Volume I of *Capital*, Marx uses, perhaps deliberately, an example of a service to illustrate the concept of productive labour in capitalist economies.

> The only worker who is productive is one who produces surplus-value for the capitalist, or in other words contributes towards the self-valorization of capital. If we may take *an example from outside the sphere of material production*, a schoolmaster is a productive worker when, in addition to belabouring the heads of his pupils, he works himself to the ground to enrich the owner of the school. That the latter has laid out his capital in a teaching factory, instead of a sausage factory, makes no difference to the relation. (Marx, 1992, p. 644, emphasis added)

To clarify this issue in some detail, let us follow Marx's analysis of transportation services in Volume II of *Capital*. Let us start out by distinguishing goods and services using the circuit of capital. The circuit of capital for goods production can be represented with the familiar formula we have seen earlier:

$$M - C \cdots (P) \cdots C' - M'$$

The key point as far as goods production is concerned is that

> the product of P [in the above circuit] is considered as a material thing different from the elements of productive capital. (Marx, 1993a, p. 134)

Thus, in the case of goods production, the use-value that is produced in the process of production is a material thing. It is separate, as a material thing, from the productive capital (the machines, the raw material, the building, and so on) that produced it. In contrast to goods, in the case of services, production and consumption coincide; hence, the product, that is, output, is not a material object separate from the productive capital that creates it. The use-value is not a material thing; rather, it is a 'useful effect' that arises by and through the use of the elements of productive capital, but cannot be separated out as a material thing from them. Hence, the circuit of capital for the production of a service is given by

$$M - C \cdots (P) \cdots M'$$

The important point to notice in the above representation is that the C' is missing, and that is precisely because, in the production of a service, there is no separate material thing appearing as the output; rather, it is

> the production process itself, and not a product separable from it, that is paid for and consumed. (Marx, 1993a, p. 135)

But this lack of material embodiment of a service does not make it any less of a commodity than a good. What is important is whether the service, that is, the useful effect, is produced for exchange or for direct use. If the service is produced for exchange, then it is a commodity as much as any good produced for exchange.

Once we have ascertained whether a service is a commodity, we need to then investigate its location in the overall social reproduction of capital. This is precisely where the distinction that we drew in a previous section between, on the one hand, production broadly construed to include transportation, storage, and so on, and, on the other, circulation, becomes salient. Since circulation involves activities that merely facilitate a change in the form of value, it cannot give rise to a change in the magnitude of value. Hence, all circulation activities, which have been referred to here as distribution, are part of non-production.[13]

---

[13]While discussing costs of circulation, Marx distinguishes two types of costs: (*a*) those that proceed 'from the mere change in form of value' and (*b*) those that 'arise from the production process that are simply continued in the circulation sphere' so that their 'productive character is merely hidden by the circulation form' (Marx, 1993a, p. 214). Examples of the latter are transportation, storage, warehousing, and so on – activities that create value. By absorbing these in the broad definition of production, I have left only the activities related to the first type of costs in the category of circulation. This allows me to make the claim that circulation is unproductive.

In concrete terms, these include wholesale and retail trade, book keeping and accounts, handling of money and financial dealings, and so on.

> It is not necessary to go into all the details of the costs of circulation here, such as packing, sorting, etc. *The general law is that all circulation costs that arise simply from a change in form of the commodity cannot add any value to it.* (Marx, 1993a, pp. 225–26, emphasis added)

On the other hand, there are many important services that should be considered part of the domain of production, an important example being transportation (and storage). Other examples are education, health care, entertainment, tourism, and so on. What the transport industry produces and sells is the useful effect of 'actual change of place' of people and things.[14] Here,

> the useful effect produced is inseparably connected with the transport process, i.e. the production process specific to the transport industry. (Marx, 1993a, p. 135)

Moreover, the useful effect produced is a commodity with value and its value is determined like that of any commodity

> by the value of the elements of production used up (labour-power and means of production), plus the surplus-value created by the surplus labour of the workers occupied in the transport industry. (Marx, 1993a, p. 135)

To summarize: all goods-production activities create value and surplus value if produced in capitalist firms; all services that are involved in the sphere of production broadly construed, including transportation, storage, warehousing, and so on are productive of value and surplus value if organized under capitalist relations of production; on the other hand, all services involved in dealing with the change of forms of value, that is, pure buying and selling of commodities, are unproductive even if organized along capitalist lines.

Using the classification of US industries used by the Bureau of Labour Statistics (BLS), we can give the following rough categorization of productive and unproductive labour:

---

[14]What the storage industry sells is the *useful effect* of preventing the loss of value of a commodity by the deterioration of its use-value.

- Productive labour is involved in the following industries:

  - Goods-producing industries: natural resources and mining; mining, quarrying and oil & gas extraction; construction; manufacturing.
  - Services-producing industries: transportation; information sector; utilities (electric power, natural gas, steam supply, water supply and sewage removal); scientific and technical services; education and health services; leisure and hospitality.

- Unproductive labour is involved in the following industries:

  - Services-producing industries: trade; financial activities; professional and business activities other than scientific and technical services; government.

Readings
- Marx's discussion of productive and unproductive labour can be found in Marx (1992, Chapter 16), Marx (1993a, Chapter 6) and Marx (1993b, Chapter 17). Useful expositions can be found in Foley (1986b, Chapter 7, pp. 118–22) and Shaikh and Tonak (1994, Chapter 2, pp. 20–37).

5.5 Interest and Fictitious Capital

5.5.1 Interest-Bearing Capital and Interest

Interest is the part of the aggregate surplus value that is appropriated by owners of money – whom Marx refers to as 'money capitalists' – who specialize in the function of lending it to industrial or commercial capital. Industrial and commercial capital use the money to appropriate surplus value, the former by generating it and the latter by helping to realize it through sale, with the two dividing the total surplus value among themselves in some fixed ratio. The appropriators of surplus value – industrial and commercial capital – then surrender a part of the surplus value to money capitalists as *interest*.

Capital that functions in this manner in the overall reproduction of the aggregate social capital, and earns interest income for this function, is known as *interest-bearing capital*. It can be represented as

$$M_0 - M - C\{MP, LP\} \cdots (P) \cdots C' - M' - M_0'$$

where M_0 represents the sum of money lent by its owner to a 'functioning capitalist', that is, either an industrial or a commercial capitalist. The functioning capitalist uses the borrowed money, possibly with other funds, in her circuit of capital, $M - C - M'$. At the end of a definite period specified in the lending contract, known as the maturity period, she returns the principal, M_0, along with an interest payment, $M_0' - M_0$, to the owner of the money.

> [I]nterest ... is thus nothing but a particular name, a special title, for a part of the profit which the actually functioning capitalist has to pay to the capital's proprietor. (Marx, 1993b, p. 460)

To understand interest, let us study the supply and demand sides of the market for loans of money? How does a capitalist economy generate a regular supply of money for the purpose of lending? Money accumulates in the hands of different capitalists during the process of the social reproduction of capital and becomes the main source of loans to other capitalists. For instance, the revenue generated from sale of finished commodities might not be immediately recommitted to fresh capital outlays because capitalist firms might be looking for a better time to invest and expand; or, a portion of the revenue might be kept aside after each cycle of the circuit as a depreciation fund (to be used several periods later for replacing a worn out machine at one go); or, capitalist households might save some of their income (which is a part of the surplus value) for the rainy season. This pool of money, constantly regenerated by the circuit of capital, creates a potential source of supply of money that can be used for capital accumulation. But where does the demand for loans of money come from? Large investments, for instance to set up a new factory or to open a whole new line of production or to purchase a new state-of-the-art machinery, often require more funds than internally generated by capitalist enterprises, that is, the revenue at the end of some cycle of their circuit of capital. Hence, the need for extra funds by capitalist enterprises creates a demand for money to finance capital outlays.

Since the lender gives the borrower – the functioning capitalist, in this case – the sum of money represented by the principal, to be used by the borrower for a specified period of time, interest can be seen as the price of getting to use money for a given period (an year, say). For instance, the industrial capitalist uses the borrowed funds to finance capital outlays, produce commodities and realize surplus value through sale of the finished products, the latter with the help of the commercial capitalist. A part of the surplus value is then surrendered to the lender as interest payment. Hence, from the perspective of the functioning capitalist, the interest payment is a deduction from the total surplus value she realizes in her circuit of capital. What remains of the surplus value, with industrial or commercial capital, after the payment of interest is known as *profit of enterprise*.

> In opposition to the interest which he has to pay to the lender out of the gross profit, the remaining part of the profit which accrues to him necessarily assumes the form of industrial or commercial profit, or to describe it with a German expression which embraces both these things, the form of profit of enterprise [*Unternehmergewinn*]. (Marx, 1993b, p. 496)

5.5.2 Interest Rate

In the circuit of interest-bearing capital, $M_0 - M_0'$, the increment, $M_0' - M_0$, is the interest income, which, expressed as a percentage of the principal, M_0, and for every year of the contract, is called the *annual interest rate*. What determines the rate of interest? There is no economic principle for the determination of the interest rate, other than possibly the pressures of demand and supply of loan capital affecting the bargaining power of money capitalists. The interest rate is largely the result of bargaining between the two fractions of the ruling class: owners of money, on the one hand, and functioning capitalists (industrial or commercial), on the other. When there is an excess of funds in the capitalist system, during recessions, for instance, the bargaining power of the lenders is low and so the interest rate tends to fall and remain at low levels. When there is an excess demand for funds relative to supply, during the peak of business cycles, for instance, the opposite happens. While these general forces of demand and supply work to strengthen or weaken one or the other party involved in the transaction, in modern capitalist economies, this relationship between the two fractions of the ruling class is mediated by actions of the Central Bank and the commercial banking system. The overall aim of the Central Bank is to ensure favourable conditions for capital accumulation, but it also can use its power to influence interest rates (through the purchase and sale of government debt) and thereby tilt the power balance between the two fractions of the ruling class: owners of money, on the one hand, and industrial or commercial capitalists, on the other.

5.5.3 Fictitious Capital

Once we have understood interest-bearing capital and the interest rate in capitalist economies, we are ready to grasp what Marx called *fictitious capital*.

> The formation of fictitious capital is known as capitalization. (Marx, 1993b, p. 597)

What does this mean? When the operation of money markets have become a regular feature of capitalist economies and the interest rate has seeped into the consciousness of all manners of economic agents, every stream of income can be 'capitalized', that is assigned a market price, with respect to the average interest rate. Consider a revenue stream which promises $100 every year into the indefinite future. If the average interest rate is 5 per cent, then the revenue stream can be capitalized as $2,000, that is, the revenue stream has a market price of $2,000. Why? This is because the annual interest income on a sum of $2,000 is $100 when the average interest rate is 5 per cent. Thus, capitalizing a revenue stream means arriving at the sum of money which, if functioning as principal in a loan contract, would generate that specific revenue stream as its interest income. If a legal ownership title to such a revenue stream – $100 every year into the indefinite future, in this example – were available in the market, it would sell for its capitalized value, $2,000 in this example. We can see immediately that the ownership titles to the revenue stream is akin to and yet different from interest-bearing capital. It functions like interest-bearing capital because, from the perspective of the buyer of the ownership title, it does represent 'the conversion of the capital he has invested into interest'. But unlike interest-bearing capital, the money used to purchase the ownership title does not participate in the circuit of either industrial or commercial capital. Assets with such properties are what Marx called *fictitious capital*.

Let us define fictitious capital as any asset with the following two properties. Fist, for its owner, the capital value of the asset functions like interest-bearing capital, that is, it has a circuit of the form, $M - M'$, where ownership of the asset gives interest-like income, $M' - M$. Second, the money used to purchase the asset is not used as capital, that is, it is not used by either industrial capital or by commercial capital. Let us consider three prominent examples of fictitious capital: government debt, stocks of shares or bonds (of capitalist enterprises) and land.

Public Debt

In capitalist countries, governments often borrow from the money market by floating bonds. A government bond is like a loan contract between the government and a lender (the entity which purchases the bond). By purchasing a government bond, the lender, in essence, lends an amount of money (which is equal to the price of the bond) to the government for a specific period (which is the maturity period of the bond). In return, the lender gets a stream of interest payments over the life of the bond and, in addition, gets back the principal when the bond matures.

Let us work with a specific example. Consider a government bond where the principal, or what is known as the face value of the bond, is $1,000 and the interest rate is 5 per cent per year. Suppose the maturity of the bond is 10 years, interest income is paid on a yearly basis and the principal is paid back at the end of the maturity period (10 years). Once there is a 'market' interest rate, one can use that to capitalize the stream of payments that is entailed in the loan contract, that is, one can calculate the monetary equivalent of the whole stream of future payments that will come to the purchaser of the bond. For instance, if the market interest rate is 4 per cent, the capitalized value of the loan contract entailed by the bond is $1,081.11. Thus, if there is a market where government bonds are sold, it will be bought for a price of $1,081.11, and by Marx's account, it is fictitious capital.[15]

The bond is fictitious capital because it has both properties listed in the definition given above. First, it functions like interest-bearing capital for the lender (the person or entity that has purchased the bond) in that it gives an interest-like income every year for 10 years. Second, and equally crucial, the money spent on purchasing the bond is not used as capital, either by an industrial or by a commercial capitalist; it is never 'laid out as capital'.

> ... the capital from which the state's payment is taken as deriving, as interest, is illusory and fictitious. It is not only that the sum that was lent to the state no longer has any kind of existence. It was never designed to be spent as capital, to be invested, and yet only by being invested as capital could it have been made into a self-maintaining value. (Marx, 1993b, pp. 595–96)

---

[15]The interest payment is $50 per year for years $1, 2, \ldots, 10$, and in year 10, the principal, $1,000, is also received. Hence, using an interest rate of 4 per cent, the capitalized value of the bond is given by $\sum_{i=1}^{10} \left[50/(1 + 0.04)^i \right] + 1,000/(1 + 0.04)^{10} = 1,081.11$.

Where does the revenue that is paid out by the government as interest come from? It comes out of the tax and non-tax revenue earned by the government, not *directly* from the surplus value generated by a capitalist firm. Of course, some of the tax revenue might come from surplus value, but some might also come from wage income. The more important point is that the interest payment does not come directly from surplus value generated by the use of the borrowed funds in a circuit of capital.

Shares of Capitalist Enterprises

Capitalist enterprises raise money, among other ways, by floating ownership shares. The money raised in this way, along with borrowed money, is used to purchase means of production and labour-power. If it is an industrial capitalist enterprise, then it is involved in generating surplus value and if it is a commercial capitalist enterprise, then it is involved in helping realize surplus value through sale of commodities. The non-depreciated value of the means of production, stocks of finished and unfinished commodities, unused raw materials and stocks of money, and financial net worth, comprise the capital of such capitalist enterprises. For this discussion, let us remove the financial net worth and focus on the real capital value. Let us call this the 'actual value of capital' laid out in the capitalist firm.

Owners of shares of capitalist enterprises receive, in a periodic and regular manner, a part of the surplus value realized by the firms in the form of *dividend payments*. Hence, ownership of shares entails a stream of revenue – dividend payments – as long as the firm is in existence. This stream of revenue can be capitalized, given the average interest rate, and the capitalized value gives the market price of the ownership share. The sum total of the market price of all outstanding shares of any capitalist enterprise gives the 'capitalized value' of the enterprise. But there is no guarantee that this capitalized value will be equal, or even related, to the value of the actual capital of the firm. The difference between the capitalized value of the outstanding stock of shares and the actual value of capital laid out in the firm shows that the money used to purchase shares is not directly related to the capital actually laid out in the production or circulation of commodities.

From the perspective of buyers of the shares, their investment gives them a stream of interest-like income (the dividend income) and by selling the share they can also recover the principal – with some loss if the selling price is lower than the price at which they purchased it, and a gain in the opposite scenario.

Hence, shares of capitalist enterprises have both the properties listed in the definition above – they provide interest-like income and the money is not used directly in a circuit of capital. Thus, they are examples of fictitious capital.[16]

> ... the capital does not exist twice over, once as the capital value of the ownership titles, the shares, and then again as the capital actually invested or to be invested in the enterprises in question. It only exists in the latter form, and the share is nothing but an ownership title, *pro rata*, to the surplus-value which this capital is to realize. (Marx, 1993b, p. 597)

Land

The final example of fictitious capital is a non-produced resource like land, which we are going to study in greater detail in section 5.6. We will see there that ownership of the land entails a stream of payments called rent. Just like any other stream of revenue, the stream of rent payments can be capitalized using the average interest rate to generate a market price of the plot of land. For the buyer of the plot of land, the price of the plot of land functions like capital investment, generating a stream of interest-like income. But the money used for purchasing the land is not used in the process of capitalist production or circulation. Hence, land is another example of fictitious capital.

A Common Misunderstanding

A common misunderstanding of the concept of fictitious capital emphasizes its *fictitious* nature by pointing to the fact that these assets represent claims on future streams of surplus value that has not yet been generated. While it is true that fictitious capital represents claims to future surplus value, that is not what makes it fictitious. What makes it fictitious is the fact that the money used to purchase the asset is not laid out as capital and does not function as a part of the total capital that is invested either in production or circulation of commodities.

---

[16] Bonds floated by capitalist enterprises to borrow from the money market are also examples of fictitious capital – for the same reasons as shares are fictitious capital. The only difference between bonds and shares is that the latter bestows ownership rights on the capital stock of the firm and the former, being just debt, does not entail any ownership rights. But in the case of bankruptcy, funds generated by selling assets of capitalist firms are first used to pay bondholders, before they can recoup the investment of the shareholders.

All these securities actually represent nothing but accumulated claims, legal titles, to future production. Their money or capital value either does not represent capital at all, as in the case of national debts, or is determined independently of the real capital they represent. (Marx, 1993b, p. 599)

This is important to keep in mind because interest-bearing capital also represents a claim on 'future production'. But it is not fictitious capital because the capital value it represents is actually laid out in capitalist production or circulation of commodities. That is why the definition given above emphasizes that fictitious capital is an asset whose capital value presents itself like interest-bearing capital without actually being so.

Readings
  • Marx's analysis of interest-bearing capital, the interest rate and fictitious capital are contained in Marx (1993b, Chapters 21–25, 29). A short exposition is available in Foley (1986b, Chapter 7, pp. 109–16). More detailed expositions are available in Lapavitsas (2013), Chesnais (2016) and Durand (2017).

5.6   Ground-Rent

5.6.1   *The Logic of Ground-Rent*

The final component of surplus value that Marx discusses in Volume III of *Capital* is ground-rent, conceptualizing it as the fragment of surplus value that is appropriated by owners of non-reproducible resources like land. Why are owners of non-reproducible resources like land able to appropriate a portion of surplus value? Marx has a simple and intuitive answer. If the use of non-reproducible resources provide cost advantages for its users, that is, capitalist producers, then this can generate what Marx calls 'surplus profit', that is, profit over and above the uniform (average) rate of profit. In such a situation, owners of the non-reproducible resource can bargain away the whole of the surplus profit as ground-rent, leaving just enough surplus value with the capitalist producer that will allow her to earn the average rate of profit on her investment. For Marx, therefore, ground-rent is the economic form of the monopoly of private ownership of non-reproducible resources; and its magnitude is the surplus profit.

Marx used the example of a waterfall to convey some of his ideas about surplus profit and ground-rent (Marx, 1993b, Chapter 38). Suppose factories in a country are mainly powered by steam-engines and that the uniform rate of profit is 15 per cent. In such a factory, suppose the capital outlay for producing one unit of output is 100. Hence, the price of production will be 115 (= 1.15 * 100). Suppose a few capitalists have access to a waterfall so that they can run their factories with water-power. The use of water-power reduces the required capital outlay, per unit of output, to 90. The output is sold at the price of production of 115. Hence, capitalists with access to the waterfall earn a profit of 25 (= 115 - 90). Note that these capitalists earn a surplus profit of 11.5, that is, a profit of 11.5 over and above what they would have earned if their capital had earned the 15 per cent (uniform) rate of profit (= 25 - 0.15 * 90).

Now imagine a change in ownership of the waterfall. Instead of capitalists owning it, suppose the waterfall is now privately owned by a different class of persons, whom we can call landlords (or water-lords). Landlords will give access to the waterfall to capitalist producers only for a monetary payment – called ground-rent. How much will the landlords charge as rent? The whole surplus profit, that is, 11.5. Why will capitalists be willing to pay a ground-rent of 11.5? If a capitalist producer pays 11.5 in rent, she will be able to make exactly 15 per cent on her capital investment of 90 per unit of the output. Hence, she will have no incentive to move her capital elsewhere if the rent is 11.5. Of course, the landlord cannot charge a rent that is higher than 11.5. If a capitalist were to pay a rent that is higher than 11.5, then she would earn a rate of profit that was lower than 15 per cent. By moving her capital elsewhere, she could earn a higher rate of profit. Hence, no capitalist producer would be willing to pay a rent that is higher than 11.5. And no landlord would be willing to lease out the waterfall for less than 11.5. In the process of bargaining between landlords and capitalist producers, the equilibrium would be represented by a ground-rent of 11.5, which is exactly equal to the surplus profit.

We are now able to see why the landlord is able to appropriate the full amount of the surplus profit as ground-rent. If the capitalist gives up all of the surplus profit to the landowner as ground-rent, she is left with exactly the amount of surplus value that ensures her an economy-wide average rate of profit. By moving her capital to a different line of production, she would earn, on average, exactly what she earns in capitalist commodity production using land (or any other non-reproducible resource). Hence, she has no incentive to deviate from the existing arrangement. The landowner has no incentive to deviate too. This is because she cannot expect to get a rental payment in excess of the surplus profit. If she asks for a rental payment that is larger than the surplus profit, the capitalist will move to another line of production. Hence, this is the best the landowner can do for herself. Thus, the equilibrium outcome of the bargaining between landowners and capitalist commodity producers leads to a contractual rental payment from the capitalist to the landowner – which is ground-rent – that is exactly equal to the surplus profit.

Marx had argued that the total ground-rent on any parcel of land could be decomposed into three components: differential rent of the first variety (DRI), differential rent of the second variety ($DRII$) and absolute rent (AR). According to Marx, DRI came from the relative quality advantage of any parcel, $DRII$ arose due to differences in capital invested on parcels and AR came from the lower-than-average OCC in agriculture. Drawing on Basu (2020a), we will now study the decomposition of ground-rent using a simple model of agricultural production that builds on and extends Basu (2018) and Das (2018).

5.6.2   A Model of Agricultural Production

The Set-Up

We conceive of the economy as being composed of an industrial sector and an agricultural sector. We take the prices of industrial products, the wage rate and, most importantly, the uniform rate of profit, as given. In agriculture, there are three classes: capitalists, workers and landlords. Capitalists organize production of corn (the homogeneous agricultural output) by leasing in land from landlords and purchasing the labour-power of workers. The lease contract between capitalists and landlords specifies a fixed period of time – one production cycle – for which the latter hands over the right to use the relevant plot of land to the capitalists in return for a monetary payment known as ground-rent. The labour contract between capitalists and workers specifies a fixed period of time – one production cycle – for which the latter gives up the use of her labour-power to the capitalists for a monetary payment known as the wage. After production is completed, the capitalist sells the corn on the open market to recoup the wage and rent payments she made earlier and, in addition, make a profit income.

The presuppositions for the capitalist mode of production [in agriculture] are thus as follows: the actual cultivators are wage-labourers, employed by a capitalist, the farmer, who pursues agriculture simply as a particular field of exploitation of capital, as an investment of his capital in a particular sphere of production. At certain specified dates, e.g. annually, this capitalist-farmer pays the landowner, the proprietor of the land he exploits, a contractually fixed sum of money ... for the permission to employ his capital in this particular field of production. This sum of money is known as ground-rent, irrespective of whether it is paid for agricultural land, building land, mines, fisheries, forests, etc. It is paid for the entire period for which the landowner has contractually rented the land to the farmer. (Marx, 1993b, pp. 755–56)

Technology of Production

Suppose the total available land used in agricultural production is divided into N plots (or parcels), a subset of which, indexed by $i = 1, 2, \ldots, n$, are in use for agricultural production. On the i-th plot of land that is in use, let total capital outlay by the capitalist producer of corn be denoted by $k_i = c_i + v_i$, where c_i and v_i are constant and variable capital, respectively. Here, c_i refers to the sum of money used by the capitalist to purchase non-labour inputs into production, and v_i refers to the sum of money used to purchase labour-power (for one production cycle). Let $f_i(.)$ denote the 'production function' on the i-th plot of land, that is, $f_i(.)$ captures the relationship between total capital invested and the quantity of corn produced on the i-th plot (which is why the function is indexed by i).

I enclose production function in quotation marks because this is not a standard production function. In a standard production function, inputs and output are related in real terms. Here, inputs are measured in nominal terms. Hence, what I am using is a pseudo production function. In using this pseudo production function, I have implicitly assumed that the technical relationships between inputs and output, and the price of the inputs are exogenously given. Under such an assumption, the relationship between capital outlay and output is a meaningful one. It is important to note that the purpose of using this analytical construct of a pseudo production function is merely to capture Marx's ideas about the distribution of the surplus value into profit and rent, and then decompose the latter into three components. It is not suitable for analysing technical change or broader price changes.

With the above caveat in mind, we will make the following assumption about the production function: as more capital is invested on any plot of land, output of corn rises but only at a declining rate. To capture this feature of the production function, we can use the concept of 'marginal product of capital', $f_i'(.)$. By the marginal product of capital is meant the extra amount of corn produced by increasing capital investment by a small amount.[17] Our assumption about the production function can now be restated as follows: the marginal product of capital declines with the level of capital investment.

The justification for this assumption is straightforward. Land cannot be 'produced' by labour. Thus, the amount of land in each plot (or parcel) is fixed, that is, land is a non-reproducible resource. The above assumption says that as more capital is invested on this fixed plot of land, the output increases but only at a declining rate. For instance, the increase in corn output is higher when capital investment is increased from 10 to 15 than when it is increased from 100 to 105. Typical examples of the marginal product curve on two plots of land, identified with the subscripts i and j, are depicted in Figure 5.2. On the horizontal axis, we measure the magnitude of capital outlay; on the vertical axis, we measure the marginal product of capital. Note that the marginal product curve on both plots of land decline as capital investment rises – in line with our assumption about the production function.

Ordering Plots by Quality
The plots of land are of unequal 'quality', that is, some plots are more fertile, or have better location, than others. This difference in the quality of plots of land will play an important role in the analysis of rent and we would now like to capture it more rigorously. The first thing to note is that we cannot arrange plots of land in increasing (or decreasing) order of productivity without taking account of the amount of capital outlay on each plot. Because the area of each plot of land is fixed and the output of corn increases at a declining rate, different amounts of capital outlay across plots can give rise to different ordering of land productivity (measured by the marginal product of capital). This is highlighted in Figure 5.2, where we can see that the marginal product curves for the i-th and j-th plots cross over. For low levels of capital outlay,

---

[17] The marginal product of capital is the derivative of the production function, which we have implicitly assumed to be differentiable.

the j-th plot has higher marginal product; at higher levels of capital outlay, the position is reversed and the i-th plot has higher marginal product. Hence, we cannot order plots of land according to quality without taking account of capital investment.

To get around this problem, we will adopt the convention of ordering plots of land by the marginal product of the very 'first' unit of capital outlay. The intuition for this is that the marginal product of capital at the very start of capital outlay on any plot of land comes closest to capturing the notion of the 'intrinsic' productivity of that plot of land. Considering a continuum of changes in capital outlay, it gives us the amount of increase in output (of corn) when capital outlay is increased from zero to a small positive amount. It is also able to capture any productivity that derives from past capital outlays on fixed capital, like irrigation, and so on, that is now part of the plot of land.

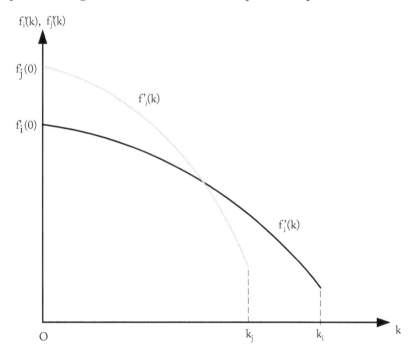

Figure 5.2   Depiction of the marginal product of capital outlay on the i-th and j-th plots of land. Note how there is a reversal of marginal productivity ranking of the two plots when we move from low to high capital outlay.

Source: Author.

Using this idea, we will order plots i and j according to intrinsic quality as follows: we will say that plot j is of *higher quality* than plot i if the marginal product of capital at zero capital investment is higher on plot j than on plot i. We can capture this easily in terms of the marginal capital curve because the curve starts from the marginal product of capital at zero capital investment. For instance, in Figure 5.2, the marginal product schedule on the j-th plot starts at a higher value than on the i-th plot. This means that the marginal product of capital at zero capital investment is higher on plot j than on plot i. Thus, we can say, following our convention, that the j-th plot is of higher quality than the i-th plot.

Pairwise comparison of all the n plots of land will allow us to arrange them all in diminishing order of quality. Once we do so, we can renumber the plots and call the most fertile plot as plot 1, the next most fertile plot as plot 2, and so on all the way to the last plot in use, plot n, which is the worst-quality plot. In terms of the marginal product curve, this will mean that plot 1 will start at the highest and plot n will start at the lowest point on the vertical axis (on a diagram like Figure 5.2).

Our analysis of ground-rent will proceed in three steps. In the first step, we will derive expressions for ground-rent and its three components, DRI, $DRII$ and AR, taking the capital outlay on each plot of land, k_i, the price of corn, p, and the economy-wide rate of profit, r, as given. In the second step, we will determine the capital outlay, k_i, by positing profit-maximizing behaviour of capitalist farmers. In the third, and final, step, we will close the model by determining the price of corn, p, by allowing the interaction of demand and supply of corn to clear the market for corn.

5.6.3 Ground-Rent with Exogenous Capital Outlays

Total Ground-Rent

Taking the uniform rate of profit, the price of corn and the capital investment on each plot as exogenously given, Figure 5.3 depicts the decomposition of ground-rent into its three components. In this figure, we have plotted the marginal product of capital outlay, $f_i'(k)$, on the vertical axis against the amount of capital outlay, k, on the horizontal axis, for the i-th plot of land (this is one of the plots currently in use for agricultural production). The total amount of capital outlay on this plot of land is given by k_i. Hence, total output of corn is given by the area under the marginal product curve, that is, $DCHO$. In Figure 5.3, $OG = AH = (1 + r)/p$, where p is the price of corn, and r is the uniform rate of profit. Thus, the area $GAHO$, which is given by $(1 + r)k_i/p$, represents the output that ensures the uniform rate of profit, r, on the total capital outlay, k_i. Hence, the area $DCAG$, being the difference between $DCHO$ and $GAHO$, represents 'surplus profit', that is, the profit over and above what capital investment of k_i could earn elsewhere in the economy (at the uniform rate of profit, r). According to Marx, ground-rent is nothing but transformed surplus profit, that is, surplus profit appropriated by the class of landlords, instead of capitalist farmers. Hence, the total ground-rent on the i-th plot of land is represented by the area $DCAG$.

Components of Ground-Rent

To decompose total ground-rent into its three components, we need to define two reference magnitudes. The first is the smallest magnitude of marginal product (of capital) across all plots of land. Let us refer to this as y^m. The second is the marginal product (of capital) on the worst plot of land at zero capital investment. Let us refer to this as $f_n'(0)$. Turning to Figure 5.3, we see that y^m is represented by the height $OF = HB$ and $f_n'(0)$ is represented by the height $OI = KJ$. In the analysis of this section, we have implicitly assumed that the marginal product of capital is larger than $(1 + r)/p$ on all plots. This assumption means that on each plot of land that is in use, the marginal product of capital outlay, $f_i'(k_i)$, is greater than the revenue that could be earned by investing each unit of capital elsewhere in the economy, $(1 + r)/p$, where r is the uniform rate of profit and p is the price of the agricultural commodity. This is a crucial assumption for the analysis of absolute rent and we will come back to it in the next section.

We are now ready to understand the decomposition of total ground-rent that is depicted in Figure 5.3. Differential rent of the first variety, DRI, is represented by the area DJI; differential rent of the second variety, $DRII$, is represented by the area $IJBF$; and absolute rent, AR, is represented by the area $FBAG$.

What is the intuition for the definition of DRI_i as the area DJI? Using the worst-quality plot of land as the benchmark, we are identifying all units of capital outlay that have higher marginal product than the 'intrinsic' quality of the worst-quality plot. When we add up all the additional output produced by these units of capital, we get DRI_i, which is represented by the area DJI.

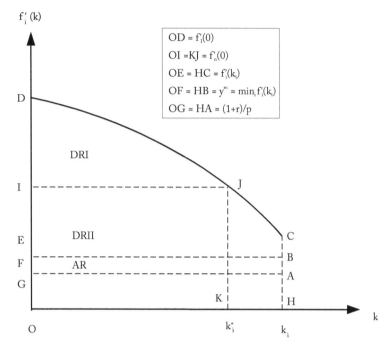

Figure 5.3 Ground-rent in agriculture on the i-th plot of land measured in units of corn. The horizontal axis measures total capital outlay; the vertical axis measures the marginal output as a function of capital outlay, $f'_i(k)$. The price of corn is p and the economy-wide rate of profit is r. Total ground-rent on the i-th plot of land is given by the area $DCAG$, differential rent by $DCBF$ and absolute rent by $FBAG$. DRI_i is given by DJI, and $DRII_i$ by $IJCBF$.

Source: Author.

Thus, this definition captures Marx's intuition that differential rent of the first variety arises due to differences in the quality (or fertility) of plots of land – the extensive margin of David Ricardo – using the worst quality plot of land as the benchmark.

What is the intuition for $DRII_i$? Total differential rent arises from a combination of productivity differences that come from differences in quality of plots of land and differences in the magnitude of capital outlay. We have seen that DRI_i arises from differences in quality of a plot with respect to the benchmark worst-quality plot of land. When we remove DRI_i from total differential rent, we are left with the component of differential rent that arises due to differences in magnitude of capital outlay. Hence, $DRII_i$ captures Marx's intuition that differential rent of the second variety arises from differences in the magnitude of capital outlay – the intensive margin of David Ricardo. But to know the total magnitude of differential rent, we first need to find the magnitude of absolute rent because total rent is the sum of differential rent and absolute rent.

What about absolute rent, AR? From Figure 5.3, we see that absolute rent on the i-th plot, AR_i, arises from the *gap* between the minimum marginal product, y^m, and the opportunity cost of capital outlay, $(1+r)/p$. As long as this gap exists, there will be positive absolute rent; if this gap is wiped out, there will be no absolute rent. This is precisely where the implicit assumption that $f_i'(k_i) > (1+r)/p$ becomes important. Since the marginal product of capital is larger than $(1+r)/p$ on all plots, this implies that the smallest marginal product, that is, y^m, is also larger than $(1+r)/p$. Hence, $y^m > (1+r)/p$ (that is, HC is larger than HA). This ensures that there is positive absolute rent on the i-th plot of land. Once we have identified absolute rent as the area $FBAG$, we also get total differential rent as the difference between total ground-rent (the area $DCHO$) and absolute rent. Thus, we see that total differential rent is given by the area $DCBF$. Once we remove DRI (the area DJI) from $DCBF$, we get $DRII$ (the area $IJBF$).

Marx had conceived of absolute rent as the total rent earned on a new plot of land that is brought under cultivation to satisfy rising demand for corn (Marx, 1993b, Chapter 45). Implicit in Marx's analysis is the idea that the new land brought under cultivation is also the least fertile plot of land, a fact that has been emphasized by Fine (1979). In Marx's analysis, the source of absolute rent is the relatively lower OCC in agriculture compared to the rest of the economy. Fine (1979, p. 263) has an algebraic expression to capture this idea. Following Marx's claim, Fine (1979) shows that if the OCC rises in the rest of the economy even as the OCC in agriculture remains unchanged, there should be an increase in absolute rent, as Marx (1993b) claims. In our model, this effect is easy to capture. The relative rise in the OCC in the rest of the economy *ceteris paribus* leads to a fall in the uniform rate of profit, r. From Figure 5.3, we can see that this will lead to a fall in the height HA, so that there will be a rise in absolute rent if y^m and p does not change.

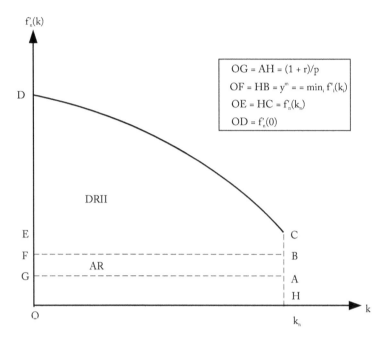

Figure 5.4 Ground-rent in agriculture on the n-th plot (that is, worst-quality plot) of land measured in units of corn. Note that DRI is zero.

Source: Author.

Worst Plot of Land

It is instructive to study the decomposition of rent on the worst-quality plot of land, that is, land n. On the worst-quality plot, which is depicted in Figure 5.4, the graph of the marginal product starts at $f'_n(0)$. This implies that what we had depicted in Figure 5.3 as the area DJI will be zero. Thus, on the worst plot of land, $DRI_n = 0$ (differential rent of the first variety is zero). By the property of the production function that each additional unit of capital investment produces a smaller amount of corn, we will have the marginal product of capital fall with capital investment. Hence, what we had depicted in Figure 5.3 as the area $IJBF$ remains positive on the worst plot of land, so that $DRII_n > 0$ (differential rent of the second variety is positive). Since the smallest marginal product is larger than $(1 + r)/p$, what we had depicted in Figure 5.3 as the area $FBAG$ remains positive on the worst-quality plot of land, so that $AR_n > 0$ (absolute rent is positive). Thus,

258

on the worst-quality plot, total rent is composed of $DRII$ and AR; there is no DRI. This is an important conclusion and worth commenting on. Marx thought that total rent on the worst-quality plot of land could be identified with absolute rent, that is, there would be no differential rent on the worst-quality plot (Marx, 1993b, Chapter 45). Our analysis shows that that is not correct. On the worst-quality plot of land, total rent is composed of both AR and $DRII$. Since $DRII$ arises from the diminishing marginal product of capital investment, Marx's conclusion seems to derive from his ignoring this latter factor when analysing rent on the worst-quality plot of land.

There is a deeper problem in the analysis presented so far. We have completely ignored the decision-making process of the capitalist farmers. In more concrete terms, by assuming a given amount of capital outlay on each plot of land, we have ignored the process and implications of the behaviour of capitalist farmers. This is a serious shortcoming because, once we allow a reasonable behaviour of capitalist farmers, there will be a serious implication for the analysis of rent. To that we now turn.

5.6.4   Ground-Rent with Endogenous Capital Outlays

On each plot of land, capitalist producers choose the amount of capital outlay that will maximize the surplus profit they can earn vis-a-vis what they can earn if they were to employ their capital elsewhere in the economy.

Since the economy-wide rate of profit is exogenously given to be r, capitalist producers can always earn the total revenue of $(1 + r)k_i$ by employing their capital, k_i, elsewhere in the economy. If they choose to employ the capital in agricultural production on the i-th plot of land, then they can expect to earn total revenue of $pf_i(k_i)$, when the price of the agricultural commodity is p. If total rent is a lump-sum monetary payment given by GR_i, then the amount of revenue a capitalist farmer can expect to earn by employing her capital in agriculture is $pf_i(k_i) - GR_i$. Hence, the extra revenue a capitalist can earn by investing her capital in agriculture is given by $pf_i(k_i) - GR_i - (1 + r)k_i$. We posit that capitalist producers choose the level of capital outlay, k_i, on the i-th plot to maximize this surplus.

How much capital investment will a capitalist farmer choose on the i-th plot of land? Since capitalist farmers are profit (or revenue) maximizers, they will choose an optimal amount of capital outlay so that the marginal product of capital outlay, $f_i'(k_i)$, is equalized to $(1+r)/p$, the revenue that they could earn by investing each unit of their capital elsewhere in the economy. If the marginal product is higher than $(1+r)/p$, then capitalist farmers can increase their profit by increasing capital investment; if the marginal product is less than $(1+r)/p$, then capitalist farmers can reduce their loss by reducing capital investment. Hence, the only equilibrium position would be equality of the marginal product of capital investment and $(1+r)/p$.

Since $(1+r)/p$ is exogenously given, because r and p are exogenously given to the capitalist farmer, this implies that the marginal product of capital outlay on each plot of land will be equalized. This is intuitively clear. If there were differences in the marginal product of capital outlay, inter-plot movement of capital would allow capitalist producers to increase surplus profit and then share it among themselves in some way to make all parties to the transaction better off. The equilibrium configuration of the distribution of capital outlays will rule this out. Hence, the marginal product of capital outlay has to be equalized across *all* plots of land.

The fact that the marginal product of capital is equalized to $(1+r)/p$ across all plots of land has an important implication. *Absolute rent will be zero.* Recall that, in the analysis in the previous section, absolute rent was positive because there was a gap between the marginal product of capital and $(1+r)/p$, the amount of revenue that can be earned by employing each unit of capital elsewhere in the economy. Once the analysis allows capital investment to be chosen by profit-maximizing capitalist farmers, the gap is completely closed. The choice of capital investment is governed precisely by the rule that the marginal product of capital outlay, $f_i'(k_i)$, is equal to $(1+r)/p$. That is why absolute rent is zero.

One strand of Marxist literature argues, in line with Marx's argument in Chapter 45 of Volume III of *Capital*, that the source of absolute rent is the low OCC in agriculture relative to the rest of the economy (Fine, 1979; Fine and Filho, 2010; Fine, 2019). The analysis in this section raises doubts on such claims. If the OCC were to rise in the rest of the economy relative to agriculture, as used in the argument in Fine (1979), then the uniform rate of profit, r, would fall to r', say. Capitalist farmers would choose the level of capital investment to ensure that the marginal product of capital, $f_i'(k_i)$, is equal to $(1+r')/p$ at the new profit rate. Hence, absolute rent would still be zero. The relatively lower OCC in agriculture does not generate any absolute rent.

To emphasize the conclusions of this section, I have visually represented the configuration of ground-rent and its decomposition, when capital outlay is endogenous, in Figure 5.5. The total amount of ground-rent on plot i is represented by the area DCE. This is, as before, the surplus profit. DRI_i is represented, just like in Figure 5.3, by the area DJI. This is the part of ground-rent that can be attributed to quality differentials across plots of land. $DRII_i$ is now represented by the area $IJCE$, and there is no AR.

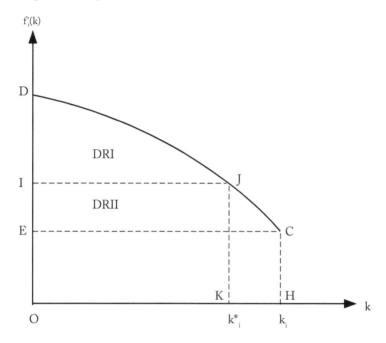

Figure 5.5 Decomposition of ground-rent in agriculture on the i-th plot of land, measured in units of corn, when rent is specified as a lump-sum monetary payment. In this case, there is no absolute rent. Total ground-rent is the sum of differential rent of first variety (DRI) and differential rent of second variety $(DRII)$.

Source: Author.

5.6.5 Price of Corn

So far we have taken the price of the agricultural commodity as given. To complete the analysis, we need to investigate how this price is determined. To do so, we look at the market for corn. Let us posit a demand function for corn, $D(p; \gamma)$, where $\partial D / \partial p < 0$ (this just means that demand and price are inversely related) and γ captures shift factors like population growth, urbanization, regulatory aspects of the corn market, and so on. The total supply of corn is the sum of the corn output on each of the n plots of land that are currently in use for agricultural production. Hence, total supply of corn can be expressed as

$$S(p) = \sum_{i=1}^{n(p)} f_i(k_i(p)) \tag{5.1}$$

Note that total supply of corn is an upward-sloping function of price because of two reasons. First, the actual number of plots in use for agricultural production is a function of p, that is, $n = n(p)$. The dependence of the number of plots of land in use is a rising function of the price of corn because, as the price of corn rises, it makes worse plots of land profitable to bring under cultivation. Second, on any plot in use, we know that k_i is an increasing function of p (because, as the price of corn rises, it becomes profitable to invest more capital), so that output is an increasing function of price. Hence, total supply, $S(p)$, is an increasing function of p. The equilibrium price of corn is the level of $p = p^*$ which bring supply and demand into balance, that is,

$$D(p^*; \gamma) = S(p^*) \equiv \sum_{i=1}^{n(p^*)} f_i(k_i(p^*)) \tag{5.2}$$

We are now ready to present the condition under which *any* plot of land will be in use in a capitalist economy with landed property, that is, private ownership of land by the class of landlords. In such a context, any plot of land that will be in use can be leased in profitably by a capitalist farmer. And it can be leased in only when it pays a positive amount of ground-rent to the landlord in addition to ensuring the uniform rate of profit on capital investment. Let us consider the most extreme case when the demand for corn is so low that even the 'best' plot of land cannot be profitably used. In this situation, there will be no corn production and, hence, there will be zero ground-rent. This immediately identifies the minimum threshold for the price, if rent is to be positive, as

$$p^{**} = \frac{1+r}{f_1'(0)} \tag{5.3}$$

where, it is to be recalled that plot 1 is the best-quality plot. If population growth, urbanization, and so on leads to growth of demand for the agricultural product such that $p > p^{**}$, this will bring land under cultivation. As soon as *any* land is brought under cultivation, this will generate positive ground-rent. As demand rises further, progressively more (worse plots of) land will come under cultivation and total rent will increase. Technical change will have a more ambiguous effect.

In our model, technical change can be captured by the upward shifts of the marginal product curves. Such upward shifts of the marginal product curves would imply that the same plots of land can satisfy rising demand. Hence, more, and worse quality, parcels will not need to be brought under cultivation as the demand for the agricultural commodity rises. This would reduce the total amount of ground-rent that would otherwise have to be paid by capitalist farmers. On the other hand, upward shifts of the marginal product curves also imply larger surplus profit on all the existing plots in use. Hence, this would have a tendency to raise the total amount of ground-rent. Therefore, the overall impact of technical change on the total ground-rent earned by the class of landlords will depend on the relative strengths of these opposing effects.

Further Readings
- Marx's analysis of ground-rent is contained in Marx (1993b, Chapters 37–45).
- For previous Marxist work on ground-rent, see Fine (1979, 2019), Ramirez (2009), Fine and Filho (2010), and Ward and Aalbers (2016).

5.7   Estimates of Surplus Value and Its Components

In this chapter, we have studied how the surplus value that is generated in production of commodities and realized through the process of circulation is then distributed among different fractions and types of capital. The various fragments of the total surplus value take the form of income streams that flow to different fragments of the non-working class as profit of enterprise, commercial profit, interest and ground-rent.

A good way to round out our discussion of surplus value and its division into various components would be to look at some real data. Towards that end, now I present estimates of surplus value and its components for the US non-financial corporate business sector (NFCB), the US corporate business (CB) sector and the Indian organized manufacturing sector.

To get an idea of the different components into which surplus value in an advanced capitalist economy is divided, let us start by looking at the different broad categories of income in the US economy. In Table 5.3, I present figures of the broad categories of income in the US CB sector for two recent years, 1998 and 2018. In 2018, net value added in the US CB sector was 9,882.5 billion USD. Of this, 6,721.8 was distributed as compensation of employees, which includes wages, salaries and supplementary benefits to employees. Thus, about 68 per cent of net value added was accounted as wage income in the US CB sector in 2018. This is no doubt an overestimate of the 'true' wage bill because it includes compensation paid to top managers, supervisory staff and chief executive officers (CEOs). From a Marxist perspective, the income earned by such persons comes out of surplus value. But for the purposes of illustration, we will ignore this complication.[18]

Table 5.3 Value added in the US CB sector (billion USD)

	1998	2018
Net value added	4,758.4	9,882.5
Taxes on production and imports	430.8	945
Compensation of employees	3,447.5	6,721.8
Net operating surplus	880.2	2,215.7
Interest payments	121.6	306.5
Net business transfer payments	52.8	130.7
Corporate income tax payments	221.8	231.3
Dividend payments	341.4	525.6
Retained earnings	142.5	1,021.5

Source: National Income and Product Account Table 1.14, US Bureau of Economic Analysis.

---

[18]For a careful empirical treatment of this issue, see Mohun (2006).

Of the 32 per cent of net value added that was the surplus value in the US CB sector in 2018, about 37 per cent went into taxes – production taxes and corporate income taxes. Interest payment was of the amount of 306.5 billion USD, or about 9.7 per cent of the surplus value. Dividend payments were in the amount of 525.6 billion USD; and retained earnings – the surplus value retained with firms after making other types of payments – was recorded as 1,021.5 billion USD. The sum of these two would give us an estimate of 'profit of enterprise', which, in this case, is about 49 per cent of the total surplus value.

In Figure 5.6, I plot the different components of surplus value in the US CB sector from 1948 to 2018. Total surplus value takes the following forms:

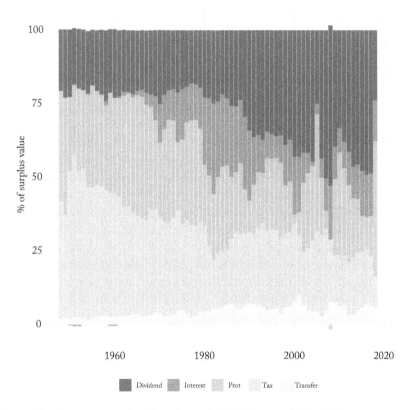

Figure 5.6 Components of surplus value in the US CB sector, 1948–2018
Source: Author's calculations from Table 1.12, National Income and Product Accounts, Bureau of Economic Analysis, USA.

interest payments (interest), corporate taxes (tax), dividend payments (dividend), net business transfer payments (transfer) and retained earnings (profit). Figure 5.6 is a stacked bar chart, where each form of surplus value is assigned a different colour. For every year, the different components of surplus value add up to 100 per cent. By tracking the patterns over time, we can see which form of surplus value has been relatively dominant over different periods.

In the period from 1948 to the early 1980s, which is often referred to as a period of regulated capitalism, retained earnings and taxes together make up the largest part of surplus value. Within this trajectory, interest income starts becoming quantitatively important since the early 1970s. Together, profits, taxes and interest account for about 75 per cent of the surplus value in the regulated period. From the early 1980s, a period of neoliberal capitalism, we see a strikingly different pattern in the division of surplus value. The most striking changes are the steady increase in the share of surplus value taking the form of dividend payments – which has reached close to 50 per cent of surplus value by mid-2000s – and the steady decline in taxes. The share of surplus value taking the form of profits (retained earnings) has been stable since the early 1980s (though this is far lower than its share in the immediate post-war period).

Figure 5.7 presents a similar stacked bar chart of the different forms of surplus value for the US NFCB sector between 1948 and 2018. The patterns regarding the trajectories of the different forms of surplus value observed for the whole CB sector is also observed for the NFCB sector. But there are some differences. First, interest income accounts for a much larger share of total surplus value since the early 1960. This shows the gradual emergence and consolidation of the financial sector of the US corporate economy: an increasingly larger share of surplus value generated in the non-financial sector of the US economy is appropriated as income of the financial sector (broadly denoted as interest income). Second, while dividend payments have increased as a share of total surplus value, it is lower than in the whole CB sector. Even at its height, it just about crosses 40 per cent.

In Figure 5.8, I present a stacked bar chart of the components of surplus value in India's organized manufacturing sector between 1981–82 to 2016–17. In this case, total surplus value is divided into interest, profit and rent. We see an interesting pattern here, which is opposite of what we saw for the US economy. In India's organized manufacturing sector, the share of surplus

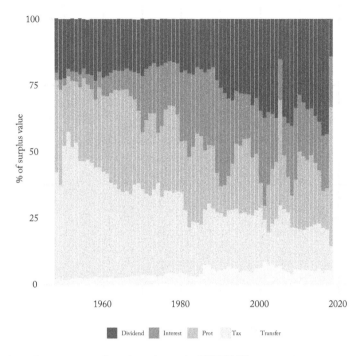

Figure 5.7 Components of surplus value in the US NFCB sector, 1948–2018
Source: National Income and Product Account Table 1.14, US Bureau of Economic Analysis.

value taking the form of interest was large in the 1980s and has declined since then. On the other hand, profits (which is the sum of dividend payments and retained earnings) have increased. Rent remains a small component of surplus value in India's organized manufacturing sector since the early 1980s.

5.8   Conclusion

The three volumes of *Capital* provide us with a comprehensive understanding of the structure and long run dynamics of capitalist economies. Volume I analyses the process of production of capital, that is, the generation and accumulation of surplus value. Volume II studies the issue of realization of surplus value through an analysis of the process of circulation of capital.

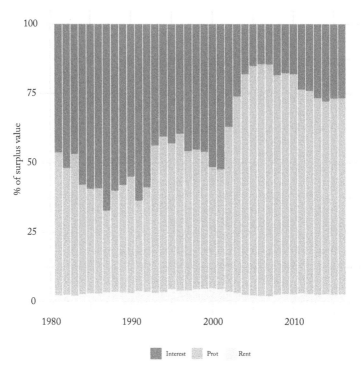

Figure 5.8 Components of surplus value in India's organized manufacturing sector, 1981–82 to 2016–17

Source: Annual Survey of Industries, 2016–17, Ministry of Statistics and Programme Implementation, Government of India.

Together, the analysis in these two volumes give us a complete picture of the important tendencies that emerge in capitalist economies on the basis of the relationship between capital and labour at the aggregate level only. In Volume III of *Capital*, Marx operates at a lower level of abstraction by analysing the totality of capitalist production from the perspective of the distribution of surplus value. The key mechanism underlying the distribution of surplus value is the competition between capitals (that takes the form of mobility of capital across sectors in search of higher rates of profit), and bargaining between industrial capital and owners of natural resources, and bargaining between different fractions of the capitalist class, for example, bargaining between industrial and merchant capital and interest-bearing capital.

By the end of Volume III of *Capital*, after we have studied the various forms in which surplus value is redistributed in capitalist economies, and grasped how portions of surplus value become the sources of income of important fractions of the ruling class, we are ready to understand the importance of the 'trinity formula', which, according to Marx, 'holds in itself all the mysteries of the social production process'. The trinity formula, or what Marx sometimes refers to as the 'trinity form', refers to the three fundamental social classes in capitalism and their income streams: capital – profit (industrial or commercial profit and interest); landowners – rent; labour – wages. From the perspective of 'vulgar economics', this trinity form is often understood as showing the share of the net output that goes to each of the three 'factors of production', that is, land, labour and capital. Each of these factors of production, argues vulgar economics, contributes to the output. Each factor get a share of the output in the proportion in which it had contributed to the output. Land gets rent; labour gets wages; capital gets profit. Hence, there is no exploitation.

The analysis of the capitalist mode of production in the three volumes of *Capital* pulls the rug from under this fairy tale. Once we have followed Marx through the three volumes of *Capital*, we know that surplus value is the result of unpaid labour of the working class involved in production. We also know that the aggregate surplus value generated in production is then distributed and redistributed, through various channels and using varied mechanisms, across capitalist society and ends up as the income streams of different fractions of the ruling class. Hence, the trinity form, according to Marx, shows that profit of enterprise (industrial or commercial profit), interest and rent are merely portions, and forms, of surplus value. Unlike the fairy tale of vulgar economics, we see clearly in *Capital* that incomes of various fractions of the ruling class do not arise to compensate them for their contribution to the production of value; it derives from the unpaid labour of the working class involved in capitalist production. Since surplus value is created by the unpaid labour of workers, the whole edifice of ruling-class incomes is based on exploitation. Capitalism, like all other class-divided societies, rests on the exploitation of one class by another. It is one of the greatest achievements of Marx that he could demonstrate this with uncanny precision and true scientific rigour.

At the end of the three volumes of *Capital*, we also get a picture of capitalism as a profoundly contradictory system. On the one hand, it is inherently progressive in terms of technological change and growth in the productivity of social labour. And in this respect, it is unlike, and far superior to, all previous modes of production. On the other, the immense possibilities opened up for human welfare by the technological progressivity of capitalism is caught up in the narrow confines of profit maximization and mindless capital accumulation. Hence, its technological progressivity is blind to the enormous costs it imposes on labour and nature, the two fundamental sources of wealth. One cannot but agree with Marx that there is no other way to realize the possibilities of human welfare opened up by capitalism than to transcend it.

Part II

Further Explorations in Political Economy

6

Capitalism and Technical Change

In section 5.2, we had studied the issue of technical change, and we now revisit the issue to deal with it in greater detail. In particular, two questions related to technical change will be addressed in this chapter. We will first make precise the definition of technical change, relate it to capitalist decision-making and then ask the following question: Does technical change adopted by capitalist firms coincide with what is best from a social perspective? The second question we will investigate relates to the relationship between technical change and the rate of profit. When does technical change in capitalist economies lead to a fall in the rate of profit?

The second question derives its importance from a long and distinguished Marxist literature on tendencies of economic crisis in capitalist economies.[1] From a Marxist perspective, *an economic crisis in a capitalist economy is a deep and prolonged interruption of the economy-wide circuit of capital.* The proximate cause of an economic crisis is a decline in the average rate of profit. The rate of profit can fall in two different, and mutually exclusive, ways, which suggest a typology of economic crises in capitalism. The first way in which the average rate of profit can fall is when the economy is marked by a chronic insufficiency of aggregate demand, so that commodities are sold at prices that are below their value (or price of production). Hence, in this case, the sale of the commodity does not realize the full surplus value (or the average rate of profit), and the realized rate of profit falls below the 'normal' rate of profit (which prevailed previously). We can refer to this as a 'crisis of excess surplus

---

[1]For a discussion of economics crisis and different Marxist explanations of the important crisis tendencies, see Basu (2019).

value' (because more surplus value was produced than could be realized through sale). The second way in which the average rate of profit can fall is when, despite the commodity selling at its full value (or price of production), the realized rate of profit declines. Thus, in this case, the problem is not one of realization of the surplus value embedded in commodities, but rather points to the production of insufficient surplus value itself. We can refer to this as a 'crisis of deficient surplus value' (because the system produces less surplus value than is necessary to ensure a 'normal' rate of profit).[2]

Two mechanisms that can account for the crisis of deficient surplus value are, first, the profit-squeeze mechanism (discussed in Chapter 25, Volume I of *Capital*) and, second, the rising OCC mechanism (discussed in Chapter 13, Volume III of *Capital*). The second mechanism is associated with Marx's law of the tendential fall in the rate of profit (LTFRP) and claims to establish the proposition that the average rate of profit has a tendency to fall with capitalist development due to rising mechanization of production, the latter being a key feature of capitalist technical change. In a famous contribution, Okishio (1961) was seen as overturning Marx's result and establishing that technical change would, in fact, lead to a rise in the average rate of profit. In this chapter, we will study the relationship between Marx's original claim and Okishio's result – both of which relate to the relationship between technical change and the rate of profit in capitalist economies. We will want to understand which position, Marx's or Okishio's, is right? Is Marx's LTFRP overturned by Okishio? In this chapter, we will see that there is less of a contradiction between Marx's and Okishio's results. We will see that both results can be reconciled in a more general framework, which includes technical change and class struggle. The main result in this respect that we want to derive and highlight is that depending on the state of class struggle, technical change can lead to either a fall or a rise in the rate of profit, a result we had briefly discussed in section 5.2 earlier.

---

[2]What I have called a normal rate of profit has been called the 'usual' rate of profit by Marx and Sweezy. The important point is that when the actual rate of profit falls below the 'usual' rate of profit in more or less all industries in an economy, the rate of capital accumulation slows down and can initiate a period of economic crisis (Sweezy, 1942, p. 142).

6.1 Technical Change

6.1.1 Basic Set-Up

To develop some of the key Marxist arguments relating to capitalism and technical change, I will use a model of a capitalist economy. This model capitalist economy produces only one commodity. Let us call this commodity, corn, and note that it can be used both for consumption and investment.[3] Such a model of the capitalist economy is very much like the model used by David Ricardo or like the one used in modern macroeconomic growth theory. It is decidedly simple, and the simplicity has both advantages and disadvantages. The advantage is its accessibility, and the disadvantage is that some issues, for example, relative price changes, cannot be studied in this model. For the purposes of discussing issues of technical change, the advantage seems to outweigh the disadvantage because many of the important aspects of technical change can be conveyed in this single-commodity model.[4]

In the one-commodity model that we are using, the inputs to production are saved-up corn and labour. Saved-up corn is owned by capitalists and labour is provided by workers – who sell their labour-power to capitalists for a money wage rate, w. Workers use the money wage to purchase and consume b units of corn per hour of labour. Hence, if the price of corn is p, then the real wage rate is related to the nominal wage rate as follows: $b = w/p$.

In this economy, a *technique of production* is a combination of two numbers: the amount of corn and the amount of labour that is needed to produce 1 unit of corn. For instance, a technique of production could be represented by the pair of numbers (n, a), in which case it would mean that n units of labour and a units of corn are needed to produce 1 unit of corn. We assume that labour is indispensable for production, so that $n > 0$, but the non-labour input can be dispensed with, so that $a \geq 0$. For the technique of production to be technologically meaningful, it must produce a positive net output, that is, $1 - a > 0$, so that $a < 1$. Otherwise, the technique of production would use up more inputs than it produces, which is clearly unviable from a purely technological viewpoint.

---

[3]Recall that we have already encountered this model in section 3.1.5.
[4]Many of the arguments developed in this section have been treated in multi-commodity models of production. For a two-commodity treatment, see Laibman (1992); for a n-commodity treatment, see Roemer (1981).

By *technical change*, we will mean the availability of new techniques of production. How new techniques of production become available is an important and interesting question, but we will not pursue it here. We will investigate the consequences of capitalist relations of production on the adoption of the new techniques of production made available by technical change. To get started, we must define certain aspects of technical change: productiveness, progressiveness, viability (in a capitalist sense) and types of technical change.

6.1.2 Productiveness

Suppose a technique of production is given by (n, a), that is, n units of labour and a units of corn are needed to produce 1 unit of corn. We will say that this technique of production is *productive* if the total output of corn is larger than the total input of corn, where the latter is the sum of the *direct* input in production as capital, a units of corn, and the *indirect* input as consumption requirement of workers, nb units of corn. Hence, the condition that makes the technique of production (n, a) productive is given by

$$a + nb < 1 \qquad\qquad (6.1)$$

The above condition is telling us that a technique of production is productive when it can produce a *net* output, that is, total output less the non-labour inputs, $1 - a$, that is, larger than the consumption requirements of the workers, nb. Since labour input is indispensable for production, that is, $n > 0$, and workers need to consume some positive amount of corn per hour of labour, that is, $b > 0$, a necessary condition for the productiveness of the technique of production is that $a < 1$. That is why we have assumed that $a < 1$, which ensures that the technique of production is not only technologically viable but also productive.

The intuition behind the definition in (6.1) is straightforward. The excess of the net output over the consumption needs of the workers is potentially available for reinvestment to improve technologies of production and ensure technological progress over time. If techniques of production were not productive in this sense, society would either stagnate (when the above relationship holds as a equality) or disintegrate and disappear (when the above inequality is reversed).[5]

---

[5]To keep the analysis simple, we are abstracting from consumption needs of capitalists, but that can be

6.1.3 Progressiveness

To make precise the notion of progressive technical change, let λ and λ' denote the value of, that is, labour embodied in, one unit of corn when the techniques of production are (n, a) and (n', a'), respectively. When the technique of production (n, a) is used, a units of corn is combined with n units of labour to produce 1 unit of corn. Hence, the equation for determining the value of a unit of corn can be written as $\lambda = \lambda a + n$ and, by a similar argument, $\lambda' = \lambda' a' + n'$. We can rewrite the equations to derive expressions for the value of corn as $\lambda = n/(1 - a)$ and $\lambda' = n'/(1 - a')$. Technical change is defined to be *progressive* when $\lambda' < \lambda$, that is, when the value of corn falls. A little algebraic manipulation shows that the following condition ensures that technical change is progressive:

$$a' < 1 - \left(\frac{1 - a}{n} \right) n' \tag{6.2}$$

What is the idea behind this definition? It is a way to make concrete the notion that reducing the overall toil of labour is in the general interest of society. When technical change is progressive it reduces the total, that is, sum of direct and indirect, labour content of commodities. Hence, the same amount of commodities can be produced with a smaller amount of labour or a larger amount of commodities can be produced with the same amount of labour. This opens up the possibility of supporting a higher material standard of living and also potentially increasing the time available for leisure. It is these important and worthy societal goals that are captured by the definition of a progressive technical change. The inequality in (6.2) gives the precise quantitative relationship between the two techniques of production that must hold if we are to have progressive technical change: net output per unit of the labour input must be higher in the new technique of production compared to the old.

6.1.4 Capitalist Viability

We have seen in previous chapters, especially in Chapter 3, that capitalism's driving force and primary motivation is rooted in profitability. The need to generate and realize surplus value structures all other aspects of the system,

---

easily added without changing the qualitative features of the analysis.

including technical change. When capitalist producers decide whether to adopt a new technique of production that has become available, their choice is based on cost and profitability calculations. It is this key idea that is captured by the definition of capitalist viability.

We will call the new technique of production, (n', a'), to be *capitalistically viable* if it reduces the cost of production at the *current* price and real wage rate. If the old technique of production, (n, a) were to be used, and the existing price is p, then the cost of producing one unit of output would be $pnb + pa$. On the other hand, if the new technique were to be used at the same existing price, p, the cost of production would be $pn'b + pa'$. Thus, the new technique of production is capitalistically viable if and only if the following condition holds:

$$bn' + a' < bn + a \qquad (6.3)$$

There are at least two conceptual motivations for introducing this definition. To begin with, the definition is a realistic, though simplified, description of actual capitalist behaviour. It seems realistic to assume that capitalist producers will be governed by cost and profitability calculations in choosing new techniques of production. But there is a deeper reason too. It is a fundamental Marxist critique of capitalism that profitability calculations are not always aligned with broader societal goals. In the domain of technical change, new techniques of production that are progressive might not be adopted by capitalist producers because they do not reduce the cost of production at current prices. If this were to happen, we would immediately see a gulf opening up between what is best for capitalism (captured by capitalist viability) and what is best for society (captured by progressiveness). To investigate if and when this might happen is the second motivation for introducing the above definition of capitalist viability (and distinguish it from progressiveness). But before we investigate this issue, let us introduce some terminology about types of technical change.

6.1.5 Types of Technical Change

We can define different types of technical change from a purely quantitative perspective regarding the two inputs that make up a technique of production. Comparing the old and new techniques of production, (n, a) and (n', a'), we see that there are four distinct possibilities – depending on whether the capital-input and labour-input requirement is smaller (or larger) in the old versus the new technique of production: $n' > n$ and $a' > a$; $n' > n$ and $a' < a$; $n' < n$ and $a' > a$; $n' < n$ and $a' < a$.[6] To identify these four types of technical change, let us introduce some terminology. Technical change is of the type

- capital-using, labour-using (CU-LU), if $a' > a$ and $n' > n$, that is, more capital and more labour is needed to produce one unit of output with the new technique of production;

- capital-saving, labour-using (CS-LU), if $a' < a$ and $n' > n$, that is, less capital and more labour is needed to produce one unit of output with the new technique of production;

- capital-using, labour-saving (CU-LS), if $a' > a$ and $n' < n$, that is, more capital and less labour is needed to produce one unit of output with the new technique of production;

- capital-saving, labour-saving (CS-LS), if $a' < a$ and $n' < n$, that is, less capital and less labour is needed to produce one unit of output with the new technique of production; a special case of the CS-LS type, when the degree of capital-saving and labour-saving is the same, is known as *Hicks neutral* technical change;

- pure labour-saving, also known as *Harrod neutral*, if $a' = a$ and $n' < n$, that is, same amount of capital and less labour is needed to produce one unit of output with the new technique of production;

- pure capital-saving, also known as *Solow neutral*, if $a' < a$ and $n' = n$, that is, less capital and same amount of labour is needed to produce one unit of output with the new technique of production.

Leading capitalist countries have almost always witnessed labour-saving technical change, that is, the labour productivity has risen over time (Foley et al., 2019, Table 2.8). For some periods, the growth of labour productivity has come along with a fall in capital productivity, so that we have had CU-LS technical change; at other periods, both labour and capital productivity have increased, so that we have had CS-LS technical change.[7] In the history of capitalism, periods of CU-LS and CS-LS types of technical

---

[6] I have ignored the various cases of equalities in these relationships because they are not interesting from the perspective of technical *change*.

[7] Note that, with reference to a technique of production (n,a), $1/n$ is the labour productivity, and $1/a$ is the capital productivity.

change have alternated, with the former dominating the latter (Foley and Michl, 1999). Over the last few decades, some countries have also witnessed CS-LU technical change, especially in the context of deindustrialization. In these cases, the shrinking of the industrial sector relative to the other sectors has probably pushed labour into low-producitivity and low-paying service sector jobs in the informal sector, so that overall labour productivity has fallen.[8]

From the perspective of capitalists, CS-LS is the most favourable type of technical change because it saves on both inputs. From a theoretical perspective, the CU-LS type of technical change is more interesting because it highlights certain trade-offs that capitalists face with respect to the choice of technique. These trade-offs open up the possibility of the divergence between not only social and capitalist goals but also between goals of individual capitalists and the capitalist class as a whole. Before looking at these important issues, it might be useful to pause and think about how one might define the types of technical change that we have discussed here, for example, CU-LS technical change, in a more general set-up with many commodities.

In a multi-sector circulating capital model of an economy with n sectors (and each sector producing only one commodity), each technique of production will be a vector of size $n + 1$. The first n elements of this vector will be the material inputs, that is, physical quantities, of the n commodities needed to produce one unit of the commodity; the last element will be the magnitude of labour input (assuming that labour is homogeneous). In such a case, there is no unique way to define, for instance, capital-using technical change. This is because there is no unique way to compare the sizes of the two n vectors of required material inputs before and after technical change. Following from the work of Morishima (1973), one approach to defining capital-using technical change has been the following: a new technique is considered to be capital-using if *every* element of the material input vector changes by non-negative amounts. While this captures the intuitive notion of 'more' capital being used in the new technique, it is clear that the definition is very restrictive (because *every* material input must rise or remain unchanged). There can be other ways to implement the intuition of 'more' capital input, for example, a larger Euclidean norm of the new material input

---

[8]For an excellent discussion of this and other issues related to technical change in capitalist economies, see Foley et al. (2019, Chapter 8).

vector, or a larger magnitude of some aggregate measure of the n vector of material inputs. One crucial advantage of working in a one-commodity model, as we have done in this section, is that we avoid this ambiguity – in a one-sector model, types of technical change can be defined uniquely and unambiguously.

6.2 Progressive Technical Change and Capitalism

The first question we wish to investigate is the relationship between progressive technical change and capitalist viability. For this analysis, we will use the diagram in Figure 6.1. In this diagram, we measure the labour input requirement, n', and the capital input requirement, a', associated with a *new technique of production* on the horizontal and vertical axes, respectively. The original technique of production, (n, a), is represented by the point O'.

The straight line AB represents the boundary (or limiting case) of progressive technical change given in (6.2). Hence, any point inside the triangle AOB represents progressive technical change, that is, they represent new techniques of production that reduce the labour embodied in a unit of corn compared to the old technique of production O'. On the other hand, the straight line CD represents the capitalist viability condition in (6.3). Hence, any point inside the triangle COD represents new techniques of production that reduce the total cost of producing a unit of corn at the existing price and wage rate, compared to the old technique of production O'. Two important results that highlight the possible technological irrationality of capitalism follow immediately from an inspection of Figure 6.1.

The first result is that there are many instance of progressive technical changes that will *not* be adopted by capitalist producers because they are not capitalistically viable. Starting from the original technique of production O', the whole set of progressive technical changes that will not be adopted by capitalist producers is represented by the triangle $AO'C$. This triangle represents all new techniques of production that are technologically progressive (because they are inside the triangle AOB) but are not capitalistically viable (because they are outside the triangle COD).

The second result is that capitalist producers might adopt new techniques of production that are *technologically regressive*. Starting from the original

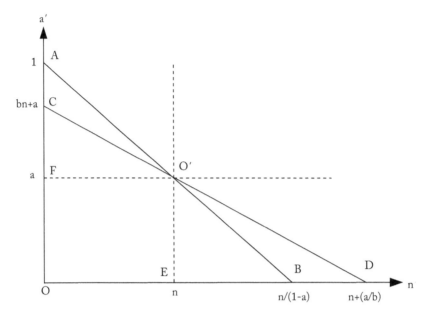

Figure 6.1 The relationship between progressive technical change and capitalistically viable technical change

Source: Author.

technique of production O', the set of technologically regressive techniques of production that might be adopted by capitalist producers is represented by the triangle $BO'D$. This triangle represents all new techniques of production that are capitalistically viable (because they lie inside the triangle COD) but are technologically regressive (because they are outside the triangle AOB).

Let us probe further. Using the original technique of production O', we can divide up the set of all the possible new techniques of production into four groups. These groups are represented by the regions to the northeast, southeast, southwest and northwest of O'. Northeast, northwest, southwest and southeast regions represent CU-LU, CU-LS, CS-LS and CS-LU technical change, respectively. From our discussion earlier, we know that the only really interesting case is the CU-LS technical change. Hence, we need to only focus on the region to the northwest of O'.

When we focus on the region to the northwest of O', we see another interesting result: for CU-LS type of technical change, all capitalistically viable techniques of production are also technologically progressive. To see this, note that the CU-LS type of technical change that involves capitalistically viable techniques of production (compared to the original one) is represented by the triangle $CO'F$; and CU-LS type of technical change that involve technologically progressive techniques of production (compared to the original one) is represented by the triangle $AO'F$. Since the triangle $CO'F$ is completely contained in the triangle $AO'F$, the result immediately follows that if we restrict ourselves to only CU-LS type of technical change, then capitalistically viable techniques of production are technologically progressive.[9]

6.3 Technical Change and the Rate of Profit

Now we turn to investigating the second question: What is the impact of technical change on the rate of profit? As I have noted in the introduction to this chapter, this question has attracted enormous scholarly attention over the past several decades.[10] Using Marx's analysis of LTFRP in Volume III of *Capital*, many scholars have understood the claim that technical change can lead to a fall in the rate of profit as a central proposition of Marxist political economy. After several decades of work on this issue, we have a fairly clear picture (Okishio, 1961; Roemer, 1981; Foley, 1986b; Laibman, 1992). Technical change cannot, on its own, lead to a fall in the rate of profit in a competitive setting if capitalists are assumed to behave in a reasonable manner, that is, if they choose to adopt new techniques if and only if it reduces the cost of production at existing prices. But the interaction of technical change and class struggle over the distribution of income *can* lead to a fall in the rate of profit. This is the main result I want to highlight in this section.

When the original technique of production, (n, a), is used, the rate of profit is given by

$$r = \frac{\text{profit}}{\text{total outlay}} = \frac{p - p\,(nb + a)}{p\,(nb + a)} = \frac{1 - nb - a}{nb + a}$$

---

[9]All the results of this section have been proved in a n-commodity model in Roemer (1977).

[10]For an introduction to the discussion of technical change and the rate of profit, see section 5.2.

where r is the rate of profit and p is the price of the commodity. A little algebraic manipulation shows that the rate of profit is given by

$$r = \frac{1}{nb + a} - 1 \tag{6.4}$$

The relationship in (6.4) can be called the *real wage rate-profit rate frontier*. It shows that, given the technique of production, (n, a), there is a negative relationship between the real wage rate, b, and the rate of profit, r. If the real wage rate rises, the rate of profit must fall, and vice versa. Thus, the income of the working class and the income of the capitalist class are negatively related to each other. That is why the relationship in (6.4) highlights the source of distributional conflict between the fundamental social classes.[11]

Suppose a new technique of production becomes available to an innovator capitalist that can produce 1 unit of corn using a' units of corn and n' units of labour, that is, the new technique of production is (n', a'). The innovator capitalist would only consider the new technique of production for adoption if it is capitalistically viable, that is, it reduces the cost of production at existing prices. Hence, the new technique of production, if it is to be adopted, must satisfy the condition given in (6.3). This will immediately imply that the innovator capitalist can earn a higher rate of profit if she adopts the new technique of production. To see this, note that if the new technique of production is used in production, it will generate a rate of profit, r', where

$$r' = \frac{\text{profit}}{\text{total outlay}} = \frac{p - p\,(n'b + a')}{p\,(n'b + a')} = \frac{1 - n'b - a'}{n'b + a'}$$

Hence, the rate of profit associated with the new technique of production is

$$r' = \frac{1}{n'b + a'} - 1 \tag{6.5}$$

so that, we have

$$r' - r = \frac{1}{n'b + a'} - \frac{1}{nb + a} \tag{6.6}$$

---

[11] A slightly different way of writing the real wage-profit rate frontier gives us what Foley and Michl (1999) have called the growth-distribution schedule. For a discussion of the real wage rate-profit rate frontier in an economy with more than one commodity, see Appendix A in Chapter 7.

Since the viability condition (6.3) must hold, this implies that $r' > r$.

The higher rate of profit provides the incentive to the innovator capitalist to adopt the new technique of production, (n', a'). Over time, the new technique, which generates a higher rate of profit, diffuses through the capitalist economy. Eventually, all capitalist producers adopt the new technique of production. When this happens, a new price of the commodity emerges, p'. At this new price, the average rate of profit in the economy now becomes

$$r'' = \frac{\text{profit}}{\text{total outlay}} = \frac{p' - p'\left(n'b + a'\right)}{p'\left(n'b + a'\right)} = \frac{1 - n'b - a'}{n'b + a'} = r' > r$$

Thus, we have a striking result: technical change that is capitalistically viable leads to a rise in the average rate of profit. In simplified form, this is the essence of the celebrated Okishio theorem (Okishio, 1961). In the one-commodity model we have been using, we have $r'' = r'$, that is, the average rate of profit after technical change was adopted by all capitalists is the same as the rate of profit earned by the innovator capitalist when she first introduces the new technique of production. That is why demonstrating the increase in the average rate of profit was easy. In a n-commodity model, like the one used in Okishio (1961), in general, the two profit rates will not be the same, that is, $r'' \neq r'$, and yet it can be demonstrated that $r'' > r$. In fact, the implication runs the other way too: if the average rate of profit rises after technical change, it must be capitalistically viable.[12]

The result described by the Okishio theorem shows that progress of capitalism will lead to a rising rate of profit.[13] It seems to contradict Marx's equally celebrated claim that the progress of capitalism will lead to a falling rate of profit (Marx, 1993b). In fact, there is less of a contradiction than seems at first sight.

6.4   A Marx-Okishio Threshold

The validity of the results of the Okishio theorem rests on a crucial, and implicit, assumption – that the real wage rate, b, remains unchanged after the new technique of production has been adopted widely in the capitalist

---

[12]This result is easy to see in the one-commodity model that we are using. It was first proved in a multi-sector model by Dietzenbacher (1989, Theorem 2).

[13]For an elegant proof of this theorem in a n-commodity model, see Roemer (1981, Theorem 4.6).

economy. In a sense, therefore, the result of Okishio's theorem is not surprising: if the real wage rate remains unchanged, then all the benefits of technological progress in terms of productivity growth are taken by capitalists. Naturally, then, the rate of profit rises.

While the assumption of a constant real wage rate might be true in some scenarios (for example, in a labour-surplus economy), it might not hold in others (for example, in a labour-constrained economy). Thus, it is interesting to revisit the Okishio theorem without this restrictive assumption. It seems intuitively clear that whether or not the rate of profit falls after the adoption of a new technique of production would depend on the magnitude of the growth of the real wage rate. After all, if the rate of profit rises with a constant real wage rate, it is equally clear that it will fall if the real wage rate rises by a large magnitude.

The idea that the rate of profit will fall even when technical change is capitalistically viable if the real wage rate rises fast enough is well known in the literature (Okishio, 1961; Roemer, 1977, 1981; Foley, 1986b; Dietzenbacher, 1989; Laibman, 1992). Once we recognize the dependence of Okishio's result on the fixity of the real wage rate, its critical thrust is significantly weakened. Since we are working with a one-commodity model, we can go one step further and derive what can be called a Marx-Okishio threshold (Basu, 2019). This is a threshold for the rate of growth of the real wage rate such that the following holds: if the growth rate of the real wage rate is higher than the threshold, the rate of profit will fall (and Marx's claim about the falling rate of profit will hold); if the growth rate of the real wage rate is lower than the threshold, the rate of profit will rise (and Okishio's claim about the rising rate of profit will be true).

To derive the value of the Marx-Okishio threshold, let us assume that the real wage rate is αb after the new technique of production is adopted, where α is some real number, that is, the real wage rate increases by $100(\alpha - 1)$ per cent. In this new situation, the rate of profit is

$$r''' = \frac{\text{profit}}{\text{total outlay}} = \frac{1 - a' - \alpha b n'}{a' + \alpha b n'} = \frac{1}{a' + \alpha b n'} - 1$$

The Marx-Okishio threshold is the value of α that ensures that $r''' = r$, that is, the rate of profit remains unchanged even after the new technique of production has been adopted. Let us denote the Marx-Okishio threshold as α^*, and note that it must satisfy the following condition,

$$\frac{1}{a' + \alpha^* bn'} - 1 = \frac{1}{a + bn} - 1$$

so that the Marx-Okishio threshold, α^*, is given by

$$\alpha^* = \frac{n}{n'} + \frac{a - a'}{bn'} = \frac{n}{n'} + \left(\frac{a}{a'} - 1\right) \frac{a'}{bn'} \tag{6.7}$$

How would a researcher calculate the Marx-Okishio threshold? Define n and n' as the reciprocal of output per person before and after technical change, respectively; define a and a' as the ratio of capital stock and net value added; finally, note that bn' is the share of wages in real value added. Once we collect data on these variables, we can use (6.7) to calculate the Marx-Okishio threshold.

Proposition 3. *If the real wage rate increases by more than $100(\alpha^* - 1)$ per cent after the new technique of production is adopted, then the rate of profit will fall; if the real wage rate increases by less than $100(\alpha^* - 1)$ per cent, then the rate of profit will rise.*

The proof follows immediately from the preceeding discussion. It is important to note that this proposition shows that both Marx and Okishio are right. What happens to the rate of profit after technical change in a capitalist economy depends on the movement of the real wage rate. If the real wage rate is sluggish, then the rate of profit will rise after technical change; if the real wage rate rises relatively rapidly, then the rate of profit will fall. Without more knowledge about the trajectory of the real wage rate, it is not possible to unambiguously predict the effect of technical change on the average rate of profit.

A useful way to summarize the whole argument presented in this section is to break down the process of technical change into four steps and see what happens to the profit rate at each step.

- Step 1: This is the initial situation. All capitalists use the old technique of production. The average profit rate is given by r.

- Step 2: A new technique becomes available to an innovator capitalist, and she evaluates whether it is profitable to adopt it. When carrying out this evaluation, she uses the existing prices and real wage rate. If the viability condition is satisfied, she adopts the new technique and her profit rate is r'. Obviously, the rate of profit she earns is higher than before, that is, $r' > r$. It is important to keep in mind that r' is the individual rate of profit (earned only by the innovator capitalist.)

- Step 3: Other capitalists adopt the new technique because of diffusion of the new technique across the economy. The average rate of profit, r'', is now equal to r' because all capitalists use the same technique of production as the innovator capitalist. Hence, the average rate of profit is higher than in the initial situation, that is, when the old technique was being used, that is, $r'' > r$. (Note that $r'' = r'$ in the one-commodity model I am using. If I used an n-commodity model, then r'' would not in general be equal to r'.)

- Step 4: There are changes in the labour market (or changes in the balance of class forces). This leads to a change in the real wage rate. If $\alpha > \alpha^*$, that is, if the real wage rate rises by more than the Marx-Okishio threshold, then the average profit rate falls, that is, $r''' < r$, where r''' is the new economy-wide, average rate of profit.

The last step, whereby the rate of profit falls, highlights an important problem faced by capitalist economies. This relates to the divergence between actions that are individually rational from those that are collectively rational. In this case, it is individually rational for a capitalist innovator to search for and adopt new techniques of production that reduce the cost of production. But under certain conditions, adopting the new technique reduces the average rate of profit and goes against the collective interests of the capitalist class.

The problem is that capitalism suffers from a *social coordination* problem (Foley et al., 2019). Being a competitive system, there is no way that capitalists can coordinate their actions. Once the innovator capitalist adopts the new technique, her rate of profit rises. Competitive pressures then lead to a diffusion of the new technique through the rest of the economy. What the individual capitalist, and the capitalist class as a whole, does not have control over is the effect of technical change on the average real wage rate. In the case when the institutional set-up allows for workers to bargain for and get a relatively higher real wage rate, the average rate of profit falls. Individually rational actions become collectively irrational!

Let us use data from the US CB sector to see the empirical relevance of the Marx-Okishio threshold. In Figure 6.2, I present a scatter plot of two variables measured annually for the period between 1979 and 2019. On the horizontal axis, I measure the difference between the ratio of the average weekly real wage rate in successive years and the Marx-Okishio threshold for each year (calculated using the expression in (6.7)); on the vertical axis, I measure the change in the annual rate of profit (measured as the ratio of net operating surplus and the replacement cost value of net fixed assets). From Figure 6.2, we see a strong negative relationship between the variables: when the actual real wage rate is higher than the Marx-Okishio threshold, the rate of profit declines, which is exactly what we expect on the basis of the discussion in this section. The average relationship is captured by the dashed line (the bivariate regression line) which has a statistically significant slope of -1.88. This means that, on average, if the ratio of actual real wage rate is higher than the Marx-Okishio threshold by unity, then the rate of profit declines by 1.88 percentage points.

6.4.1 Marx-Okishio Threshold for Different Types of Technical Change

To see how the Marx-Okishio threshold changes according to the type of technical change, let us go back to (6.7). Using the expression for the Marx-Okishio threshold, we see that,

$$\alpha^* - 1 = \left(\frac{n}{n'} - 1\right) + \left(\frac{a}{a'} - 1\right)\frac{a'}{bn'} \tag{6.8}$$

is composed of three parts: the rate of change of labour productivity,

$$\frac{(1/n' - 1/n)}{(1/n)} = \frac{n}{n'} - 1$$

the rate of change of capital productivity,

$$\frac{(1/a' - 1/a)}{(1/a)} = \frac{a - a'}{a'} = \left(\frac{a}{a'} - 1\right)$$

and the composition of capital of the new technique of production at the original real wage rate,

$$\frac{a'}{bn'}$$

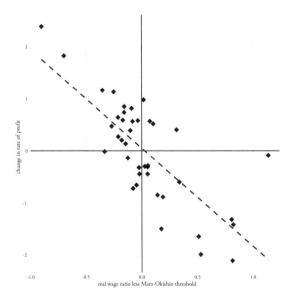

Figure 6.2   Scatter plot for the US CB sector between 1979 and 2019 of (a) the difference between ratio of real wage rate in consecutive years and the Marx-Okishio threshold for that year and (b) change in the rate of profit

Source: Author's calculations using data from NIPA Table 1.14, US Bureau of Economic Analysis, and FRED, Federal Reserve Bank of St. Louis.

For CS-LS technical change, since $0 < a' < a$ and $0 < n' < n$, all the terms on the right-hand side of (6.8) are positive, that is, $a^* > 1$.[14] This means that there is a whole range of positive growth rates of real wage rate, including, of course, zero real wage growth, that is, compatible with a rising rate of profit: this range is given by $0 \leq \alpha < \alpha^*$, where $\alpha - 1$ is the actual growth rate of the real wage rate. Only if the actual growth rate of the real wage is larger than $\alpha^* - 1$ will the rate of profit fall.

On the other hand, CU-LS technical change highlights a trade-off that capitalists face. Here, technical change reduces the labour input, but only at the cost of increasing the capital input. This is a case that was discussed by Marx and has been highlighted in the work of Duncan Foley and Tom Michl, who call it Marx-biased technical change (Foley and Michl, 1999). It opens up the possibility that technical change, the key strength of capitalism, might

---

[14]We rule out $a' = 0$ to avoid division by zero.

also reduce profitability, the driving force of capitalism. This is, therefore, a peculiar way in which capitalism undermines itself.

To see this, let us note that the last expression on the right-hand side of (6.8) is negative for CU-LS technical change (this is because $a' > a$). If we also have

$$\left(\frac{n}{n'} - 1\right) < \left(1 - \frac{a}{a'}\right)\frac{a'}{bn'}$$

then this shows that $\alpha^* - 1 < 0$. This condition tells us that if the growth rate of labour productivity, $(n/n') - 1$, is less than negative of the change in capital productivity, $1 - (a/a')$, multiplied by the OCC of the new technique (evaluated at old prices), $(a'/bn') = (pa'/wn')$, then $\alpha^* - 1 < 0$. In such a case, we have a situation where *any* increase in the actual real wage rate, including a zero growth, will lead to a fall in the rate of profit. The relevant range is captured by the condition $\alpha^* < 1 \leq \alpha$, where $\alpha - 1$ is the actual growth rate of the real wage rate. In fact, it is striking to note that there is a whole range of negative values of the growth rate of the real wage rate that is also compatible with a fall in the rate of profit. This range is given by $\alpha^* < \alpha < 1$, where $\alpha - 1$ is the actual growth rate of the real wage rate. Only if the real wage rate is *pushed down* far enough, that is, $\alpha < \alpha^*$, will the rate of profit rise. Of course, in this case, the capital–labour conflict over the distribution of income is bound to be intense.

At the end of the previous section, we had computed the Marx-Okishio threshold for the US CB sector between 1979 and 2019. When we compute the average value of the Marx-Okishio threshold between 2000 and 2019, we get 0.915. Thus, here we have a case where the Marx-Okishio threshold is lower than unity. In such a situation, even a zero growth of the real wage rate would have led to a decline in the rate of profit.

6.5 Constant Rate of Exploitation

We have seen earlier that if the wage rate grows at a rate that is larger than the Marx-Okishio threshold, then the rate of profit will fall after technical change. Here we wish to investigate a special case, one that Marx used in his analysis, where the rate of exploitation remains constant before and after technical change. This is a special case of the analysis with a rising real wage rate because, in a context of rising labour productivity, the rate of exploitation can remain constant only if the real wage rate rises. It is under this assumption that Marx had worked out his LTFRP (Marx, 1993b, Chapter 13). The next proposition shows that Marx's claim is correct even when we consider capitalistically viable technical change.

Proposition 4. *Consider capitalistically viable technical change that is of the CU-LS type. If the rate of exploitation does not change, then the rate of profit will fall.*

To see the proof, recall that the rate of exploitation, denoted by e, is the ratio of surplus value and variable capital. Let us denote by λ the value of one unit of corn when the old technique of production, (n, a), is in use. As before, let us assume that the real wage rate is b. Then, the variable capital per hour of labour is $nb\lambda$ and the surplus value is $(\lambda - (nb + a)\lambda)$. Hence, the rate of exploitation is given by

$$e = \frac{1 - (nb + a)}{nb} \tag{6.9}$$

Suppose the new technique of production is given by (n', a') and the value of a unit of corn using this new technique of production is given by λ'. If the real wage rate changes to αb, an argument similar to the one used above shows that the rate of exploitation, after technical change, is given by

$$e' = \frac{1 - (n'\alpha b + a')}{n'\alpha b}$$

For the rate of exploitation to be constant, that is, $e' = e$, the value of α must be given by:

$$\bar{\alpha} = \frac{(1 - a')\, n}{(1 - a)\, n'} \tag{6.10}$$

To see what happens to the rate of profit, in this case, we need only compare $\bar{\alpha}$ with α^*, the Marx-Okishio threshold given in (6.7). A little algebraic manipulation shows that

$$\bar{\alpha} - \alpha^* = \frac{(bn + a - 1)\,(a - a')}{nb\,(1 - a)} \tag{6.11}$$

Since $a < 1$, the denominator of the expression on the right-hand side is positive. Since technical change is of the CU-LS type, we have $a' > a$ and

$n' < n$. Hence, $a - a' < 0$. Moreover, capitalist producers will only adopt techniques of production that are productive. This applies to the old technique of production, as much as to the new. Hence, $bn + a < 1$. Hence, both terms in the numerator of (6.11) are negative. Since the denominator is positive, this shows that the fraction is positive, so that $\bar{\alpha} > \alpha^*$. Using Proposition 3, we see that the rate of profit will fall after technical change.

What is the intuitive meaning of this result? Proposition 4 tells us that when a capitalist economy undergoes CU-LS technical change and socio-economic forces manage to keep the rate of exploitation (or the ratio of profit and wage income) constant, then the rate of profit will fall. How can this come about? Let us imagine a new cost-reducing technique of production being adopted by an innovator capitalist. As the new technique diffuses in the capitalist economy, other producers adopt it too. Over time, the new technique becomes universally used. Parallel to this process of technical change, the economy also witnesses changes in the labour market. In the context of the rise in labour productivity coming from the adoption of the new technique of production, workers are able to bid up the real wage rate. In fact, they manage to push up the real wage to the extent that is necessary to keep the rate of exploitation (or the profit–wage ratio) constant, that is, to keep the balance of class forces unchanged.

If workers manage to do so, the new technique of production, which has already been universally adopted, is no longer cost-reducing when compared to the original technique of production. This last point can be seen by comparing the cost of production with the new technique of production at the new real wage rate, with the cost of production with the original technique of production at the old real wage rate:

$$(n'\alpha b + a') - (nb + a)$$

Plugging the value of α from (6.10), we get

$$n'\alpha b + a' - (nb + a) = \frac{bn(1 - a')}{(1 - a)} + a' - nb - a$$
$$= \frac{(a' - a)(1 - a - nb)}{1 - a} > 0$$

because technical change is CU-LS, so that $a' - a > 0$, and the original technique of production is productive, so that $1 - a - nb > 0$. That is why the rate of profit falls.

6.6 Conclusion

In this chapter, we have studied the relationship between capitalism and technical change. We have highlighted two important results. First, technical change in a capitalist context is crucially impacted by profitability considerations because only those new techniques of production are adopted that are capitalistically viable. This creates the possibility of divergence between societal needs and capitalist profitability. Many techniques of production that are desirable from a societal point of view will not be adopted because they do not increase the rate of profit. Similarly, many new techniques of production might be adopted that are inimical to broader societal interests.

Second, we have presented an approach to the vexed issue of the impact of technical change on the rate of profit. We have argued that there is no necessary contradiction between the claims advanced by Marx and Okishio. Both can be accommodated in a more general framework where we allow the real wage rate to be impacted by class struggle. In that case, which seems quite realistic, whether or not the rate of profit falls after technical change in a capitalist economy will depend crucially on whether workers are able to force a rise in the real wage rate parallel to technical change.

One special case of this general discussion regarding the effect of technical change on the rate of profit was discussed by Marx in Volume III of *Capital*. This is the case where the rate of exploitation (also the wage–profit ratio) remains constant over the process of technical change. This is not implausible. In many advanced capitalist countries, institutions of collective bargaining might allow workers to keep the wage share of national income, that is, the wage–profit ratio, constant. In this institutional context, if technical change is of the CU-LS type, which Foley and Michl (1999) have called Marx-biased technical change, then the average rate of profit will fall.

There is an interesting technical issue that is worth highlighting. In the one-commodity model that we have worked with in this chapter, the rate of exploitation is also equal to the ratio of profits and wages. To see this, note that profit income per unit of output is $p - p(nb + a)$ and nominal wages per unit of output is pnb. Hence, the ratio of profits and wages is equal to e, the rate of exploitation, as defined in (6.9). The identity of the rate of exploitation, which is defined in terms of value, and the profit–wage ratio, which is defined in terms of prices, is no longer true in models with more than one commodity. In fact, in general linear models, where the nominal wage rate is the numeraire, the scale of production in each sector enters into the definition of the profit–wage ratio (Roemer, 1981, Chapter 6). On the other hand, the rate of exploitation can be defined without referring to the scale of production. Hence, in general, the two will not be equal. There is one special case, the New Interpretation of Marx's labour theory of value, which I discuss in detail in the next chapter, where the equality obtains even in a general n-commodity model.

Further Readings
- An insightful discussion of various aspects of technical change can be found in Laibman (1992, Chapters 5–8). In these chapters, the effect of technical change on the rate of profit when the rate of exploitation remains unchanged is worked out in a two-commodity model.

- A rigorous treatment of the issues discussed in this section within the context of a n-commodity model can be found in Roemer (1981, Chapters 4–6).

- An analysis of the effect of technical change on the rate of profit when the profit–wage ratio remains constant is worked out in a two-commodity model in Roemer (1977, 1981). An important finding is that only sectoral profit-wage ratios, but not the aggregate profit–wage ratio, can be defined without reference to the scale of production. Moreover, sectoral profit-wage ratios can remain constant only when the real wage varies across sectors, that is, we need to assume non-competitive labour markets. The main result in Roemer (1977, 1981) is that the rate of profit falls (or remains unchanged) if there is cost-reducing CU-LS technical change in the capital goods (consumer goods) sector. This result has been generalized to the case of a n-commodity model in Chen (2019), which shows that when there is cost-reducing CU-LS technical change in any sector with sectoral profit-wage ratios remaining constant, the equilibrium profit rate falls.

7

The Transformation Problem

The relationship between 'value' and 'price' of commodities has been an important issue of investigation in the classical-Marxian tradition for more than two centuries.[1] By 'value' we mean, as in the previous chapters, the socially necessary abstract simple labour directly and indirectly needed to produce a commodity, and by 'price' we mean prices of production, that is, the set of prices that can ensure a uniform rate of profit in all industries (see section 5.1). The transformation problem refers to attempts to offer consistent conceptualizations of the relationship between value and price, as defined here.

Along with the literature on the impact of technical change on the rate of profit, which we discussed in the previous chapter, the literature on the transformation problem is arguably one of the largest in Marxist political economy. In this chapter, I reinterpret the vast literature on the transformation problem as consisting of attempts to provide meaningful answers to two questions.

- Can a set of prices of production be calculated consistently that avoids mistakes made by Marx?
- If a consistent set of prices of production can be calculated, is there any role left for value magnitudes? Are value magnitudes redundant?

The first question relates to the computation of a set of prices of production that avoids some mistakes Marx made. The second question relates to the

---

[1] The discussion in this chapter draws on Basu (2017).

nature of possible relationships between value and price magnitudes, given that the latter can be calculated in a consistent manner. In this chapter, I provide both a brief survey of the existing literature on, and detailed treatments of two approaches to, the transformation problem by organizing the discussion around these two questions. I will discuss how these two questions emerged and how the Marxist tradition addressed the questions.[2]

The two approaches I take up for detailed treatment are the Standard Interpretation (SI) and the New Interpretation (NI). The SI was the traditional approach to the transformation problem until the 1970s. It emerged in the early 1900s in the work of the German statistician-economist Ladislaus von Bortkiewicz, and was popularized by Paul Sweezy and beautifully formalized by scholars like Nobuo Okishio, Michio Morishima and John Roemer. The SI offered a strong answer to the first question by showing that a consistent set of prices of production could be calculated. It provided a weak answer to the second question in the form of the Fundamental Marxian Theorem (FMT). The FMT is an important result and captures a key Marxist intuition: surplus value (which arise from the exploitation of the working class) and profits are inextricably linked; one cannot have profits without surplus value, and vice versa. But this provides only a qualitative relationship between the price system and the value system. The SI could not provide, due to conceptual problems I discuss in detail in the chapter, a robust quantitative relationship between price and value.

The approach that I think has the most promise is the NI, which was developed independently in the late 1970s by Gérard Duménil and Duncan Foley. It offered a way to move beyond the conceptual problems of the SI by redefining a key concept: the value of labour-power. In this chapter, I offer a new way to understand the motivation for this redefinition, and show how the NI offers robust answers to both questions that have framed discussions of the transformation problem. I also point out that there is an incompleteness in the NI, but that addressing the incompleteness is both feasible and opens up fruitful avenues of research.

Throughout the chapter, I use a simple example of an economy that produces three commodities to explain all the concepts of the SI and the NI. I use numbers to illustrate the computation of all key magnitudes, and I offer algorithms to carry out calculations of value and price magnitudes for an economy of an arbitrary size, that is, which produces n commodities. The

---

[2]A good companion reading for this chapter is Mohun and Veneziani (2017).

discussion in the text of the chapter is kept relatively less technical. I present a formal analysis of a general linear economy, both with homogeneous and heterogeneous labour, in Appendix 7.A. Code to implement the examples discussed, and the algorithms presented in the text, in the R statistical environment are given in Appendix 7.B.

7.1 Ricardo, Marx and Bortkiewicz

It is useful to begin the discussion of the transformation problem with David Ricardo and Karl Marx. Both these scholars were aware of the fact that prices (of production) and values of commodities were related to each other in complicated ways and that they need not necessarily coincide. While they shared this understanding, they had different ways of conceptualizing the correspondence between value and prices of production.

Ricardo thought that the ratios of prices and and ratios of values were *approximately equal* for individual commodities. After examining ample textual evidence, Stigler (1958) summarized this contention with the famous quip that Ricardo had a 93 per cent labour theory of value, with the 93 per cent figure capturing the degree of approximation involved in the value-price correspondence. On the other hand, as we have seen in section 5.1, Marx understood that profit rate equalization in conjunction with different OCCs across industries would necessarily lead to a deviation of prices (of production) from values of individual commodities. Hence, he conceptualized the correspondence between values and prices at the aggregate level, as we have emphasized throughout this book. For him, the process of equalization of the rate of profit was driven by the movement of capital across industries in search of higher rates of profit. This process tended to push the economy, in the long run, towards a state where all industries earned a uniform rate of profit and commodities exchanged at prices of production. Since industries differed in their OCC, this meant that prices (of production) and values of individual commodities necessarily diverged from each other.

For Marx, emergence of a uniform rate of profit (and the corresponding set of prices of production) was primarily a way of conceptualizing the redistribution of surplus value across industries enforced by competitive pressures (Baumol, 1974). He referred to this process as the 'transformation' of values into prices of production, and thought that both surplus value and total value would be preserved in this process of transformation. That is why he proposed the value-price equivalence underlying his labour theory of value in Volume III of *Capital* in terms of two aggregate equalities: (*a*) total value = total price and (*b*) total surplus value = total profits. We can see that these equalities hold in the example that we discussed in Tables 5.1 and 5.2. Total value and surplus value before the computation of the prices of production in Table 5.1 are 610 and 110, respectively; and total price and total profit after the 'transformation', that is, after the computation of the prices of production in Table 5.2 are, respectively, 610 and 110. They remain unchanged.

7.1.1 Getting Units Right

Before we proceed further, it is important to clarify one dimensional issue. How could Marx have claimed the equivalence between total value and total price, or total surplus value and total profits, when the quantities on the two sides of these equalities are measured in different units? After all, values are measured in units of labour hours and prices are measured in units of a currency (dollars, say). So, how can we meaningfully assert that 610 units of value is equal to 610 units of revenue computed with prices (of production), or that 110 units of surplus value is equal to 110 units of profits? The answer lies in the fact that Marx implicitly used, all through the three volumes of *Capital*, a monetary expression of value (MEV), as we saw in section 3.2, to freely move between value and price magnitudes.

In the examples given in the quotations in section 3.2.4, Marx asserts equivalence between value and price magnitudes at the aggregate level (highlighted by the word 'average' in many cases). Recall from our discussion in section 3.2 that the MEV is defined as the quantity of money (that is, units of the currency) that is equivalent to one hour of social labour. Thus, a value magnitude (measured in units of labour hours) could be multiplied with the MEV to generate its price (monetary) equivalent (measured in units of the currency). Thus, implicitly using the MEV, Marx could freely move between values and prices so that when he discusses price–value deviations, both terms (of the equality or inequality) are expressed in terms of the same units. In the examples discussed in Tables 5.1 and 5.2, we have implicitly used a MEV of $1 per hour of social labour.

While the dimensional problem was explicitly noted by Michio Morishima, he did not propose the concept of a MEV to resolve the problem. Instead, he suggested 'normalizing prices so that they are dimensionally identical with values' (Morishima, 1973, p. 73). His method of normalizing prices was to express all prices in terms of the nominal wage rate. Thus, for any commodity, the 'normalized' price is the ratio of the price of production and the nominal wage rate, that is, $p_w = p/w$, where p, w and p_w, refer to the vector of price of production, the scalar nominal wage rate and the vector of normalized price, respectively. According to Morishima, this would solve the dimensional problem because, on the one hand, values were expressed in units of labour hours, and the normalized price of any commodity 'expresses the amount of labour which can be obtained by offering a unit of that commodity' on the market. While this does solve the dimensional issue, it commits another conceptual mistake. What is purchased on the market is labour-power and not labour. The nominal wage rate is the price of one unit of labour-power. Hence, the normalized price expresses the amount of labour-power which can be obtained by offering a unit of any commodity. It is true that both labour-power and labour are expressed in the same unit, for example, hours. Hence, the dimensional issue is addressed by Morishima's proposal, but only at the cost of importing the conceptual mistake of conflating labour and labour-power.[3]

7.1.2 Marx's Errors

With this small but necessary detour on units of measurement, let us return to the main narrative. Immediately upon the publication of Volume III of *Capital* in 1894, critics like the Austrian economist Eugen von Böhm-Bawerk discovered two problems in Marx's transformation procedure: (*a*) inputs had not been transformed from value to price magnitudes, even as outputs had been and (*b*) the rate of profit had been calculated using value magnitudes, whereas a consistent procedure would need to calculate it in terms of prices of production. Going back to the examples discussed in Tables 5.1 and 5.2, we see both these problems (as was noted at the end of section 5.1).

---

[3] Another way to state this problem is to note that value of commodities come from labour embodied in them, while the nominal wage rate gives a measure of labour-power commanded on the market. It is a mistake, coming right from Adam Smith, to equate labour-power commanded with labour embodied.

Since the prices (of production) of the output from all the sectors are different from their values, and since the outputs of some or all these sectors are precisely the non-labour inputs into the production of all the (other) sectors, the constant capital used to purchase the means of production would no longer be equal to its value. But Marx's procedure of computing prices of production does not take this into account (in the computations of Table 5.1, inputs have been valued in terms of labour embodied, not in terms of prices of production). In effect, therefore, Marx is using two sets of prices for the same commodity – one price at which it is bought as an input (this price is proportional to the value of the commodity), and another price at which it is sold as an output (this is the price of production and is not proportional to the value of the commodity). This is clearly problematic: a commodity cannot be bought and sold at different prices because purchase and sale are two sides of the same transaction. Moreover, the rate of profit needs to be computed with price magnitudes and not value quantities. For instance, the uniform profit rate of 22 per cent in Table 5.2 is computed as the ratio of total surplus value and total capital outlay (constant + variable capital). In general, this aggregate value rate of profit is not equal to the uniform rate of profit computed with price magnitudes.[4]

7.1.3   *The First Question and Its Answer*

This leads to the first question around which I want to organize the discussion of the transformation problem.

Question 1 (Transformation Problem). *Can a uniform rate of profit and a corresponding set of prices of production be computed consistently that avoid Marx's mistakes?*

The answer is in the affirmative. In 1907, the German statistician-economist Ladislaus von Bortkiewicz demonstrated that the two errors in Marx's procedure could be easily corrected (von Bortkiewicz, 1949). But to do so, one would need to make the *use-value basis of production* in all sectors explicit, that is, one would need information about input–output ratios – how many units of the output of a sector is used as an input into the production

---

[4]In fact, the aggregate value rate of profit and the uniform price rate of profit are both weighted harmonic means of sectoral value rates of profits, where the weights are given by the direct labour-time expended in production in a sector under a given gross output vector (for the aggregate value rate of profit) and the specific von Neumann golden age output vector (for the uniform price rate of profit) (Roemer, 1981, Theorem 4.1 and Corollary 4.2).

process in every other sector, including that sector itself? Note that in the price of production calculations in Tables 5.1 and 5.2, the use-value basis of production is hidden – it has not been made explicit by Marx. Thus, in doing this, we would necessarily go beyond the procedure adopted by Marx.

Once the input–output information is available, and under the assumption that these input–output ratios are exogenously given, we can use prices of production in computing the monetary magnitudes of inputs used in the production process in each sector. Thus, a linear system of *simultaneous equations*, with each equation representing a different sector, could be solved to correctly compute the prices of production for the output of all sectors – with each sector earning the same rate of profit. Since this was a 'simultaneous' equation system, the procedure ensured that a commodity is bought and sold at the same price.

Moreover, the linear equation system would be written to ensure that each sector earned the same rate of profit – the uniform rate of profit – where the latter was computed using the same set of prices (of production). Hence, there is no possibility of making Marx's errors. Under certain plausible conditions, the simultaneous equation system could be solved to arrive at a uniform rate of profit and the corresponding set of relative prices. Thus, we could correct Marx's errors and compute a consistent set of prices of production. But discussions of the transformation problem did not end there because the solution highlighted another issue: *only one* of Marx's aggregate value-price equalities could hold (von Bortkiewicz, 1949). When the simultaneous equation system is solved to compute prices of production, it is no longer possible to derive *both* aggregate value-price equalities that Marx had asserted.

7.2 The Standard Interpretation

Revival of interest in Marxist economics in the 1960s and 1970s saw further development and elaboration of the Bortkiewicz argument in the works of, among others, Francis Seton, Nobuo Okishio and Michio Morishima. The Seton-Okishio-Morishima contribution recast the question about the computation of prices of production in the Leontief-Sraffa input–output framework, thereby making explicit the use-value basis and sectoral interdependence of capitalist production – something that was already implicit in von Bortkiewicz (1949). At the same time, it generalized the analysis of Marx (who had worked with five-industry numerical examples) and Bortkiewicz (who has worked with a three-department algebraic model) to a general n-commodity economy. The Seton-Okishio-Morishima contribution responded to the first question in the transformation problem debate by demonstrating that in a general n-sector circulating capital model of a capitalist economy with no joint production, *relative* prices of production and a uniform rate of profit could be derived rigorously from data on technology, that is, input–output ratios, and the real wage (commodity) bundle.

Before moving to the next step of the debate on the transformation problem, let me illustrate the methodology of the SI with an example that is based on, and extends, the example discussed in Pasinetti (1977, pp. 144–49). Working through the example will clarify many important concepts in the labour theory of value. It will also point to the strengths and limitations of different interpretations developed by Marxist scholars. R code to implement the example can be found in Appendix 7.B.1.

7.2.1   An Example of a Three-Sector Economy

Consider an economy with three industries, where each industry produces only one output and there is no fixed capital. The second assumption means that all the capital inputs are used up in one cycle of production, that is, we only have circulating capital. To be concrete, let us call the output of Industry 1 as 'wheat', the output of Industry 2 as 'iron' and the output of Industry 3 as 'meat'. We assume that the economy is in a state of simple reproduction, that is, all its net output is consumed, and there is no net investment to increase the scale of production.

Technology and Real Wage Bundle

Let us start by specifying the technology in this economy, that is, specifying the amounts of each commodity required in the production of all the commodities, and the amount of direct labour input required in each commodity's production. The first is given by the 3×3 matrix, A, where

$$A = \begin{bmatrix} 0.413 & 2.571 & 0.500 \\ 0.027 & 0.286 & 0.050 \\ 0.020 & 0.286 & 0.250 \end{bmatrix} \tag{7.1}$$

and the second by the 1×3 vector,

$$l = \begin{bmatrix} 0.040 & 0.571 & 0.500 \end{bmatrix} \tag{7.2}$$

The columns of the A matrix give us non-labour input requirements in each industry, and the corresponding element of the l vector gives us the labour input requirement. For instance, the above specification of technology tells us that

- to produce 1 unit of wheat (Industry 1), this economy requires 0.413 units of wheat, 0.027 units of iron, 0.020 units of meat and 0.04 units of labour;

- to produce 1 unit of iron (Industry 2), the economy requires 2.571 units of wheat, 0.286 units of iron, 0.286 units of meat and 0.571 units of labour; and

- to produce 1 unit of meat (Industry 3), the economy requires 0.5 units of wheat, 0.05 units of iron, 0.25 units of meat and 0.5 units of labour.

An important variable in the SI is the real wage bundle. This gives the amounts of each commodity workers can purchase with their wage income for every hour of labour-power sold to capitalists. We will work with the classical savings assumption, that is, workers do not save. Hence, in this example economy, workers spend all their income on consumption. This will mean that the monetary amount used to purchase the real wage bundle will be equal to the total wage income.

We also need to decide which commodities workers consume. It seems realistic to assume that workers do not consume all commodities produced in any capitalist economy. After all, capital goods are not meant for consumption. Since iron can be considered such a capital good, it will not figure in the consumption basket of workers. Thus, the real wage bundle will have positive quantities of only the other two commodities, wheat and meat, while the amount of iron in the real wage bundle will be zero. Let us make these ideas concrete by specifying the real wage bundle as the following 3×1 vector,

$$b = \begin{bmatrix} 2.000 \\ 0.000 \\ 0.167 \end{bmatrix} \tag{7.3}$$

What does this tell us? The nominal wage rate in this economy is such that workers, by spending all their wage income, are able to purchase 2 units of wheat and 0.167 units of meat for every hour of labour-power that they sell to capitalist producers.

Gross and Net Output

To facilitate the analysis, we will need to specify the size of the economy. Suppose the *net* output of this economy consists of 180 units of wheat, 0 units of iron and 30 units of meat, then the net output vector can be written as

$$y = \begin{bmatrix} 180 \\ 0 \\ 30 \end{bmatrix} \tag{7.4}$$

The difference between gross and net output is an important one. To see this clearly, note that production of each commodity requires inputs of all the commodities in the economy. The input requirements are captured precisely by the A matrix. Hence, for this economy to be viable and functioning, the total (that is, gross) output of each commodity must be the sum of two magnitudes: (*a*) the amount of the commodity that is required as input in the production of all the commodities and (*b*) the amount of net output (which, in this example, is consumed, because there is no investment).

If we denote the gross and net outputs by the 3×1 vectors

$$x = \begin{bmatrix} x_1 \\ x_2 \\ x_3 \end{bmatrix} \tag{7.5}$$

and

$$y = \begin{bmatrix} y_1 \\ y_2 \\ y_3 \end{bmatrix} \tag{7.6}$$

respectively, where subscripts identify sectors, we will have

$$x = Ax + y$$

To see this clearly, let us write the equation for the first commodity:

$$x_1 = a_{11}x_1 + a_{12}x_2 + a_{13}x_3 + y_1$$

Note that a_{11} is the amount of commodity 1 required for producing 1 unit of itself. Hence, if x_1 is the total output of commodity 1, then $a_{11}x_1$ amount of commodity 1 will be needed as input. Similarly, a_{12} is the amount of commodity 1 needed to produce each unit of commodity 2. Since x_2 amount of commodity 2 is produced as output, that will require $a_{12}x_2$ amount of commodity 1 as input. In exactly the same way, we can see that $a_{13}x_3$ is the amount of commodity 1 required to produce the output of commodity 3, that is, x_3. Hence, $a_{11}x_1 + a_{12}x_2 + a_{13}x_3$ is the total amount of commodity 1 used up as inputs in the production process. Since x_1 is the total (gross) output of commodity 1, the net output is given by $y_1 = x_1 - (a_{11}x_1 + a_{12}x_2 + a_{13}x_3)$. The same logic holds for the second commodity, so that

$$x_2 = a_{21}x_1 + a_{22}x_2 + a_{23}x_3 + y_2$$

and for the third commodity, so that

$$x_3 = a_{31}x_1 + a_{32}x_2 + a_{33}x_3 + y_3$$

Together, the three equations give us the above relationship between the matrix A and the vectors x and y. If the technology is productive, that is, capable of producing positive amount of net output of some commodity, then the matrix $(I - A)$ is invertible, and we get $x = (I - A)^{-1}y$. Using our chosen net output vector in (7.4) and the A matrix in (7.1), we get the gross output vector as

$$x = \begin{bmatrix} 450 \\ 21 \\ 60 \end{bmatrix} \tag{7.7}$$

Note that the gross output is a strictly positive vector, that is, the gross output of all commodities is strictly greater than 0. This is as it should be in any meaningful (and productive) system. What is the interpretation of the gross output vector in this example? It tells us that the system produces a total of 450 units of wheat, 21 units of iron and 60 units of meat. Of this, 180 units of wheat, 0 units of iron and 30 units of meat are the net output, that is, the magnitudes of the three commodities left after all input requirements have been taken care of. While all the iron is used up as inputs in the production process, there is a net output of both wheat and meat. These are consumed by workers and capitalists (since there is no investment).

The Value System

What is the amount of labour embodied in, that is value of, each commodity? If we denote the 1×3 vector of values by Λ,

$$\Lambda = \begin{bmatrix} \Lambda_1 & \Lambda_2 & \Lambda_3 \end{bmatrix} \tag{7.8}$$

then we will have $\Lambda = \Lambda A + l$. To see this, let us write out the value equation for the first commodity:

$$\Lambda_1 = \Lambda_1 a_{11} + \Lambda_2 a_{21} + \Lambda_3 a_{31} + l_1$$

Since a_{11} units of commodity 1 is used as input into producing each unit of itself, the value transferred from the input is $\Lambda_1 a_{11}$. Again, since a_{21} is the amount of commodity 2 used as input for producing each unit of commodity 1, the value transferred from the input is $\Lambda_2 a_{21}$. In a similar way, $\Lambda_3 a_{31}$ is the value transferred by the input of commodity 3. Hence, $\Lambda_1 a_{11} + \Lambda_2 a_{21} + \Lambda_3 a_{31}$ is the total amount of value transferred from the material inputs, and l_1 is the amount of value added, to each unit of commodity 1. That is what gives us the above equation. The same logic gives us equivalent equations for the other two commodities, that is for commodity 2, we have

$$\Lambda_2 = \Lambda_1 a_{21} + \Lambda_2 a_{22} + \Lambda_3 a_{23} + l_2$$

and for the third commodity, we have

$$\Lambda_3 = \Lambda_1 a_{31} + \Lambda_2 a_{32} + \Lambda_3 a_{33} + l_3$$

We put these together in the matrix equation, $\Lambda = \Lambda A + l$.

If the technology is productive, that is, capable of producing some positive amount of net output, then the matrix $(I - A)$ is invertible, and we get $\Lambda = l(I - A)^{-1}$. When we use the numbers for this example, we see that the value vector is given by

$$\Lambda = \begin{bmatrix} 0.182 & 1.818 & 0.909 \end{bmatrix} \tag{7.9}$$

With this value vector, we can calculate the value of the real wage bundle, $\Lambda b = 0.515$. What does this tell us? It shows that for every hour of labour-power sold by workers, they get back 0.515 hours of social labour-time equivalent in their real wage bundle. If every hour of labour-power gives 1 hour of labour in the production process, we see the immediate source of exploitation: every hour of labour of the workers creates, on average, 1 unit of value (social labour-time); workers get back in wages, on average, 0.515 hours of social labour-time. The surplus value appropriated by capitalist producers is $1 - 0.515$ per hour of labour-power purchased. Hence, the rate of exploitation, that is, the ratio of what the capitalist appropriates to what she pays, is given by $e = (1 - \Lambda b)/\Lambda b = (1 - 0.515)/0.515 = 0.9412$. This means that capitalists appropriate 48.49 per cent (=0.9412/(1+0.9412)) of the value created by the labour of workers, that is, the unpaid labour of workers is about 49 per cent of their total labour.

The Price System

The three-sector capitalist economy will be in long run equilibrium when capital invested in each sector earns the same rate of profit. Let us call this the uniform (or average) rate of profit and denote it by r. The set of prices which can support the uniform rate of profit in each sector are known as the prices of production. In the context of this example, the price (of production) is a 1×3 vector,

$$p = \begin{bmatrix} p_1 & p_2 & p_3 \end{bmatrix} \tag{7.10}$$

and is specified by the following system of equations,

$$p = (1 + r)(pA + wl)$$

where r is the uniform rate of profit, w is the nominal wage rate and p is the vector of prices of production.

To see where this equation system came from, note that the cost of the non-labour inputs for producing one unit of commodity 1 is $p_1 a_{11} + p_2 a_{21} + p_3 a_{31}$, and the cost of purchasing the labour input is wl_1. Hence, total cost of production per unit of commodity 1 is

$$p_1 a_{11} + p_2 a_{21} + p_3 a_{31} + wl_1$$

on which the capitalist producer must earn the uniform rate of profit, r. Hence, total profit income per unit of commodity 1 needs to be

$$r(p_1 a_{11} + p_2 a_{21} + p_3 a_{31} + wl_1)$$

The price of the commodity must be such as to cover not only the total cost of production but also the required profit income. Hence, we must have

$$p_1 = (1+r)(p_1 a_{11} + p_2 a_{21} + p_3 a_{31} + w l_1)$$

The same logic shows us that the price of the second commodity must be

$$p_2 = (1+r)(p_1 a_{12} + p_2 a_{22} + p_3 a_{32} + w l_2)$$

and the price of the third commodity must be

$$p_3 = (1+r)(p_1 a_{13} + p_2 a_{23} + p_3 a_{33} + w l_3)$$

Writing these three using matrix notation, we get

$$\boldsymbol{p} = (1+r)(\boldsymbol{p}\boldsymbol{A} + w\boldsymbol{l}) = (1+r)(\boldsymbol{p}\boldsymbol{A} + \boldsymbol{p}\boldsymbol{b}\boldsymbol{l})$$

where we have used the fact that workers use their nominal wage income, w, entirely for consuming the real wage bundle, $\boldsymbol{b}$, so that

$$w = p_1 b_1 + p_2 b_2 + p_3 b_3 = \boldsymbol{p}\boldsymbol{b}$$

Maximal Rate of Profit
In this capitalist system, the maximum possible uniform rate of profit, R, will be generated if the wage rate is pushed down to 0, in which case, the price system will become

$$\boldsymbol{p} = (1+R)\boldsymbol{p}\boldsymbol{A}$$

A well-known theorem from mathematics, known as the Perron–Frobenius theorem, allows us to calculate R, whenever the matrix $\boldsymbol{A}$ is indecomposable (which is ensured when no subset of industries can form a sub-system that is completely independent of the rest of the economy), as follows:

$$R = \frac{1}{\lambda_M(\boldsymbol{A})} - 1$$

where $\lambda_M(\boldsymbol{A})$ is the maximal eigenvalue of the matrix $\boldsymbol{A}$.[5]

---

[5] For any square matrix $\boldsymbol{A}$, if on multiplying it with a vector $\boldsymbol{x}$, we get λ times the vector $\boldsymbol{x}$, where λ is a scalar, then we say that λ is an eigenvalue and $\boldsymbol{x}$ is the eigenvector of $\boldsymbol{A}$ associated with that eigenvalue. If the number of rows (and columns) of $\boldsymbol{A}$ is n, then there are n eigenvalues. The eigenvalue which is greatest in magnitude is the maximal eigenvalue. A statement of the Perron–Frobenius theorem and its proof can be found in Debreu and Herstein (1958).

The example we are working with, which I have borrowed from Pasinetti (1977), has constructed the A matrix in such a way that the maximal eigenvalue is less than 1 (which is also what makes the technology productive). This ensures that the uniform rate of profit is always positive. Using figures of the example, we get the maximal eigenvalue of A to be 0.675, which then gives us the maximum rate of profit as $R = 48.25$ per cent. This tells us that if the workers in our example capitalist economy could be forced to work without wages, the capitalist producers would be able to earn, in the long run, a 48.25 per cent rate of profit on their investments.

Actual Rate of Profit

Of course, workers will not work for zero wages. In fact, we have already specified the real wage bundle. Hence, we need to compute the uniform rate of profit that emerges when the real wage bundle is what is given in (7.3). To do this, we first need to compute the augmented input matrix, $M = A + bl$. This is because we can write the price system using M as follows:

$$p = (1+r)(pA + pbl) = (1+r)p(A + bl) = (1+r)pM$$

For the example we are working with, we get

$$M = \begin{bmatrix} 0.493 & 3.714 & 1.500 \\ 0.027 & 0.286 & 0.050 \\ 0.027 & 0.381 & 0.333 \end{bmatrix} \tag{7.11}$$

Using the same mathematical theorem as before, we can now calculate the average rate of profit as

$$r = \frac{1}{\lambda_M(M)} - 1$$

where $\lambda_M(M)$ is the maximal eigenvalue of the matrix M. Carrying out the calculation for the matrix M, we see that its maximal eigenvalue is 0.844, and so we get $r = 18.54$ per cent. Thus, the uniform rate of profit earned by capitalists in this economy, in the long run, given the technology and the real wage bundle, is 18.54 per cent.

Relative Prices

The next step is to calculate the prices of production, that is, the set of prices that support the uniform rate of profit of 18.54 per cent in each sector. To find the vector of prices, let us go back to the price equation

$$p = (1 + r)pM$$

and use the fact we have just learned, that is, $1 + r = 1/\lambda_M(M)$, to get from the above equation, upon a little manipulation,

$$p \left[I - \frac{1}{\lambda_M(M)} M \right] = 0$$

where I is a 3×3 identity matrix, and we know that $\lambda_M(M) = 0.844$. Hence, to solve for the vector of prices of production, p, we need to solve the following equation system:

$$\begin{bmatrix} p_1 & p_2 & p_3 \end{bmatrix} \left[\begin{bmatrix} 1 & 0 & 0 \\ 0 & 1 & 0 \\ 0 & 0 & 1 \end{bmatrix} - \frac{1}{0.844} \begin{bmatrix} 0.493 & 3.714 & 1.500 \\ 0.027 & 0.286 & 0.050 \\ 0.027 & 0.381 & 0.333 \end{bmatrix} \right] = 0$$

This can be rewritten as:

$$\begin{bmatrix} p_1 & p_2 & p_3 \end{bmatrix} \begin{bmatrix} 0.415 & -4.403 & -1.778 \\ -0.032 & 0.661 & -0.059 \\ -0.032 & -0.452 & 0.604 \end{bmatrix} = 0$$

Multiplying out the matrix system gives us the following equation system:

$$0.415p_1 - 0.032p_2 - 0.032p_3 = 0$$
$$-4.403p_1 + 0.661p_2 - 0.452p_3 = 0$$
$$-1.778p_1 - 0.059p_2 + 0.605p_3 = 0$$

An important property of this equation system is that the equations are linearly dependent – in fact, that is the condition for the system to have a non-zero solution vector. To understand why this is the case, recall that the equation system that is meant to solve for the vector p and the profit rate, r, is given by: $pM = 1/(1 + r)p$. This is a system of n equations in $n + 1$ unknowns (the n prices and the rate of profit, r). Hence, we can solve for at most n unknowns. Using the Perron–Frobenius theorem, we have solved for r. We get the above equation system by plugging the value of r back into the system of equations: $pM = 1/(1 + r)p$. By doing so, we get n equations (in the example, three equations). If they were linearly independent, then we would be able to solve for all the n prices (in the example, three prices). In which case, we would have solved for $n+1$ unknowns using n equations. But that is not possible. The linear dependence of the equation system is just another way of ensuring this.

This fact that the three equations are linearly dependent means that we can solve for the price vector only up to a factor of proportionality, that is, we can use only any two equations to solve for two prices in terms of the third price. For instance, using the first two equation,

$$0.415p_1 - 0.032p_2 = 0.032p_3$$
$$-4.403p_1 + 0.661p_2 = 0.452p_3$$

we can solve for p_1 and p_2 in terms of p_3. On solving this two-equation system, we get the following:

$$p_1 = 0.267p_3 \tag{7.12}$$

and

$$p_2 = 2.462p_3 \tag{7.13}$$

Thus, the price vector, up to a factor of proportionality, is given by

$$p = \begin{bmatrix} 0.267p_3 & 2.462p_3 & p_3 \end{bmatrix} \tag{7.14}$$

What we have solved so far are *relative prices*, that is, prices relative to the price of the third commodity. To solve for the level of prices, that is, absolute prices, we will need to use one more equation. This additional equation can come from either choosing a numeraire or from what Seton (1957) has called an 'invariance postulate'. I will call the latter an invariance principle and would like to emphasize the key difference between closing the system with a numeraire versus closing the system with an invariance principle.

7.2.2 Closing the System with a Numeraire

A numeraire is a unit to express all prices. By furnishing another equation, it allows us to solve for the price of production vector. By its very nature, the choice of a numeraire is arbitrary. One can choose the numeraire in many different ways, and there are no theoretical reasons to prefer one over the other. For instance, we could choose to express all prices in terms of the first commodity, that is, wheat in our example; or, we could choose the numeraire as the second commodity, that is, iron in the example, or even the third commodity, meat in this example.

Once we fix the numeraire as one of the commodities in the system, all prices will be expressed in units of that commodity. In the analysis of the transformation of values into prices by early theorists like von Bortkiewicz (1949) and Sweezy (1942), the equation system included one commodity that was set-up to function as a numeraire, that is, gold. By choosing gold (one of the commodities produced by the system) as a numeraire, all prices were expressed in terms of gold. An appealing feature of this approach was that it seemed to be close to the classical treatment of the commodity money system.

Let us see how the commodity money approach works in our example. To see this, let us choose the third commodity as the numeraire, that is, all prices are expressed in units of meat. If we write 'gold' in place of 'meat', we have a commodity money system and all prices are expressed in terms of 'gold'. It is easy to implement this solution in our example. All we need to do is to set $p_3 = 1$. Once we use this equation, we immediately get the vector of prices of production from (7.14) as

$$p = \begin{bmatrix} 0.267 & 2.462 & 1 \end{bmatrix}$$

Later theorists working within this approach switched to a different numeraire: the nominal wage rate. Use of the nominal wage rate as the numeraire is ubiquitous in Sraffian and Analytical Marxist approaches (Morishima, 1973; Pasinetti, 1977; Roemer, 1981). When the nominal wage rate is chosen as the numeraire, all prices are expressed in units of the nominal wage rate. Since the nominal wage rate is the price of the commodity labour-power, this gives us what can be considered a *labour-power money system*. In terms of solving the system of equation, this choice of numeraire functions as well as any other.

Some of the scholars using this numeraire have misinterpreted it, as I have pointed out above, for example, Morishima (1973). They have interpreted this as a *labour money system*. But the commodity purchased by the nominal wage rate is labour-power and not labour. In fact, this is a key distinction that allowed Marx, as we have seen in Chapter 3 earlier, to identify the source of surplus value in the exploitation of workers, a task that earlier classical economists were unable to accomplish.[6] Hence, giving up the conceptual distinction between labour-power and labour seems a heavy price to pay and should be avoided at all costs.

To implement this choice of numeraire, we need to set the nominal wage rate, w, to a value of 1. Since the nominal wage rate is spent on purchasing the real wage bundle, assuming workers do not save, this means

$$1 = p_1 b_1 + p_2 b_2 + p_3 b_3$$

Hence, the choice of the nominal wage rate as a numeraire to express prices gives us the above equation. In the context of the example we are working with, we know $b_1 = 2$, $b_2 = 0$, and $b_3 = 0.167$. Thus, the numeraire equation becomes

$$1 = 2p_1 + 0.167 p_3$$

We can now use this equation, along with (7.12) and (7.13), to solve for the price vector as

$$p = \begin{bmatrix} 0.381 & 3.512 & 1.427 \end{bmatrix} \tag{7.15}$$

7.2.3 Closing the System with Invariance Principles

An invariance principle is an alternative device to close the system of prices and calculate the prices of production vector (Seton, 1957). In an accounting sense, choosing an invariance principle is similar to choosing a numeraire because both choices give us another equation and allow us to solve for absolute prices (of production). But the conceptual underpinning of invariance principles are very different from choosing a numeraire.[7] An invariance principle gives us a relationship of equality, *at the aggregate level*, between some suitably defined value and price magnitudes.

In positing such a relationship, the invariance principle gives expression to some key intuition about the labour theory of value and also *defines* a conversion factor between value and price magnitudes to capture that

---

[6] For a discussion of the importance of this distinction in Marx's work, see Engels' introduction to the 1849 pamphlet, *Wage Labour and Capital*.

[7] Seton (1957, p. 152) did not distinguish clearly between choosing a numeraire and an invariance principle. His discussion can be interpreted as suggesting that there is no essential difference between closing the system with a numeraire and an invariance principle. I think that is a mistake.

intuition. In effect, therefore, an invariance principle establishes a theoretical link between value and price magnitudes. On the other hand, the choice of a numeraire has no such theoretical underpinning – it is a mere accounting device that allows us to solve a system of equations; it does not provide any link between value and price magnitudes at the aggregate level and, hence, it cannot be used to give expression to any intuition about the labour theory of value.

There are several invariance principles available in the literature, and here we will work with four important ones. Each invariance principle is anchored in an understanding of what constitutes the core of Marx's labour theory of value. Moreover, each unique invariance principle is incompatible with other invariance principles, in the sense that the set of absolute prices of production will differ across the choice of invariance principles (even though each is compatible with the *same* set of relative prices). As we work through the details of price calculations, it is important to pay attention to the intuitive understanding that underlies each invariance principle.

Invariance Principle 1

The first invariance principle we will use is the following: *the net output expressed in price terms is equal to the net output expressed in value terms.* This invariance principle states that the net output is invariant to the transformation from values to prices. Another way to understand this invariance principle is to see that it *defines* a conversion factor between value and price magnitudes at the aggregate level.

Recall that such a conversion factor was always implicitly used by Marx, and has been called a monetary expression of value (MEV) by Foley (1986b). In fact, without such a conversion factor, it is not even possible to state that the net output expressed in price terms is equal to the net output expressed in value terms, because the two sides of the asserted equality would be expressed in different units. In fact, the first invariance principle defines the MEV in the following way,

$$MEV = \frac{\text{money value added (\$)}}{\text{labour embodied in the net output (hours)}}$$

which then ensures that the MEV, understood as a conversion factor, multiplied by the value of (or labour embodied in) the net output (measured in hours of social labour) is exactly equal to the monetary value added (measured in units of money). Of course, in this case, the invariance principle also implies that this particular MEV=1.

Using the net output vector in (7.4), we see that the value of (or labour embodied in) the net output (measured in hours of social labour) is, using (7.9), $180 * 0.182 + 0 * 1.818 + 30 * 0.909 = 60$; and the value added expressed in money terms is $180 * p_1 + 0 * p_2 + 30 * p_3$. Thus, the first invariance principle is captured by equating the two: $180p_1 + 30p_3 = 60$. This becomes

$$6p_1 + p_3 = 2 \tag{7.16}$$

If we add this equation to the two-equation system, (7.12) and (7.13), we used above to solve for the price vector, we get

$$0.415p_1 - 0.032p_2 - 0.032p_3 = 0$$
$$-4.403p_1 + 0.661p_2 - 0.452p_3 = 0$$
$$6p_1 + p_3 = 2$$

which is a three-equation system in three unknowns. On solving the above, we get the price vector as

$$p = \begin{bmatrix} 0.203 & 1.886 & 0.782 \end{bmatrix}$$

Invariance Principle 2
A second invariance principle comes from one of Marx's equalities, and has been used by Winternitz (1948): *the gross output expressed in price terms is equal to the gross output expressed in value terms*. Note that the key difference between this and the previous invariance principle relates to the difference between net and gross output. While the previous invariance principle would keep the net output invariant to the transformation from values to prices, the second invariance principle means that the gross output is invariant to the transformation from values to prices. Just as in the previous case, this invariance principle also *defines* a MEV, understood as a conversion factor between value and price magnitudes:

$$\text{MEV} = \frac{\text{total revenue from sale of the gross output (\$)}}{\text{labour embodied in the gross output (hours)}}$$

And in this case too, we have this MEV = 1. Using the gross output vector in (7.7), this invariance principle can be expressed through the following equation,

$$450p_1 + 21p_2 + 60p_3 = 174.55 \tag{7.17}$$

where the left-hand side is the gross output evaluated in prices and the right-hand side is the value of (labour embodied in) the gross output. Following the same steps as in the case of invariance principle 1, we now get the vector of price of production as

$$p = \begin{bmatrix} 0.199 & 1.850 & 0.767 \end{bmatrix}$$

Invariance Principle 3
The third invariance principle is one used by Pasinetti (1977, p. 147): *the real wage bundle per worker expressed in price terms is equal to the real wage bundle per worker expressed in value terms.* This principle of invariance means that the real wage bundle is invariant to the transformation from values to prices.[8] The conversion factor defined by this invariance principle is:

$$\text{MEV} = \frac{\text{money cost of real wage bundle (\$)}}{\text{labour embodied in real wage bundle (hours)}}$$

Note, once again, that this MEV=1. Using the vector of values in (7.9) and the real wage bundle in (7.3), we can express the third invariance principle as

$$2p_1 + 0.167p_3 = 0.52 \tag{7.18}$$

where the left-hand side is the money cost of the real wage bundle and the right-hand side is the labour embodied in the real wage bundle. Using the same procedure as earlier, we get the vector of prices of production as

$$p = \begin{bmatrix} 0.198 & 1.827 & 0.742 \end{bmatrix}$$

Invariance Principle 4
Let us use another of Marx's equalities as an invariance principle: *total surplus value is exactly equal to total profits.* In essence, this invariance principle keeps

---

[8]While the other invariance principles have some intuitive appeal, this invariance principle seems quite arbitrary. There is no intuitive reason why the real wage bundle should be invariant between price and value accounting.

the surplus value invariant to the transformation from values to prices. It defines the following MEV:

$$\text{MEV} = \frac{\text{total monetary profits (\$)}}{\text{total surplus value (hours)}}$$

which, like in the previous three cases, also implies that this MEV = 1.

To implement this fourth invariance principle, note that the row vector of monetary profits is given by $rp\boldsymbol{M}$. Since $\boldsymbol{x}$ is the gross output (column) vector, we see that total monetary profits is given by $rp\boldsymbol{M}\boldsymbol{x}$. Using a similar reasoning, we can see that total surplus value is given by $(1 - \boldsymbol{\Lambda b})\boldsymbol{l x}$. Using the numbers for this example, and equating the two we get the following equation:

$$390p_1 + 21p_2 + 40p_3 = 323.67$$

Using the same procedure as earlier, we get the vector of prices of production as

$$p = \begin{bmatrix} 0.438 & 4.067 & 1.686 \end{bmatrix}$$

7.2.4 A Solution Algorithm

We have seen earlier that there are various ways to close the model and solve for the uniform rate of profit and the vector of prices of production. The numerical aspects of the earlier discussion can be captured in the following algorithm to solve for the uniform rate of profit and the prices of production in the SI of the labour theory of value. R code presented in Appendix 7.B.1 can be used to implement this algorithm for any economy.

- Gather information about the following: $\boldsymbol{A}$ ($n \times n$ input–output matrix), $\boldsymbol{l}$ ($1 \times n$ labour input vector), $\boldsymbol{b}$ ($n \times 1$ vector of the real wage bundle).
- Calculate the eigenvalues of $\boldsymbol{A}$ and check if the maximum eigenvalue, $\lambda_M(\boldsymbol{A}) < 1$. Proceed to the next step if the answer is in the affirmative. If the maximum eigenvalue of $\boldsymbol{A}$ is greater than or equal to 1, something is wrong with the input–output matrix. Check for errors.
- Calculate the $1 \times n$ vector of values: $\boldsymbol{\Lambda} = \boldsymbol{l}(\boldsymbol{I} - \boldsymbol{A})^{-1}$. When n is large, this step will be computationally intensive.

- Calculate rate of exploitation: $e = (1 - \boldsymbol{\Lambda b})/\boldsymbol{\Lambda b}$.
- Calculate the maximum rate of profit: $r = (1/\lambda_M(\boldsymbol{A})) - 1$.
- Calculate the $n \times n$ augmented input matrix: $\boldsymbol{M} = \boldsymbol{A} + \boldsymbol{bl}$.
- Calculate the $n \times n$ 'new' augmented input matrix:

$$\boldsymbol{M_1} = \boldsymbol{I} - (1/\lambda_M(\boldsymbol{A})) * \boldsymbol{M}$$

where $\boldsymbol{I}$ is the $n \times n$ identity matrix.

- Choose a numeraire or invariance principle to close the system. Write out the numeraire condition or the invariance principle as,

$$c_1 p_1 + c_2 p_2 + \cdots c_n p_n = d$$

and collect the coefficients $c_1, c_2, \ldots, c_n$, noting that some of these might be zero. Form a $1 \times n$ row vector,

$$\boldsymbol{c} = \begin{bmatrix} c_1 & c_2 & \cdots & c_n \end{bmatrix}$$

- Form a new matrix, $\boldsymbol{M_2} = \boldsymbol{M_1^T}$, that is, $\boldsymbol{M_2}$ is the transpose of $\boldsymbol{M_1}$.
- Form a new matrix, $\boldsymbol{M_3}$, by replacing the last row of $\boldsymbol{M_2}$ with the vector $\boldsymbol{c}$.
- Solve the linear system of equations given by $\boldsymbol{M_3 p^T} = \boldsymbol{d_1}$, where $\boldsymbol{d_1}$ is the $n \times 1$ vector

$$\begin{bmatrix} 0 \\ 0 \\ \vdots \\ 0 \\ d \end{bmatrix}$$

and $\boldsymbol{p}^T$ denotes the transpose of the price of production vector.

- The vector of price of production is given by the $1 \times n$ vector from the previous step, $\boldsymbol{p}$.
- The solution consists of the scalar r (the uniform rate of profit) and the $1 \times n$ vector $\boldsymbol{p}$ (the prices of production).

7.2.5 Numeraire versus Invariance Principles

Since there are many invariance principles to close the system of prices, that is, calculate the absolute magnitude of prices of production, a natural question to ask is this: Which invariance principle should a researcher use? Before attempting to answer this question, let us note some important points common to all invariance principles.

The choice of invariance principles does not affect the value of commodities, the rate of exploitation, the uniform rate of profit and the vector of relative prices. Once technology is given in the form of the input–output matrix, A, and the labour input vector, l, we can solve for the vector of values. If we now add information about the real wage bundle, b, we can compute the rate of exploitation, the uniform rate of profit and relative prices (of production). Hence, even *without choosing either a numeraire or an invariance principle*, we can calculate many of the important Marxist variables pertaining to the capitalist economy and can demonstrate a set of key results that, following Morishima (1973), we can together call the Fundamental Marxian Theorem (FMT):

- the rate of profit is positive if and only if the rate of exploitation is positive (Roemer, 1981, Theorem 1.1);

- whenever the rate of exploitation is positive, the rate of profit is always less than the rate of exploitation (Pasinetti, 1977, p. 128);

- the rate of profit is a strictly increasing function of the rate of exploitation and vice versa (Pasinetti, 1977, p. 128).

The FMT is a powerful result because it establishes the tight link between exploitation and profits in a capitalist system. It demonstrates that in a capitalist system, the rate of profit and the rate of exploitation are reflections of each other: if there is no exploitation, that is, the rate of exploitation is zero, there can be no profit, that is, the rate of profit will be zero, and vice versa. To be sure, the FMT does not demonstrate that the rate of exploitation and the rate of profit are numerically equal. Neither does it explain why positive profits exist (Steedman, 1977). But it does establish an indissoluble, qualitative link between the two: if there is no exploitation, there will be no profit.

Once we add the nominal wage rate as the numeraire, we can solve for the vector of prices of production, that is, absolute prices as opposed to relative prices. In this system of wage-prices or labour-power prices, we can demonstrate an additional result (Morishima, 1973, p. 71):

- whenever the rate of profit is positive, the vector of prices of production is, element by element, larger than the vector of values (labour embodied).

While the approach of closing the system with a numeraire solves for prices of production and establishes some key results of the labour theory of value, it leaves unaddressed the possible *quantitative* link between values and prices. In fact, in the numeraire approach, there is no such necessary link even at the aggregate level (other than under fairly restrictive assumptions). Some scholars have accepted this as an apt characterization of Marx's labour theory of value (Morishima, 1973; Roemer, 1981). But that is not the only option open to Marxist political economy.

An alternative approach would use one of the invariance principles to establish a quantitative link between values and prices at the aggregate level. It is important to note that the invariance principle should only posit the link between values and prices at the *aggregate level*. This is because the analysis of the system of prices of production establishes that there cannot be any proportionality between prices and values at the individual level other than in two restrictive cases: (*a*) when all sectors have the same OCC, or (*b*) when the rate of profit is zero. Since neither of these cases are realistic, one has to necessarily abandon any price–value relationships at the individual level. Hence, invariance principles can only give us price–value links at the aggregate level.

It is also important to be clear that an invariance principle is an assumption we impose on the model; it is not a relationship derived from more primitive assumptions, rather it can be thought of as an axiom of the theory. It might seem that this is a drawback of our analysis. Instead of deriving a relationship of equality between value and price magnitudes, we are assuming it. But this drawback is only apparent. If we choose to work with a labour theory of value, then we cannot avoid the fact that there are two accounting systems in our analysis – a value (labour-time) and a price (monetary) accounting system. The only way these two accounting systems can be quantitatively linked is when a theorist imposes that link in her model of the capitalist economy. An invariance principle is precisely a way to do so.

Of course, at a technical level, the invariance principle is an alternative closure of the system of equation defining prices of production. But at a deeper, conceptual level, it is a way to express some key intuition about the labour theory of value. Hence, the way to choose between alternative invariance principles will ultimately come down to accepting the underlying intuition that animates its understanding of the labour theory of value.

7.2.6 Which Invariance Principle to Use?

Let us return to the four invariance principles that we have used earlier and uncover the underlying intuitions. The first invariance principle asserts that the net output expressed in price terms is exactly equal to the net output expressed in terms of values (labour embodied). This captures the key intuition of the labour theory of value that, over a given period of time, labour expended in producing *new* commodities is expressed in the aggregate price (or revenue) of those commodities, that is, the money value added. Prices are a way to express the value (labour embodied) of commodities. But since prices and values do not coincide at the individual level, the equivalence between the two that is a core intuition of the labour theory of value can only be posited at the aggregate level.

This way of posing the question also indicates why the second invariance principle differs fundamentally from the first. Recall that the second invariance principle tries to capture the same intuition as the first but posits the equivalence for the gross, rather than the net, output. The difference between the gross and net output is the labour indirectly used in production. In valuational terms, the total output is the sum of the intermediate inputs used up, including depreciation of fixed capital, and the value added. It is conceptually appealing to identify the latter with the direct labour involved in production, and to use this as the key intuition of the labour theory of value, that is, value added in money terms is a reflection, in price terms, of the direct labour involved in production.

The same equivalence cannot be asserted in a conceptually clean manner for the total output because the value of the total output, that is, gross output, includes the value transferred by the intermediate inputs used up in production. The value of the intermediate inputs is the result of past labour, it does not arise from current labour. There is no straightforward way to establish equivalence between magnitudes of past labour and current labour.

Hence, it makes conceptual sense to limit the key intuition of the labour theory of value to the net output, and not try to extend it to the gross output. That is why, it seems to me, that we should choose the first over the second invariance principle.

This brings us to the third invariance principle used above – which asserts that the real wage bundle expressed in price terms is exactly equal to the value of, that is, labour embodied in, the real wage bundle. This assertion does not have the intuitive appeal of the first invariance principle. Workers do not consume all commodities produced in any capitalist economy. Hence, if we used the third invariance principle, we would be leaving out some commodities, for example, capital goods, from the ambit of the value-price aggregate equivalence. There is no compelling theoretical reason for doing that. If we want to express our intuition about the labour theory of value with a value-price equivalence, it seems best to do it for the whole net output – because the whole net output has absorbed the whole of the direct labour expended in production. Hence, the first invariance principle is superior to the third.

Now we take up the fourth and final invariance principle, which equates the total monetary profits to the total surplus value. This invariance principle has lot of intuitive appeal. After all, one of the key claims of Marx's labour theory of value is that profits are nothing but a form of surplus value. We can capture this equivalence, at the aggregate level, precisely with the fourth invariance principle. But this creates a serious difficulty for us.

On intuitive grounds, both invariance principle 1 and 4 seem to be important to retain for any labour theory of value, especially one that is close to Marx's key intuitions. Using the framework for the labour theory of value we have been working with, that is, the SI, we cannot retain both invariance principle 1 and 4. This is because each invariance principle gives rise to a different vector of prices of production. On the one hand, a coherent theory cannot allow for non-unique prices. On the other, we do not want to sacrifice either invariance principle 1 or 4 – because both capture key intuitions about the labour theory of value. How can we deal this theoretical difficulty? The NI offers a framework to answer this question. But before we turn to the NI, we need to quickly look at the Sraffian critique.

7.3 Sraffa-Based Critique

The SI of the labour theory of value was subjected to a serious Sraffa-based critique in the 1970s, most prominently by Steedman (1977). The main thrust of the critique was an argument about redundancy of value, an issue we briefly touched upon in Appendix 3.C. Since the main focus of the Seton-Okishio-Morishima contribution had been a demonstration of the existence of a positive uniform rate of profit and strictly positive relative prices of production, Steedman (1977) argued that this did not require us to deal with any notion of value. Given data on technology and the real wage bundle, one could calculate the uniform rate of profit and prices of production, as we have seen earlier in our discussion of the FMT. Hence, there was no need for value categories. Value was conceptually redundant.

One way to respond to the charge of redundancy would have been to use some invariance principle to link prices and values – and we saw four possible candidates above – but the problem with SI was that it did not see the problem this way. Hence, it did not work towards developing any theoretical grounds for choosing one invariance principle over any other. Even more damaging was the fact that choosing *any* one seemed to militate against some key intuitions of the labour theory of value. Naturally, then the notion of value could not be defended in a logically satisfactory manner from within the SI framework – other than in a weak qualitative sense captured by the FMT. Even though the essence of the Sraffa-based critique was not new – the same point had been made previously by Samuelson (1971) and seven decades earlier by the Russian economist Dmitriev (1974) – it was forceful and provocative.

Let us summarize the key point of the Sraffian critique as the second question in the long discussion on the transformation problem.

Question 2 (Transformation Problem). *How can a consistent set of prices of production be computed that does not, at the same time, undermine the relevance of value magnitudes?*

In responding to this challenge of the Sraffa-based critique, Marxist political economy renewed itself. By the early 1980s, one could discern several strands of Marxist political economy that had emerged as a response to the Sraffa-based critique. Many of these strands opened up new, or continued older, lines of scholarly work and research, and all of them, in their own ways reconfirmed the centrality of value. The most promising of these strands, in my opinion, is the NI that was developed independently by Gérard Duménil and Duncan Foley in the late 1970s. But before I present the details of the NI, let us briefly look at some of the other strands.

7.4   Marxist Responses to the Sraffa-Based Critique

One response that developed in the 1970s through the work of scholars like Ben Fine, Laurence Harris, Simon Mohun and others emphasized the difference between the Ricardian understanding of value as 'embodied labour' and the Marxist understanding of value as 'abstract labour' (for a recent exposition of this strand, see Fine et al. (2004)). This important point about the difference between embodied (or concrete) and abstract labour was incorporated in all later Marxist work.

Another response came from SI in the form of the FMT, as we have already seen earlier. A third response emerged in the work of Shaikh (1977, 1984), who continued to use a SI of the labour theory of value. His main claim was similar to Ricardo's: value and price magnitudes are approximately equal at the level of individual commodities. In his 1984 paper, Shaikh developed a theoretical argument demonstrating that the deviation of prices from values would be 'small' and then used data from the Italian and US economies to show that his claim is empirically valid. There are both methodological and measurement issues in this approach, as highlighted in Basu (2017).

Another response came from the work of two mathematicians, Emmanuel Farjoun and Moshé Machover, who brought a probabilistic approach to political economy. Farjoun and Machover (1983) argued that most economic variables – like price, rate of profit, wage – are non-degenerate random variables, each with their own probability distribution functions. This means that equilibrium in a capitalist economy should be characterized by a distribution of the rate of profit, instead of a single, uniform rate of profit. Looked at from within a probabilistic perspective, the Sraffa-based critique is based on the erroneous postulate of a uniform rate of profit as characterizing long run equilibrium; hence, its conclusions are invalid. In addition to offering a rebuttal of the Sraffa-based critique, Farjoun and Machover (1983) also developed a positive theory of the distribution of the rate of profit and value-price deviations. This approach, which I will call Probabilistic Political Economy, has seen some recent interesting work that significantly extends the original work of Farjoun and Machover (1983).[9] The final response to the Sraffa-based critique, which is the most relevant for our discussion here, was the NI, and to that we now turn.

7.5 The New Interpretation

The New Interpretation (NI) of Marx's labour theory of value introduced two conceptual innovations – value of money (or its reciprocal, the MEV that we have already seen in Chapter 3) and value of labour power (Foley, 1982b; Duménil, 1983–84). These twin innovations anchored the aggregate equivalence between value and monetary magnitudes, and created a theoretically informed and consistent accounting framework for theoretical and empirical analysis. This accounting framework allowed one to consistently compute prices of production, addressing the first question related to the transformation problem; and the aggregate value-price equivalence that was asserted at the very beginning meant that value magnitudes are no longer peripheral, *ad hoc* or redundant, thereby addressing the second question of the transformation problem. In addition, the novel definition of the value of labour-power ensured that the apparent contradictions between key intuitions of Marx's labour theory of value that plagued the SI are also resolved.

7.5.1 Value of Money

The first conceptual innovation introduced by the NI is the notion of the value of money. It is defined, for any economy, as the ratio of total productive labour (measured in units of hours) and the total money value added (measured in units of dollars or some other currency), both referring to some period of time (say, a year):

$$\text{value of money} = \frac{\text{total productive labour}}{\text{total money value added}}$$

---

[9]For a brief survey of this new literature, see Basu (2017).

Thus, the value of money is the reciprocal of the MEV that we have seen earlier in Chapter 3:

$$\text{MEV} = \frac{\text{total money value added}}{\text{total productive labour}}$$

As we have noted several times in previous sections of this book, there is ample textual evidence that Marx implicitly used this, or a similar, concept all through the three volumes of *Capital*. Our discussion of the SI shows that this particular way of defining the MEV is one of the invariance principles that had been used previously by Marxist scholars (Seton, 1957). Thus, the contribution of the NI, on this score, was mainly to bring this concept to the fore.

Computing either of these quantities, the MEV or value of money, is a way of conceptually asserting the equivalence between value added (measured in monetary units) and productive labour (measured in labour hour units) *at the aggregate level*. It is a meaningful quantity to compute not only for the convenience it affords us in freely converting value into monetary units and vice versa, but more importantly, because it captures Marx's idea that money is a form of value. Thus, it is meaningful to claim that the aggregate of value added (measured in monetary units) should be equal to the aggregate productive labour that created that value added. But to operationalize this equivalence, we need to have a conversion factor between labour hours and units of money, and the value of money (or its reciprocal, the MEV) is precisely that.

7.5.2 *Value of Labour-Power*

The second conceptual innovation of the NI defines the value of labour-power as the product of the nominal wage rate and the value of money, that is,

value of labour-power = nominal wage rate × value of money

In doing so, as we have seen in section 3.3.3, it departs from the conventional way of defining the value of labour-power as the value of the commodity bundle consumed by the average worker. Recall that in the SI, the value of labour-power is defined as the value of (or labour embodied in) the worker's real wage bundle. Since workers are assumed to not save, the real wage bundle is also the consumption bundle (see section 7.2.1). We have encountered these two alternative ways of defining the value of labour-power in Chapter 3, and it is now necessary to dwell further on that difference. What could be the theoretical justification for departing from the standard definition of the value of labour-power?

One might think that the reason to accept the NI definition comes from the fact that wage bargaining between workers and capitalists is over the price of the commodity labour-power, that is, the bargaining is over a monetary magnitude, the nominal wage, and not over some bundle of commodities (Foley, 1982b; Lipietz, 1982). While this is true, it does not detract from the fact that workers do convert their money wage income into real commodities. Hence, if we short circuit the bargaining process and think directly in terms of the real wage bundle – as is done in the SI or in the Sraffian tradition – there is hardly any conceptual error involved.

Another reason that is often advanced to accept the NI definition is related to the issue of the deviation of price and value. If we use the standard definition of the value of labour-power – the value of the commodities in the average worker's consumption bundle – then the price of the real wage bundle will not be equal to the value of the bundle of commodities in the real wage bundle. This is because, in general, relative prices and relative values of commodities do not coincide – other than in the special case where the production process of all commodities have the same OCC or when the rate of profit is zero. It is to avoid the divergence between the price and value of the real wage bundle, the argument goes, that we should not use the standard definition (Mohun, 2004). But this is not a convincing argument for abandoning the standard definition of the value of the commodity labour-power. If we accept the standard definition for the value of labour-power, then all we will be allowing for is that the price of labour-power will deviate from its value. That happens to be the case for all commodities. So that cannot be a serious enough problem to force us to abandon the standard definition.

To my mind, the real justification for accepting the NI definition over the standard definition of labour-power is that it is the *only way* in which we can retain two aggregate equivalences, that is, two invariance principles, that are crucial for an intuitive appeal of the labour theory of value:

- the equivalence between total monetary value added and total productive labour, and

- the equivalence between total monetary profits and total surplus labour (unpaid productive labour).

To see this, let us look at production from two perspectives: from the perspective of monetary magnitudes and from the perspective of the labour involved in production. Let Y, W and Π denote the value added, wage bill and profits, all measured in monetary units. Then, by definition, we have

$$Y = W + \Pi \tag{7.19}$$

Let the column vector $\boldsymbol{x}$ and $\boldsymbol{y}$ denote the gross and net output, and let $\boldsymbol{l}$ denote the row vector of labour inputs. Then, $L = \boldsymbol{lx}$ denotes the total productive living labour in this economy, that is, the total labour used in the production, and the monetary value added is given by $Y = \boldsymbol{py}$. If the value of money is denoted by vm, then we have,

$$vm = \frac{L}{Y} = \frac{\boldsymbol{lx}}{\boldsymbol{py}} = \frac{\boldsymbol{\lambda y}}{\boldsymbol{py}} \tag{7.20}$$

where the last equality follows from the fact that

$$\boldsymbol{lx} = \boldsymbol{l}\left(\boldsymbol{I} - \boldsymbol{A}\right)^{-1}\boldsymbol{y} = \boldsymbol{\lambda y}$$

because the gross and net output are related as $\boldsymbol{x} = \left(\boldsymbol{I} - \boldsymbol{A}\right)^{-1}\boldsymbol{y}$, and the vector of values is given by $\boldsymbol{\lambda} = \boldsymbol{l}\left(\boldsymbol{I} - \boldsymbol{A}\right)^{-1}$. Thus, the value of money is equal to the ratio of total living labour and monetary value added, which, in turn, is equal to the total value of the net output and the monetary value added.

Suppose the total productive labour-time is composed of two parts, L_N and L_S, which denote, respectively, necessary labour and surplus labour, so that

$$L = L_N + L_S \tag{7.21}$$

We want to see under what conditions the ratio of surplus labour and monetary profits is exactly equal to the ratio of total labour and monetary value added, that is,

$$\frac{L_S}{\Pi} = \frac{L}{Y}$$

The Conventional Definition

From the definition of profits, we have

$$\Pi = Y - W = \frac{L}{vm} - W$$

where we have used (7.20) to substitute for Y. According to the conventional definition, necessary labour, or the value of labour-power, is equal to the value of the real wage bundle. If b denotes the column vector of the real wage bundle, λ denotes the row vector of values and p denotes the row vector of prices, then, according to the conventional definition,

$$L_N = \lambda b L = \lambda b \frac{pb}{pb} L = \frac{\lambda b}{pb} W$$

where we have used the fact that the nominal wage bill is given by $W = pbL$, because workers spend all their income on the real wage bundle, b. Hence, the nominal wage bill is related to necessary labour as follows:

$$W = \frac{L_N}{vm_0}$$

where,

$$vm_0 = \frac{\lambda b}{pb} \tag{7.22}$$

A little algebra shows that

$$\Pi = Y - W = \frac{L}{vm} - \frac{L_N}{vm_0} = \frac{L_N + L_S}{vm} - \frac{L_N}{vm_0}$$

so that

$$\Pi = L_N \left(\frac{1}{vm} - \frac{1}{vm_0} \right) + \frac{L_S}{vm}$$

Hence, on rearranging the above, we have

$$\left(\Pi - \frac{L_S}{vm} \right) = L_N \left(\frac{1}{vm} - \frac{1}{vm_0} \right) \tag{7.23}$$

Using (7.20) and (7.22), we see that, in general,

$$vm = \frac{\lambda y}{py} \neq \frac{\lambda b}{pb} = vm_0$$

Since $L_N > 0$, this shows that, in general, the right-hand side of (7.23) is not zero. Hence, in general, using the conventional definition of the value of labour-power (or necessary labour), will imply that

$$\frac{L_S}{\Pi} \neq \frac{L}{Y}$$

that is, the ratio of surplus labour and monetary profits will not be equal to the ratio of total labour and monetary value added.

There are two special, and rather restrictive, cases in which we will have $vm = vm_0$. First, if prices are proportional to values of commodities, then $p = \mu_1 \lambda$, where $\mu_1 > 0$ is some scalar. In this case, it is easy to see that

$$vm_0 = \frac{\lambda b}{pb} = \frac{\lambda b}{\mu_1 \lambda b} = \frac{1}{\mu_1} = \frac{\lambda y}{\mu_1 \lambda y} = \frac{\lambda y}{py} = vm$$

Second, if the vector of real wage bundle is a scaled-down version of the net output vector, then $b = \mu_2 y$, where $0 < \mu_2 < 1$ is some scalar. In this case also, it is easy to see that

$$vm_0 = \frac{\lambda b}{pb} = \frac{\mu_2 \lambda y}{\mu_2 py} = \frac{\lambda y}{py} = vm$$

But neither of these special cases can be expected to hold in general. Hence, they should not be of much concern. The general conclusion holds: if we use the conventional definition of the value of labour-power (or necessary labour), then the ratio of surplus labour and monetary profits will *not* be equal to the ratio of total labour and monetary value added.

The NI Definition
Let us again start from the definition of profit,

$$\Pi = Y - W = \frac{L}{vm} - W$$

and now use the NI definition of the value of labour-power as the product of the nominal wage rate and the value of money. Thus, using the NI definition, we have

$$L_N = w * vm * L = W * vm$$

where w is the nominal wage rate and W is the nominal wage bill. Hence, we see that

$$\Pi = Y - W = \frac{L}{vm} - W = \frac{L}{vm} - \frac{L_N}{vm} = \frac{L_S}{vm}$$

Hence, $L_S/\Pi = L/Y = vm$, that is, the ratio of surplus labour and monetary profits is exactly equal to the ratio of total labour and monetary value added.

This analysis shows that we cannot use the standard definition of the value of labour-power as the labour embodied in the consumption bundle of the working class. If we do so, we will no longer be able to ensure, at the same time, the proportionality between money value added and total productive labour, and the same proportionality between monetary profits and surplus labour. The only way to ensure that both these proportions are equal is to use the NI definition of the value of labour-power as the product of the money wage rate and the value of money (defined for the whole economy).

An interesting implication of the NI definition of the value of labour-power, v, is that it is equal to the wage share in money value added,

$$v = vm * w = \frac{wL}{Y} = \frac{W}{Y}$$

because $W = wL$, and also equal to the ratio of necessary labour and total labour

$$v = vm * w = \frac{vm * W}{L} = \frac{L_N}{L}$$

because $W = vm * L_N$ (according to the NI definition of the value of labour-power). This implication is important for empirical analysis because we can use the wage share in money value added, an observable quantity, to measure the value of labour-power.

7.5.3 Answering the Two Questions

Let us now return to the two questions that define the transformation problem and see how the NI addresses them. Starting with the second question – the redundancy charge – we can see that the NI is designed to address that issue. Since the value of money is defined to bring the total money value added and the total productive labour into a relationship with each other, and since the value of money is then used to define the value of labour-power, one cannot dispense with value magnitudes. In fact, the definition of the value of money is *the* way to operationalize the two fundamental claims of the labour theory of value that productive labour creates value and that value is expressed in money.

The final step of the argument is to return to the first question regarding the computation of prices of production. Following Foley (1982b, footnote 8) and Lipietz (1982, pp. 78–79), it is relatively easy to demonstrate that we can use the NI to calculate the uniform rate of profit and the corresponding set of prices of production that not only correct Marx's errors but also retain two of Marx's key insights about the labour theory of value: (*a*) the monetary value added is an expression of the total productive labour and (*b*) total profit is an expression of total surplus labour.[10]

7.5.4 Incompleteness

The NI has introduced two related concepts – the MEV and the value of labour-power. The two are linked through the nominal wage: value of labour-power is the ratio of the nominal wage rate and the MEV. Even if we take the nominal wage rate as given, we still need a theory for the determination of either the MEV or the value of labour-power. Hence, to close the system, we still need one more equation – either to determine the MEV or to determine the value of labour-power.[11] As it currently exists, the NI analysis is *incomplete*.

One strand of literature has developed a theory of the determination of the MEV using various notions of the quantity of money in, or required for, circulation. An initial attempt was presented in Saros (2007), which was significantly strengthened in Moseley (2011b), and has been used in Rieu et al. (2014). The basic idea in this approach is most clearly articulated in

---

[10]For a formal treatment and a solution algorithm, analogous to the one discussed for the SI, see Appendix 7.A.

[11]Mohun and Veneziani (2017) also note the incompleteness of the NI in these two respects. They think both aspects need to be theorized to deal with the incompleteness. Since the two are definitionally linked, dealing with one, that is, either the value of money or with the value of labour-power, is enough.

Moseley (2011b) and is relatively straightforward to explain.[12] Recall that the MEV is defined as the ratio of money value added and total productive labour-time,

$$m = \frac{py}{lx}$$

where p, y, l, x denote the vector of prices, the vector of net output, the vector of direct labour inputs and the vector of gross output, respectively. The equation of exchange from macroeconomics shows that the money supply (quantity of money) times the velocity of circulation of money is equal to nominal gross domestic product. If we denote by M^S the quantity of money in circulation and by V the velocity of circulation, then the equation of exchange tells us that $py = M^S V$. Hence, using the equation of exchange, we see that

$$m = \frac{M^S V}{lx}$$

If we knew the values of M^S and V, we could determine the MEV and address the incompleteness of the NI. While the quantity of money is a known magnitude in most capitalist countries with a developed monetary and financial system, the velocity of circulation is not observed. Hence, to implement this approach, we need to develop a theory of the determination of the velocity of circulation of money. Thus, the incompleteness is just pushed down one further level.

An alternative approach might be to develop a theory of the determination of the value of labour-power. Recall that an implication of the NI accounting system is that the value of labour-power is exactly equal to the share of wages in national income. Thus, if we could develop a theory of the determination of the wage share in national income, for example, through a specification of class struggle over the distribution of income, we could address the incompleteness of the NI. In fact, the discussion about the value of labour-power in Volume I of *Capital* suggests its determination is impacted by social, cultural and historical factors. Thus, developing a theory of the determination of the value of labour-power using a class struggle

---

[12]Moseley (2011b) derives this result in a more circuitous way using gold (commodity) money. One of the key steps in his argument relies on the equation of exchange for gold money. A direct application of the equation exchange to any form of money, as I have done here, gives the same result.

framework is both intuitive and in line with Marx's insights. While some work has happened in the other, that is, monetary approach, to addressing the incompleteness of the NI, this other class struggle–based approach has not yet been explored in sufficient detail. This seems like a fruitful area for future research.

7.6 Three Less Appealing Approaches

Before concluding the discussion of the transformation problem, I would like to discuss three other Marxist approaches to the question. These three approaches share a commonality, which also distinguishes them from the SI and NI in that they define the concept of 'value' in a non-standard manner. In both the SI and the NI, the value of a commodity is defined as the sum of the value transferred from non-labour inputs used up and the direct labour used in the production of a commodity. In this conventional way of defining value, prices do not play any role in the determination of value. Once we have information on technology, that is, the physical magnitudes of all commodities and labour needed to produce 1 unit of a commodity, we can calculate its value. The three approaches that I discuss now abandon this conventional way of defining value. In their own ways, each of these approaches bring in price magnitudes to define value.

The first approach is associated with the work of Fred Moseley and is known as the macro-monetary interpretation (MMI) of Marx's value theory (Moseley, 2000, 2011a, 2016). The second approach is associated with the work of several scholars and is known as the temporal single system interpretation (TSSI) of Marx's value theory (Carchedi and Freeman, 1996; Kliman and McGlone, 1999; Kliman, 2006). The third approach is known as the simultaneous single system interpretation (SSSI) approach and is associated with the work of several scholars, including Richard Wolff and Bruce Roberts (Wolff et al., 1982).

The key motivation in these approaches seem to be the desire to derive both of Marx's equalities. Recall that in presenting his analysis of the transformation of values to prices in Volume III of *Capital*, Marx had claimed that two aggregate equalities will be preserved through the process of transformation: total price = total value; total profit = total surplus value. Starting with von Bortkiewicz (1949), numerous scholars have demonstrated that both these equalities cannot hold. The three approaches I discuss now have been motivated, in their own ways, to counter this claim.

7.6.1 Macro-Monetary Interpretation

The MMI and TSSI share a key idea, which allows them to show that both aggregate equalities of Marx hold. This idea is explained very clearly in Kliman and McGlone (1999) and can be expressed through the following four equations:

$$p = C + V + \Pi \tag{7.24}$$
$$\Lambda = C + V + S \tag{7.25}$$
$$g = \Pi - S \tag{7.26}$$
$$gx = 0 \tag{7.27}$$

The first equation determines the vector of prices, p, as the sum of the vector of constant capital, C, the vector of variable capital, V, and the vector of profits, Π. The second equation determines the vector of values, Λ, as the sum of the vectors of constant capital, C, variable capital, V, and surplus value, S. The third equation defines a vector g as the difference between profits and surplus value, and the fourth equation asserts that, at the aggregate level, profits are equal to surplus value, that is, $gx = 0$, where x is the gross output vector, and a MEV of 1 is implicitly used. By definition, we also have $p - \Lambda = g$. Hence, we immediately see that $px = \Lambda x$, so that total value and total price are also equal.

Thus, the above equation system shows that if we can define the price and value of commodities in such a way that *the constant and variable capital appear identically in both definitions*, then we will always be able to derive both of Marx's equalities: total price = total value; total profit = total surplus value. We need to assume one of the equalities, which is perfectly legitimate as an invariance principle, and the other will immediately follow. Therefore, the important question is whether we are justified in defining the vector of values and prices in this way, that is, using the *same* magnitudes for constant capital and variable capital in both value and price equations.

Moseley (2011b, 2016) argues that we are justified in doing this because Marx took the constant and variable capital from the analysis in Volume I of *Capital* as given when he developed his argument in Volume III of *Capital*.

Moseley (2016) primarily presents textual evidence to make his case. But I find the whole argument unconvincing because there does not seem to be any reason to accept it other than that Marx might have used it. In fact, even that is not a matter of consensus. There are some passages in Volume III of *Capital*, which even Moseley (2000) has quoted, which shows, to my mind convincingly, that Marx was struggling with this issue. He seems to have been aware that some sort of change was needed to be incorporated into his calculations of prices of production at the input end of the equation, and that he could not just use the value magnitudes of constant and variable capital in price of production calculations. It also seems to be the case that he had probably not had the time to work it all out. There is textual evidence that Marx had contradictory ideas about this – at places he argued that it was not necessary to transform the inputs; at other places, he argued that it was necessary to do so.

Given this, it would be a mistake to base the whole analysis on textual evidence *only*, if one cannot provide some independent justification, either theoretical or empirical. Note, moreover, that to incorporate the change that Marx was trying to work out, it would be essential to make explicit the use-value basis of production. Transforming inputs would have required Marx to explicitly bring in the physical aspects of production and then re-compute the price of the physical inputs (that is, commodities) using prices of production. Since Moseley (2016) does not do so, he can ignore the difference between the magnitudes of constant and variable capital in the value equations from their counterparts in the price equations. But the whole procedure seems theoretically questionable.

7.6.2 *Temporal Single System Interpretation*

The TSSI and the SSI do make the use-value basis of production explicit in the standard manner, that is, by using an input–output matrix, A (like the one used in the discussion earlier). Once the use-value basis of production has been made explicit, the only way to arrive at both of Marx's equalities is to give up the conventional manner of defining value, and allow value to be determined by price. To see this, note that the main equation system of the TSSI is given as

$$p_{t+1} = p_t A + l + g_t \tag{7.28}$$
$$\Lambda_{t+1} = p_t A + l \tag{7.29}$$
$$g_t x_t = 0 \tag{7.30}$$

where time subscripts identify periods and capture the temporal aspect of the argument. For instance, the first equation shows that the price vector in period $t + 1$ is determined by the cost of purchasing inputs in period t; the second equation shows that the value of the commodities in period $t + 1$ is determined by the *prices* of the non-labour inputs and the direct labour input in period t. The vector of labour input, l, is broken up into variable capital, $p_t bl$, and surplus value, $l - p_t bl$, where b is the real wage bundle. Thus, the value determination equation (7.29) is written as

$$\Lambda_{t+1} = p_t A + p_t bl + (l - p_t bl)$$

where variable capital is $p_t bl$ and surplus value is $l - p_t bl$. Similarly, the price determination equation (7.28) is written as

$$p_{t+1} = p_t A + p_t bl + (l - p_t bl + g_t)$$

where the same expression for variable capital is used in the price determination equation, $p_t bl$, as in the value determination equation, and profit is defined as $(l - p_t bl + g_t)$. Hence, just like in the previous section, g_t is both the difference between price and value, and between profit and surplus value. Hence, we again have both of Marx's equalities, as in the MMI. But now there is an additional complication. The vector of values in period $t + 1$, Λ_{t+1}, is now determined by the *price* of the constant capital, $p_t A$, in the previous period. How is this justified? This issue goes back to Wolff et al. (1982), and I will deal with it in the next section.

When the TSSI discusses prices of production, some additional conceptual problems emerge. To see this, let us write down the price of production equation system of the TSSI:

$$p_{t+1} = (1 + r) \, p_t \, (A + bl) \tag{7.31}$$

where the uniform rate of profit is defined as

$$r = \frac{lx - p_t blx}{p_t \, (A + bl) \, x} \tag{7.32}$$

The equation system in (7.31) has $2n + 1$ unknowns (the two price vectors and the uniform rate of profit). To solve it, the TSSI insists that both p_t and r are given, so that only n unknowns remain. This is the reason for the TSSI insistence that p_t and r are not solved simultaneously with the price vector, p_{t+1}. That is why (7.32) is so important – it shows that the rate of profit is determined *before* the prices of the output have been formed. But this formulation throws up two conundrums.

Notice that in (7.32), profit is defined even before commodities are sold (because all the variables entering the determination of the rate of profit have the time subscript t). In standard understanding, the sale price determines the rate of profit realized by the seller. That is why lower prices lead to lower profit rates, and higher prices can lead to higher profits. This simple intuition is lost in the TSSI.

Another strange aspect of the equation system in (7.31) and (7.32) is that even as prices are in disequilibrium, the rate of profit is in equilibrium. If the price vector were the same in periods t and $t + 1$, then we would say that the price vector has attained its long run equilibrium value, that is, it is the price of production vector, and that would justify thinking of the corresponding rate of profit as the uniform rate of profit. But in the TSSI, the price vector cannot be the same in periods t and $t + 1$. If it were to coincide, then we would have simultaneous valuation, and not temporal valuation, according to TSSI terminology. Thus, the prices keep changing from one period to the next, even as the profit rate has attained its long run equilibrium!

7.6.3 Simultaneous Single System Interpretation

Many of the conceptual confusions in the TSSI go back to the SSSI developed by Wolff et al. (1982). This SSSI can be captured in the following equations,

$$p = (1 + r)\, p\,(A + bl) \tag{7.33}$$
$$\Lambda = pA + l \tag{7.34}$$
$$r = \frac{lx - pblx}{pAx + pblx} \tag{7.35}$$

A comparison of the SSSI with TSSI equation system for prices of production (7.31) and (7.32) shows that they are identical, other than the fact that the TSSI use time subscripts to emphasize the sequential determination of prices and the SSSI does not, which is therefore dubbed a 'simultaneous' interpretation.

The key question that we encountered earlier in the TSSI and which figures here too is captured in the value determination system in (7.34). This equation asserts that the value of any commodity is determined by the price of the non-labour inputs, in addition to the direct labour input. In conventional thinking, which is shared by both SI and NI, the value of commodities are determined by the value of the non-labour inputs that are transferred to the output, and the value that is added by living labour. To highlight the difference, let us recall this:

$$\Lambda = \Lambda A + l \tag{7.36}$$

What is the justification for abandoning this definition and mixing up price and value? According to SSSI, as the analysis moves from Volume I to Volume III of *Capital*, a new form of value emerges and so 'the quantity of labour time in money form which each capitalist must actually advance to get his constant capital goods (their respective prices of production) becomes a constituent part of the *value* of the commodities produced with those capital goods' (Wolff et al., 1982, p. 574, original emphasis). There is no argument here; the authors are merely asserting what needs to be explained.

In other parts of the same text, the authors seem to argue that as the analysis moves from a higher to a lower level of abstraction, that is, as the analysis moves from Volume I to Volume III, the *meaning* of the term 'value' itself changes. If this is the rationale for the non-standard definition of value, then it seems to arise from a serious misunderstanding of what Marx has in mind when he presents his analysis at different levels of abstraction. As the analysis moves from a higher to a lower level of abstraction, new determinations (or aspects of reality) are incorporated into the analysis (Marx, 1993c). Marx's methodology does not involve changing the meaning of terms and concepts midway through the analysis. That would lead to theoretical incoherence! In Wolff et al. (1984), the authors argue that even though value-form is a price, it must still be denominated in labour-time, rather than in money. If this is the reason for using the non-standard definition of value, then this is, again, a serious theoretical misunderstanding. Marx was quite clear that prices cannot *directly* express labour-time (Marx, 1992, Chapter 3, footnote 1). The expression of value has to be mediated through money. This would be especially relevant in the context of

Volume III, where value and prices diverge. In sum, there are no convincing theoretical reasons offered by the SSSI for using the non-standard definition of value.

Since the same issue is relevant for the TSSI, let us try to understand the reason they give for using this unconventional definition of value. The TSSI also asserts this definition of value as one of the two differences between the TSSI and dual-system interpretations. 'The temporal single-system interpretation of Marx's theory, in contrast, holds that the value of capital advanced depends on the prices, not the values, of the inputs ...' (Kliman and McGlone, 1999, p. 34). Later on in the text, this assertion is stated in mathematical terms,

$$\Lambda_{t+1} = p_t A + l$$

and it is explained that this is what makes this interpretation a 'single-system' interpretation 'since the values of outputs depend on the prices of inputs' (Kliman and McGlone, 1999, p. 37). Much like in the case of SSSI, no argument is offered for the determination of value by price. It is merely asserted as a feature of the TSSI.

7.7 Conclusion

The transformation problem refers to a consistent procedure for relating values and prices of commodities in a capitalist economy. It has gained prominence because, among other things, it has been advanced as a claim of logical inconsistency in the conceptual structure of Marxist political economy. In this chapter, we have seen that there is a way to interpret Marx's value theory, that is, the NI, that consistently computes long run prices of production and restores a quantitative link between value and price magnitudes. As it exists, the NI is incomplete because it lacks a theory of the determination of the value of money or the value of labour-power. Developing a theory for the determination of either of these variables can easily deal with that incompleteness. My own understanding is that working out a theory of the determination of the value of labour-power using a class-struggle framework is a more fruitful avenue for future research than developing a theory of the value of money.

The Marxist literature on the transformation problem has divided existing approaches into dual-system and single-system approaches. While a dual-system approach is supposed to have two accounting systems, one in value terms and another one in price terms, a single-system approach is supposed to have just one unified accounting system. I think this is a misleading classification. All approaches, including the SI and the NI, have two accounting systems, one in terms of values and another in terms of prices. In what is referred to as a single-system approach, a link between value and price magnitudes is *posited* as a theoretical construct or an underlying assumption of the analysis. For instance, the theoretical construct of the value of money (or its reciprocal, the MEV) used in the NI is precisely such an assumption – what I have called, following Seton (1957), an invariance principle.

I have argued in this chapter that there is nothing intrinsically wrong about positing such a link, that is, an invariance principle, between value and price magnitude. In fact, there is no other way that the two accounting systems can be *quantitatively* linked to one another. The claim of Samuelson (1971) that the Marxist transformation procedure is akin to writing down one system, erasing it and then filling in with the other system is no longer true: the invariance principle, as a theoretically informed postulate, prevents the complete delinking of the two systems. Hence, it is best to do away with the dual-system and single-system terminology and instead focus explicitly on the invariance principle that links the two accounting systems. This makes the assumptions of the analysis transparent and will allow researchers to judge for themselves the reasonableness or otherwise of the crucial assumption that is posited to quantitatively link the value and price systems.

I have also argued that the key drawbacks of the SI were, first, its inability to distinguish a *numéraire* closure from an *invariance principle* closure of the price system and, second, its inability to generate a coherent theoretical framework of invariance principle closures which could retain key intuitions of the labour theory of value. From this perspective, the strengths of the NI are obvious. First, it is explicitly rooted in a meaningful invariance principle (which defines the MEV). Second, it is able to redefine the value of labour-power in such a way that two important invariance principles, those between living labour and monetary value added, and between surplus labour and monetary profits, can be simultaneously satisfied.

Some scholars have followed Baumol (1974) and Sen (1978) in distinguishing between a profit-exploitation orientation and a price-profit rate orientation to value theory (Mohun and Veneziani, 2017). The underlying idea seems to be that it is useful and meaningful to distinguish between a labour theory of value geared towards explaining profit in capitalist economies as arising from, or linked to, the exploitation of workers, and a labour theory of value primarily geared towards explaining prices of production and linking them to values. All prominent approaches to Marx's labour theory of value deal with both prices of production and with exploitation. Hence, the distinction is moot. In fact, it cannot be otherwise. The phenomenal world of capitalism is unavoidably linked with prices; and a key Marxist claim, deriving from its materialist conception of history, is that capitalism, like other class-divided societies, is based on the exploitation of direct producers. Marx's labour theory of value encompasses both, tries to provide explanations for both, tries to even link the world of prices and profit with the world of labour and exploitation.

The claim of Steedman (1977) that value magnitudes are redundant is only, and trivially, true when one focuses solely on magnitudes that do not require value magnitudes for their definition. Marxist economics is keenly interested in not only the qualitative but also the quantitative aspects of exploitation. For the latter aspect, the rate of exploitation is key, and the rate of exploitation has a quantitative dimension that cannot be ignored. Moreover, the rate of exploitation can only be meaningfully defined with value magnitudes. Hence, if we are interested in the rate of exploitation, how it changes across industries or countries and how it varies over time, then we *must* use value magnitudes.

Further Readings

- For a discussion of the transformation procedure worked out by Marx, see Marx (1993b, Chapter 13).

- For the SI, see Sweezy (1942), Morishima (1973) and Roemer (1981).

- For the NI, see Foley (1982b) and Foley (1986b).

- For an informative and rigorous survey of existing approaches to the transformation problem, see Mohun and Veneziani (2017). This paper provides a fairly comprehensive set of references to the previous literature. It covers stochastic approaches to value theory that I have not discussed in this chapter. My presentation in this chapter has lot of overlaps with Mohun and Veneziani (2017), but there are important differences in interpretation and emphasis.

7.A Appendix A: General Treatment

7.A.1 Technology

Consider a capitalist economy with n sectors, each producing a single commodity using labour and all commodities. There are no joint products and there is no fixed capital. The technical conditions of production in each sector are taken as given and are captured by the $n \times n$ matrix of input–output coefficients,

$$A = \begin{bmatrix} a_{11} & a_{12} & \cdots & a_{1n} \\ a_{21} & a_{22} & \cdots & a_{2n} \\ & & \vdots & \\ a_{n1} & a_{n2} & \cdots & a_{nn} \end{bmatrix}$$

and the corresponding $1 \times n$ vector of direct labour inputs

$$l = \begin{bmatrix} l_1 & l_2 & \cdots & l_n \end{bmatrix}$$

where a_{ij} is the physical magnitude of the i-th commodity used to produce 1 unit of the j-th commodity, and l_j is the quantity of direct labour used to produce 1 unit of commodity j.

Let x and y denote $n \times 1$ vectors of gross and net output. Since y_i and x_i are the net and gross output of commodity i, and

$$x_1 a_{i1} + x_2 a_{i2} + \cdots + x_n a_{in}$$

is the amount of commodity i used as input in the production of all other commodities, we have

$$y_i = x_i - (x_1 a_{i1} + x_2 a_{i2} + \cdots + x_n a_{in})$$

which captures the definitional relationship between gross and net output, that is, net output is gross output less the amount used up as inputs in production. Thus, for $i = 1, 2, \ldots, n$, we have,

$$x_i = (x_1 a_{i1} + x_2 a_{i2} + \cdots + x_n a_{in}) + y_i$$

Writing this in matrix notation, we get

$$x = Ax + y \tag{7.37}$$

which implies that

$$(I_n - A)\,x = y$$

where I_n is the identity matrix of size n.

The matrix $(I_n - A)$,

$$\begin{bmatrix} 1 - a_{11} & -a_{12} & \cdots & -a_{1n} \\ -a_{21} & 1 - a_{22} & \cdots & -a_{2n} \\ & & \vdots & \\ -a_{n1} & -a_{n2} & \cdots & 1 - a_{nn} \end{bmatrix}$$

deserves some comment. To begin with, note that each column of this matrix is completely determined by the technical requirements of producing a commodity, in terms of the quantities of different commodities required to produce one unit of the commodity represented by the given column. Thus, the columns of the matrix are likely to be linearly independent – because, for $i, j = 1, 2, \ldots, n$, the technical requirements of producing commodity i are likely to be independent of the technical requirements of producing commodity j. This implies that the matrix $(I_n - A)$ has full rank and, hence, is invertible (Pasinetti, 1977, p. 56). Hence, we will be able to write the gross output as

$$x = (I_n - A)^{-1}\,y$$

For the economic system represented by these equations to be meaningful, we need to ensure that the gross output vector is strictly positive, that is, each element of x must be larger than zero.[13] Now, we know that the vector of net output, y, and the input–output matrix, A, is non-negative, that is, some elements can be zero but none can be negative.[14] Therefore, if the matrix $(I_n - A)^{-1}$ were to be strictly positive, then that would ensure that the gross output vector is strictly positive.

Definition 1. *The non-negative matrix A is said to be productive if there exists a non-negative vector, $x \geq 0$, such that $x > Ax$.*

---

[13]We will use the following convention for vector and matrix orderings. If $x \geqq y$, that means $x_i \geq y_i$ for all components of the vectors. If $x \geq y$, that means $x \geqq y$ and $x \neq y$. If $x > y$, that means $x_i > y_i$ for all components of the vectors.

[14]A negative net output of any commodity does not make economic sense (Pasinetti, 1977, p. 62).

Proposition 5. *Suppose the non-negative matrix A is productive. Then,*

1. $\lambda_M(A) < 1$, *where $\lambda_M(A)$ denotes the maximum eigenvalue of the matrix A.*

2. $(I_n - A)^{-1} > 0$.

These are standard results in matrix algebra (Pasinetti, 1977, Appendix). The economic intuition is more important and can be understood by looking at the definition of a productive matrix. If the vector x is the level at which each sector is operated, then the vector Ax is the amount of inputs used up in producing each commodity. Hence, when the former is larger than the latter, it tells us that all commodities have positive net output when the technology is given by the matrix A. If this condition were not satisfied, then we would be dealing with a technology which could not produce more output than it used up as inputs. Hence, it would be technologically unviable, that is, unproductive.

Proposition 6. *(Hawkins–Simon) The necessary and sufficient condition for the matrix A to be productive is that all the principal minors of $I_n - A$ are strictly positive.*

This result is known as the Hawkins-Simon condition and was first proved in Hawkins and Simon (1949). It provides the necessary and sufficient conditions for the matrix A to be productive, in the sense defined above, that is, for a non-negative gross output vector to exist that can produce any given level of a positive net output vector. Suppose we want to produce a net output vector f. Since A is productive, we know that $(I_n - A)^{-1} > 0$. Hence, the correct gross output vector is given by $(I_n - A)^{-1} f$.

What is the intuition for this result? 'The condition that all principal minors must be positive means, in economic terms, that the group of industries corresponding to each minor must be capable of supplying more than its own needs for the group of products produced by this group of industries' (Hawkins and Simon, 1949, p. 248). A more economical version of the same result was later proved in Georgescu-Roegen (1966).

Proposition 7. *(Georgescu-Rogen) The necessary and sufficient condition for the Hawkins-Simon condition to be satisfied is that all the leading principal minors of the matrix $I_n - A$ are strictly positive.*

While the Hawkins-Simon condition refers to all principal minors of $I_n - A$, the Georgescu-Roegen result shows that considering the leading principal minors is enough.[15]

7.A.2 *The Value System*

Let Λ be the $1 \times n$ vector of value of the commodities. Since the value of a commodity is the sum of the value of the inputs used up and the direct labour used in producing the commodity, we have, for $i = 1, 2, \ldots, n$,

$$\Lambda_i = \Lambda_1 a_{1i} + \Lambda_2 a_{2i} + \cdots + \Lambda_n a_{ni} + l_i$$

so that, collecting terms, we have

$$\Lambda = \Lambda A + l \tag{7.38}$$

Thus, the vector of values of commodities is given by

$$\Lambda = (I_n - A)^{-1} l$$

where we are justified in inverting the matrix $(I_n - A)$ because, as we have seen earlier, it is invertible if it is productive (which we assume).

If we post-multiply (7.38) by x and pre-multiply (7.37) by Λ and compare the two, we see immediately that

$$lx = \Lambda y \tag{7.39}$$

which shows that the total labour involved in producing the gross output, which is the left-hand side, is equal to the total labour embodied in the net output which is the right-hand side.

7.A.3 *Standard Interpretation*

Rate of Exploitation

Let b denote the $n \times 1$ vector of the real wage bundle per hour of labour-power sold. If $L = \sum_i l_i$, then the total amount of commodities purchased and consumed by the working class is Lb. Here, we operate with the classical savings assumption, that is, we assume that the working class as a whole does

---

[15]For a proof of these results, see Nikaido (1968, Theorem 6.1).

not save, so that their income and consumption are equal. We can now define the rate of exploitation as follows:

$$e = \frac{L - L\Lambda b}{L\Lambda b} = \frac{1 - \Lambda b}{\Lambda b} \tag{7.40}$$

Relative Prices

Let p denote the $1 \times n$ vector of prices of production and w denote the nominal wage rate. Let us consider the production of the i-th commodity. The cost of non-labour inputs to produce 1 unit of the i-th commodity is $(p_1 a_{1i} + p_2 a_{2i} + \cdots + p_n a_{ni})$, and the cost of the labour input is given by wl_i.

Let r denote the uniform rate of profit. The price of production of the i-th commodity must be such as to ensure that the total capital outlay, that is, the sum of constant capital and variable capital, earns the uniform rate of profit, that is,

$$p_i = (p_1 a_{1i} + p_2 a_{2i} + \cdots + p_n a_{ni} + wl_i)(1 + r)$$

Given the classical savings assumption, the nominal wage is equal to the inner product of the real wage bundle and the price vector, that is, $w = pb$, and we will have

$$p_i = (p_1 a_{1i} + p_2 a_{2i} + \cdots + p_n a_{ni} + pbl_i)(1 + r)$$

Since this profitability condition must be ensured for the production of all commodities, we have, using matrices,

$$p = (1 + r)p(A + bl) \tag{7.41}$$

where r denotes the uniform rate of profit.

To see if the system of equation in (7.41) can be solved, let us use a simple counting argument. In this system of linear equation, there are n equations and $(n + 1)$ unknowns – the n prices *and* the average (uniform) rate of profit. Hence, we need to impose one restriction to make the system potentially solvable. The standard practice has been to choose a *numeraire* commodity, that is, set the price of the numeraire to 1 and, hence, express all prices in terms of this commodity. Once we choose a numeraire, we are left with n unknowns – the $n - 1$ relative prices and the uniform rate of profit –

and n equations. Hence, the counting argument suggests that it is possible for this system to have a solution – for average rate of profit and $n-1$ *relative prices*.

To solve the equation system (7.41) with economically meaningful solutions, we will rewrite it as a eigenvalue problem for the matrix $M = A + bl$, that is,

$$pM = \frac{1}{1+r}p \tag{7.42}$$

The rewritten system in (7.42) is an eigenvalue problem, that is, when we pre-multiply the matrix M by the vector p, we get back the vector p multiplied by a scalar, $1/(1+r)$. The matrix M is known as the augmented input matrix because it gives the total input of each commodity needed for sustaining production, where inputs include not only the material inputs used in the production process, captured by the matrix A, but also the amount of commodities consumed by workers, given by the real wage bundle, b. The augmented input matrix is non-negative because each of its element is a sum of two non-negative numbers. If m_{ij} denotes the (i, j) element of M, then we have

$$m_{ij} = a_{ij} + b_i l_j \geq 0$$

because the amount of the i-th commodity used in producing a unit of the j-th commodity is non-negative, $a_{ij} \geq 0$, the amount of the i-th commodity in the wage bundle is non-negative, $b_i \geq 0$, and the amount of labour needed to produce the j-th commodity is strictly positive, $l_j > 0$.

For any economically meaningful solution, we would need to ensure that the relative price vector p is strictly positive. Hence, with the restriction that the price vector p is strictly positive, we can use the Perron–Frobenius theorem to assert that the maximum eigenvalue of M is positive and unique, that is, $\lambda_M(M) > 0$.[16]

We have established that there is a unique positive value of $\lambda_M(M) = 1/(1+r)$. But this is not enough. We also need to ensure that the $r > 0$. Hence, we need to ensure that $\lambda_M(M) < 1$. From Proposition 5, we see that

---

[16]The Perron–Frobenius theorem shows that the maximum eigenvalue of any indecomposable, non-negative matrix is real and positive, and the associated eigenvector is strictly positive. Moreover, the maximal eigenvalue is a continuous and strictly increasing function of the elements of the matrix (Debreu and Herstein, 1958; Pasinetti, 1977; Roemer, 1981).

this is ensured as long as the M is productive. Since we have already assumed that A is productive, we only need to ensure that the real wage bundle is not 'too large', that is not so large as will make the maximal eigenvalue of M greater than or equal to 1.[17]

Thus, if the system is able to produce a physical net product for the capitalists, which is ensured as long as the M is productive, then (7.42) has a unique rate of profit, r, with $0 < r$. The corresponding eigen vector gives the vector of prices of production, p (up to a factor of proportionality). Since the n-vector of prices of production, p, can only be solved up to a factor of proportionality, that is, only relative prices can be found, we need an additional equation to solve for the absolute prices. But before we do that, let us discuss the FMT.

Fundamental Marxian Theorem

The FMT is a key result in the SI and was first highlighted by M. Morishima. There are two important points about the FMT that are worth emphasizing. First, it is true for any choice of numeraire or invariance principle. Second, it establishes a well-defined, qualitative link between values and prices that can go a long way in expressing some key intuitions about the labour theory of value. The main intuition is that the rate of profit is positive if and only if the rate of exploitation is positive.

Theorem 1. *Let $M = A + bl$ be the augmented input matrix; let r be the uniform profit rate associated with M; let $e = (1/\Lambda b) - 1$ be the rate of exploitation. Then, we have:*

1. *$r > 0$ if and only if $e > 0$;*

2. *if $e > 0$, then $r < e$;*

3. *r is an increasing function of e, and vice versa.*

Proof. For the first part, see Roemer (1981, Theorem 1.1); for the second and third parts, see Pasinetti (1977, p. 128). □

The relationship between the rate of profit and the rate of exploitation was further clarified by Roemer (1981), who showed, first, that every real

---

[17]Using the Perron–Frobenius theorem, we know that $\lambda_M(M)$ is a strictly increasing function of the elements of M. Hence, given A and l such that $\lambda_M(A) < 1$, we can always find a $b \geqq 0$ which makes $\lambda_M(M) \geq 1$.

wage bundle which gives a positive rate of exploitation can be uniquely associated with a uniform profit rate and, second, that if the real wage bundle is allowed to vary while keeping the rate of exploitation fixed, the corresponding uniform rate of profit will not attain a unique magnitude, but will vary over a range. Thus, while there is strictly increasing relationship between the rate of profit and the rate of exploitation, it is not unique if the real wage bundle is allowed to vary so as to keep the rate of exploitation fixed. Roemer (1981, Chapter 8) called such a relationship a 'transformation correspondence'. Using the transformation correspondence, it is possible to establish some well-defined qualitative relationships between values and prices at the individual level. These relationships give upper and lower bounds for the maximum and minimum deviation between values and prices across sectors (Roemer, 1981, Corollary 8.6).

Real Wage Rate-Profit Rate Frontier

In Chapter 6, we have seen the real wage rate-profit rate frontier in a single-commodity economy. In the one-commodity model, we saw that the real wage rate-profit rate frontier gives a negative relationship between the real wage rate and the profit rate. We understood this relationship as capturing the conflict of interest between the working class (who are the wage earners) and the capitalist class (whose members earn profit income) over the distribution of the national income. Now, we would like to derive the real wage rate-profit rate frontier in a general model with n commodities.

Our first task is to define the 'real wage rate', which is no longer obvious in a n-commodity model.[18] Given the real wage bundle, b, we define the real wage rate as a real number, ω, such that the consumption bundle of the workers is given by ωb, that is, ω captures the scale of consumption once the real wage bundle, b, is given. Thus, for the real wage rate ω, the price system in (7.41) can be written as

$$p = (1+r)\,(pA + p\omega bl)$$

which, using the normalization that $pb = 1$, becomes

$$p = (1+r)\,(pA + \omega l)$$

so that,

$$p = (1+r)\,\omega l\,[I - (1+r)\,A]^{-1}$$

---

[18]This sub-section draws on Cogliano et al. (2018, pp. 96–97).

The real wage rate-profit rate frontier is then given by plugging this expression of the price vector into the normalization equation, $pb = 1$, that is,

$$(1+r)\,\omega l\,[I - (1+r)\,A]^{-1}\,b = 1 \qquad (7.43)$$

The relationship in (7.43) implicitly defines the wage-profit frontier. It is a non-linear relationship between the real wage rate, ω, and the profit rate, r. We want to show that this implicit relationship is a negative one. Note, first, that when $\omega = 0$, we have

$$p = (1+r)\,pA$$

which defines the maximal rate of profit, R. When $0 \leq r < R$, we have

$$p = (1+r)\,(pA + p\omega bl)$$

If we define $M(\omega) = A + \omega bl$, then the above equation becomes the following eigenvalue problem:

$$pM(\omega) = \frac{1}{1+r}p$$

Using the Perron–Frobenius theorem, we know that

$$1 + r = \frac{1}{\lambda_M(M(\omega))}$$

where $\lambda_M(M(\omega))$ is the maximal eigenvalue of $M(\omega)$. The Perron–Frobenius theorem also tells us that $\lambda_M(M(\omega))$ is an increasing function of ω. This immediately shows that the rate of profit, r, is a decreasing function of the real wage rate, ω.

Absolute Prices

Let us return to the price system and see how we can compute absolute prices. One way to do so, that is, close the system, is to use a numeraire, that is, a unit to express all prices. For instance, if we choose the first commodity as the numeraire, then all prices will be expressed in units of the first commodity. This can be implemented by assuming $p_1 = 1$. This will provide the extra equation to now solve for absolute prices. Yet another numeraire that could be used is the nominal wage rate, that is, all prices would now be expressed in units of labour-power. This numeraire could be implemented as $pb = 1$, which would now provide another equation to solve for absolute prices.

The other way to close the system is to use invariance principles. Two obvious candidates to choose from are: (a) total money value added is equal to the total labour embodied in the net output and (b) total monetary profits is equal to the total surplus value. The first invariance principle – total money value added is equal to the total labour embodied in the net output – can be written as

$$py = \Lambda y \tag{7.44}$$

and the the second – total monetary profits is equal to the total surplus value – can be written as

$$p\left(I_n - A - bl\right)x = \Lambda\left(I_n - A - bl\right)x \tag{7.45}$$

Any of these invariance principles can be used to close the system and solve for absolute prices. But more than one cannot be used because that would render the system of equations overdetermined. Intuitively, each of these invariance principles is a way to express an intuition of the labour theory of value, and each define the MEV in a specific way.

7.A.4 New Interpretation with Homogeneous Labour

Closing the System
Given the $n \times n$ input–output coefficient matrix, A, the $1 \times n$ labour input vector, l, and the nominal wage rate, w, a system of equation for the $1 \times n$ vector of prices of production, p, can be written, as before:

$$p = (1 + r)(pA + wl) \tag{7.46}$$

The system of equation has n equations and $n + 1$ unknowns (the n elements of the price vector, p, and the average rate of profit, r). Hence, we need one more equation to solve for the $n + 1$ unknowns. In the NI framework, this additional equation is generated by using the relationship between the nominal wage rate, w, the value of labour-power, v, and MEV, m.

Value of Labour-Power
Unlike the SI, the NI does not specify the real wage bundle. Instead, it takes either the MEV or the value of labour-power as the exogenous variable. Here,

I will take the nominal wage rate and the value of labour-power as *exogenously fixed* by institutional factors or by the state of class struggle. Since the value of labour-power is defined as the ratio of the nominal wage rate and the MEV, that is, $v = w/m$, we have,

$$m = \frac{w}{v}$$

But, the MEV is the ratio of the aggregate money value added and total labour embodied in the net output, where the latter is also equal to the total labour involved in production of the gross output. Hence,

$$m = \frac{p\left(I_n - A\right)x}{lx}$$

where x is gross output. Hence,

$$\frac{v}{w} = \frac{lx}{p\left(I_n - A\right)x}$$

This gives us the extra equation to solve for the vector of absolute prices:

$$vp\left(I_n - A\right)x = wlx \tag{7.47}$$

Thus, given the input–output coefficient matrix, A, the vector of direct labour inputs, l, the gross output vector, x, the nominal wage rate, w, and the value of labour-power, v, a simple counting argument suggests that the vector of prices of production, p, and the average rate of profit, r, can be computed using (7.46) and (7.47).

To show that a solution exists, we can begin by writing the expression for the price vector that comes from the price system in (7.46):

$$p = (1+r)\,wl\left[I_n - (1+r)\,A\right]^{-1}$$

From (7.47), we get

$$\frac{1}{v} = \frac{p\left(I_n - A\right)x}{wlx}$$

which, on using the expression for the price vector, becomes

$$\frac{1}{v} = \frac{(1+r)\,l\left[I_n - (1+r)\,A\right]^{-1}\left(I_n - A\right)x}{lx} \tag{7.48}$$

There is a serious difficulty lurking here. Given the value of all the known variables appearing in (7.48), it reduces to a polynomial equation in r of degree n. From the fundamental theorem of algebra, we know that this equation has n roots. Hence, there will be n different values of the uniform rate of profit that will solve (7.48). There is no unique root. Moreover, the n roots of (7.48) can be real or complex numbers. How do we know that a meaningful uniform profit rate exists? How do we know that it is a unique, real, positive number? The Perron–Frobenius theorem comes to the rescue again.

Since the matrix A is productive, its maximal eigenvalue, $\lambda_M(A)$, is less than 1, that is, $\lambda_M(A) < 1$ (see Proposition 5). If we define the maximal rate of profit of this economy as R, where $1 + R = (1/\lambda_M(A))$, we see immediately that $R > 0$, that is, the economy has a positive maximal rate of profit. As long as $r < R$, each element of the matrix $[I_n - (1+r)\,A]^{-1}$ is strictly positive and an increasing function of r (Pasinetti, 1977, Mathematical Appendix). This implies that the right-hand side of (7.48) is a monotonically increasing and unbounded function of r, as long as $r < R$. Moreover, when $r = 0$, the right-hand side of (7.48) is 1. This implies that for any $v < 1$, there exists a positive and unique value of r between 0 and R that solves (7.48). Since v is the value of labour-power, it always lies between 0 and 1 by assumption. Hence, a solution for (7.48) always exists, is unique and lies in the range given by $0 < r < R$. For this value of the uniform rate of profit, r, the price vector can be solved from the following equation system:

$$p = (1+r)\,wl\,[I_n - (1+r)\,A]^{-1}$$

This completes the demonstration that the NI can solve for a set of prices of production and the uniform rate of profit consistently. Moreover, since the calculation is nested within the NI framework, we get back two key aggregate equalities: (a) the monetary value added is an expression of the total productive labour and (b) total profit is an expression of the total surplus labour.

Fundamental Marxian Theorem

The FMT is easily proved in the NI framework. In the NI, the rate of exploitation is defined as

$$e = \frac{1-v}{v}$$

where e is the rate of exploitation and v is the value of labour-power. Unlike the SI, the determination of the value of labour-power does not involve the bundle of commodities consumed by the working class. Rather, it is defined as the social labour-time equivalent of the nominal wage rate. Thus, the value of labour-power denotes the fraction of an hour of social labour-time that the workers get back through their wage income. Hence, $1 - v$ is the surplus labour, so that $(1 - v)/v$ is the rate of exploitation.

Using the definition of the rate of exploitation, we can rewrite (7.48) as

$$1 + e = \frac{(1+r)\, l\, [I_n - (1+r)\, A]^{-1}\, (I_n - A)\, x}{lx} \tag{7.49}$$

which, by the argument presented above to demonstrate existence of a solution, immediately establishes the FMT: $r > 0$ if and only if $e > 0$. This is because the right-hand side of (7.49) is a monotone strictly increasing function of r, which takes the value of 1 at $r = 0$ and increases in an unbounded manner as $r \to \infty$.

A Solution Algorithm

The following algorithm can be used to compute the uniform rate of profit and the vector of prices of production for the NI of Marx's labour theory of value with homogeneous labour. For this algorithm, I take the value of labour-power as an exogenous variable, and treat the MEV as endogenous. An alternative closure is to instead take the MEV as the exogenous variable and treat the value of labour-power as endogenous.

- Gather information about the following: A ($n \times n$ input–output matrix), l ($1 \times n$ labour input vector), w (nominal wage rate, which is a positive scalar) and v (value of labour-power, which is a fraction lying between 0 and 1).

- Calculate the eigenvalues of A and check if the maximum eigenvalue, $\lambda_M(A) < 1$. Proceed to the next step if the answer is in the affirmative. If the maximum eigenvalue of A is greater than or equal to 1, something is wrong with the input–output matrix. Check for errors.

- Calculate the maximal rate of profit: $R = (1/\lambda_M(A)) - 1$.

- Define a univariate function of r:

$$f(r) = (1+r)\, wl\, [I_n - (1+r)\, A]^{-1}\, (I_n - A)\, x - \frac{wlx}{v}$$

We use this particular function because finding the root of this function leads to the solution of the uniform rate of profit, as shown by (7.48).

- Use a numerical method to find the unique root of $f(r)$ over the range $0 < r < R$. Uniqueness is guaranteed because the function is strictly increasing and increases from 1 to ∞ over the range $0 < r < R$. Make sure to specify the upper bound of the range as slightly less than R (because the function becomes infinite at R). When n is large, this step will be computationally intensive because of the matrix inversion: $[\boldsymbol{I_n} - (1+r)\,\boldsymbol{A}]^{-1}$.

- Calculate the vector of prices of production:

$$\boldsymbol{p} = (1+r)\,wl\,[\boldsymbol{I_n} - (1+r)\,\boldsymbol{A}]^{-1}$$

- Calculate $1 \times n$ vector of values: $\boldsymbol{\Lambda} = l\,(\boldsymbol{I_n} - \boldsymbol{A})^{-1}$. When n is large, this step will also be computationally intensive.

- Calculate the MEV:

$$\mathrm{MEV} = \frac{py}{ly}$$

and use it to freely convert between monetary and labour hour magnitudes.

An Example

Let us continue working with the three-commodity economy that was used in the example of the SI. Thus, technology is the same as in the previous example, that is, $\boldsymbol{A}$ and $\boldsymbol{l}$ are as given in (7.1) and (7.2), respectively; and, the net and gross output vectors are also as given in (7.4) and (7.7), respectively. Whereas in the the SI, we need to specify the real wage bundle, in the NI, we need to provide information about the nominal wage rate and the value of labour-power (or the MEV). We choose a nominal wage rate, $w = 1$, and a value of labour-power, $v = 0.33$ (which is approximately the wage share in national income in the US).

The first step is to compute the maximal rate of profit, $R = (1/\lambda_M(\boldsymbol{A})) - 1$, where $\lambda_M(\boldsymbol{A})$ is the maximal eigenvalue of the matrix $\boldsymbol{A}$. Since the $\boldsymbol{A}$ matrix has remained unchanged from the previous example, we have $\lambda_M(\boldsymbol{A}) = 0.675$. Hence, $R = 0.483$. This is important information because it tells us that the uniform rate of profit, r, will lie between 0 and R, that is, $0 < r < 0.483$. To calculate the uniform rate of profit, we will define the following function of the single variable, r,

$$f(r) = (1+r) \, wl \left[I_n - (1+r) \, A \right]^{-1} (I_n - A) \, x - \frac{wlx}{v}$$

and find the root of this function over the following range, $0 < r < 0.483$, using standard numerical methods. Using this method, we find that, in this example, $r = 0.2859$, that is, the uniform rate of profit is 28.59 per cent. The next step is to compute the vector of prices of production. We can do this as follows:

$$p = (1+r) \, wl \left[I_n - (1+r) \, A \right]^{-1}$$

Using the magnitudes for this example, we get

$$p = \begin{bmatrix} 0.648 & 5.775 & 2.109 \end{bmatrix}$$

The final step is to compute the value of money (or its reciprocal, the MEV). To do so, let us compute the vector of values,

$$\Lambda = l \, (I_n - A)^{-1}$$

In this example, we get

$$\Lambda = \begin{bmatrix} 0.182 & 1.818 & 0.909 \end{bmatrix}$$

Now we can calculate the MEV as

$$\text{MEV} = \frac{py}{ly}$$

In our example, we have $MEV = (179.97/60) = 2.99$. Thus, every hour of social labour is expressed as 2.99 dollars. Using the MEV as a conversion factor, we can move back and forth between monetary and labour hour magnitudes.

7.A.5   New Interpretation with Heterogenous Labour

The presentation of the NI in the previous section assumes that there is only one type of labour in the economy, that is, homogeneous, simple labour.[19]

---

[19]This section follows, but also modifies, Duménil et al. (2009).

Of course, this is unrealistic because in any actual capitalist economy, there is a *heterogeneity of labour*, that is, there are many different types of complex or heterogeneous labour. If, instead of homogeneous, simple labour, we are given m types of complex labour, where $m > 1$, this fact can be easily incorporated into the analysis. The key analytical difference with the previous analysis will relate to the specification of the labour input. Instead of the labour input in each sector being a scalar, it will now be given by a m-vector, each element of which will specify the amount of the j-th type of labour, with j running from 1 to m, needed to produce 1 unit of the commodity.

Technology and Value
In an economy with heterogeneous labour, technology will be defined by the $n \times n$ input–output coefficient matrix, $\boldsymbol{A}$, as before, and a $m \times n$ matrix, $\boldsymbol{l}$, of labour inputs,

$$\boldsymbol{l} = \begin{bmatrix} l_{11} & l_{12} & \cdots & l_{1n} \\ l_{21} & l_{22} & \cdots & l_{2n} \\ & & \vdots & \\ l_{m1} & l_{m2} & \cdots & l_{mn} \end{bmatrix}$$

where l_{jk} gives the amount of j-th type of labour used in producing 1 unit of the k-th commodity.

Since complex labour creates, in each hour, a multiple of the value created by simple labour, specifying the m types of labour requires that we also specify the differential value-creating capacities of heterogeneous labour. Given the value-creating capacity, that is, the magnitude of value created in 1 hour, by the m types of labour, we can choose to arrange them in ascending order, and then choose the *productive labour* with the lowest value-creating capacity as 'simple labour'.[20] Hence, we can represent this differential value-creating capacity of heterogeneous labour as the $1 \times m$ vector

$$\boldsymbol{\mu} = \begin{bmatrix} 1 & \mu_2 & \cdots & \mu_m \end{bmatrix} \tag{7.50}$$

---

[20]In this framework, we can accommodate the difference between productive and unproductive labour by assigning $\mu_j = 0$ for types of labour that are unproductive. That is why it is important to emphasize that the type of labour chosen as simple labour is productive. That will ensure that $\mu_1 > 0$ and will allow us to divide all the other μ_j by μ_1.

where value created by each unit of the $m - 1$ types of complex labour, indexed by $2, 3, \ldots, m$, should be understood as multiples of the value created by each hour of simple labour.[21]

Let Λ denote the $1 \times n$ vector of values of the n commodities. Then, we have

$$\Lambda = \Lambda A + \mu l$$

This equation tells us that the value of a unit of any commodity comes from the value transferred by constant capital, that is, the non-labour inputs used up in producing the commodity, and the value added by various types of complex labour. It is worth noting that we are here adding up units of complex labour after reducing them to the correct units of simple labour, as must be done according to Marx's labour theory of value (see Appendix 3.A for details). To see this clearly, let us write the value equation for the i-th commodity:

$$\Lambda_i = (\Lambda_1 a_{1i} + \cdots + \Lambda_n a_{ni}) + (l_{1i} + \mu_2 l_{2i} + \cdots + \mu_m l_{mi})$$

Now we can see that the expression in the second parenthesis above is the sum of complex labour reduced to correct multiples of simple labour.[22]

Average Nominal Wage Rate
The price of a unit of the j-th type of labour-power, which provides the j-th type of labour when used in production, is denoted by w_j, so that the nominal wage rate in this economy is given by w, a $1 \times m$ vector:

$$w = \begin{bmatrix} w_1 & w_2 & \cdots & w_m \end{bmatrix}$$

If x is the gross output, then the total wage income is given by wlx, and total labour input is given by ilx, where i is a $1 \times m$ vector of 1s. Hence, the average nominal wage rate can be defined as

$$\overline{w} = \frac{wlx}{ilx} \tag{7.51}$$

---

[21] The vector μ is therefore nothing other than the vector of reduction coefficients discussed in the appendix to Chapter 3.

[22] Since Duménil et al. (2009) use a different normalization, the reduction of complex to simple labour, whereby each unit of complex labour adds a multiple of the value added by each unit of simple labour, seems to be less transparent in their account.

Prices of Production
With information on technology and the nominal wage rates for the different types of labour-power given, the price system can be written as

$$p = (1+r)(pA + wl) \tag{7.52}$$

where p is the $1 \times n$ vector of prices of production, A is the $n \times n$ matrix of input–output coefficients, w is the $1 \times m$ vector of nominal wage rates for the m types of labour, l is a $m \times n$ matrix of direct labour input requirements and r is the uniform rate of profit. Algebraic manipulation gives us the expression of the price of production vector in terms of technology, wage rates and the uniform rate of profit,

$$p = (1+r) wl [I_n - (1+r)A]^{-1} \tag{7.53}$$

Monetary Expression of Value
To find an expression for the MEV, we need to divide total monetary value added by total value-creating (socially necessary abstract simple) labour. Aggregate monetary value added is given by $p(I_n - A)x$. To find the total magnitude of value-creating labour, note that total complex labour is given by lx, and the differential magnitude of value-creating capacity of these complex labours is given by μ, expressed in units of simple labour. Hence, total magnitude of value-creating labour, expressed in units of simple labour, is given by μlx. Thus, the MEV is given by

$$m = \frac{p(I_n - A)x}{\mu lx} \tag{7.54}$$

Existence of Solution and FMT
To close the system, that is, solve for the uniform rate of profit and the price of production vector, we need another equation. We will follow the same methodology as proposed in this chapter and take the *value of labour-power as given by the state of class struggle*. Let v denote the value of labour-power at the aggregate level, which can be defined as

$$v = \frac{\overline{w}}{m}$$

where $\overline{w}$ is the average nominal wage rate defined earlier in (7.51) and m is the MEV. Hence,

$$\frac{1}{v} = \frac{m}{\overline{w}} = \frac{(1+r)\,\boldsymbol{wl}\left[\boldsymbol{I_n} - (1+r)\,\boldsymbol{A}\right]^{-1}(\boldsymbol{I_n} - \boldsymbol{A})\,\boldsymbol{x}}{\overline{w}\mu l\boldsymbol{x}}$$

where I have used (7.53) and (7.54) to substitute for the MEV in the above equation. Since $0 < v < 1$ is *given to us*, the above equation allows us to solve for the unique and positive uniform rate of profit – using the same argument as used above to prove existence of a unique solution in the model with homogeneous labour. It also demonstrates the FMT. Moreover, for this particular uniform rate of profit, we can then use (7.53) to solve for the price of production vector.

7.A.6 Unequal Rates of Surplus Value

In general, the value of labour-power, and hence the rate of surplus value, will vary across types of labour-power. This is because the social labour-time equivalent of the nominal wage rate earned by a certain type of complex labour might be different from the value added by that type of labour-power. This is because the social labour-time equivalent of complex labour is computed with the aggregate MEV, whereas the value added by any type of complex labour is computed with the reduction coefficient of that type of complex labour-power. There is no reason why these two calculations should come up with the same number. In a similar way, the rate of surplus value will, in general, vary across industries because the social labour-time equivalent of the average nominal wage rate in any industry might be different from the value added by the different types of labour in that industry.

The long-period method of analysis implies that the mobility of labour across sectors lead to an equalization of the rate of exploitation. But redistribution of surplus value across sectors means that the rate of (realized) surplus value can, and do, differ across sectors. What we have with heterogeneous labour is another mechanism for the divergence of the rate of surplus value across sectors and types of complex labour-power. The main mechanisms at play seem to be the different types of impediments to the supply (production) of the different types of complex labour-power. If such impediments are strong, they can account for the existence of differential rates of surplus value across types of complex labour – in addition to the mechanisms of redistribution of surplus value that come from mobility of capital and bargaining between, on the one hand, industrial capital and, on the other, money capitalists and resources owners. Using a very different framework, Wright (1997) has argued that wage differentials arise due to monopolies of various types that restrict the production of complex labour-power. For instance, market and non-market impediments exist in the supply of doctors or engineers, which then lead to a significantly higher wage rate earned by these types of workers, that is higher than what would be earned if there were no such impediments. In our framework, we could perhaps draw on the existence of such societal monopolies to explain the continuation of differential rates of surplus value in a long run equilibrium.

7.B Appendix B: R Code for Examples Discussed in Text

Here, I give R code for the examples discussed in this chapter about the transformation problem, that is, about the methods for solving for the uniform rate of profit and the vector of prices of production.

7.B.1 Standard Interpretation

This is the R code to implement the example discussed in section 7.2.1.

```
# ------------------------------------------------ #
# ----- Quantities that are taken as given ------- #
# These quantities will need to be changed
# to implement the algorithm for any economy.

# -- Input-output matrix
A <- matrix(c(186/450, 12/450, 9/450,
54/21, 6/21, 6/21,
30/60, 3/60, 15/60),
ncol = 3)

# -- Labour input vector
l <- c(18/450, 12/21, 30/60)

# -- Real wage bundle
```

```
b <- c(2, 0, 1/6)

# -- Net output
y <- c(180, 0, 30)

# Check the dimensions of vectors and matrix
# If number of columns of A is not equal
# to the length of the other three vectors
# do not proceed. Check data.
(dim(A))
(length(l))
(length(b))
(length(y))

# ------------------------------------------------- #
# ------- Quantities that are calculated --------- #

# ---- Gross Output Vector ------- #
# Create identity matrix
n <- ncol(A)
I <- diag(n)

# The "solve" function gives the inverse,
# and %*% is used for matrix multiplication
# The result will be displayed on screen
(Q <- solve(I - A) %*% y)




# ------ The Value System --------- #

# Vector of values
(lambda <- t(l)%*%solve(I - A))

# Value embodied in the net product ...
(lambda %*% y)
```

```
# Is equal to the total labour to produce gross output
(l%*%Q)

# Value of real wage bundle (value of labour power)
(vrb <- lambda %*% b)

# Rate of exploitation
(e <- (1/vrb)-1)




# --------- Price System: 1 --------- #
# -- Rate of profit calculations

# Maximum eigenvalue of A
jj_A <- eigen(A)$values
(lambda_mA <- max(jj_A))

# Maximal rate of profit
(R <- (1/lambda_mA)-1)

# Augmented input matrix
(M <- A + b%*%t(l))

# Maximum eigenvalue of M
jj_M <- eigen(M)$values
(lambda_mM <- max(jj_M))

# Uniform rate of profit
(r_e <- (1/lambda_mM)-1)




# --------- Price System: 2 --------- #
# -- Relative price calculations

# M1 matrix
(M1 <- I - (1/lambda_mM)*M)
```

```
# Pre-multiply M1 with a price vector
# Choose any two equations
# Solve for relative prices
# Here we solve in terms of p3
A1 <- M1[1:2,1:2]
b1 <- M1[3,1:2]
(p12 <- solve(t(A1),b1))

# Relative price vector in terms of p3
(p <- c(-p12,1))


# --------- Price System: 3 --------- #
# -- Using numeraire to close system

# Numeraire = third commodity, i.e. p3=1
# We have solved this above and the answer is
(p <- c(-p12,1))

# Numeraire = nominal wage rate
# Equation capturing this numeraire:
# 2 * p_1 + 0.167 * p_3 = 1
# To solve for prices, we will
# replace one equation with the
# numeraire equation.

# Transpose of M1
(M2 <- t(M1))

# Create new matrix by appending
# vector of coefficients of numeraire equation
ncoef <- c(2, 0, 0.167)
(M3 <- rbind(M2[1:2,1:3],ncoef))

# Create new right hand side vector
(bn <- c(0,0,1))
```

```
# Solve: M3 * p = bn
# To get the vector of prices of production
(solve(M3,bn))


# --------- Price System: 4 --------- #
# -- Using invariance principles to close system

# -- Invariance principle 1
# Net output remains unchanged with transformation
# Equation: 6 * p_1 + 1 * p_3 = 2

# Transpose of M1
(M2 <- t(M1))

# Create new matrix by appending
# vector of coefficients of numeraire equation
inv1coef <- c(6, 0, 1)
(M4 <- rbind(M2[1:2,1:3],inv1coef))

# Create new right hand side vector
(binv1 <- c(0,0,2))

# Solve: M4 * p = binv1
# To get the vector of prices of production
(solve(M4,binv1))


# -- Invariance principle 2
# Gross output remains unchanged with transformation
# Equation: 450*p_1 + 21*p_2 + 60*p_3 = 174.55

# Transpose of M1
(M2 <- t(M1))

# Create new matrix by appending
```

```
# vector of coefficients of numeraire equation
inv2coef <- c(450, 21, 60)
(M5 <- rbind(M2[1:2,1:3],inv2coef))

# Create new right hand side vector
(binv2 <- c(0,0,174.55))

# Solve: M5 * p = binv2
# To get the vector of prices of production
(solve(M5,binv2))


# -- Invariance principle 3
# Gross output remains unchanged with transformation
# Equation: 2*p_1 + + 0.167*p_3 = 0.52

# Transpose of M1
(M2 <- t(M1))

# Create new matrix by appending
# vector of coefficients of numeraire equation
inv3coef <- c(2, 0, 0.167)
(M6 <- rbind(M2[1:2,1:3],inv3coef))

# Create new right hand side vector
(binv3 <- c(0,0,0.52))

# Solve: M6 * p = binv3
# To get the vector of prices of production
(solve(M6,binv3))


# -- Invariance principle 4
# Surplus value = profit

# Total surplus value
((1-vrb)*(1 %*% Q))
```

```
# Total profit = r p MQ
# Pre-multiply the vector below with
# the price vector to get total profit
(r_e*M%*%Q)

# Equation for invariance principle:
# 390*p1 + 21*p2 + 40*p3 = 323.67

# Transpose of M1
(M2 <- t(M1))

# Create new matrix by appending
# vector of coefficients of numeraire equation
inv4coef <- c(390, 21, 40)
(M7 <- rbind(M2[1:2,1:3],inv4coef))

# Create new right hand side vector
(binv4 <- c(0,0,323.67))

# Solve: M4 * p = binv1
# To get the vector of prices of production
(solve(M7,binv4))
```

7.B.2   New Interpretation

This is the R code to implement the example discussed in section 7.A.4.

```
# ----------------------------------------------- #
# ----- Quantities that are taken as given ------- #
# These quantities will need to be changed
# to implement the algorithm for any economy.

# A = input output matrix
# l = labour input vector
# w = nominal wage rate
# v = value of labour power
```

```
# Q = gross output vector

# -- Input-output matrix
A <- matrix(c(186/450, 12/450, 9/450,
54/21, 6/21, 6/21,
30/60, 3/60, 15/60),
ncol = 3)

# -- Labour input vector
(l <- c(18/450, 12/21, 30/60))

# -- Nominal wage rate
(w <- 1)

# -- Value of labour power
(v <- 0.515)

# -- Net output
y <- c(180, 0, 30)

# -------------------------------------------------- #
# ----- Quantities that are computed ------------ #

# -- Compute Gross Output
I <- diag(3)
(Q <- solve(I - A) %*% y)



# -- Maximum eigenvalue of A
jj_A <- eigen(A)$values
(lambda_mA <- max(jj_A))

# -- Maximal rate of profit
(R <- (1/lambda_mA)-1)


# -- Define Univariate Function of rate of profit
```

```r
myfunc <- function(r2){

# Given variables
D2=(I-A)%*%Q
l2=l
A2=A
L2=(l%*%Q)/v

# Compute value of function
C2 = solve(I-(1+r2)*A2)
E2 = C2%*%D2
B2 = (1+r2)*l2%*%E2
i2 = B2-L2
return(i2)
}

# Find root to get uniform rate of profit
# Note: upper bound should be kept less than
# R because the function blows up at R
(r <- uniroot(myfunc,c(0,R-0.1))$root)

# Solve: p = (1+r)wl*[I-(1+r)A]^{-1}
# To get the vector of prices of production
(p <- (1+r)*w*l%*%(solve(I-(1+r)*A)))

# --- Calculating the MEV
# Create identity matrix
n <- ncol(A)
I <- diag(n)

# Vector of values
(lambda <- t(l)%*%solve(I - A))

# MEV
(mev <- (p%*%y)/(lambda %*%y))
```

8

Exploitation and Oppression

The concept of exploitation is a central one in Marxism. A key claim of Marxism is that capitalism, like previous class-divided societies, rests on the exploitation of the class of direct producers. Just like the slave system was built on the exploitation of the slaves, the direct producers in a slave system, and the feudal system rested on the exploitation of the serfs, who were the direct producers in feudalism, the capitalist system rests on the exploitation of the working class, the direct producers in capitalism. In Chapter 3, we had encountered the concept of exploitation when we were discussing Marx's argument about the origins of surplus value. In this chapter, we revisit the issue and discuss it in greater detail. We will also discuss two important issues related to the question of exploitation. First, we will study the Analytical Marxist (AM) critique of the labour theory of value (and exploitation of labour) that can be called a commodity theory of value (and exploitation of commodities). Second, we will study the relationship between exploitation and oppression, and the related question of the relationship between exploitation and distributive injustice.

Recall that Marx's labour theory of value rests on the argument that labour is the substance of value (Marx, 1992, Chapter 1). In the first volume of *Capital*, Marx refined and extended the classical labour theory of value (LTV) and used it to demonstrate that capitalism rests on the exploitation of the working class. An influential strand of AM thinking has challenged this basic argument with what I would like to call a commodity theory of value (CTV). There are two key claims of the CTV: first, that any basic commodity can be used to construct a consistent value theory, where a basic commodity is one which is used directly or indirectly to produce all other commodities; and second, that the rate of profit is positive if and only if the basic commodity is exploited. This means that there is nothing special in labour so far as it can be considered the substance of value. Basic commodities can as well function as a substance of value. Moreover, just like labour is exploited if we choose to use Marx's LTV, it can also be demonstrated that when a basic commodity is chosen as the candidate substance of value, it is also necessarily exploited in a capitalist economy. Hence, labour does not have a special function to play even in a theory of exploitation (Roemer, 1982, 1985). In this chapter, we will see that these claims rest on rather shaky theoretical foundations.

We will also see that while exploitation gives rise to class oppression, there are many other forms of oppression that we can identify in capitalist societies. Some of these oppressions come from the process of expropriation of segments of populations from productive resources; others arise from, and reproduce, inequalities of income, wealth and power along dimensions of caste, gender, race & ethnicity, and citizenship. Fighting against these oppressions can be understood as a struggle against expropriation, against injustice and for equality. What, then, is the relationship of these myriad forms of oppressions to class oppression? Is it useful to conceptually distinguish exploitation and oppression? Is exploitation merely a matter of distributive injustice? We will investigate these questions in the last section of this chapter.

8.1 Theories of Exploitation

In this first section, we want to understand the debates that have occurred in the past few decades on the *theories* of exploitation. To facilitate comprehension. we will divide the discussion on exploitation theory into two parts. In the first part, we will discuss some of the key qualitative issues involved in the definition, meaning and implication of exploitation. In the second part of this section, we will turn to the quantitative angle and engage with the question about the measurement of exploitation.

8.1.1   Qualitative Issues

Let us start with a basic question: What is exploitation? We will follow Erik Olin Wright and define a relationship to be exploitative if the following three criteria are satisfied (Wright, 2000, p. 1563):

1. *The inverse interdependence of welfare principle*: An increase in the material welfare of exploiters is causally dependent on a decline in the material welfare of the exploited.

2. *The labour appropriation principle*: The inverse interdependence of welfare of the exploiter and exploited comes about because exploiters can appropriate the labour or the fruits of labour of the exploiters.

3. *The exclusion principle*: The exploiters are able to appropriate the labour of the exploited because the exploited are excluded from access to key productive resources of the economy.

The definition of exploitation offered here highlights the fact that it always refers to a *relationship*, that is, it is a characteristic of a relationship. The relationship in question could be between individuals or between suitably defined groups of individuals. In this chapter, our focus is on groups and we consider individuals only as much as they can be considered representatives of groups. Whenever a relationship of exploitation exists, it defines the two parties involved in that relationship as representatives of two groups – one as a member of the exploited group, and the other as a member of the exploiting group. We will refer to these two groups as *fundamental social classes*. In our discussion of historical materialism in section 2.1.3, we had claimed that relations of production, that is, economic power over means of production and labour-power, define fundamental social classes. Now we are drawing out one important implication of that definition: relations of production define two large groups of people such that one exploits the other.

Let us consider the three principles in the definition of exploitation. The inverse welfare interdependence principle tells us that exploiters and exploited are linked to each other in such a way that the former benefits at the expense of the latter. Benefiting 'at the expense of' is a key feature of an exploitative relationship so that increase in material welfare of the exploiters is causally dependent on the decrease in the material welfare of the exploited. Thus, there is a zero-sum interaction involved in exploitative relationships and that is what captures the conflict of material interests between the two classes. But an inverse interdependence of welfare, by itself, will not be enough to define exploitation. For a relationship to be exploitative, the inverse interdependence of welfare must arise from the *appropriation of labour* (or the fruits of labour) of the exploited by the exploiters. This is an important point and will allow us to distinguish different types of oppression. Finally, the third principle tells us that the appropriation of labour must be made possible by, that is, must rest on, the systematic exclusion of the exploited from key productive resources of the economy. If labour appropriation occurs without relying on systematic exclusion from some key productive resource, we will not be able to identify that as exploitation. Only when all the three principles are satisfied can we identify a relationship as exploitative. It is also important to note the causal linkage between the three principles involved in the definition of exploitation: exclusion from productive resources leads to labour appropriation, which, in turn, leads to the inverse welfare interdependence.

Forms of Oppression

This way of defining exploitation allows us to distinguish different forms of oppression. *By oppression, we mean the systematic subordination of the interests of one group by another.* Exploitation, in the sense defined earlier, which identify fundamental social classes, leads to one form of oppression that we may call as 'class oppression', or to be more precise, exploitative oppression. We can then identify all other forms of oppression as non-class oppression or non-exploitative oppression. It is useful to further distinguish between two categories of non-exploitative oppression.[1]

- *Oppression of expropriation*: This form of non-exploitative oppression occurs when one group benefits at the expense of the other without any appropriation of labour effort but due to forcible expropriation of the latter from productive resources. The canonical example of this form of non-exploitative oppression is the relationship observed between European colonial settlers and indigenous populations.

- *Oppression of distributive injustice*: This form of non-exploitative oppression also occurs when one group benefits at the expense of

---

[1]Wright (1997) distinguishes exploitative and non-exploitative oppressions. I am proposing a further distinction between two types of non-exploitative oppression, one based on expropriation and the other based on distributive injustice.

another group without any appropriation of labour effort. It comes from systematic advantages that one group has over another with respect to key distributive conflicts – over income, wealth, resources and other aspects of material life. The canonical examples of this form of non-exploitative oppression are those based on relatively stable social identities defined by, for instance, caste, race, ethnicity, gender, citizenship, language, and so on.

Consider the relationship between European colonial settlers and the indigenous people of the New World, which was based on expropriation of the latter from the key productive resources of those economies: land (and other natural resources). The exclusion of the indigenous people from access to land (and other natural resources) gave rise to the inverse interdependence of welfare between the European colonial settlers and the indigenous people. But the inverse interdependence of welfare did not rest on the labour of the indigenous people, that is, it did not involve appropriation of labour of the indigenous people. Here, oppression does not come along with exploitation. Hence, we can identify this as *non-exploitative oppression* of expropriation. Now consider the relationship between workers and capitalists in modern Europe. In this relationship, the exploiter and exploited are inversely related in terms of material welfare – the increase in welfare of the former depends on the decline in welfare of the latter – as in the case of the relationship between European colonial settlers and the indigenous people. But there is also a very important difference: the inverse interdependence of welfare rests on the appropriation of labour effort of the workers by the capitalists. In this case, there is systemic or structural exclusion of workers from the productive resources of society, that is, the capital stock, and that makes possible the appropriation of labour of the workers by capitalists. Here, oppression goes hand in hand with exploitation. Hence, this is a case of *exploitative oppression.*

The difference between exploitative oppression and non-exploitative oppression of expropriation is important from the perspective of social conflict. In the case of non-exploitative oppression of expropriation, since the exploiters do not need the labour effort of the exploited for their material welfare, the interaction can be extremely violent and can take the form of genocidal assaults on the exploited. In the case of exploitative oppression, on the other hand, the exploiters and the exploited are linked in a relationship marked both by conflict of interests *and* mutual dependence – a relationship that Marx would call, following Hegel, a contradiction. The dependence of the exploiter on the labour of the exploited also gives power to the latter, a power that has to be negotiated in the labour process and gives rise to a whole technology to extract labour effort of the exploited. The mutual dependence also means that the exploiter does not have any interest in exterminating the exploited, unlike in the case of non-exploitative oppression of expropriation.

Non-exploitative oppression of distributive injustice is more complex because it is intertwined with exploitation. In this case, the systematic group advantage with regard to key distributive conflicts impacts the very economic structure of society. For instance, one group might be able to prevent members of another group from becoming part of the exploiting class (and thereby appropriating surplus from the exploited class). Or, the advantaged group might be able to impact the share of the net output that is received as income by the members of the disadvantaged exploited group. Or, the advantaged group might be able to force members of the disadvantaged group to locate themselves at the lower rungs of employment relationships. Take the example of race-based oppression in the US. In ante-bellum US, the vast majority of Blacks were slaves. For historical reasons, Whites were able to force Blacks to become part of the exploited class of slaves. In the post-bellum Southern US, the vast majority of Blacks were systematically prevented from becoming independent farmers, entrepreneurs and capitalists. They were prevented from accessing the higher education system and were therefore systematically prevented from accessing professional, managerial, skilled or other well-paying white-collar jobs. When some Blacks did get employed in professional or skilled jobs, their wages were systematically lower than Whites doing the same job.[2] A similar logic applies to lower-caste persons, especially Dalits, in India.

In cases of non-exploitative oppression of distributive injustice, group-based inequalities of power overlay the underlying class relations. When we restrict ourselves to capitalist societies, this means that the group-based inequalities overlay the capital-labour relation. The group-based inequalities do not change the basic logic of capitalist exploitation. Rather, they impact how the share of income, wealth and other material benefits that come from capitalist production is distributed between different groups in society. Capitalists still earn income from ownership of means of production; and workers still earn income from selling their labour-power. But the

---

[2]For details, see Leiman (2010).

income earned by capitalists of the advantaged group, for example, Whites, is systematically higher than other capitalists, for example, Blacks; wage income earned by workers of the advantaged group, for example, White, is, again, systematically higher than other workers, for example, Blacks and Hispanics. The systematic advantages of the privileged group is maintained over time with control over state and non-state institutions. Over time, inheritance and the income generation process lead to enormous differences in wealth and other aspects of material life.

Centrality of Exclusion

The definition of exploitation that has been presented earlier accords a central role to *exclusion from access to productive resources*. One can conceive of scenarios where appropriation of labour effort takes place but which we would not want to designate, on intuitive grounds, as exploitative. For instance, we might help our elderly neighbours by running errands for them. In this case, there is clearly some labour effort appropriated by my neighbours from me. But we would not like to identify this as an exploitative relationship because I run errands for them voluntarily. Such voluntary appropriation of labour is also involved in gift giving or social and political work. All these cases are starkly different from the situation of a worker in capitalism because the worker is not free to choose to not work for a capitalist. While it is true that the worker can choose not to work for some particular capitalist, the worker, individually, and workers as a class, cannot choose to not work for the capitalist class. Workers, therefore, are structurally constrained to enter into the wage-labour relationships with capitalists, that is, they are forced to sell their labour-power for a wage. The structural constraint that does the work of coercion, in this case, is the systematic exclusion of workers from access to the means of production.[3] Structural exclusion gives rise to a vulnerability of the working class, which is then used or instrumentalized by the capitalist class for their gain. According to Marxist philosophers Allen Wood and Nicolas Vrousalis, the aspect of vulnerability is essential in any exploitative relationship – and we capture this by emphasizing the centrality of exclusion of the exploited from access to productive resources of society (Wood, 2004; Vrousalis, 2018a,b).

---

[3]This point has been argued forcefully by Cohen (1986c).

Market Power Is Not Essential

An important point to note about the definition of exploitation is that it does *not* rely on forms of market power, like monopoly or monopsony. Exploitation is not only possible but its key features truly emerge in a competitive capitalist economy. In fact, the challenge Marx had set himself, as we have seen in Chapter 3, was to explain the existence of exploitation in a competitive capitalist economy. In such a set-up, there is no monopoly power and yet exploitation of workers arise because they are forced to work for capitalists due to their structural exclusion from access to the means of production.

Scholars using variants of a neoclassical framework often use the competitive outcome as a benchmark and departure from that benchmark is understood as giving rise to different types of rent, the latter understood as a marker of exploitation.[4] In such theoretical descriptions, the benchmark situation, that is, competitive capitalism without market power, is free of exploitation – by definition. A Marxist account does not deny the existence of monopoly power in various input and output markets. In fact, the general accumulation of capital gives rise to concentration and centralization of capital. Monopoly of ownership of land, and other natural resources, might give rise to rent. But, in the Marxist account, exploitation in capitalism theoretically precedes, and does not need the existence of, monopoly or monopsony power – exploitation exists even in a competitive capitalist economy. Hence, a Marxist perspective would assert that curbing monopoly or monopsony power of large capitalist firms through various kinds of regulation, or even abolishing monopolies of all types, cannot do away with capitalist exploitation.

So far, the discussion of exploitation has only investigated its qualitative aspects. We have so far said nothing about how, if at all, we can quantify exploitation. In the next section, we will turn to the strand of the literature which has dealt with the quantitative aspect. But before we do so, let us note that the qualitative discussion stands on its own. Even if we are not able to come up with a consistent and convincing way to quantify exploitation in capitalism, that would not nullify the qualitative discussion. We would still be able to assert, on the basis of solid qualitative arguments, that capitalism is an exploitative system, that it rests on the exploitation of the working class.

---

[4]For instance, see Brooks et al. (2019).

Hence, we will be able to engage in meaningful discussions about the harm of exploitation – even if we are unable to quantify the latter.

8.1.2 Quantitative Issues

In Volume I of *Capital*, Marx's presentation of capitalist exploitation involved both qualitative and quantitative dimensions. As we have seen in Chapter 3, in capitalist economies, exploitation arises because the value *added by* each hour of labour is larger than the value *of* each hour of labour-power (the capacity to do useful work). The difference between the value added by labour and value of labour-power is the surplus value, a quantitative measure of exploitation. Since the value of labour-power is the variable capital, we can also define the degree or *rate* of exploitation as follows:

$$e = \frac{\text{surplus value}}{\text{variable capital}} = \frac{1-v}{v} = \frac{1}{v} - 1$$

where e denotes the rate of exploitation, $s = 1 - v$ denotes surplus value and v denotes the value of labour-power per hour of labour. Each hour of labour adds to the objects of labour, by definition, 1 unit of value. Since v is the value of labour-power, this means that surplus value is given by $1 - v$, the portion of the value added by labour that is appropriated by the capitalist.

Standard Interpretation
The SI of the Marxist labour theory of value defines the value of labour-power as the value of the real wage bundle per hour of labour. The real wage bundle comprises the vector of the physical quantities of commodities that are purchased with the nominal wage income. Adding up the value of each commodity in the real wage bundle gives us the value of labour-power according to the SI. This definition of the value of labour-power had been used by Marx and was adopted by many theorists who used the SI (Sweezy, 1942; Okishio, 1963; Morishima, 1973).

In the SI, the theory of exploitation is captured by the Fundamental Marxian Theorem (FMT). Taking the real wage bundle as exogenously given, the FMT links exploitation and profitability of capitalist economies in the form of the following proposition: the uniform rate of profit is positive if and only if the economy-wide rate of exploitation is positive (Okishio, 1963; Morishima, 1973). The FMT is an important result because it links the profitability of capitalist economies with the exploitation of the working class, as we have discussed in Chapter 7. The FMT shows that exploitation and profitability are inextricably linked in a capitalist economy; one cannot exist without the other.

When our model of the economy features a Leontief technology without choice of technique, all capital is circulating capital and there are no joint products, then it is possible to calculate the values of the commodities and add them up to get the value of labour-power as the sum of the values of the commodities in the real wage bundle.[5] But the FMT runs into problems when the description of technology in the model capitalist economy is generalized beyond the Leontief specification. A generalization of Leontief to a von Neumann specification, which allows for fixed capital, choice of technique and joint products, leads to the result that labour values of commodities, defined in the standard manner as the sum of direct and indirect labour needed to produce one unit of a commodity, can no longer be guaranteed to be positive or unique (Morishima, 1974; Steedman, 1977). This means that the labour value of the real wage bundle can no longer be defined meaningfully. Hence, the above definition of the rate of exploitation, and with it the FMT, breaks down. Faced with this difficulty, Morishima (1974) redefined the concept of 'necessary labour' and thereby restored the FMT in a von Neumann specification.

To understand Morishima's argument, we need to distinguish between a *production process* and an output.[6] In the Leontief specification, each production process has a single output. Hence, we could identify the production process with the output (commodity), and the latter with the industry. Once we allow for each production process to have more than one output, which is what we mean by saying that there are *joint products*, the identification of production process and output (commodity) breaks down. For instance, think of the production process in the cement industry as producing cement (the main commodity) and also cement kiln dust (CKD). Here, the production process has two outputs; hence, we can call the output as a joint product. Fixed capital, that is, machines, plant and equipment, can be easily incorporated into the category of joint products. We only need to

---

[5] See the appendix to Chapter 7 for details.
[6] For a discussion of fixed capital, joint products and the von Neumann specification, see Steedman (1977, Chapters 10–13).

think of fixed capital both as an input and output, that is, at the end of each production cycle, we can think of the undepreciated fixed capital as one of the joint products.

In a Leontief specification of the model economy, the value of labour-power, defined as the value of the real wage bundle, is equal to necessary labour, where necessary labour is equal to the amount of social labour-time actually needed to produce the real wage bundle (vector) of commodities.[7] Hence, surplus labour is the part of the working day over and above whatever is needed to produce the real wage bundle. In a von Neumann specification of the model economy with multiple production processes and many commodities, Morishima (1974) redefined the concept of necessary and surplus labour. Instead of defining necessary labour as the *actual* labour-time needed to produce the real wage bundle, Morishima (1974, p. 617) defined necessary labour as the *minimum* amount of labour needed to produce it, where the minimum is computed over all the possible feasible ways of producing a net output vector that is at least as large as the real wage bundle of commodities. Surplus labour was then defined as the difference of total labour-time and necessary labour. The rate of exploitation, which is defined as the ratio of surplus labour and necessary labour, could be computed once again. With this redefinition, the FMT is restored in this more general setting of a von Neumann technology and we have the following result: the uniform rate of profit is positive if and only if the economy-wide rate of exploitation is positive (Morishima, 1974, Theorem 1). Following Morishima, let us call this the Generalized Fundamental Marxian Theorem (GFMT).

An important point worth highlighting here is the implicit notion of long run equilibrium. The uniform rate of profit, and the associated vector of prices of production, define the notion of classical, long run equilibrium that is implicit in both the FMT in Okishio (1963) and its more generalized version in Morishima (1974). The long run equilibrium is conceptualized as the state of a capitalist economy when the distribution of capital across sectors is such that the *rate of profit* is the same in all branches of production. The underlying understanding is that differential rates of profit across sectors cannot characterize a long run equilibrium because that will create incentives for the mobility of capital from a lower to a higher profit rate sector. This idea, and the centrality of the rate of profit in this conception of long run

---

[7]See the discussion in section 3.3.3 and especially the box diagram.

equilibrium, is important to keep in mind as we look at the next important contribution in this discussion about exploitation by John E. Roemer (Roemer, 1980, 1981, 1982).

The key result in Roemer (1980) can be read both as a generalization and a critique of the GFMT. The generalization consisted in moving from a von Neumann technology to a general convex economy and the critique consisted of the demonstration that the GFMT would hold in a convex economy only under a rather restrictive assumption. By a 'convex economy' is meant a description of the production possibilities of an economy using production sets rather than through linear relationships between quantities of inputs and outputs (as was the case in the von Neumann or Leontief description of production technologies), and then specifying certain plausible properties of the production sets. The most important property that is postulated for production sets is that it is convex – which lends its name to the whole technology. The assumption of convexity is a standard one in mainstream microeconomics and captures two intuitions about production possibilities. First, it rules out increasing returns to scale, that is, convexity means that if all inputs are increased by a certain multiple, then output cannot increase by more than that multiple.[8] Second, it asserts that an unbalanced combination of inputs cannot be more productive than a balanced one.

In this more general setting, Roemer (1980) defines exploitation in a similar way as in Morishima (1974) and then proves that a GFMT-type result will hold only if the following technical condition is satisfied: there are no goods which can only be produced as joint products in fixed proportion with other goods (Roemer, 1980, p. 519). Here, the link of exploitation and profitability relies on a technical condition that does not seem to have any intuitive backing. Why must a capitalist economy exclude such goods (which can only be produced as joint products in fixed proportion with other goods)? There is no answer provided in the literature. Does this mean that the link between exploitation and profits in a capitalist economy, a fundamental claim of Marxist economics, should be abandoned? Yoshihara (2017) rightly notes that such a conclusion is not warranted. The fact that the GFMT-type result in Roemer (1980) relies on an unintuitive technical condition does not so much raise questions about the existence of exploitation in capitalist economies as about Morishima's and Roemer's specific ways of defining it.

---

[8]If there are fixed costs involved in production, then there will be increasing returns to scale. Hence, the convexity assumption rules out the presence of fixed costs.

The Axiomatic Approach

Over the past decade, Roberto Veneziani and Naoki Yoshihara have developed an interesting strand of the literature on exploitation theory (Veneziani and Yoshihara, 2017; Yoshihara, 2017). Deriving inspiration from social choice theory and the literature on income inequality, they argue for an axiomatic approach to exploitation theory. In this approach, authors would (and they do) begin by setting out, or agreeing with, a small number of axioms that any definition of exploitation must satisfy. Any definition of exploitation can then be evaluated to see if it satisfies the axioms. This method potentially allows us to choose between multiple definitions because a definition which satisfies all (more) of the axioms can be understood to be 'better' than one that satisfies none (fewer) of the axioms. A surprising result that has emerged out of the axiomatic approach is that the NI definition of exploitation is superior – in the sense just defined – to all other existing definitions, including the Morishima (1974) and Roemer (1980) definitions, of exploitation.

To understand the details, let us start by noting that Veneziani and Yoshihara (2017) offer two axioms that must be satisfied by any definition of exploitation.

- Axiom 1 (Labour exploitation). A propertyless worker is exploited if and only if the labour contributed by the worker through wage-labour is larger than the labour received by the worker, where the latter is defined as the labour content of the exploitation reference bundle (ERB). The ERB is a consumption bundle of commodities that has two properties. First, it can be purchased with the wage income of the worker; and second, it can be produced as a net output of an efficient production process (that is, available with the existing technology).

- Axiom 2 (Profit-exploitation correspondence). At the aggregate level, positive profit exists if and only if all the propertyless workers are exploited in the sense of Axiom 1.

The first axiom defines the meaning of exploitation. It follows the earlier literature, for example, Okishio (1961), Morishima (1973) and Roemer (1981), in defining the exploitation status of any worker by evaluating the difference between the 'labour contributed' by the worker and the 'labour received' by the worker. All workers for whom the labour contribution is larger than the labour received are identified as being exploited. As we have noted earlier, it is relatively straightforward to measure the labour contribution – this is just the total labour performed by the worker in capitalist production. With regard to this aspect, Veneziani and Yoshihara (2017) extend the discussion to a situation where each worker is conceived of as possessing potentially a large number of types of labour-power. Assuming a given wage rate associated with each type of labour-power, they aggregate the different types of labour by multiplying each type of labour with its associated wage rate and summing across all types of labour.[9] This aggregate is then identified as the 'labour contributed' by the worker.

The measurement of 'labour received' is more complicated. Here, Veneziani and Yoshihara (2017) ask us to first conceive of an ERB for each worker. This is a bundle of commodities that the worker *can*, but need not, purchase with her wage income. Moreover, this commodity bundle must also be technologically feasible, that is, it must be possible to produce this commodity bundle as the net output (total output minus the intermediate inputs used up) of a technologically efficient production process available with the current technology. Once we find the ERB, we then need to measure its labour content using particular definitions of 'value' or 'labour content'.[10]

The second axiom captures the important intuition in Marxist political economy that profits and exploitation of workers are tightly linked in capitalist economies. This axiom requires that any definition of exploitation satisfy the property that aggregate profits in the economy be positive if and only if *every* propertyless worker is exploited – in the sense defined by the first axiom. This axiom is related to but also different from the FMT. While the FMT establishes the link between positive profits and exploitation, this axiom treats it as a property that must be satisfied by any definition of exploitation. The axiom is certainly intuitively appealing, but it allows for some curious cases. For instance, a definition of exploitation which allows for zero profits even when *some*, but not all, propertyless workers are exploited (in the sense of Axiom 1) would not violate this axiom. But this is

---

[9]In essence, Veneziani and Yoshihara (2017) use the nominal wage rates as the reduction coefficients of complex labour. See the discussion in the appendix to Chapter 3.

[10]Recall that in a Leontief technology set-up, we can define the labour content of a commodity bundle (vector) as the sum of direct and indirect labour needed to produce the commodity bundle. In a von Neuman technology set-up, we can define the labour content of a commodity bundle as the minimum amount of direct labour needed to produce the commodity, with the minimum computed over all production processes that produce a net output vector that is at least as large as the commodity bundle (Morishima, 1974, p. 617).

clearly counter-intuitive. If some workers are exploited, it must show up as positive profit at the aggregate level.

After setting up these two axioms, Veneziani and Yoshihara (2017) evaluate three definitions of exploitation. The first is a generalization of the Morishima definition (Morishima, 1973), the second is a generalization of the Roemer definition (Roemer, 1980) and the third is their own definition. Morishima's definition rests on defining the labour content of any commodity bundle as the minimum amount of labour-time necessary to produce the commodity bundle as the net output when we search over all possible production processes; Roemer's definition is a refinement of Morishima's definition in that it restricts the search over production processes that are also profit-maximizing; Veneziani and Yoshihara (2017) depart from both and define the labour content of any commodity bundle in a novel way.

Generalizing the New Interpretation

Given any aggregate production activity, Veneziani and Yoshihara (2017) define a *fraction* associated with any commodity bundle, c, that costs less than the net output vector, both evaluated at market prices, as the ratio of the cost of the commodity bundle and the money value added of the net output, that is,

$$\tau^c = \frac{\text{cost of commodity bundle}}{\text{cost of net output}} = \frac{pc}{py}$$

where p is the price vector and y is the net output vector.[11] The labour content of the commodity bundle, $l.c.\,(c)$, is then defined as the product of that *same fraction* and total social labour necessary to produce the net output vector, that is,

$$l.c.\,(c) = \tau^c \times \text{total social labour-time}$$

Note what this definition of 'labour content' is accomplishing. It is setting the ratio of the monetary value of *any* commodity bundle and the monetary value of the net output vector to be exactly equal to the ratio of the 'labour content' of that commodity bundle and the 'labour content' of the net output vector

---

[11] This definition was proposed by them in their previous work, for example, Yoshihara and Veneziani (2009).

(= total social labour-time necessary to produce the gross output), that is,

$$\frac{l.c.\,(\boldsymbol{c})}{\text{total social labour-time}} = \frac{\text{market price of commodity bundle}}{\text{market price of net output}}$$

which, on rearranging terms, becomes

$$l.c.\,(\boldsymbol{c}) = \frac{\text{total social labour-time}}{\text{market price of net output}} \times \text{market price of commodity bundle}$$

Recall from our discussion of the NI in Chapter 7 that the definition of the value of money is the ratio of total social labour-time and the total money value added. Using this definition of the value of money, we see that the Veneziani-Yoshihara definition of the labour content of any commodity bundle is equivalent to the following:

$$l.c.\,(\boldsymbol{c}) = \text{value of money} \times \text{market price of commodity bundle}$$

There are several important implications of this definition that are worth noting. First, it is a generalization of the intuition of the NI to a setting where it might not be possible to consistently define labour values of commodities in the standard way (as the sum of direct plus indirect labour necessary to produce any commodity). Recall that as soon as we allow for joint products and fixed capital, we get paradoxical results if we define labour values of commodities in the standard way.[12] By defining the labour content of commodity bundles, and hence also of individual commodities, in the way proposed by Veneziani and Yoshihara (2017), we can avoid those paradoxes in this more general setting (which allows for joint products, fixed capital, and so on). This is a significant advantage because we not only can define labour content consistently but can also retain the key insights of the NI in terms of linking market prices and labour content. The link, it is to be noted, is established by using the value of money (or its reciprocal, the MEV) to convert monetary magnitudes (labour-time magnitudes) to labour-time magnitudes (monetary magnitudes).

The second implication is that we are now able to define the value of labour-power in exactly the same way as in Foley (1982b). If workers do not save, as is common to assume in the classical tradition, and spend their wage income on a commodity bundle, then the market price of the commodity bundle is equal

---

[12] See discussion in the previous section and in Steedman (1977, Chapters 10–13).

to the nominal wage bill. If we define the value of each hour of labour-power as the labour content of the commodity bundle purchased by the worker with the nominal wage rate, then we see that *the value of each hour of labour-power is the value of money multiplied by the nominal wage rate* – which is exactly the same definition as in Foley (1982b). The key advantage of defining the value of labour-power in this manner, as we have seen in Chapter 7, is that we are able to establish two important quantitative equivalences: (*a*) between total money value added and total social labour and (*b*) between total monetary profits and total unpaid labour. The great advantage of the Veneziani-Yoshihara definition of labour content is that it will preserve both these equivalences in a general setting with convex production sets.[13]

The final implication is related to the identification of the exploitation status of any worker. To do so, we compare the labour contributed by any worker through wage labour with the labour content of her consumption bundle. If the former is larger than the latter, we say that she is exploited.

Superiority of the New Interpretation

Let us return to the discussion of exploitation. After setting up the two axioms discussed above, Veneziani and Yoshihara (2017) evaluate three definitions of exploitation: the Morishima definition, the Roemer definition and the Veneziani-Yoshihara definition (which, as we have just seen, is based on a generalization of the NI definition of value). The striking result in Veneziani and Yoshihara (2017) is that the NI definition always satisfies the second axiom (profit-exploitation correspondence) but there are economic states where the Morishima and the Roemer definitions do not satisfy the second axiom. This means that there are economic states where the intuition captured by the second axiom, that is, aggregate profit is positive if and only if all propertyless workers are exploited, would not hold if we used either Morishima's or Roemer's definition of exploitation. But we would never face such a situation if we used the generalized NI definition of exploitation. Since all three definitions satisfy the first axiom (labour exploitation), this establishes the superiority of the NI framework. The superiority of the NI extends beyond the theory of exploitation, as I have argued here. The Veneziani-Yoshihara definition of the labour content of commodities, in

---

[13] Of course, if workers save some fraction of their wage income, then the labour content of the consumption bundle will no longer coincide with the value of labour-power (= value of money × nominal wage rate).

conjunction with the classical savings assumption (workers do not save), would also allow us to recover the key equivalences between labour-time and monetary magnitudes in general settings with convex production sets: (*a*) total monetary value added is equal to the total social labour-time and (*b*) total monetary profits is equal to total unpaid labour. Thus, and this is my conjecture, the transformation problem is also solved in general convex economies if we use the Veneziani-Yoshihara definition of the labour content of commodities.

8.2 A Critique of the Commodity Exploitation Theorem

The Marxist labour theory of value is built on the premise that labour is the *only* substance of value. This understanding comes from a deeper understanding of the role of labour in the history of humankind, and of the role of the process of exchange in enforcing a social division of labour in a society of independent, private producers (see Appendix 3.C.5). After developing it, the labour theory of value is used by Marx to demonstrate the exploitative nature of capitalism.

A strand of Marxist thinking, which I will call Analytical Marxist (AM) for lack of a better term, developed a whole set of arguments in the 1970s and 1980s that was interpreted as raising serious doubts on the labour theory of value. This argument has two important claims. First, that any basic commodity can be used to construct a consistent theory of value, that is, we can have a commodity theory of value (CTV). Second, we can use a CTV to show that, in a capitalist economy, the basic commodity (which is the substance of value) is exploited, that is, we can establish a commodity exploitation theorem (CET) (Gintis and Bowles, 1981; Roemer, 1982). In Appendix 3.C, I had pointed out that this argument rests on two conceptual fallacies, and now I will flesh out the details of my critique drawing on Basu (2020b).

8.2.1   Summary of AM Argument

A key ingredient of the AM argument is the notion of a 'basic'.

> We define an input into production to be a *basic* if it enters directly or indirectly (via its being an input into another production input) into the production of all commodities. (Gintis and Bowles, 1981, p. 18)

With this definition in place, the AM argument can be presented in terms of two propositions (Gintis and Bowles, 1981, Appenidix I).

- Proposition 1: If the wage rate is positive, then labour is not the only basic in the economy.
- Proposition 2: Any basic is a consistent basis for value theory.

The first proposition attempts to show that once we abstract from the physical characteristics of commodities, labour is still not the only production input that is common to all commodities. Hence, this proposition, if correct, would nullify Marx's claim in Chapter 1, Volume I of *Capital* that labour should be considered the basis of value because it is the only thing that is common to all commodities when looked at from the perspective of production. In the next section, I will present a simple critique of Proposition 1.

The second proposition shows that any basic can be a consistent basis for constructing a value theory. A consistent value theory demonstrates the following proposition: in a capitalist economy, the rate of profit is positive if and only if the basic is exploited.[14] Since the first proposition has established that there will always be some basic (because the wage rate is bound to be positive), the two propositions, taken together, show that we can always find an alternative basis for value theory, that is, alternative to labour. Thus, we can conclude that any basic can be used to construct a value theory and to show that, in a capitalist economy, the existence of positive profits is equivalent to the exploitation of the basic commodity. For our purposes, it is important to note that nested within Proposition 2 is the claim that commodities can be exploited, a claim that can be called a commodity exploitation theorem (CET). In the following section, I will critically evaluate the CET; I will not be concerned with the rest of Proposition 2.

8.2.2   A Critique of Proposition 1

Proposition 1 is key in establishing the chain of claims captured by the two propositions given earlier. It is instructive to carefully study its proof.

---

[14]Recall that this proposition in the case of labour is known as the Fundamental Marxian Theorem (Morishima, 1973); see Chapter 7 for details.

We shall assume that labour is a basic input. If the wage rate is positive, then there is some commodity or resource in the wage bundle. This commodity or resource is thus indirectly embodied in any commodity produced by labour. Thus, any element of the wage bundle is also a basic. It follows that labour is not the only basic. (Gintis and Bowles, 1981, p. 19)

The key step in the above proof is the following sentence: 'This commodity or resource is thus indirectly embodied in any commodity produced by labour'. Let us ask: Is this statement true? To be concrete, let us suppose that the wage bundle has a commodity called 'food'. Why might 'food' be indirectly embodied in another commodity, say steel? The answer seems to be the following: 'food' is used to produce labour; labour is used to produce steel; hence, 'food' is indirectly embodied in steel through its being used in the production of labour, an input into the production of steel. We can immediately see why this argument is false.

If 'food' is part of the wage bundle, this simply means that 'food' is consumed by the worker. This, in turn, means that 'food' is used to produce labour-power, the capacity to do useful work. In the labour market, workers sell labour-power to the capitalist. When labour-power is used in the production process, we get labour. Thus, the input into the production of steel, that is, labour, is *different from* what is sold by workers on the labour market, that is, labour-power. Hence, the chain of arguments that would establish that 'food' is embodied in steel is broken. This is because 'food' is not used to produce labour, it is used to produce labour-power. This means that 'food' is not a 'basic' as defined by Gintis and Bowles (1981).

What is the key source of error in the proof of Proposition 1? It is the inability to distinguish between labour-power and labour. It is worthwhile recalling that classical political economists before Marx had not been able to conceptually distinguish between labour-power and labour. It is this inability to distinguish between labour-power and labour that led to the failure of political economists before Marx to clearly understand the source of surplus value. This point was highlighted by F. Engels in the introduction to the 1849 pamphlet, *Wage Labour and Capital* (Engels, 1891), as I have pointed out earlier. It is important not to make that same error once again.

What is the implication of this critique? I have shown that the claim made by Gintis and Bowles (1981) that any element of the wage bundle is a basic is false. This means that, following their definition, there is only one basic: labour. This also means that Proposition 2 loses its force. This is because Proposition 2 requires the theoretical support of Proposition 1. After all, if one cannot demonstrate that there exists some basic (other than labour), then the claim that a basic (other than labour) can be a consistent basis of value theory is vacuous. Hence, the fact that Proposition 1 is false means that one cannot construct a CTV in the way proposed by Gintis and Bowles (1981).

While I note this to draw attention of the reader, I will nonetheless proceed to develop a critique of CET, a key component of Proposition 2. I do so for two reasons. First, the CET has been presented in the literature as a stand-alone result (Roemer, 1982, Appendix 6.1):

> Marx believed that labour power was the commodity which produced a surplus under capitalism. In this appendix I show that one can define embodied value in terms of any commodity numeraire, with the result that the technology is productive if and only if each commodity is exploited when it is taken as numeraire. Steel is exploited if the steel value embodied in a unit of steel is less than one. Labour power is not special in having this property. (Roemer, 1982, Appendix 6.1, p. 186)

Hence, a critical engagement with the CET is called for irrespective of the status of Proposition 1. Second, Proposition 2 highlights another conceptual flaw in the AM argument: the inability to distinguish between labour-power and all other commodities.

8.2.3   A Critique of the CET

Recall that the CET claims that the basic commodity that is used as a basis for value theory is also exploited in capitalist economies. I will evaluate this claim by working with a simple example discussed in Gintis and Bowles (1981, p. 19) where the economy produces two commodities.[15] The economy in this example has two goods, food (F) and jewellery (J), where F is a *basic* and J is not. The technology for producing the two goods is specified as follows:

> Food is used to produce all goods, and is in the wage bundle, while jewelry is consumed only by nonworkers and is not used in

---

[15] My critique also holds for the similar argument in Roemer (1982, Appendix 6.1). For details, see Basu (2020b).

production (i.e. it is not a basic). Specifically, suppose $1/2$ bushel of F and $1/2$ hour of labour are used to produce one bushel of F, and $1/2$ bushel of food is in the wage bundle. Also suppose $1/4$ bushel of food and one hour of labour is used to produce one unit of J. (Gintis and Bowles, 1981, p. 19)

Labour Values: Definition and Two Intuitions

Let Λ_F, Λ_J and Λ_{LP} represent the labour values of food, jewellery and labour-power. From the specification of the technology for producing F and J, and the fact that the real wage bundle contains $1/2$ units of food, we see that their labour values must be determined by the following equations,

$$\frac{\Lambda_F}{2} + \frac{1}{2} = \Lambda_F \tag{8.1}$$

and

$$\frac{\Lambda_F}{4} + 1 = \Lambda_J \tag{8.2}$$

and

$$\Lambda_{LP} = \frac{\Lambda_F}{2} \tag{8.3}$$

On solving the three equations, (8.1), (8.2) and (8.3), we get: $\Lambda_F = 1, \Lambda_J = 5/4, \Lambda_{LP} = 1/2$. Thus, the labour value of food is 1, the labour value of jewellery is $5/4$ and the labour value of labour-power is $1/2$.

These equations capture two different intuitions about the concept of labour value. The first intuition is related to the idea that the labour value of one unit of any commodity is the labour embodied in a unit of the commodity, which, in turn, is the sum of the direct and indirect amounts of labour needed to produce it (Marx, 1992, Chapter 1). For instance, in (8.1), the labour value of one unit of F, Λ_F, is the sum of the amount of direct labour, $1/2$, and the amount of indirect labour, $\Lambda_F/2$, used in the production of 1 unit of F. The same logic holds for the equation determining the value of jewellery, Λ_J, in (8.2). Finally, the value of labour-power, $\Lambda_F/2$, is, using the SI of Marx's value theory, equal to $\Lambda_F/2$ because the wage bundle has $1/2$ units of F. The implicit understanding is that in the production of labour-power, value accounting will only include the indirect input, food (F), because the labour that is used in the production of labour-power falls outside the domain of capitalist commodity production.

A different intuition is also embedded in the earlier equations (8.1), (8.2) and (8.3). According to this second intuition, the value of one unit of the output is equal to the sum of the *value transferred* by the non-labour inputs used up and the *value added* by labour (Marx, 1992, Chapter 8). For instance, in the production of F, the non-labour input transfers $\Lambda_F/2$ units of value and the labour input (that is, use of labour-power) adds $1/2$ units of value. This second intuition is important because it allows us to see the source of surplus value. The value *added by* labour-power is larger than the value *of* labour-power, and this difference is the source of surplus value. For instance, in the production of food, the value added by labour-power is $1/2$, but the value of labour-power is $\Lambda_{LP}/2$. Hence, the surplus value generated in the production of food is given by $(1/2 - \Lambda_{LP}/2) = 1/4$. The same intuition applies to the equation determining the value of jewellery, that is, (8.2).

Food Values: First Intuition
Let us now follow Gintis and Bowles (1981) and use food as the substance of value. We can do so, according to Gintis and Bowles (1981), because food is a basic. This means that we can meaningfully define the value of all commodities in terms of food. Let μ_F, μ_J, μ_{LP} denote the F-value (food value) of food, jewellery and labour-power, respectively.

According to the first intuition discussed earlier, the F-value of any commodity is the sum of the direct and indirect amounts of food used in producing 1 unit of the commodity. Using the technology for food production given above, we can implement this definition through the following value determination equation for food as,

$$\frac{1}{2} + \frac{\mu_{LP}}{2} = \mu_F \tag{8.4}$$

Here, the direct input of food is $1/2$ and the indirect input of food is $\mu_{LP}/2$. In a similar way, we can implement the definition of the food value of jewellery, using information about the technology of jewellery production, as

$$\frac{1}{4} + \mu_{LP} = \mu_J \tag{8.5}$$

Since the wage bundle has $1/2$ bushel of food, we finally get the value equation for labour-power as

$$\mu_{LP} = \frac{1}{2} \tag{8.6}$$

Solving the three equations in (8.4), (8.5) and (8.6), we get $\mu_F = 3/4, \mu_J = 3/4$ and $\mu_{LP} = 1/2$. Thus, we see that the F-value of every commodity is a positive number. Moreover, these calculations show that the F-value of food is less than 1 (because $\mu_F = 3/4$). This is interpreted by Gintis and Bowles (1981, p. 19) as demonstrating that food (the basic input, in this case) is exploited. To complete their argument, Gintis and Bowles (1981) show that a positive profit rate is implied by and implies positive exploitation of the basic commodity. But that demonstration is not relevant for my argument. I want to look critically at the argument that has apparently demonstrated that food is exploited. To do so, I will return to the calculation of food values and look at the equations determining value using the second intuition.

Food Values: Second Intuition

Let us start with the equation for the determination of the F-value of food given in (8.4): $1/2 + \mu_{LP}/2 = \mu_F$. Let us look at the left-hand side of this equation from the perspective of value transferred and value added. Since $1/2$ units of food is used as an input, and since each unit of food has F-value of μ_F, the F-value transferred by food is $\mu_F/2$. Similarly, $1/2$ units of labour-power is used in production. We know that each unit of labour-power has F-value of μ_{LP}. Hence, the F-value transferred by labour-power is $\mu_{LP}/2$. Thus, total F-value transferred by the two inputs is given by $\mu_F/2 + \mu_{LP}/2$.

Comparing with (8.4), we see the following: if we add $1/2 - \mu_F/2$ and $\mu_F/2 + \mu_{LP}/2$ (total F-value transferred by the two inputs), we get the expression on the left-hand side of (8.4). This means that, in the production of food, *surplus* F-value of $1/2 - \mu_F/2$ units has been generated – because this amount of F-value is in excess of the F-value transferred by both inputs. We see immediately that surplus F-value is positive if and only if $\mu_F < 1$. Hence, if we can show that $\mu_F < 1$, as was shown by Gintis and Bowles (1981) and as we have confirmed earlier (recall: we found $\mu_F = 3/4$), then we would be justified in claiming that surplus F-value has been generated. But just by demonstrating that $\mu_F < 1$, we are not yet able to answer the question as to which commodity is exploited. To answer that question, we need to answer another question: Does food add this surplus F-value or does labour-power add this surplus F-value? If it is the former, then we would be justified in claiming that food is exploited, and the CET would be established; if it is the latter, we will not be so justified, and the CET would not be established.

There are two options to answering the question: Which commodity adds the surplus F-value? The first option is to argue that labour-power adds the surplus F-value. In this case, we could rearrange (8.4) and write it as

$$\frac{\mu_F}{2} + \left[\frac{\mu_{LP}}{2} + \frac{1}{2}\left(1 - \mu_F\right)\right] = \mu_F \tag{8.7}$$

which clearly shows that the F-value added by labour-power, the term in the square bracket, is larger than the F-value of labour-power, $\mu_{LP}/2$. In this case, the fact that $\mu_F < 1$ does not imply that food is exploited. In fact, in this case, since labour-power adds the surplus F-value, we are justified in asserting that labour is exploited (even though we compute values in units of food). Hence, the claim of Gintis and Bowles (1981) that $\mu_F < 1$ implies that food is exploited is false.

The second option is to argue that food adds the surplus F-value. In this case, we could rearrange (8.4) and write it as

$$\left[\frac{\mu_F}{2} + \frac{1}{2}\left(1 - \mu_F\right)\right] + \frac{\mu_{LP}}{2} = \mu_F \tag{8.8}$$

which shows that the F-value added by food, the term in the square bracket, is larger than the F-value of food, $\mu_F/2$. If this is the case, then we are certainly justified in claiming that food is exploited. But it is not legitimate to claim that food adds the surplus F-value. To claim that food adds the surplus F-value would imply that food adds more F-value than it has. But this is absurd: food cannot add more F-value than food has. I look at this argument in greater detail in the next section. Here, let us understand the nature of the error that underlies the claim that food is exploited.

In using equation (8.4) to claim that food is exploited, one is implicitly confounding terms, that is, one is making a *category error*. Instead of attaching the surplus F-value that is generated by the use of labour-power to the commodity labour-power, we are instead attaching that surplus F-value to the commodity food. It is this confounding of terms, this category error, that generates the surprising result: food is exploited.

The same reasoning applies to the equation for determining the F-value of jewellery. To begin, note that in the production of jewellery, the F-value transferred by food is $\mu_F/4$ and the F-value of labour-power is μ_{LP}. With these magnitudes in mind, we can see that equation (8.5) can be equally written as

$$\frac{\mu_F}{4} + \left[\mu_{LP} + \frac{1}{4}\left(1 - \mu_F\right)\right] = \mu_J$$

or as

$$\left[\frac{\mu_F}{4} + \frac{1}{4}\left(1 - \mu_F\right)\right] + \mu_{LP} = \mu_J$$

In the first version, we are correctly attaching the surplus F-value, $1/4 - \mu_{LP}/4$, to the commodity labour-power; in the second, we are incorrectly attaching the surplus F-value to the commodity food. The second version is what takes us to (8.5) and the claim that food is being exploited, and it is now clear why that is conceptually problematic.

8.2.4 Commodity Exploitation: Conceptual Problem

What *is* the conceptual problem of any commodity exploitation theorem? As a technical matter, there is no problem with defining something called 'food value' or 'steel value' – as done by Gintis and Bowles (1981) or by Roemer (1982, Appendix 6.1). Following these scholars, one can certainly define something called food value or steel value, if one so wishes. One can write equations to determine these values and show that the equation system can be solved to get a positive number for such values. One can then also demonstrate that the food (steel) value of food (steel) is less than 1. So far there is no problem – it is just a technical matter of defining an odd quantity called food (steel) value and then solving a system of equations.

When the finding that the food (steel) value of food (steel) is less than 1 is used to conclude that food (steel) is exploited, it is then that a conceptual error creeps into the argument. This is because the food (steel) value of food (steel) being *less than* 1 rests on positive exploitation of labour, that is, on the fact that the food (steel) value added by labour-power is greater than the food (steel) value of labour-power. Only by an accounting trick is the surplus value generated by the use of labour-power instead added to the food (steel) value transferred by food (steel). Thus, even when the food (steel) value of food (steel) is less than 1, it is still labour that is exploited. Food (steel) is not exploited.

This brings me to the source of the conceptual problem in the CET. The key problem, as I see it, is associated with the attempt to treat labour-power symmetrically with all other commodities, that is, to fail to distinguish between labour-power and all other commodities. Labour-power is the capacity to do useful work; labour is the outcome when that capacity is used. As a qualitative matter, no such distinction can exist for any other commodity, including food (steel). It is meaningless to try to define 'food-power' ('steel-power') as distinct from food (steel). This is because the capacity of food (steel) to be used is not distinct from the commodity itself. Food, or any other commodity, does not have the will, consciousness or incentive to resist its use in whatsoever way its possessor wants. In the case of labour-power, that is not the case. The possessor of labour-power, the worker, can and does, resist the way her employer, the capitalist, uses her labouring capacity. Hence, while it is meaningful to distinguish labour-power (the labouring capacity) from labour, it is meaningless to do so for *any* other commodity. Moreover, only because it is meaningful to distinguish between labour-power and labour, does it make sense to claim that there can be a difference between the value of labour-power and the value added by labour-power.

Gintis and Bowles (1981, p. 7) would not agree with this argument because, for them, it is meaningful to define something called 'lathe-power' of the commodity lathe.

> But clearly every commodity has an abstract form as a commodity and a concrete form as a physical entity engaged in production. A lathe can be considered a union of lathe-power, its abstract potential to perform useful functions, and as lathing, the concrete activity of the lathe engaged in production. (Gintis and Bowles, 1981, p. 7)

As a logical and philosophical statement, the above assertion is probably correct. But in terms of political economy and social analysis, the difference between lathe-power and lathe only makes sense if by purchasing the former, that is, lathe-power, the capitalist does *not* automatically get the latter, lathing. But that is clearly impossible unless we are ready to impute consciousness and will to the lathe.

The point to note is that there is a fundamental difference between lathe-power and labour-power. The difference relates to the latter being a capacity of a human being and the former being the abstract capacity of an inanimate object. The difference between a human being and an inanimate object comes from the will and consciousness possessed by the former, which is absent in the latter. Hence, the attempt to use lathe-power in a parallel way to the concept of labour-power does not stand scrutiny.

From a quantitative angle, it is important to note that labour, the input in production, has no value, but labour-power, the commodity purchased by the capitalist, does have value, and that the value added by labour-power was greater than the value of labour-power. To repeat this logic in the case of food (steel), we would have to say that food (steel), as an input in production, has no food (steel) value, but food (steel), as the commodity purchased by the capitalist, does have food (steel) value. Furthermore, we would have to assert that each unit of food (steel), used as an input in production, adds more food (steel) value than the food (steel) value of each unit of food (steel) that was purchased by the capitalist. Clearly, these are absurd propositions – because we are talking about the same entity, food (steel), in both cases. No wonder then that the whole attempt to define the concept of 'food-value' (or 'steel-value') and to use it to identify exploitation of 'food' ('steel') leads to conceptual conundrums.

8.3   Manifold Exploitations?

An influential strand in the critical social science literature argues that the Marxist definition of exploitation, and its tight link with class, is too narrow. It is necessary, this strand argues, to expand the definition of exploitation to include other dimensions of social power, inequality and disadvantage. One way to develop this argument is to give up the distinction between exploitation and oppression, or the distinction between exploitative and non-exploitative oppression, and consider all, or most, forms of oppression as exploitation. Folbre (2020) makes a sophisticated intersectional political economy argument along these lines and asks us to think in terms of 'manifold exploitations'.

Drawing on a rich feminist literature, Folbre (2020) argues for expanding the traditional definition of production. In addition to what is included in the standard understanding of production, that is, production of goods and services, the expanded definition of production includes 'reproduction' and 'social reproduction'. Reproduction refers to the development and maintenance of human capabilities; and, social reproduction is the development and maintenance of social groups to which individuals can identify and thereby pursue interests of the group (as opposed to the individual's) as its own. This theoretical move to expand the definition of production is a welcome one, and we have seen this in great detail in our discussion of the commodity labour-power in Chapter 3. But in Folbre (2020), it has a different purpose. It is meant to focus the analysis of exploitation on *distributional conflict* in the domain of reproduction – as a way to develop the intersectional political economy of 'manifold exploitations'.

> The organization of reproduction is profoundly influenced by complex forms of distributive conflict reflecting collective efforts to advance the well-being of specific social groups at the expense of others. Class conflict represents one very important dimension of this larger process of contestation, but it is not the only dimension. Groups defined by race/ethnicity, gender, and citizenship (among others) also establish institutional structures that determine access to economic assets, including rights over bodies, protection against violence and harassment, rights to health care and education, and access to employment and retirement benefits. Membership in an economically advantaged group is itself an economic asset, linking group identities with group interests. (Folbre, 2020, p. 7)

The key claims here are the following: (*a*) class conflict is a type of group conflict over distribution, (*b*) class is one type of social group, like those defined by race/ethnicity, gender and citizenship and (*c*) the focus of the analysis of exploitation should be on distributive justice. Since there are, no doubt, many forms of distributive conflict, once we identify exploitation with distributive injustice, we will have 'manifold exploitations'. Exploitation, as defined in the Marxist tradition, will be just one – albeit an important one – form of exploitation.

The theoretical framework to understand *exploitation as distributive injustice*, or 'group-based economic inequalities', is built on an understanding of production, in the broad sense discussed earlier, as cooperation between groups of human beings that generate gains from cooperation. The term 'cooperation' seems to give a misleading impression that we are referring only to voluntary cooperation. This is not the case. Some groups are, or might be, coerced in various ways to enter into the cooperative venture and, hence, it is better to refer to this as 'coerced cooperation'. Looked at from the perspective of the outcome, such activities give rise to gains from coerced cooperation. Since it is difficult to precisely assess the contribution of different individuals or groups involved in the cooperative venture, the division of the gains from cooperation are determined by a process of 'bargaining'. Unequal fall-back positions of the groups then lead to unequal distribution of the gains from coerced cooperation – arrived at through bargaining. Is the unequal distributional outcome exploitation? We can identify the unequal distribution as exploitation, argues Folbre (2020), when either the outcome or the process of bargaining or both are 'unfair'. In a nutshell, exploitation is distributive injustice.

To pin down this analysis, one will need to define the meaning of the term 'unfair'. What is an unfair distribution? Folbre (2020) offers no answer to this important question. The problem is that there is a circularity in the argument. Since powerful, or advantaged, groups can *define* what is 'fair' and what is 'unfair', there is no independent way to assess the unfairness of any distributional outcome which is not already enmeshed in the relative power positions of the groups involved in the bargaining process. Folbre (2020) is acutely aware of this problem. Hence, she notes that this issue cannot be settled by philosophical arguments alone; it will require democratic deliberation. But democratic deliberation can itself be subverted, or unduly influenced, by the relative power of groups involved in the democratic deliberation. Socially and economically powerful groups can ensure that the outcome of 'democratic' deliberations are broadly in their interest. Therefore, the problem of circularity persists.

8.4 Exploitation and Distributive Justice

The attempt to identify exploitation with distributive injustice has deeper philosophical problems and it is worth discussing some of these issues in

401

detail. To begin, let me offer the apparently counter-intuitive idea: Marx was clear in his writings that exploitation is not about distributive injustice. To be sure, Marx did not write extensively on this issue. But on the basis of whatever we know from his extant writings, it is clear that Marx did not offer his critique of exploitation on the basis of distributive injustice. In fact, there is some evidence that Marx was decidedly opposed to conceptualizing working-class politics in the idiom of justice and equality. For Marx, the goal of working-class politics was the abolition of classes. Moreover, Marx was sure that the abolition of classes, and thereby the end of exploitation, did not have much to do with distributive justice.[16]

Marx commented most extensively on the issue of justice and equality in 'critical marginal notes' that he wrote in 1875 about the programme of the United Worker's Party of Germany (UWPG). He sent the critical notes, along with a letter, to W. Bracke and intended it to be shared with other leading members of the party 'for examination' of his arguments. Marx's notes, along with the letter, were published in 1891 by Engels as *The Critique of the Gotha Program*. In Part 3 of this text, Marx engages with questions of 'fair distribution' and 'equality'.

The UWPG programme wanted to enshrine a principle of 'fair distribution' in a post-capitalist, communist society. Such a society was understood to be one where the 'instruments of labour are common property and total labour is co-operatively regulated'. The principle of 'fair distribution' espoused by the UWPG, for such a society, was that 'the proceeds of labour belong undiminished with equal right to all members of society'. Since the focus of the UWPG proposal is on *distribution*, Marx needs to first clarify the important point that even in a post-capitalist, communist society, the whole 'proceeds of labour' cannot be distributed to the workers. Why is that so?

From the total social product, the following will need to be deducted: (*a*) what is needed for replacement of used-up, and expansion of new, means of production, (*b*) what goes into a reserve fund for insurance against accidents and natural calamities, (*c*) what is used for general costs of administration (as opposed to production) – this portion, notes Marx, will diminish as we move beyond capitalism and (*d*) what is used for fulfilling social needs like publicly-provided education, health care, entertainment, and so on – this portion will increase as we transcend capitalism. Only after

---

[16]This section draws on Wood (1986a, 2004).

these deductions have been made will we arrive at the portion of the total social product that is potentially available for 'distribution' to workers to fulfil their individual consumption needs. This clarification drives home an important point: even in socialist societies, a surplus product will exist; the wage equivalent of the workers' income will be smaller than the total net product (that is, even after deducting depreciation needs), so that a surplus product will exist.[17] Without the surplus product, post-capitalist societies will not be able to carry out investments to increase the quantity and quality of the capital stock; it will not be able to support scientific and artistic activities. By defintiion, a socialist society will not have classes in the Marxist sense of the word because the means of production will not be privately owned. Thus, in a socialist society, there will be a surplus product but there will be no classes. This means that the existence of a surplus product is necessary but not sufficient for the existence of a class-divided society. Of course, in a socialist society, the surplus product is neither appropriated nor is its use determined by a particular class, as happens in capitalism or any class-divided society. The use to which the surplus product will be put is decided in a democratic fashion by the collective institutions of society.

With this necessary clarification, let us return to the main question. Let us suppose that socialists of the UWPG have accepted the necessity of the deductions Marx pointed to. Taking this into account, they reformulate their principle of fair distribution to refer to the part of the total social product that is destined for individual consumption. Now their principle of 'fair distribution' can be stated as follows: distribution in proportion to labour contribution. Thus, according to this principle, every worker has an equal right to a share of the total social product devoted to individual consumption that is in proportion to their contribution to total social labour. What is Marx's critique of *this* principle of fair distribution? There are two parts to Marx's critique. The first part highlights the defects of this principle; the second part argues for a different basis of socialist politics.

To implement the principle of distribution according to labour contribution, there must be available some mechanism to compare labour of different types (for example, different degrees of complexity), duration and

---

[17] If we remove from the total social product the amount of means of production used up as intermediate inputs, we arrive at the net social product. From the net social product, if we remove the depreciation allowances to replace the fixed capital used up and the consumption of the workers, we arrive at the surplus product.

intensities. These are non-trivial problems. In commodity production, the process of exchange takes care of these issues 'behind the back' of producers. Let us assume that socialist society has some mechanism to address this problem and to carry out meaningful comparisons of labour. Even if we assume that this problem is solved, we have to deal with a more difficult problem. There are bound to be significant differences between workers in terms of age, ability, health status, family structure, and other characteristics, all of which translate into *significant differences in needs*. If socialist society uses the principle of 'distribution according to labour contribution', the end result will be inequality in well-being, that is, an inequality in need satisfaction. Thus, equal right (to a share of society resources) leads to unequal outcomes.

According to Marx, this problem is a general one. Every right is a right of equality in form but a right of inequality in content.

> Right by its very nature can consist only in the application of an equal standard; but unequal individuals (and they would not be different individuals if they were not unequal) are measurable by an equal standard insofar as they are brought under an equal point of view, are taken from one *definite* side only, for instance, in the present case, are regarded *only* as workers and nothing else is seen in them, everything else being ignored . . . *It is therefore a right of inequality in its content, like every right.* (Tucker, 1978, pp. 530–31)

Consider the principle of 'equality of income' or 'equality of wealth'. Since individuals are fundamentally different in terms of their needs, the equality of income or wealth will lead to an inequality of well-being or satisfaction or utility. This is because the conversion of income or wealth into well-being depends on individual characteristics, and these are different across individuals. That is why an application of the principle of equality of income or wealth will necessarily lead to an inequality of well-being. If it is objected that the equality of well-being, and not the equality of income or wealth, is the principle we ought to champion, then it must mean that we are ready to accept the inequality of income or wealth or access to resources or even basic goods of the philosopher John Rawls. Only by allowing an inequality of income or wealth can we hope to attain equality of well-being.

Marx's point in highlighting these defects of the principle of 'fair distribution' is, of course, not to argue for inequality, rather it is to argue for a different basis for conceiving socialist politics. Consistent with his historical materialist understanding, the driving force of large-scale historical change is the contradiction between productive power and the relations of production. The mechanism of this change is class struggle.[18] From this understanding follows the basic and fundamental thrust of socialist politics: the abolition of classes. Looked at from this perspective, that is, from the perspective of historical materialism, a politics of rights and equality is limited because it falls short of the fundamental goal of socialist politics, as conceived by Marx, which is the abolition of classes.

Various kinds of 'group-based economic inequalities' that Folbre (2020) wants to make the basis of an intersectional political economy are overlaid on the basic class structure of capitalist society, as I have argued earlier. According to a historical materialist understanding, the class structure broadly corresponds to the level of development of the productive power of society. The three fundamental classes, as we have seen in Part I of this book, are the capitalists, the workers and the owners of land (or other natural resources). The total value added is divided into the basic income streams of these classes: wage income for workers; profit income, in the broadest sense, for capitalists and ground-rent for landowners, where profit and ground-rent are the division of surplus value, the monetary expression of the unpaid labour of the workers. Various kinds of group-based economic inequalities, deriving from race, caste, gender, religion or citizenship, can impact the divisions of these three basic forms of income among different social groups. It can also impact the distribution of persons across classes. But removing those inequalities will do nothing to change the basic class structure of capitalist society; neither will it change the basic forms of income earned by the three classes. That is why, emphasizes Marx, a politics of rights and equality is always circumscribed by a bourgeois vision of politics. Its limit is a well-functioning bourgeois society, free from discriminations and inequalities. But it never transcends bourgeois horizons. In fact, the basic principle of exchange in bourgeois society is an exchange of equivalents – the transaction that occurs when two commodity owners come face to face on the market. The politics of equality enshrines that principle in all spheres of life. That is why such a politics is located within bourgeois horizons.

Let us take the example of caste-based inequalities, which are extremely important in India. The dominance of the state and other social institutions

---

[18]See Chapter 2.

by the upper and middle castes has led to perpetuation of income and wealth inequalities among different castes. The functioning of the state and the functioning of social institutions have systematically prevented lower castes and Dalits from accessing the educational system, have prevented them from accessing well-paying occupations, have perpetuated discrimination of wage income within the same occupations and have prevented ownership of land and other kinds of productive resources. These forms of historical and contemporary discrimination have led to relative deprivation of lower castes and Dalits in all aspects of material and social life. If a political movement were able to force through the abolition of all these caste-based inequalities in education, the labour market, access to land and capital, and social life more broadly, such a politics would still leave the basic class structure of contemporary Indian society – a class structure coming from a mixture of capitalist and petty commodity production – intact.

Does this mean Marx was a champion of inequality? The answer is a resounding no. The fact that Marx pointed out the limitations of a politics of rights and equality does not mean that he championed a politics of inequality. Marx was well aware of and, in fact, positively appreciative of the politics of rights and equality as a stage in the historical evolution of progressive politics. At the stage when the bourgeoisie was fighting against feudalism, the politics of rights and equality was a revolutionary slogan – because it had the potential to bring about fundamental social change, that is, a change in the class structure of society. But when we come to the struggle of the working class against the capitalists, which is a higher stage in the historical evolution of progressive politics, a politics of rights and equality represents a back-sliding, a retrogression – because the abolition of classes has already come on the historical horizon.

Even though the abolition of classes has come on the historical horizon, it does not in any way diminish the importance of the politics of rights and distributive justice. Inequalities of various kinds, especially group-based economic inequalities, give rise to social oppression. And Marx was a lifelong and implacable foe of all forms of social oppression. Using this understanding, we can argue for the continuing role for and importance of the politics of distributive justice, even as we recognize its limitation, that is, its firm location within bourgeois politics. Every form of opposition to social oppression advances progressive politics and that would undoubtedly be championed by Marx.

8.5 Conclusion

In this chapter, we have studied several aspects of exploitation in capitalist economies. We have seen that a definition of exploitation involves both qualitative and quantitative aspects. The qualitative aspects involve three principles: inverse interdependence of welfare between exploiters and exploited; appropriation of the labour effort of the exploited by the exploiter; structural exclusion of the exploited from key productive resources of society. On the quantitative side, we have seen that a new and promising line of research has been opened up by the axiomatic approach to exploitation. A startling result of this literature is that the NI definition of exploitation has desirable properties that none of the other alternatives in use, that is, the Morishima and the Roemer definitions, have.

In this chapter, we have also critically engaged with two strands of literature on exploitation. The first strand is the Analytical Marxist tradition that has developed a critique of Marx's labour theory of value by demonstrating that there is nothing special in labour so far as it is the substance of value. This strand has attempted to show that any basic commodity (or input) can be used to construct a consistent value theory. Even more striking is the result that emerged within this tradition which attempts to show that there is nothing special about labour even with respect to exploitation. Just like labour is exploited if we use a labour theory of value, a commodity will be exploited if we use a commodity theory of value. In this chapter, I have argued that both claims rest on elementary conceptual flaws: the inability to distinguish labour and labour-power, and the inability to distinguish labour-power from all other commodities.

The second strand that we have engaged with is one which espouses intersectional political economy and manifold exploitations. We have seen that the argument suffers, at one level, from a problem of circularity. But more importantly, it rests on the attempt to collapse exploitation into distributive injustice. In this chapter, I have argued that the move to conceptualize exploitation as distributive injustice suffers from philosophical and political problems. Without denying the importance of distributive justice in any way, it is important to point out that a politics organized around distributive justice is limited in the precise sense that it is never able to transcend bourgeois horizons. The goal of eliminating exploitation, on the other hand, can only be accomplished through the abolition of classes, the latter necessarily taking us beyond bourgeois society.

Further Readings

- For a discussion of the qualitative issues involved in theories of exploitation, see Wright (1997, 2000), Wood (2004) and Vrousalis (2018a,b).

- For a discussion of the quantitative issues involved in theories of exploitation, see Yoshihara (2017).

- For a discussion of the GCET, see Gintis and Bowles (1981).

- For an argument in favour of intersectional political economy, see Folbre (2020). For an analysis of Marx's position on distributive justice, see Wood (1986a, 2004).

Bibliography

Alemi, Piruz, and Duncan K. Foley. 1997. 'The Circuit of Capital, U.S. Manufacturing, and Non-Financial Corporate Business Sectors, 1947–1993'. Unpublished paper. Available at https://docs.google.com/a/newschool.edu/viewer?a=v&pid=sites&srcid=bmV3c2Nob29sLmVkdXxk dW5jYW4tZm9sZXktaG9tZXBhZ2V8Z3g6MTBhNjg4YWNmMTA2 MTczNA. Accessed on 2 March 2021.

Basu, Deepankar. 2013. 'The Reserve Army of Labour in the Postwar U.S. Economy'. *Science & Society* 77 (2): 179–201.

———. 2014. 'Comparative Growth Dynamics in a Discrete-Time Marxian Circuit of Model'. *Review of Radical Political Economics* 46 (2): 162–83.

———. 2017. 'Quantitative Empirical Research in Marxist Political Economy: A Selective Review'. *Journal of Economic Surveys* 31 (5): 1359–86.

———. 2018. 'Marx's Analysis of Ground-Rent: Theory, Examples and Applications'. Working paper 2018–04, Department of Economics, University of Massachusetts Amherst, Amherst.

———. 2019. 'Reproduction and Crisis in Capitalist Economies'. In *The Oxford Handbook of Karl Marx*, edited by Matt Vidal, Tony Smith, Tomas Rotta and Paul Prew, 281–98. New York, NY: Oxford University Press.

———. 2020a. 'Marx's Analysis of Ground-Rent: A Suggested Reformulation'. Working Paper Series 296, Department of Economics, University of Massachusetts Amherst, Amherst.

———. 2020b. 'Exploitation of Labour or Exploitation of Commodities'. Working Paper Series 297, Department of Economics, University of Massachusetts Amherst, Amherst.

———. 2021. 'Reserve Army of Labour'. In *Global Political Economy: A Critique of Contemporary Capitalism*, edited by V. Upadhyay and Paramjit Singh, 140–57. New Delhi: Aakar Books.

Basu, Deepankar, and Debarshi Das. 2018. 'Profitability in India's Organized Manufacturing Sector: The Role of Technology, Distribution, and Demand'. *Cambridge Journal of Economics* 42 (1): 137–53.

Basu, Deepankar, and Duncan K. Foley. 2013. 'Dynamics of Output and Employment in the U.S. Economy'. *Cambridge Journal of Economics* 37 (5): 1077–106.

Basu, Deepankar, Cameron Haas, and Athanasios Moraitis. 2021. 'What Is the Impact of an Intensification of Labour on the Rate and Form of Exploitation'. Economics Department Working Paper Series 298, University of Massachusetts Amherst. Available at https://scholarworks.umass.edu/econ_workingpaper/298.

Basu, Deepankar, and Ramaa Vasudevan. 2013. 'Technology, Distribution and the Rate of Profit in the U.S. Economy: Understanding the Current Crisis'. *Cambridge Journal of Economics* 37 (1): 57–89.

Baumol, W. J. 1974. 'The Transformation of Values: What Marx "Really" Meant: An Interpretation'. *Journal of Economic Literature* 12 (1): 51–61.

Bowles, Samuel, and Herbert Gintis. 1977. 'The Marxian Theory of Value and Heterogeneous Labour: A Critique and Reformulation'. *Cambridge Journal of Economics* 1 (2): 173–92.

Bowles, Samuel, David M. Gordon and Thomas E. Weisskopf. 1983. *Beyond the Waste Land: A Democratic Alternative to Economic Decline*. New York, NY: Anchor Doubleday.

Boyce, James K. 2002. *The Political Economy of the Environment*. Cheltenham, UK: Edward Elgar.

Braverman, Harry. 1998. *Labour and Monopoly Capital: The Degradation of Work in Twentieth Century*. 2nd ed. New York, NY: Monthly Review Press.

Brooks, Wyatt J., Joseph P. Kaboski, Yao Amber Li and Wei Qian. 2019. 'Exploitation of Labor? Classical Monopsony Power and Labor's Share'. NBER working paper no. 25660, National Bureau of Economic Research, Cambridge MA.

Burnette, Joyce. 2008. 'Women Workers in the British Industrial Revolution'. In *EH.Net Encyclopedia*, edited by Robert Whaples. Available at http://eh.net/encyclopedia/women-workers-in-the-british-industrial-revolution/.

Callinicos, Alex. 2006. 'G. A. Cohen and the Critique of Political Economy'. *Science & Society* 70 (2): 252–74.

Carchedi, Guglielmo, and Alan Freeman, eds. 1996. *Marx and Non-Equilibrium Economics*. Cheltenham, UK and Brookfield, US: Edward Elgar.

Carver, Terrell. 1975. *Karl Marx: Texts on Method*. Oxford: Basil Blackwell.

Chase-Dunn, C. K. 1998. *Global Formation: Structures of the World-Economy*. Lanham, MD: Rowman and Littlefield.

Chen, Weikai. 2019. 'Technical Change, Income Distribution, and Profitability in Multisector Linear Economies'. Working Paper Series 273, Department of Economics, University of Massachusetts Amherst, Amherst.

Chesnais, Francois. 2016. *Finance Capital Today: Corporations and Banks in the Lasting Global Slump*. Boston: Brill.

Cogliano, Jonathan, Peter Flaschel, Reiner Franke, Nils Frohlich and Roberto Veneziani. 2018. *Value, Competition and Exploitation: Marx's Legacy Revisited*. Cheltenham, UK: Edward Elgar.

Cohen, G. A. 1980. 'Cohen on Marx's Theory of History'. *Political Studies* 28 (1): 129–35.

———. 1982. 'Reply to Elster on "Marxism, Functionalism and Game Theory"'. *Theory and Society* 11 (4): 483–95.

———. 1986a. 'Forces and Relations of Production'. In *Analytical Marxism*, edited by John E. Roemer, 11–22. Cambridge, UK: Cambridge University Press.

———. 1986b. 'Marxism and Functional Explanation'. In *Analytical Marxism*, edited by John E. Roemer, 221–34. Cambridge, UK: Cambridge University Press.

———. 1986c. 'The Structure of Proletarian Unfreedom'. In *Analytical Marxism*, edited by John E. Roemer, 237–59. Cambridge, UK: Cambridge University Press.

———. 2001. *Karl Marx's Theory of History: A Defence*. Princeton, NJ: Princeton University Press. First published 1978.

Das, Debarshi. 2018. 'A Model of the Marxist Rent Theory'. Working paper 2018–10, Department of Economics, University of Massachusetts Amherst, Amherst.

Debreu, Gerard. 1959. *Theory of Value: An Axiomatic Analysis of Economic Equilibrium*. New York: John Wiley & Sons.

Debreu, Gerard, and I. N. Herstein. 1958. 'Nonnegative Square Matrices'. *Econometrica* 21 (4): 597–607.

Dietzenbacher, Erik. 1989. 'The Implications of Technical Change in a Marxian Framework'. *Journal of Economics* 50 (1): 35–46.

Dmitriev, V. K. 1974. *Economic Essays on Value, Competition and Utility*. Edited with an Introduction by D. M. Nuti; translated by D. Fry. Cambridge, UK: Cambridge University Press. First published in Russian in 1902.

dos Santos, Paulo L. 2011. 'Production and Consumption in a Continuous-Time Model of the Circuit of Capital'. *Metroeconomica* 62 (4): 729–58.

Dumenil, Gerard. 1983–84. 'Beyond the Transformation Riddle: A Labour Theory of Value'. *Science & Society* 47 (4): 427–50.

Dumenil, Gerard, and Dominique Levy. 2002. 'The Field of Capital Mobility and the Gravitation of Profit Rates (USA 1948–2000)'. *Review of Radical Political Economics* 34 (4): 417–36.

Dumenil, Gerard, Duncan Foley and Dominique Levy. 2009. 'A Note on the Formal Treatment of Exploitation in a Model with Heterogeneous Labor'. *Metroeconomica* 60 (3): 560–67.

Durand, Cedric. 2017. *Fictitious Capital: How Finance Is Appropriating Our Future*. New York, NY: Verso.

Eaton, John. 1963. *Political Economy*. New York, NY: International Publishers.

Elster, Jon. 1980. 'Cohen on Marx's Theory of History'. *Political Studies* 28 (1): 121–28.

———. 1982. 'Marxism, Functionalism and Game Theory'. *Theory and Society* 11 (4): 453–82.

———. 1985. *Making Sense of Marx*. Cambridge, UK: Cambridge University Press.

Emmanuel, Arghiri. 1972. *Unequal Exchange: A Study of the Imperialism of Trade*. New York, NY: Monthly Review Press.

Engels, Fredrich. 1869. 'Karl Marx'. Available at https://www.marxists.org/archive/marx/bio/marx/eng-1869.htm. Accessed on 23 August 2017.

———. 1877. 'Karl Marx'. Available at https://www.marxists.org/archive/marx/works/1877/06/karl-marx.htm. Accessed on 23 August 2017.

———. 1891. 'Introduction to Karl Marx's Wage Labour and Capital'. Available at https://www.marxists.org/archive/marx/works/1847/wage-labour/. Accessed on 21 August 2017.

Farjoun, Emmanuel, and Moshe Machover. 1983. *Laws of Chaos: A Probabilistic Approach to Political Economy*. London, UK: Verso.

Fine, Ben. 1979. 'On Marx's Theory of Agricultural Rent'. *Economy and Society* 8 (3): 241–78.

———. 2019. 'Marx's Rent Theory Revisited? Landed Property, Nature and Value'. *Economy and Society* 48 (3): 450–61.

Fine, Ben, and Alfredo Saad Filho. 2010. *Marx's Capital*. 5th ed. London, UK: Pluto Press.

Fine, Ben, Costas Lapavitsas and Alfredo Saad Filho. 2004. 'Transforming the Transformation Problem: Why the "New Interpretation" Is a Wrong Turning'. *Review of Radical Political Economics* 36 (3): 3–19.

Flaschel, Peter, Reiner Franke and Roberto Veneziani. 2013. 'Labour Productivity and the Law of Decreasing Labour Content'. *Cambridge Journal of Economics* 37 (2): 379–402.

Folbre, Nancy. 2020. 'Manifold Exploitations: Toward an Intersectional Political Economy'. *Review of Social Economy* 78 (4): 451–72.

Foley, Duncan K. 1982a. 'Realization and Accumulation in a Marxian Model of the Circuit of Capital'. *Journal of Economic Theory* 28 (2): 300–19.

———. 1982b. 'The Value of Money, the Value of Labour Power and the Marxian Transformation Problem'. *Review of Radical Politics Economics* 14 (2): 37–47.

———. 1986a. *Money, Accumulation and Crisis: Fundamentals of Pure and Applied Economics*. Oxon, UK: Routledge.

———. 1986b. *Understanding Capital: Marx's Economic Theory*. Cambridge, MA: Harvard University Press.

Foley, Duncan K., and Thomas R. Michl. 1999. *Growth and Distribution*. Cambridge, MA: Harvard University Press.

Foley, Duncan K., Thomas R. Michl and Daniele Tavani. 2019. *Growth and Distribution*. 2nd ed. Cambridge, MA: Harvard University Press.

Foster, John Bellamy, Robert McChesney and R. Jamil Jonna. 2011. 'The Global Reserve Army of Labor and the New Imperialism'. *Monthly Review* 63 (6). Available at https://monthlyreview.org/2011/11/01/the-global-reserve-army-of-labor-and-the-new-imperialism/. Accessed on 21 August 2017.

Friedman, Milton. 1970. 'The Counter-Revolution in Monetary Theory'. IEA occasional paper no. 33, Institute of Economic Affairs, London.

Gabriel, Mary. 2011. *Love and Capital: Karl and Jenny Marx and the Birth of a Revolution*. New York, NY: Back Bay Books.

Georgescu-Roegen, N. 1966. 'Analytical Economics'. In *Some Properties of a Generalized Leontief Model*, edited by N. Georgescu-Roegen, 316–37. Cambridge, MA: Harvard University Press.

Gintis, Herbert, and Samuel Bowles. 1981. 'Structure and Practice in the Labor Theory of Value'. *Review of Radical Political Economics* 12 (4): 1–26.

Harris, D. J. 1978. *Capital Accumulation and Income Distribution*. Stanford, CA: Stanford University Press.

Harvey, David. 2004. 'The New Imperialism: Accumulation by Dispossession'. In *Socialist Register 2004: The New Imperial Challenge*, edited by Leo Panitch and Colin Leys, 63–87. New York, NY: Monthly Review Press.

Hawkins, H. D., and H. A. Simon. 1949. 'Note: Some Conditions of Macroeconomic Stability'. *Econometrica* 17 (3/4): 245–48.

Heinrich, Michael. 2012. *An Introduction to the Three Volumes of Karl Marx's Capital*. New York, NY: Monthly Review Press.

Helliwell, J. F., and H. Huang. 2014. 'New Measures of the Cost of Unemployment: Evidence from the Subjective Well-Being of 3.3 Million Americans'. Working paper 16829, National Bureau of Economic Research, Cambridge, MA.

Hilferding, Rudolf. 1949. 'Bohm-Bawerk's Criticism of Marx'. In *Karl Marx and the Close of His System*, edited by Paul M. Sweezy, 119–96. New York, NY: Augustus M. Kelley.

Horrell, S., and J. Humphries. 1995. 'Women's Labour Force Participation and the Transition to the Male-Breadwinner Family'. *The Economic History Review*, New Series, 48 (1): 89–117.

Huberman, Leo. 1936. *Man's Worldly Goods: The Story of the Wealth of Nations*. New York, NY: Monthly Review Press.

Kliman, Andrew. 2006. *Reclaiming Marx's Capital: A Refutation of the Myth of Inconsistency*. Lanham, MD: Lexington Books.

Kliman, Andrew, and Ted McGlone. 1999. 'A Temporal Single-System Interpretation of Marx's Value Theory'. *Review of Political Economy* 11 (1): 33–59.

Kotz, David. 1991. 'Accumulation, Money and Credit in the Circuit of Capital'. *Rethinking Marxism* 4 (2): 119–33.

———. 2009. 'The Financial and Economic Crisis of 2008: A Systemic Crisis of Neoliberal Capitalism'. *Review of Radical Political Economics* 41 (3): 305–17.

Krause, Ulrich. 1981. 'Heterogeneous Labour and the Fundamental Marxian Theorem'. *The Review of Economic Studies* 48 (1): 173–78.

Laibman, David. 1992. *Value, Technical Change and Crisis: Explorations in Marxist Economic Theory*. Armonk, NY: M. E. Sharpe, Inc.

Lapavitsas, Costas. 2013. *Profiting without Production: How Finance Exploits Us All*. New York, NY: Verso.

Leiman, Melvin. 2010. *The Political Economy of Racism*. Chicago, IL: Haymarket Books.

Lenin, Vladimir Ilyich. 1913. 'The Three Sources and Three Component Parts of Marxism'. Available at https://www.marxists.org/archive/lenin/works/1913/mar/x01.htm. Accessed on 21 August 2017.

———. 1915. 'On the Question of Dialectics'. Available at https://www.marxists.org/archive/lenin/works/1915/misc/x02.htm. Accessed on 6 July 2018.

Levien, Michael. 2011. 'Special Economic Zones and Accumulation by Dispossession in India'. *Journal of Agrarian Change* 11 (4): 454–83.

Lewis, W. A. 1954. 'Economic Development with Unlimited Supplies of Labour'. *The Machester School* 22 (2): 139–91.

Lipietz, Alain. 1982. 'The So-Called "Transformation Problem" Revisited'. *Journal of Economic Theory* 26 (1): 59–88.

Loranger, Jean-Guy. 1989. 'A Re-Examination of the Marxian Circuit of Capital: A New Look at Inflation'. *Review of Radical Political Economics* 21 (1–2): 97–112.

Marx, Karl. 1976. *A Contribution to the Critique of Political Economy*. Edited with an Introduction by Maurice Dobb. New York: International Publishers. First published in 1859.

———. 1992. *Capital: A Critique of Political Economy*, vol. I. London, UK: Penguin. First published in 1867.

———. 1993a. *Capital: A Critique of Political Economy*, vol. II. London, UK: Penguin. First published in 1885.

———. 1993b. *Capital: A Critique of Political Economy*, vol. III. London, UK: Penguin. First published in 1894.

———. 1993c. *Grundrisse: Foundations of the Critique of Political Economy* (Rough Draft). London, UK: Penguin Books in association with New Left Review. Translated with a Foreword by Martin Nicolaus.

Marx, Karl, and Friedrich Engels. 1998. *The Communist Manifesto*. Foreword by Paul M. Sweezy. New York: Monthly Review Press. First published in 1848.

Matthews, Peter H. 2000. 'An Econometric Model of the Circuit of Capital'. *Metroeconomica* 51 (1): 1–39.

Mohun, Simon. 2004. 'The Labour Theory of Value as Foundation for Empirical Investigations'. *Metroeconomica* 55 (1): 65–95.

———. 2006. 'Distributive Shares in the U.S. Economy, 1964–2001'. *Cambridge Journal of Economics* 30 (3): 347–70.

Mohun, Simon, and Roberto Veneziani. 2017. 'Value, Price and Exploitation: The Logic of the Transformation Problem'. *Journal of Economic Surveys* 31 (5): 1387–420.

Morishima, Michio. 1973. *Marx's Economics: A Dual Theory of Value and Growth*. Cambridge, UK: Cambridge University Press.

———. 1974. 'Marx in the Light of Modern Economic Theory'. *Econometrica* 42 (4): 611–32.

Moseley, Fred. 2000. 'The "New Solution" to the Transformation Problem: A Sympathetic Critique'. *Review of Radical Politics Economics* 32 (2): 282–316.

———. 2011a. 'Recent Interpretations of the "Transformation Problem"'. *Rethinking Marxism* 23 (2): 186–97.

———. 2011b. 'The Determination of the "Monetary Expression of Labor Time" ("Melt") in the Case of Non-Commodity Money'. *Review of Radical Political Economics* 43 (1): 95–105.

———. 2016. *Money and Totality: A Macro-Monetary Interpretation of Marx's Logic in Capital and the End of the 'Transformation Problem'*. Boston, MA: Brill.

Nikaido, Hukukane. 1968. *Convex Structures and Economic Theory*. New York, NY: Academic Press.

Ochsen, C., and H. Welsch. 2011. 'The Social Cost of Unemployment: Accounting for Unemployment Duration'. *Applied Economics* 43 (27): 3999–4005.

Okishio, N. 1961. 'Technical Changes and the Rate of Profit'. *Kobe University Economic Review* 7: 85–99.

———. 1963. 'A Mathematical Note on Marxian Theorems'. *Weltwirts Archiv* 289–99.

———. 1988. 'On Marx's Reproduction Scheme'. *Kobe University Economic Review* 34: 1–24.

Ollman, Bertell. 1981. 'What Is Marxism: A Bird's Eye-View'. Available at https://www.nyu.edu/projects/ollman/docs/whatismarxism.php. Accessed on 6 July 2018.

Pasinetti, Luigi L. 1977. *Lectures on the Theory of Production*. New York, NY: Columbia University Press.

Postone, Moishe. 1993. *Time, Labour and Social Domination: A Reinterpretation of Marx's Critical Theory*. Cambridge, UK: Cambridge University Press.

Ramirez, M. D. 2009. 'Marx's Theory of Ground Rent: A Critical Assessment'. *Contributions to Political Economy* 28 (1): 71–91.

Resnick, Stephen A., and Richard D. Wolff. 1987. *Knowledge and Class: A Marxian Critique of Political Economy*. Chicago, IL: University of Chicago Press.

Rieu, Dong-Min, Keonbeom Lee and Hyeon-Hyo Ahn. 2014. 'The Determination of the Monetary Expression of Concrete Labor Time under the Inconvertible Credit Money System'. *Review of Radical Political Economics* 46 (2): 190–98.

Roemer, John E. 1977. 'Technical Change and the "Tendency of the Rate of Profit to Fall"'. *Journal of Economic Theory* 16 (2): 403–24.

———. 1978. 'The Effect of Technical Change on the Real Wage and Marx's Falling Rate of Profit'. *Australian Economic Papers* 17 (30): 152–66.

———. 1980. 'A General Equilibrium Approach to Marxian Economics'. *Econometrica* 48 (2): 505–30.

———. 1981. *Analytical Foundations of Marxian Economic Theory*. Cambridge, UK: Cambridge University Press.

———. 1982. *A General Theory of Exploitation and Class*. Cambridge, MA: Harvard University Press.

———. 1985. 'Should Marxists Be Interested in Exploitation?' *Philosophy and Public Affairs* 14 (1): 30–65.

Rosdolsky, Roman. 1977. *The Making of Marx's Capital*. New York, NY: Pluto Press. First published in 1968.

Rowthorn, Bob. 1974. 'Skilled Labour in the Marxist System'. *Bulletin of the Conference of Socialist Economists* 8: 25–45.

Rubin, I. I. 1978. 'Abstract Labour and Value in Marx's System'. *Capital & Class* 2 (2): 109–39.

———. 1990. *Essays on Marx's Theory of Value*. Translated by Milos Samardzija and Fredy Perlman. New York: Black Rose Books. First published in Russian in 1928.

Samuelson, Paul. 1971. 'Understanding the Marxian Notion of Exploitation: A Summary of the So-Called Transformation Problem between Marxian Values and Competitive Prices'. *Journal of Economic Literature* 9 (2): 399–431.

Sanyal, Kalyan. 2007. *Rethinking Capitalist Development: Primitive Accumulation, Governmentality & Post-Colonial Capitalism*. New Delhi: Routledge.

Saros, Daniel. 2007. 'The Price-Form as a Fractional Reflection of the Aggregate Value of Commodities'. *Review of Radical Political Economics* 39 (3): 407–15.

Sen, Amartya. 1978. 'On the Labour Theory of Value: Some Methodological Issues'. *Cambridge Journal of Economics* 2 (2): 175–90.

Seton, F. 1957. 'The "Transformation Problem"'. *The Review of Economic Studies* 24 (3): 149–60.

Shaikh, Anwar. 1977. 'Marx's Theory of Value and the "Transformation Problem"'. In *The Subtle Anatomy of Capitalism*, edited by Jesse Schwartz, 106–39. Santa Monica, CA: Goodyear Publishing Company Inc.

———. 1978. 'Political Economy and Capitalism: Notes on Dobb's Theory of Crisis'. *Cambridge Journal of Economics* 2 (2): 233–51.

———. 1984. 'The Transformation from Marx to Sraffa'. In *Ricardo, Marx, Sraffa*, edited by E. Mandel and A. Freeman, 43–84. London, UK: Verso.

Shaikh, Anwar, and E. Ahmet Tonak. 1994. *Measuring the Wealth of Nations: The Political Economy of National Accounts*. Cambridge, MA: Cambridge University Press.

Smith, Adam, ed. 1991. *Wealth of Nations*. New York: Prometheus Books. First published in 1776.

Smith, Paul. 1978. 'Domestic Labour and Marx's Theory of Value'. In *Feminism and Materialism: Women and Modes of Production*, edited by Annette Kuhn and Annemarie Wolpe, 198–219. Oxon, UK: Routledge and Kegan Paul.

Starosta, G. 2012. 'Cognitive Commodities and the Value-Form'. *Science & Society* 76 (3): 365–92.

Steedman, Ian. 1977. *Marx after Sraffa*. London, UK: New Left Books.

Stigler, G. J. 1958. 'Ricardo and the 93% Labour Theory of Value'. *American Economic Review* 48 (3): 357–67.

Sweezy, Paul M. 1942. *The Theory of Capitalist Development*. New York, NY: Monthly Review Press.

Trigg, Andrew B. 2006. *Marxian Reproduction Schema: Money and Aggregate Demand in a Capitalitst Economy*. New York, NY: Routledge.

Tse-tung, Mao. 1937. 'On Contradiction'. Available at https://www.marxists.org/reference/archive/mao/selected-works/volume-1/mswv117.htm. Accessed on 6 July 2018.

Tucker, Robert C., ed. 1978. *The Marx-Engels Reader*. New York: W. W. Norton & Company.

Vasudevan, Ramaa. 2016. Financialization, Distribution and Accumulation: A Circuit of Capital Model with a Managerial Class'. *Metroeconomica* 67 (2): 397–428.

Veneziani, Roberto, and Naoki Yoshihara. 2017. 'One Million Miles to Go: Taking the Axiomatic Road to Defining Exploitation'. *Cambridge Journal of Economics* 41 (6): 1607–26.

Vogel, Lise. 2000. 'Domestic Labour Revisited'. *Science & Society* 64 (2): 151–70.

———. 2013. *Marxism and Oppression of Women. Towards a Unitary Theory*. Boston, MA: Brill.

von Bortkiewicz, Ladislaus. 1949. 'On the Correction of Marx's Fundamental Theoretical Construction in the Third Volume of Capital'. In *Karl Marx and the Close of His System*, edited by Paul M. Sweezy, 199–221. New York, NY: Augustus M. Kelley.

Vrousalis, Nicholas. 2018a. 'Exploitation, Vulnerability, and Social Domination'. *Philosophy & Public Affairs* 41 (2): 131–57.

———. 2018b. 'Exploitation: A Primer'. *Philosophy Compass* 13 (2).

Wallerstein, Immanuel. 1974. 'The Rise and Future Demise of the World Capitalist System: Concepts for Comparative Analysis'. *Comparative Studies in Society and History* 16 (4): 387–415.

Ward, Callum, and Manuel B. Aalbers. 2016. 'Virtual Special Issue Editorial Essay: "The Shitty Rent Business": What's the Point of Land Rent Theory?' *Urban Studies* 53 (9): 1760–83.

Weisskpof, Thomas E. 1979. 'Marxian Crisis Theory and the Rate of Profit in the Postwar U.S. Economy'. *Cambridge Journal of Economics* 3 (4): 341–78.

Wen, Yi. 2006. 'The Quantity Theory of Money'. *Economic Synopses*, Federal Reserve Bank of St. Louis. Available at https://files.stlouisfed.org/files/htdocs/publications/es/06/ES0625.pdf.

Wheen, Francis. 2001. *Karl Marx: A Life*. New York, NY: Norton.

Winternitz, J. 1948. 'Value and Prices: A Solution of the So-Called Transformation Problem'. *Economic Journal* 58 (230): 276–80.

Wolff, Edward N. 2003. 'What's behind the Rise in Profitability in the US in the 1980s and 1990s?' *Cambridge Journal of Economics* 27 (4): 479–99.

Wolff, Richard, Antonio Callari, and Bruce Roberts. 1982. 'Marx's (Not Ricardo's) "Transformation Problem": A Radical Reconceptualization'. *History of Political Economy* 14 (4): 564–82.

———. 1984. 'A Marxian Alternative to the Traditional Transformation Problem'. *Review of Radical Political Economics* 16 (2–3): 115–35.

Wood, Allen. 1986a. 'Marx and Equality'. In *Analytical Marxism*, edited by John E. Roemer, 283–303. Cambridge, UK: Cambridge University Press.

———. 1986b. 'Historical Materialism and Functional Explanation'. *Inquiry* 29 (1–4): 11–27.

———. 2004. *Karl Marx*. 2nd ed. New York, NY: Routledge.

Wright, Erik Olin. 1997. *Class Counts: Comparative Studies in Class Analysis*. Cambridge, UK: Cambridge University Press.

———. 2000. 'Class, Exploitation and Economic Rents: Reflections on Sorenson's "Sounder Basis"'. *American Journal of Sociology* 105 (6): 1559–71.

———. 2015. *Understanding Class*. New York, NY: Verso.

Yoshihara, Naoki. 2017. 'A Progress Report on Marxian Economic Theory: On the Controversies in Exploitation Theory since Okishio (1963)'. *Journal of Economic Surveys* 31 (2): 632–59.

Yoshihara, Naoki, and Roberto Veneziani. 2009. 'Exploitation as the Unequal Exchange of Labour: An Axiomatic Approach'. CCES Discussion Paper Series. Center for Research on Contemporary Economic Systems, Graduate School of Economics, Hitotsubashi University.

Index

absolute surplus value, 125
abstract labour, 57
accumulation of capital, 136

Bowles, S., 389

capital, 102
    circulating, 188
    constant, 120
    fixed, 188
    variable, 120
centralization of capital, 136
circuit of capital, 103
circulating capital, 188
circulation of capital, 181
circulation of money, 101
class, 28, 374
class struggle, 35
Cohen, G. A., 27
commercial profit, 228
commodity, 48
commodity capital, 184
commodity exploitation theorem,
    389, 397
commodity fetishism, 94
commodity money, 82
commodity value theory, 389

competition, 211
complex labour, 61
composition of capital
    organic, 121
    value, 198
concentration of capital, 136
concrete labour, 56
constant capital, 120
cooperation, 131
credit money, 84

Das, D., 250
dialectic
    Hegel, 23
    Marx, 25
dividend payments, 246
Duménil, G., 297

economic structure, 28
embodied labour, 116
Engels, F., 22, 38
equation of exchange, 80
exchange value, 52
expanded reproduction, 136, 199
exploitation, 116, 118, 238

fictitious capital
    definition, 244

land, 247
ownership shares, 247
public debt, 245
Fine, B., 257
fixed capital, 188
Folbre, N., 399
Foley, D. K., 12, 86, 94, 112
formal subsumption, 133
Fundamental Marxian Theorem,
  320

generalized commodity
    exploitation theorem,
    174
Gintis, H., 389

heterogeneous labour, 359
Hilferding, R., 160
historical materialism, 27
hoard, 80

inconvertible paper money, 83
intensity of labour, 69
interest, 241
interest rate, 243
invariance principle, 320, 322

Kautsky, K., 38

labour productivity, 66
labour theory of value, 54
labour-power, 106, 107
    market component, 109
    non-market component, 109
    value of, 112
Laibman, D., 275
long-period method, 94, 165

machine production, 132

Macro-Monetary Interpretation,
  336
Mandel, E., 12
manufacture, 131
Marx, K., 19
Marxian exchange rate, 91
materialist conception of history,
  26
means of payment, 81
measure of value, 79
medium of circulation, 79
MEV, 86
mobility of capital, 212
monetary expression of value, 86
money, 78
    forms of, 82
    functions of, 78
money capital, 184
Morishima, M., 302, 350, 380

New Interpretation, 326

Okishio, N., 285, 302
oppression, 375
organic composition of capital,
  121

price, 78
prices of production, 213
primary accumulation of capital,
  157
productive capital, 184
productive labour, 236
productive power, 28
productivity of labour, 66
profit of enterprise, 243

quantity theory of money, 80

rate of profit, 121
rate of surplus value, 121
real subsumption, 133
reduction coefficient, 62, 163
relative surplus value, 125
reproduction
    expanded, 199
    simple, 195
reproduction schemas, 194
Roemer, J. E., 275

services production, 238
Shaikh, A., 232
simple circulation, 101
simple labour, 61
simple reproduction, 136, 195
Simultaneous Single System
    Interpretation, 339
socially necessary, 64
Sraffa-based critique, 324
Steedman, I., 324
substance of value, 170
superstructure, 29
surplus product, 176
surplus value, 106
Sweezy, P. M, 12

technical change, 276

technique of production, 275
Temporal Single System
    Interpretation, 337
transformation problem, 299
trinity form, 269
turnover of capital, 186

universal equivalent, 78
unproductive labour, 236
    exploitation, 237
use value, 51

value, 53
value of labour-power
    new interpretation, 112, 327,
        331
    standard interpretation, 112,
        330
variable capital, 121
Veneziani, R., 384
Vogel, L., 108
von Bortkiewicz, L., 301

wage-profit frontier, 284, 351
Wood, A. W., 22, 402
Wright, E. O., 374

Yoshihara, N., 384

www.ingramcontent.com/pod-product-compliance
Ingram Content Group UK Ltd.
Pitfield, Milton Keynes, MK11 3LW, UK
UKHW010248140625
459647UK00013BA/1731

* 9 7 8 1 0 0 9 4 1 8 1 1 9 *